SHAPING EDUCATION POLICY

Shaping Education Policy is a comprehensive overview of education politics and policy during the most turbulent and rapidly changing period in American history. Respected scholars review the history of education policy to explain the political powers and processes that shape education today. Chapters cover major themes that have influenced education, including the civil rights movement, federal involvement, the accountability movement, family choice, and development of nationalization and globalization. Sponsored by the Politics of Education Association, this edited collection examines the tumultuous shifts in education policy over the last six decades and projects the likely future of public education. This book is a necessary resource for understanding the evolution, current status, and possibilities of educational policy and politics.

Douglas E. Mitchell is Professor of Education at the University of California, Riverside.

Robert L. Crowson is Professor of Education and Policy at Peabody College, Vanderbilt University.

Dorothy Shipps is Associate Professor of Public Affairs and Education at Baruch College, City University of New York.

SHAPING EDUCATION POLICY

Power and Process

*Edited by Douglas E. Mitchell,
Robert L. Crowson, and Dorothy Shipps*

NEW YORK AND LONDON

First published 2011
by Routledge
711 Third Avenue, New York, NY 10017

Simultaneously published in the UK
by Routledge
2 Park Square, Milton Park, Abingdon, Oxon OX14 4RN

Routledge is an imprint of the Taylor & Francis Group, an informa business

Library of Congress Cataloging in Publication Data
Mitchell, Douglas E.
    Shaping education policy : power and process / edited by Douglas E.
    Mitchell, Robert L. Crowson, Dorothy Shipps. — 1st ed.
    p. cm.
    1. Education and state—United States. 2. School management and
    organization—United States. 3. Community and school—United
    States. 4. Home and school—United States. I. Crowson, Robert L. II.
    Shipps, Dorothy. III. Title.
    LC89.M56 2011
    379.73—dc22
                                                   2011000349

ISBN 13: 978-0-415-87504-2 (hbk)
ISBN 13: 978-0-415-87505-9 (pbk)
ISBN 13: 978-0-203-83735-1 (ebk)

Typeset in Bembo and Stone Sans by
EvS Communication Networx, Inc.

Printed and bound in the United States of America on acid-free paper by
Walsworth Publishing Company, Marceline, MO.

SUSTAINABLE
FORESTRY
INITIATIVE

Certified Sourcing

www.sfiprogram.org
SFI-00555
The SFI label applies to the text stock.

In memoriam …

William Lowe Boyd
1935–2008

We remember his leadership,
His insightfulness,
His mentorship of young scholars,
His appreciation of music, and
Above all, his generous and gentle character.

CONTENTS

FOREWORD

Paul Peterson

In the late 1950s, the American educational system was the envy of the world. Though it had many warts—southern schools were racially segregated, disabled students were excluded, and school facilities were often hopelessly inadequate—the nation's schools could boast a larger high school graduation rate than that of any other major industrial country. Secondary schooling attendance had exploded in the 1920s and 1930s so that already, by 1940, some 72% of adolescents were going to school, a percentage that grew to 90% by 1960. College enrollment rates more than doubled between 1940 and 1970. (These and the following statistics are taken from Peterson, 2010). Schools had helped propel the United States from a developing country to the world's superpower.

Today, elementary and secondary schools in the United States no longer appear exceptional. In recent decades, other countries have been encouraging their young people to remain in school for ever longer periods of time, but U.S. graduation rates have remained constant. Once the world leader, the United States now stands at just the industrial world average. Nor are those who remain in school learning more. According to various international measures of high school student performance, America's schools range from just average in reading to well below that level in science and math. At age 17, White students score no better in reading in 2004 than they did in 1971. African Americans and Hispanic high school students made noticeable progress in reading during the 1970s and 80s, but their performance has slipped since then. The story is much the same in math.

Why has a once-dynamic educational system turned stagnant, or worse? Has it been a change in pedagogical practice? Have the necessary resources been lacking? Was it the racial turmoil that accompanied the efforts to desegregate the schools? Was it the rise of powerful teacher unions who won the right to bargain collectively? Have school systems become overly centralized, professionalized, legalized and bureaucratized? Did the school reforms of the past half century have consequences their advocates never anticipated? Answers to such questions are explored in the pages that follow, though no predetermined conclusion is forced. But on one fact almost all authors agree: Power over schooling has over the last 50 years shifted steadily from lower to higher levels of government.

From Local Schools to Central Control

The system the reformers sought to reform was in the beginning modeled on Scottish and English arrangements marked by voluntary enrollments, fee-based education, religious instruction, and local control. A march toward a more centrally regulated, secular, bureaucratized educational system has taken place through a series of struggles, each of which shifted control of education away from parents and localities to professionals operating within larger legal entities—large districts, collective bargaining agreements, state governments, court jurisdictions, and federal executive agencies. Centralization became the almost inevitable byproduct of school reform, simply because reformers sought maximum power to carry their desires into effect.

If the drive to centralize was pervasive, so was the demand for a customized education. Dewey tried to replace the standardized, rote learning taking place in the schools of his childhood with a child-centered system. His less creative followers customized the educational experience by putting students into tracks—academic, vocational, and general (with a heavy dose of life-adjustment courses). Class size reduction was promoted on the grounds that teachers could meet the needs of each child more effectively if they had fewer to instruct. Customization reached its zenith in 1974 when Congress said that every child with a disability needed an "individualized education plan," a tailored set of resources and programs appropriate for his or her particular situation. The idea was also applied to those who came from non-English speaking families; each was to be taught in their native tongue, an extraordinary expectation given the multiplicity of languages immigrants were bringing to the United States. The accountability movement has had its own approach to customization. The federal law, No Child Left Behind, did not just ask that for progress by all students, on average. Rather, no child could be left behind, and it had to be shown that all types of students—boys, girls Blacks, Whites, Latinos and all other ethnic minorities, the disabled, and even immigrants—were all moving toward educational proficiency.

Ironically, customization of American education was to be accomplished through centralization, its seeming opposite. To overcome resistance by vested interests, those who wished to save the schools found it easier to do so if they could shift power upward toward more central organs of government. But centralized power did not necessarily yield the customized education reformers desired. Nor did it create the efficient, egalitarian, quality educational institutions they envisioned.

The steps toward centralized control are well described, from multiple vantage points, in the superb collection of essays that follow. Yet to be told, however, is a coming reform struggle—one that seeks to customize education through the provision of virtual learning opportunities by means of new, fast-changing technologies—lap-top computers, broadband, on-line social networking, 3-dimensional programming, and much more. Either within brick and mortar schools or outside of them, or by a combination of both venues, students will be able to access high quality materials of their own choosing—from colleges, private entrepreneurs, and, perhaps, even from fellow students. It is unlikely that this coming restructuring of American education will in the near term yield fairy tale results. But the direction of change will be hostile to standardized approaches established through still more centralized political power. Instead, new educational technologies are creating for the first time the possibility of an on-line learning experience that can reach each student at the level of accomplishment he or she has reached. If multiple providers are given equal access to public resources, and students and their families are able to choose among the available options, control over learning opportunities will be radically decentralized. By the middle of the 21st century, public education in the United States may have a look decidedly different from that of the centralized, stagnant behemoth it became during the closing decades of the 20th century

Reference

Peterson, P. E. (2010). *Saving schools: From Horace Mann to virtul reality.* Cambridge MA: Harvard University Press.

PREFACE

Soon after William Lowe Boyd passed away in late 2008, members of the *Politics of Education Association* (PEA) decided to honor his memory through this edited volume of essays on education policy and politics. We recognize and value Bill Boyd's many intellectual contributions to the study of education, and his formative influence upon the development of educational politics and policy. We, the editors, are indebted to the then-President of PEA, Lora Cohen-Vogel, for initiating this project

William Boyd's outline, and accompanying ideas for a book that he had intended to be the capstone of his distinguished professional career, served the editors as an excellent guide in the course of fashioning this volume. Boyd's desire was to produce a thoughtful review and analysis of the extraordinary evolution of education politics and policy over the roughly 60-year period of 1950 to the present. This edited book, commissioned by the PEA, attempts to carry out that unfinished, half-century or more, review. The editors and chapter-authors contributing to this volume have agreed to distribute any royalties earned from sales of the book to support the Politics of Education Association.

William Lowe Boyd began his professional career as a high school band director in Loudon County (eastern Tennessee), in 1957. Bill earned a masters degree in Music Education from Northwestern University in 1961— and continued to pursue a lifelong interest in music even with the change in career that accompanied earning a Ph.D. in educational administration at The University of Chicago in 1973. Throughout academic appointments at the University of Rochester (1970–1980) and Pennsylvania State University (1980–2008), Bill spent every summer of his career (over 50-year period) in

Interlochen, Michigan, serving as a Director of Camp Life with the Interlochen Center for the Arts.

At Pennsylvania State University, Bill occupied the Harry L. Batchelet Chair of Educational Administration, the University's first awardee of that honor. Other major recognitions include the first Stephen K. Bailey Award (in 1994) for his work in helping to shape an intellectual and research agenda for the study of educational politics and the Roald F. Campbell Lifetime Achievement Award (in 2002) from the University Council for Educational Administration (UCEA). Bill published more than 140 articles and co-edited 17 books over the course of his extraordinarily productive career

In his life of professional service across more than a half-century, Bill was a leader among his academic colleagues in experiencing, studying, analyzing, explaining, and helping to establish an academic discipline in the politics of public education. "Surprising" is a summary word Bill Boyd used in his outline for the volume that he had in mind as early as 2008. It is a word that fits well into the many events, twists and turns, and dramatic changes in educational governance and policymaking accompaning the nation's entry into the 21st century

Collectively, the editors and chapter authors assembled in this volume attempt to make sense of 60-year period in the spirit of Bill's outline and the questions that drove his curiosity. Each of the chapters in this book constitutes an original contribution to the 60-year review, providing a truly state-of-the-art work that draws upon some of the best education policy scholars of this generation

Major policy themes in the first decade of the 21st century were unimaginable in 1950. Quickly following recognition of how surprising the twists and turns of policy making have been, however, we are likely to hear the words "dramatic" and "disappointing." Education organization, governance, policy and program changes have unfolded in rapid succession in response to startling national events and harsh and relentless critiques of the nation's public schools. There were critiques during the first half of the twentieth century, of course, but they do not compare with the breadth and rapidly changing focus of criticisms washing over the schools in the last half century. Prior to 1950, public schooling was a growth industry as enrollments expanded, staff became more skilled and more bureaucratically organized, new curricula were developed, and psychological and achievement testing were introduced. During this growth period, local school systems learned to cope with inadequate funding, religious controversies and rural/urban tensions over policy. Historian David Tyack labeled this mid-century pattern of development and accommodation the "One Best System" to characterize (and to criticize) the widespread confidence in America's ability to implement a Progressive agenda through its schools that had emerged by mid-century. All was not wonderful, of course. The emergent system largely ignored special needs students and displayed strong biases toward White families, males,

Protestants, property rich communities, and the moral and social norms of the middle class. The system was rather more inclined toward political and moral socialization than toward rigorous intellectual development. The wealthy and the religiously committed tended to form private school systems to preserve their own social and class values. Nevertheless, by the start of the 1950s it was generally taken for granted that the public schools were on a par with families, churches, corporations, and civic community life in providing the fundamental building blocks of the grand American Dream of moral righteousness, economic prosperity, and civic democracy.

The chapters of this book explore the evolution of the politically controversial and increasingly complex public/private school system we have today. They offer insights into why changes in policy direction have often been surprising and dramatic. They also examine how and why the social and political forces shaping and re-shaping the nation's educational policies and programs have failed to elevate confidence in the nation's public school system. Additionally, they outline some promising ways of re-thinking past events and envisioning future directions.

Finally, we must note that, while Bill Boyd has been an inspiration for our collective effort to interpret the political powers and policymaking processes shaping education governance, our work does not always adopt his conclusions. Of course, any errors are certainly our own.

ACKNOWLEDGMENTS

As editors, we appreciate the insights and assistance provided by a large number of people who have contributed to the success of this volume. We have already noted, in the preface and on our dedication page, the inspiration of William Lowe Boyd, but we are also profoundly grateful for the hard work of the contributing authors who have offered wise and detailed analyses of America's education policy systems. The authors all responded with care and diligence to editorial suggestions and the result is a singularly powerful body of scholarly insights. We also want to thank our Taylor and Francis Group editors at Routledge—Lane Akers who helped nurture the book proposal and shepherded it through the Publications Committee, and Heather Jarrow who provided editorial guidance and brought the work to publication. Special thanks goes to Lora Cohen Vogel who, as President of the Politics of Education Association, encouraged us to propose this work and negotiated its approval by the Association. Dr. Tedi Mitchell also deserves a note of thanks. In addition to being the senior author for one chapter, she helped extensively with copy editing, checking references, and otherwise facilitating the editorial process for the entire volume.

PART I

Historical and Theoretical Context

Douglas E. Mitchell

Shaping education policy is a matter of increasingly high priority for political leaders and professional educators as well as an enduring concern for families and local communities. All this policy attention is not, however, leading to broad agreement about the most desirable policies or developing a consensus regarding whether schools are responding appropriately to adopted policies. Some see schools as virtually impervious to change while others see them as adopting faddish and rapidly changing practices without regard to their effectiveness. This book takes a fresh look at how education policy is shaped and how, once shaped, it is affecting school organizations. The core ideas developed here are about power and process. The authors explore the powers inherent in political positions, in socio-political coalitions, in historical precedents and in cultural beliefs. Our authors are equally concerned about processes: the often surprising processes of policy formation and implementation, the processes of organizational and institutional change, and the processes by which political power and influence are created, allocated and exercised.

From a variety of theoretical and empirical perspectives, the chapters of this book explore the transition from what David Tyack dubbed public education's "One Best System"—laboriously framed in the first half of the 20th century—to the politically controversial, persistently challenged, closely scrutinized, and increasingly hybridized public/private school system of today. They offer insights into why changes in policy direction have been so surprising and dramatic, examine how and why the social and political forces shaping and re-shaping the nation's education policies and programs have largely failed to elevate confidence in the nation's public school system and they outline some promising ways of thinking about future directions.

The book is divided into six parts. Part I is composed of two chapters that introduce in broad strokes some of the reasons why policy changes have been so surprising and incoherent over the last several decades, and provide a framework for discussing fundamental changes occurring in school governance systems. In Chapter 1, Douglas Mitchell concentrates on the reasons why policy developments have been disjointed and surprising, developing three lines of interpretation for the unpredictable character of policy change. He describes how the identification of educational problems interacts with the entrepreneurial promotion of policy solutions and the political opportunities for action to provide for the opening and closing of brief "windows of opportunity" that provide concrete, but often unpredictable, opportunities for policy change. The chapter also summarizes competing paradigms of social explanation which serve to make some policy options seem reasonable and others quite inappropriate. Because these competing explanatory paradigms rely on different conceptions of educational purposes as well as differing beliefs about how policy and governance might be expected to secure an education system that works, shifting from one paradigm to another makes it appear that radical educational reform is desperately needed. This first chapter concludes with a brief discussion of four core public values that are in constant competition for endorsement and support and which require differing conceptions of the proper role and function of public education.

In Chapter 2, Betty Malen concentrates on how the complex American school governance system interacts with our historic commitments to democratic policy control and distributed influence among key actors at the federal, state, and local levels. This chapter highlights the dramatic shift in the locus (and scope) of policy making power, highlighting the dramatic expansions of federal and state influence, still weak and incoherent in the 1950s. Though the chapter notes the substantial contraction of local policy control mechanisms, it argues persuasively that policy making power is not a "zero sum game" in which expansion of influence by one level or agency of government *must* be matched by diminishing influence by others. To the contrary, this chapter argues, policy control can be seen as having expanded at all levels—perhaps leaving the school systems overly controlled and unable to adapt to local circumstances and needs. The chapter concludes by reflecting on the nature and effectiveness of democratic political control over schools as compared with the potential for market mechanisms for allocating policy influence.

Together, these first two chapters set out the problems and issues that many of the subsequent chapters explore in some detail. Later chapters provide diverse perspectives and detailed analyses aimed at clarifying the social forces and political processes by which public schools are being shaped, challenged, and redirected to serve both local and national purposes in the 21st century.

1

THE SURPRISING HISTORY OF EDUCATION POLICY 1950 TO 2010

Douglas E. Mitchell

Schooling in America: Taking a 1950 Perspective

The chapters in this book examine the tumultuous waves of education policy and politics that rolled over America's schools in the six decades from 1950 to 2010. The work was prompted by an unfinished book outline developed initially by William L. Boyd (1935–2008) who passed away leaving several ideas and insights in draft form. Members of the Politics of Education Association (PEA) saw in his draft outline a framework for tracing recent history and projecting the likely future of public education—not only in America but throughout the developed world. With encouragement from the PEA leadership, the three editors set about to build on these ideas and to create an edited volume analyzing key issues and interpreting the underlying storyline of the last six decades.

The chapters document the historical developments in education policy over the last six decades, and place those developments within theoretical frameworks that explain their dynamics and trace their trajectory. The story begins in 1950 as the Baby Boom generation is just entering the public schools and the remarkably powerful Progressive Education and Urban Reform movements are fading from the political landscape. Experience with the Great Depression as well as with World War II had significantly recast the American Psyche. And inner city racial and poverty ghettos had become the norm under the impact of financial "red lining" and a dramatic rise in migration of ethnic minorities and low income families, primarily from the rural South. It was a time before the *Brown* decisions, the *Sputnik* launching, and aggressive teacher unions shattered the "apolitical myth" (Iannaccone, 1967) that enabled a previous generation to move both civic and education policy making substantially out of the hands lay community leaders and into those of professional educators and city managers. It was a time of economic liberation from the wartime economy that had produced scarcity and rationing of all sorts of commodities, but equally a time of growing fear of the "Red Menace" of international communism. The horrors of atomic warfare were settling into the American spirit making civil defense drills and building bomb shelters seem like reasonable community participation activities. Local community life was fairly robust, and the belief that education policy should be handled strictly by local communities was an extraordinarily powerful political belief. Also important at this time was the entry of returning service men (and a few women) into school teaching and administration, directly and through the educational opportunities created under the GI Bill. The themes of this adjustment were heavily influenced by concerns with cost control, Taylorism's scientific management, and the "Cult of Efficiency" (Callahan, 1962).

As soon would become evident, however, this was a period of political calm before a storm of political controversy and policy innovation that broke by the middle of the 1950s and has been raging ever since. The 1950s saw schools in America rocked by three dramatic events whose continuing impact is still reverberating through the educational policy systems of the nation. These events were: (a) the *Brown v. Board of Education* desegregation decisions rendered by the U.S. Supreme Court (1954); (b) the 1957 *Sputnik* launching by the Soviet Union and the resulting sense of academic crisis in American schools leading to adoption of the National Defense Education Act (NDEA) in 1959, and (c) the militant unionization of teachers symbolized by the 1960 strike by the American Federation of Teachers in New York. These themes have remained important throughout the ensuing decades placing schools at the cross-roads of energetic and sometimes even violent struggles over racial and social class integration, reform and improvement of curricula, and systemic restructuring of school organizations.

There were dramatic changes afoot throughout society during this period (e.g., the feverish cold war with the Soviet Union, accompanied by a hot war in Korea and then Vietnam, a revolution in popular music and the rise of the "free speech," and "beat generation" rebellions against formal social institutions). But it was these three fundamental shocks during the 1950s that directly impacted the schools and substantially destroyed a broad post-war consensus regarding how schools should be organized, what they should teach and how they should separate or integrate student groups—what Tyack (1974) summarized as the "one best system." What followed was a tumultuous, half-century long crash program to "fix" the public schools. The "shock and awe" unleashed by these startling events prompted a widespread conviction that the nation needed to make real changes in basic school design and operations. As Bill Boyd started to summarize, education policy and the politics driving policy changes moved dramatically:

- From a logic of productive processes, to a logic of confidence, to a logic of accountability for outcomes
- From a focus on resources and inputs to a focus on outcomes and achievement
- From teachers as civil servants to teachers as organized employees
- From *in loco parentis* student management to students with constitutional rights
- From little federal concern to No Child Left Behind federal dominance
- From education as cultural belief to evidence based educational treatments
- From student tracking and achievement gaps to disaggregated Annual Yearly Progress monitoring
- From educator professional control to civic political domination of school governance
- From education as secular gospel to education as national security and economic necessity

Looking into the future in 1950, even the most sophisticated of observers never expected the dramatic policy changes that have dominated the ensuing decades. The first big surprise is that the federal government could penetrate the gospel of localism in America and adopt programs of general support for public schools. The National Defense Education Act of 1959 was a cold war response to the Russian *Sputnik*, but a more fundamental policy shift occurred with the 1965 adoption of the Elementary and Secondary Education Act, which provided much more money and was targeted toward broader and more general support to the schools. With race and poverty as core issues, the judiciary became a much more visible player in day to day school policy and practice—"legalizing" decision making procedures and formalizing educational governance.

A second surprise is that the civil rights emphasis and resource augmentation thrust of 1960s education policy could give way so dramatically to an emphasis on accountability for educational outcomes with the accompanying threats to forcibly reorganize schools and punish unproductive educators. This surprising shift in emphasis is partly grounded in the belief that quality educational research can make schooling a more technical and less cultural enterprise, reinforced by a fairly sharp global turn toward fiscal and social conservatism in mainstream politics. This shift calls for changes in how research is conducted, re-grounding policy in research evidence, and making educational practices more transparent and standardized.

A third big surprise is that a significant proportion of public school enrollments came to be controlled by family choice. A shift from political to economic rationales for action produced an expectation that, when required to compete for students and teachers, competition among education service providers would ratchet up the academic quality of their programs.

The degree of nationalization and even globalization of education policy is a fourth surprising development of the last half century. A half-century ago it was a central article of faith that local communities, through their local school boards and under the leadership of local professional educators, should control the cost, the quality, the content, and the distribution of children's education. By the beginning of the 21st century, it had become equally taken for granted that education was too important to both national security and economic development to be left to either educators or local community leaders. The national security theme began with the NDEA support for new curricula and teacher training in the wake of the *Sputnik* launching, and gained a full-throated demand for reform with the 1983 *Nation at Risk* report. Economic themes have become more important over the years as national policy shifted from a cold war mentality to a recognition that our economy was being challenged by developments in Germany and Japan and more recently by China.

A fifth important, and somewhat surprising, development has been a fundamental shift in the preparation and supervision of teachers. In addition to the development of formal collective bargaining and ongoing informal labor management negotiations that turned teachers into employees, there have been significant efforts to differentiate teaching roles, create multiple compensation and certification systems, and move control of teacher certification away from universities and into the hands of other agencies of governance.

Despite the energy behind these surprising turns of policy, there have been some surprisingly big disappointments in the last several decades. Despite more than three decades of unequivocal support from the U.S. Supreme court, schools did not become either fully desegregated or approach equality of educational opportunities for many important population groups. Moreover, the current Court has largely abandoned judicial use of constitutional legal principles for doing so. These "savage inequalities" (Kozol, 1992) are not limited to the schools, of course. Unequal economic opportunities remain high, resistant to change, and, by some measures, getting worse. The provision of occupational or career access education for the majority of students who are not headed for four-year colleges and universities has also been disappointingly slow to materialize, despite the fact that this group was the target of the first major federal policy initiative in the 1917 Vocational Education Act (Smith-Hughes Act). As with health care for low income families, early childhood support and education has also remained largely out of reach, and no national policy initiatives have come close to succeeding in improving this situation. Above all, despite its centrality in policy debates and major initiatives, the achievement gaps between rich and poor, between White and non-White, between English speakers and English learners remain largely untouched.

Prior to 1950, Progressives and Urban Reformers had largely succeeded in persuading educators, policy makers and most members of the public that education policy requires explicitly non-political civic interest and support. Indeed, the Urban Reform and Progressive Education movements, having successfully challenged some of the nation's most notorious political "machines" came to dominate civic and educational politics at the local level for much of the first half of the 20th century in many parts of the country. These leaders explicitly rejected partisan politics as a proper method for resolving policy issues, favoring instead expanding and empowering *professional* control over both local government and public education. Civic elites and business interests dominated these local political regimes, significantly buffering the schools from partisan and patronage politics (there were, of course, notable exceptions to their general success, especially in the nation's largest cities). The primary mechanisms for this were civil service and teacher tenure laws to protect workers and the use of non-partisan, off-year elections for trustees expected to govern out of civic interest rather than partisan ideologies.

Only after the Second World War, as the cold war raised concern with academic effectiveness and the civil rights movement demanded school desegregation, did it become obvious that school policy making is inherently political and that questions of social equity, educational effectiveness, and the securing of democratic rights for students, families and professional educators are fundamentally political concerns. Once the essentially political character of these questions was recognized, education policy became a key component in political debates over national security, community and economic development, and the role of government in guaranteeing social opportunity and equality among citizens.

There were, of course, important education policy issues that roiled public schooling prior to mid-century. How much schooling should be compulsory; what curricula to require; how to accommodate religious interests; fiscal and social tensions between rural and urban perspectives; conflicts over funding; and the introduction of business principles and practices had kept schools under continuous cross-pressures throughout this earlier period. What changed was a dramatic erosion of the belief among local elites that these and other issues should be handled by professionals leading local, civic-minded, school trustees to consensus on the best system for schooling the nation's children. Education became too important to be left to educators as political actors at all levels began to focus on the larger civic and economic purposes of schooling.

With the emergence of explicitly political and often partisan concern with education, school policies became harder to anticipate or predict. Major policy initiatives were surprising to both educators and politicians—surprising in both direction and intensity. This chapter lays the groundwork for the chapters that follow by summarizing some of the reasons why school policy has been so disjointed and characterized by surprising and dramatic changes in direction. As these underlying political dynamics are described, it will be easier to see how change in policy has become separated from coherent reorganization of practice in the schools.

This chapter raises issues to be addressed in the other chapters of this volume. It poses questions regarding the extent to which policy issues are being informed by economic realities and/or political ideologies. It argues that policy goals and mechanisms are transformed by divergent social paradigms. And it directs attention to the ways in which education policies become objects of political debate or are deflected and sublimated by political conflicts too hot to be addressed directly. Reflections on the origins of policy content draws attention to policy entrepreneurs who initiate and advocate specific policy options, seek political support for their intended goals, mobilize fiscal and human resources, and challenge the presuppositions of competing interest groups. Finally, this chapter explores why, in the face of creative and unprecedented policy initiatives and intense political pressure for change, public schools still look a lot like they did in 1950, leaving the half-century old issues of educational opportunity, academic excellence, and social cohesion very close to the center of contemporary political debates.

Dramatic and Surprising Policy Shifts Produced but Halting School Change

While there has been a deluge of policy initiatives proposed, debated, adopted, and often abandoned over the last six decades, the pace of change in school organizations and operations has been far less dramatic. Indeed, one of the most intriguing aspects of education policy over the last 60 years is how sharply and surprisingly policy topics and directions changed while school organizations and practices barely moved. In *Tinkering toward Utopia* Tyack & Cuban (1995) focus on this disconnect by distinguishing "policy action" from "policy talk." These authors report that, while policy talk has been dramatic, policy action has proven exceedingly slow because what they call the "grammar of schooling"— agreement that elementary schools should be neighborhood-based and age-graded, with self-contained classrooms occupied by one teacher and 20 to 40 pupils, and that high schools should be departmentally organized with students taking instruction in approximately one-hour blocks divided by subject matter and moving from one classroom to another according to schedule—was largely fixed by the start of the 20th century and has not been seriously challenged since. They assert that this basic structure reasserts itself, despite dramatic changes in policy talk, in ways that have tended to nullify most school reform efforts.

House (1998) offers a rather different explanation for why so many high profile policy initiatives fail to get past the proverbial "classroom door." Borrowing from Williamson's (Williamson & Masten, 1999) conceptualization of "transaction costs," House identifies three explicit transaction cost problems that limit the willingness and ability of educators to incorporate the changes that seemed so compelling to policy makers. First, he argues, like all ordinary mortals, educators respond to opportunities or mandates for change in professional practice in "opportunistic" ways. That is, they seek to keep demands on their time and effort to a manageable level and will generally make a cost/benefit analysis of policy demands and find that failing to comply with policy expectations often results in reduced workloads and no noticeable costs to work satisfaction. Second, educators, like other workers, have "bounded rationality." That is, they have a limited ability to know exactly what will happen when they try new professional practices and will often miss various important details in program designs simply because they cannot distinguish critical elements from accidental ones. Policy makers and social scientists also suffer from "bounded rationality" in not being able to see clearly what will happen when a new policy if promulgated. Thus, for example, Texas policy makers did not seem to recognize that detailed specification of curriculum content standards and matching tests would lead many teachers to adopt what McNeil (2000) describes as "defensive teaching"—a withdrawal of commitment to make sure that students actually learn a curriculum the teachers have not chosen and may not embrace. The third transaction cost element is identified by House as "specific assets"—learned attitudes and skills and accumulated teaching materials that are substantially devalued when educators are asked to change instructional technologies and curriculum content. Taken together, the costs associated with opportunism, bounded rationality, and specific asset devaluation are often, House argues, significantly greater than the needed resources of time, money, training, and supervisory support provided when new school policies are adopted. The result is not so much overt resistance to change as passive neglect of its demands.

Theoretical Explanations

There are at least three important and more elaborated theoretical accounts for why education policy actions change in dramatic and surprising ways while school practices change only slowly and largely out of sync with the policies intended to produce them.

Opening and Closing Policy Windows

The first theory of uncertain and abrupt policy actions was suggested by Kingdon (2003) in his provocative study of federal policy making. Kingdon argues persuasively that getting a new policy onto the political agenda so that it can be considered for acceptance or rejection requires the convergence of three distinct streams of activities—streams that involve different actors, rely on different decision-making processes and criteria, and are competing for attention in ways that typically keep a "window of opportunity" for action open for only a brief period before the focus of political interest shifts and different topics take up the policy system's attention.

The first and most easily recognized of these activity streams is "problem identification." At any given moment a great variety of policy problems are being identified by individuals or groups in society who feel that, "something oughta be done" to relieve their troubles by conferring a benefit, removing a danger, or relieving some pain or suffering. As sociologist C. Wright Mills observed, politics is the business of "turning personal troubles into public issues" by urging policy makers to take responsibility for problem solving. However, as Kingdon notes, most problems don't ever get acted upon. Clearly, problem recognition is not enough to get policy action.

This brings us to the second of Kingdon's (2003) critical activity streams— developing problem solutions. Before policy proposals can be considered, a case must be made that there is some reasonable solution for the problem which has been identified. Problems that have no solutions cannot be put on the political action agenda. It is important to note that problem solution development differs from the problem identification process in a number of important ways. Problem solutions are typically produced by specialists who parse the problem carefully, consider alternative lines of attack, and formulate and recommend policy actions that promise to solve the problems without unduly disrupting other aspects of the social system. The solution development process is often quite complex and always value laden. It generally takes much more time and sustained effort than does the identification of the problems being addressed. So, while the mass media and politicians play prominent roles in problem identification, a different group of players—staff members, think tank specialists, university research staff, etc., are typically the solution providers. When, for example, the Columbine High School massacre took place in Littleton, Colorado, in 1999, a problem—school violence—was quickly and widely recognized by the media and by political leaders at all levels of government. But the solution to this problem was far from obvious. Those working on solutions had to be concerned with issues of constitutional rights, detection of probable offenders, creation of effective emergency procedures, etc. And nothing about the problem, itself, shed much light on how to deal with these important dimensions of solution development.

As Kingdon (2003) noted, the separation among players, with some highlighting problems needing attention, and others working on and advocating potential solutions, often results in a situation where aggressive policy entrepreneurs are offering ready-made "solutions in search of a problem." As a result, these policy entrepreneurs often seek to re-define policy problems so that they fit the policy solutions which have already been developed. Sometimes this is done because the solutions really were developed in anticipation that pre-existing problems would be identified and addressed. Just as often, however, the link is made by solution advocates in hopes of getting their policy proposals enough attention to get on the action agenda in order to solve problems that are not the focus of political attention at the moment.

The third stream of activities highlighted by Kingdon (2003) is the stream of political events that provide regular occasions for policy action. Elections, budget cycles, key personnel changes, program evaluation reports, regular social survey or census data reports, sunset dates for existing laws, along with imposed events like strategic planning processes and political platform development, all serve to create specific opportunities for action. And, because these actions tend to be relatively brief, policy actors, like comedians, have to be sensitive to timing their actions appropriately. Policy entrepreneurs seeking action on a preferred solution who act too soon or too late in reference to the political stream are much less likely to be successful than those who understand the rhythms of the system and time their actions accordingly. As with the problem and solution streams, the political stream is typically managed by different players with different criteria for action and inaction. Elected, and more often, appointed officials serve as political gatekeepers facilitating some and resisting other policy problems and their solutions. Rarely, however, can these actors create the political power needed to bring an issue onto the action agenda without potent problem identifiers and expert solution developers.

Since policy action depends on the convergence of these three streams of action, substantial policy change is quite rare compared to the volume of talk about policy problems and alternative policy solutions. So, the "cycles of policy talk" that intrigue Tyack and Cuban (1995), from Kingdon's (2003) perspective, would mean only that there was not a convergence between awareness of problems, identification of solutions and a propitious moment for political action. Moreover, Kingdon's framework leads us to expect that quite often political action is taken to endorse a problem solution that is not very compatible with the policy problem that is the intended target of action.

Competing Paradigms of Social Explanation

While Kingdon's (2003) framework approaches the problem of explaining surprising and discontinuous policy changes through a study of political agenda setting, other scholars focus instead on how policy proposals are grounded in competing social paradigms—intellectually divergent attempts to account for how social systems work. Ever since the seminal work in which Kuhn (1970) demonstrated that the physical sciences have moved in discontinuous revolutionary leaps of logic to construct and re-construct interpretations of critical data, the concept of scientific and social theoretical paradigms has featured prominently in discussions of public policy formation. Policy developments are rendered surprising when a successful proposal is grounded in a social paradigm that diverges significantly from the one used to formulate its predecessors. The Progressive reforms of the early 20th century, for example, were surprising because they were grounded in a new paradigm of child development—one confident in natural curiosity, active learning by doing, and democratic classroom processes. The National Defense Education Act and *A Nation at Risk* reforms were surprisingly potent because they reconceptualized education as an ingredient in international political power struggles.

The civil rights reforms post-*Brown* were surprising because they challenged the concept of race and social class neutrality assumed by the Progressives. Organizational decentralization and school choice reforms were surprising because they abandoned the "one best system" assumptions of the Progressives in favor of a pluralistic paradigm that grounded adequacy in private and very local preferences. The voucher movement was surprising because it sought to replace political with economic decision making. Industrial labor unionization of teachers was surprising because it reconceptualized teachers as vulnerable and exploited workers rather than dedicated civil servants. These shifts in underlying social paradigms are central in the conception of policy formation developed by Stone (2002, p. 11):

> The essence of policy making in political communities [is] the struggle over ideas. Ideas are a medium of exchange and a mode of influence even more powerful than money and votes and guns.

At this point in our history, there appear to be only a handful of truly divergent and incompatible social paradigms that are reasonable and compelling. Collins (1994) identifies four different paradigms which he calls "sociological traditions." In a highly popular organizational management text, Bolman and Deal (2008) identify four alternatives which they refer to as analytic "frames" for interpreting managerial and policy differences. In an early paper, I identified four social theories which I described as grounded in four distinctive "generative metaphors" (Mitchell, 1986). In work I did with William Spady (Mitchell & Spady, 1983), we traced these four competing social paradigms to an underlying theory of social power and authority. In repeated editions of his major text on the structure of sociological theory, Turner (2003, 1998, 1974, 1978, 1982) has evolved from an initial framework of four theoretical schools of thought to seven. In any event, it is clear that there at least four competing frames of reference and that they are grounded in very different assumptions about how social systems work with the result that analysts give priority to very different social problems, and endorse very different social policy strategies even when they are addressing the same problems. And Tyack (1976) gave early expression to the application of four paradigm differences to describe schooling in his essay, "Ways of Seeing: An Essay on the History of Compulsory Education." Space does not allow for a detailed review of competing paradigms, but the following few paragraphs will give a sense of what a fuller development would entail. Table 1.1 provides a brief road map to some of the essential differences among four core social system paradigms. Each of these four social paradigms makes its own assumptions about the essential nature of organized social action systems.

Table 1.1 Four Contrasting Social Paradigms

	Goal Oriented Functionalism	Power Based Conflict	Marketplace Exchange	Symbolic Interaction
Underlying Discipline	Functionalist Sociology	Political Science	Supply & Demand Economics	Cognitive Psychology
Generative Metaphor	An Organism	A Machine	A Commercial Market	A Conversation
Modernity Drawn From	Medieval Church Reforms	Military Discipline	Economic Productivity	University Knowledge
Overall Social Pursuit	Social Goal Attainment	Social Power Equity	Individual/ Group Opportunity	Cultural Identity
School Emphasis	Institutional Effectiveness	Equal Opportunity	Competitive Achievement	Cultural Development

Goal-Oriented Functionalism

The first, and most widely embraced, paradigm is one which assumes that society is formed by individuals who are engaged in cooperative pursuit of mutually appreciated goals. National constitutions typically specify the purposes of government and serve to articulate one set of basic civic goals. Thus, for example, the Preamble to the U.S. constitution (Yudof, Kirp, Levin, & Moran, 2002, p. 1001) says that this nation's government is needed:

> … in Order to form a more perfect Union, establish Justice, insure domestic tranquility, provide for the common defense, promote the general Welfare, and secure the Blessings of Liberty to ourselves and our Posterity …

Similarly, business, industry and civic organizations almost always begin the planning and policy-making processes by establishing "mission" or "goal" statements that are used as the basis for designing programs and justifying structures. Functionalist analysis does not specify the goals of action, but is a very powerful framework for identifying, deliberating, and deciding how to proceed once goals have been agreed upon. That is, functional analyses can reveal whether a policy or program might be effective in reaching established goals, and estimate how efficiently it would be in contributing to realization of those goals, but it cannot tell us whether appropriate goals have been chosen. Goal selection requires acceptance of a cultural value system and alignment with existing power relationships and/or democratic preferences to give concrete expression to those values.

Sociology, with its emphasis on explaining how social behavior is coordinated, provides the underlying social science discipline for this paradigm.

It draws many of its insights through reliance on an organismic metaphor for analysis. Just as organisms have as their prime principle of action survival and propagation, functional sociologies see social organizations as coordinating their actions in order to survive and prosper. Organizational structures are analyzed in terms of their functional contribution to empowering survival.

The medieval Catholic Church, the only social institution to survive the societal disintegration of the so-called Dark Ages, provides the archetypical template or generative metaphor for functionalist social action systems. In the face of sweeping social disintegration, the medieval church evolved the system of hierarchical command and control mechanisms that have been emulated in private sector corporations and public sector bureaucracies. Acceptance of membership in a corporate community, development of specialized functional roles, coordination through a central executive function, adaptations deployed to create a symbiotic relationship between the organization and its environment were all held together by cultural myths and ritualized actions providing participants with a sense of identity and community as the organization moved through history to maintain itself and socialize new generations of participants into its coordinated action system. All these features are taken for granted by the functionalist paradigm. And, where these characteristics are not found, organizations are seen as dysfunctional and individuals rejecting them are seen as deviant.

The dominant criteria for functional effectiveness are efficiency in pursuing established goals and a reliable system of administrative management. It was the emergence and elaboration of this social paradigm which led to the development of what Tyack (1974) identified as the "one best system" of schooling and led to powerful support for the professionalization of school, business and civic managers during the middle decades of the 20th century. Progressive movement policy advocates used a functionalist paradigm to focus reform efforts. Their goals, however, were broader and more democratic than those being used by the professional "scientific management" executives who typically endorsed narrower academic learning goals. Dewey articulated the Progressive education goals and helped lead the effort to make schools professional and efficient. Business leaders articulated functional management criteria that were folded into the Progressive framework.

Conflict Theory

The functionalist conception of social organizations that assumes cooperative goal pursuit by individuals whose loyalty and cooperation springs from their endorsement of collective goals contrasts dramatically with the social conflict paradigm identified in the middle column of Table 1.1. This second paradigm begins with the assertion that society is composed of groups of people with essentially incompatible needs and interests and are, therefore, locked in a perpetual struggle to protect their interests, to dominate other groups, or at least to defend their interests against the encroachment of competitors. The assumption is that interests are given by one's location in society and that these interests are in such conflict that we cannot expect the social system to satisfy them all. Karl Marx and Friedrich Engels (see discussion in Collins, 1994) are credited with making this paradigm a permanent part of Western social thought as they conceptualized fundamental and permanent contradiction between the interests of economic owners and economic workers. But the same basic idea of irreconcilable conflicts of interest can be seen in conflicts between genders, racial groups, social classes, religious groups, and any other social structures where group membership is associated with fundamental disagreements regarding rights, status, privilege, or access to resources.

Beginning with Machiavelli's *The Prince* (2008), political science has been the underlying social science discipline informing this paradigm. There is, of course, a long tradition of conflict sociology, and economic analysis has also tended to highlight irreconcilable conflicts, but political science has put social power at the center of the problem and has consistently pursued social analysis to examine how conflicts of interest might be managed is such a way as to prevent anarchic civil wars of each against all. The underlying metaphor for this type of social organization is the productive power of the modern machine. Machines work well when their parts are honed for the specific task to which they are assigned—which is probably why well-trained armies are often called "fighting machines." But machines are not functionally adaptive (at least not until the artificial intelligence capacities of advanced computers). The parts are ignorant of their purposes, and they are not coordinated by goals but rather by the specifics of their design.

Rather than the institutional life of the medieval church, it is the modernization of military tactics that provides the organizational archetype for this paradigm. As medieval foot soldiers developed discipline—learning to accept without question their position in rank and to collaborate against a foe—they learned the essence of conflict rather than cooperation based coordination of social action. The primary analytic questions for conflict theorists are focused on how social equilibrium is produced, not how goals are reached. The two broad political answers to this question of social equilibrium are the establishment of democracies and dictatorships. Democracies are created by power balancing— providing all citizen groups with enough power to pursue and protect their own interests, but not enough to be able to dominate others. Dictatorships, by contrast, exist when one group in a society manages to dominate all others and to coerce or manipulate others into meeting their desires. Of course, all actual societies have a mix of democratic and dictatorial impulses and arrangements. Who has dictatorial powers and who is being victimized by some mechanism of power-based domination becomes a central political concern, and policy debates center on how to limit exploitation and liberate the oppressed. Hence, this paradigm is particularly favored by those for whom social equity is a primary concern. Policy actions can take dramatic and surprising turns when policy advocates using a conflict paradigm gain enough power to overcome the managerial efficiency orientation of functional analysts.

Marketplace Exchange Theory

The third paradigm, one that has had a variety of strong advocates beginning with Friedman's seminal work (1962), sees social action systems in terms of marketplace exchanges. With economics as the underlying social science discipline, analysts taking this perspective emphasize cost/benefit models of policy formation and implementation. They assume that behavior is controlled through incentives and that social routines are generated through the creation of reliable (though not perfectly predictable) systems of rewards and incentives made available to those who are expected to comply with policy-maker preferences. The marketplace metaphor is generally articulated by asserting that individuals and groups come together with bundles of preferences for benefits (and desires to influence the behavior of others), and bring with them a bundle of resources which they have to offer in exchange for the desired outcomes. Historically, it was the birth of the modern bourgeois money and credit economy that made it possible to believe that this model of human action plausibly explains all important social transactions. Game theory, public choice analysis, studies of principal-agent relationships, and the inquiries into social transaction costs all rely on this market exchange paradigm for explaining how social action systems evolve and become more or less stabilized.

This paradigm is particularly well suited to analyzing the ways in which social systems succeed or fail in delivering liberty of choice, and providing ways for individuals and groups to pursue their preferences and self-interests. In the last quarter of a century, the prominence of this paradigm has made it appear completely self-evident that market place competition will provide the greatest public and private goal attainment for the largest number of people. Only in recent years has substantial consideration been given to the prospects of market failures that might undermine the public and/or private benefits generated through market competition. With the world-wide economic collapse of 2008, however, it has become apparent we cannot confidently know when marketplace competition will be undermined by the political exploitation of some groups and individuals by others. One thing that has become evident is that market theory does not automatically lead to the breakup of monopoly control mechanisms, and that the creation of very small market units (like individual charter or voucher supported schools) does not guarantee that there will be either competition for excellence in service delivery or independence from political and social domination by political factions or special interests.

Symbolic Interaction Theory

The fourth basic paradigm of social action starts from the simple recognition that individuals and groups hold divergent interpretations of the meaning and significance of various action possibilities, and that they act on the basis of their interpretations, not on "objective" interpretations of events. In its most extreme form, analysts using this paradigm deny that there is any "objective" reality, but only the interpretations that constitute meaning systems that are socially constructed to provide various "taken-for-granted" themes and typifications of objects, persons and events. In less radical formulations, this paradigm holds that the cultural interpretations of social actions, whatever their status as objective realities, powerfully orient groups and individuals toward the meaning and possibilities available to them, and that the culture interprets through language and other symbol systems our physical environment and orients us to social action.

The social science underpinning this paradigm is psychology with its recognition that experiential sensations are turned into perceptions of an objective world only through significant mental actions—objects are constituted and their meanings construed by inference and deduction, fitting fragmentary experiences into an inferred and imagined world of action and meaning. Thus, to a substantial degree, the world is "what we make of it" not just "how we experience it." This becomes a social action paradigm when we recognize that the construing of meaning arises through social interaction and is not a merely private construction. Or, to put the point differently, individuals who live in a privately constructed world are presumed to be mentally deranged—sane people are able to find others with mental constructions of their experience that are compatible in fundamental ways. The basic generative metaphor for this kind of social analysis is a conversation. In conversations individuals share their constructions of experience, seeking and offering confirmation that the shared constructions adequately represent the realities that have been experienced.

The social institution that best exemplifies worlds built through symbolic interaction is the modern university. With the birth of the modern university, societies learned to systematically engage in exploratory and confirmatory conversations regarding how our experience of natural and social phenomena should be construed in ways that enabled us to live without undue surprises and disappointments regarding the effects of various social actions. Many analysts see the public school as similarly exemplifying this symbolic interaction character of human social experience. Guttmann (1987), for example, sees social interaction in the school as fundamental to the development and perseveration of democratic polities. Thus, within the conversational interchanges typified and structured as universal knowledge development, the primary social pursuit is seen as meaningful social and individual fulfillment. In educational terms, this generally means urging upon the schools the quality of intellectual development generally referred to as "higher order thinking."

The Paradigms Clash

The point of these last several paragraphs has not been to develop or document clearly any of these four social action paradigms, or even to claim that these four are the definitive set of fundamental alternatives. The point has been to show that how an individual or group conceives of the basic mechanisms (paradigms) of social action will have a very powerful effect on how they define social problems and what they will consider potential policy fixes for social problems once they are identified. When there is a clash of paradigms, that is, when socially active groups adopt different fundamental explanatory schemas, groups will be baffled by each other's views of policy problems and solutions. Moreover, when control over policy decisions slips from one paradigm to another, the result will be disconcerting and surprising to those who are continuing to view the world from the earlier paradigmatic perspective.

Core Social Values

A third theoretical accounting for the surprising twists and turns of education policy during the last half-century arises from the fact that social policy always involves a struggle over which among a set of core public values should be given the highest priority. This perspective is substantially embedded in the social paradigms discussed above. That is, each of the social paradigms tends to make it easier to address some social values rather than others. But the recognition of four core public values does not require appreciation of the divergent paradigms. Indeed, Stone (2002) and Marshall, Mitchell, and Wirt (1989) have identified very similar sets of core social values without needing to discuss their links to specific social action paradigms. Using the Marshall et al.'s nomenclature, the four core values are: Liberty, Quality, Efficiency and Equity. A credible argument that one or more of these values should be addressed through a change in policy or program design tends to increase a policy advocate's access to the policy making process. It does not assure success, of course—competing and often more powerful interests and ideas will also be raised within the debate. But, as Schattschneider (1960) famously pointed out, in politics the most important argument is always "the argument about what the argument is about." And credible showing that a core public value is at stake frames participation in that argument. The following paragraphs provide a brief thumbnail sketch of each of the four core public values.

Liberty, the Basic Value

In democratic societies, liberty is the bedrock public value. Whether we think of how the ratification of constitutions and the adoption of agency regulations constrains our liberties or examine how some political decisions create new liberties where none had previously existed, all law defines or circumscribes some citizen liberties. Where no intrusion into citizen liberties are necessary, no laws are justified—citizens and group members will voluntarily cooperate with one another. These intrusions are justified by credible claims that the resulting social order creates an overall improvement in the lives of citizens; an improvement whose benefits outweigh the value of the liberty being sacrificed. For example, the adoption of compulsory school attendance laws ended citizen liberty to choose no education for their children, but the adoption of compulsory schooling was grounded in confidence that both the society and the individual students gained in terms of social and economic values much more than they had to give up in terms of the liberty to escape formal education. Education policy debates have often included proposals to expand liberty within the compulsory schooling mandate through tolerance of private or home schooling, vouchers and charter school arrangements, open enrollment and elective program options within the schools. Some Libertarians have proposed to disestablish the public schools entirely and make all participation in education a matter of freedom of choice.

Quality, the Justification for Policy

When considering how policies might reshape citizen liberties, the first value-based argument used to justify a proposed policy change is that it will improve the overall quality of life—an improvement whose value exceeds the cost in social liberty. There are, of course, perpetual and fundamental arguments over what qualities are preferred. At a very broad level, wealth is preferred over poverty, security over exposure to risk, education over ignorance, and privacy over public scrutiny. But these general preferences are not equally embraced by all citizens and there are many occasions when even these general preferences have to be balanced or prioritized. And, of course, many policies provide a better quality of life to some citizens at the expense of others. Nevertheless, access to a policy debate facilitated by making a credible argument regarding how much a given proposal enhances or degrades quality, or by showing that the sacrifice of liberty imposed by the policy is more valuable than whatever quality of life it might enhance.

In the decades since 1950, the definition of "quality education" has shifted quite dramatically. At its zenith, the Progressive movement sought to define quality in terms of "life adjustment"—helping children to be ready for entry into civic and economic adulthood through development of practical attitudes and skills. With adoption of the post-*Sputnik* National Defense Education Act, quality shifted sharply toward science, mathematics, and a more aggressive political socialization agenda. Since then there has been a continuing debate between an emphasis on "the basics" and the development of "higher order thinking." Despite differences in the meaning of the term, however, calls to improve the "quality" of education have proven an enduring feature of political agendas at local, state, and national levels.

Efficiency, the Critique of Quality

Policies that improve the quality of social life are appropriately challenged with regard to whether they do so efficiently, that is whether they use only a minimum of scarce resources and avoid producing unnecessary constraints on citizen liberties. Frederick Taylor's (1911) name is historically associated with a sweeping and profound endorsement of the efficiency value in business, industry, and government. His *Scientific Management* treatise developed the concept of fragmenting work tasks into the smallest and simplest component parts and then studying the most efficient way of performing each task. Throughout the Progressive era a visible emphasis on scientific management efficiency was felt throughout the school systems. Dewey and the Progressives pushed for a qualitative reform to the content of public education, but they also cooperated with the business community in supporting strong executive leadership, careful analysis of instructional processes, and reliance on surveying and testing to allocate education resources in the most efficient possible manner. Indeed, as Callahan (1962) noted, the business community's "Cult of Efficiency" has to be seen as more effective and long lasting in their emphasis on efficiency rather than quality criteria for promulgation of reforms.

Equity, the Redress Value

A fourth core public value is assuring that policies have an equitable effect on the citizens that they affect. Equity is last in this sequence of values both because it is the value most often neglected and because it logically arises only after the policy system has found a qualitative reasons to impose on citizens' liberties and after there is enough efficiency in the policy that it can be expected to deliver benefits worth its cost. Equity, in other words, is a *redress* value, not an *address* value. Equity arguments arise and are accepted when there is credible evidence that the social paradigm logic being used to analyze a proposed policy is shown to impose unfair burdens on some citizens because they much carry more than their share of the social and/or financial costs, or because deserving citizens are not given equal access to the benefits the policy produces.

The redress nature of social equity issues accounts for why the judiciary has played such a prominent role in trying to overcome inequality in educational opportunities. Racial and ethnic minorities, women, educationally handicapped children, students protesting unpopular social policies, families seeking equal protection for their children's constitutional rights regarding religious expression, freedom of speech, and disciplinary due processes have all turned to the courts for relief—and sometimes with remarkable and surprising success. It is equally true that equality of educational opportunity has often been a neglected issue and, not infrequently, an intentionally abused right.

Shifting Values Make for Surprising Policies

The fact that the four core values highlighted in the preceding paragraphs are broadly supported throughout democratic societies does not mean that everyone agrees about either their content or their relative priorities. From time to time political priorities shift creating surprising support for policies that previously did not seem very important. Efficiency dominated the Progressive Era reforms, giving way quite dramatically during the late 50s and 60s to a belief that equity values had been trampled on for far too long. By the release of the *Nation at Risk* report in 1983, another sharp shift in value priorities occurred as Americans were persuaded that their schools were not of sufficient quality to guarantee either national security or economic competitiveness. Although the No Child Left Behind rendition of the Elementary and Secondary Education Act remains strongly committed to improving educational quality through the twin pressures of standards-based accountability and charter or voucher schools of competitive choice, the latest Gallup poll (Bushaw & McNee, 2009, p. 10) suggests that pressure for test-score defined educational quality may no longer be the nation's number one educational value problem.

Conclusion

This chapter has been designed to introduce the more specific policy analyses presented in the remainder of this volume. Beginning with a brief sketch of how American education looked in 1950, I've noted the dramatic and surprising shifts in policy debates in the ensuing decades. The primary concern of this chapter has been to develop an understanding of why policy shifts have appeared to be abrupt and unpredictable. Of course, school organizations and programs are sufficiently similar to what was happening 60 years ago that a "Rip Van Winkle" who fell asleep in 1950 wouldn't have much trouble recognizing the elementary and secondary schools of today. The policy debates have shifted often and dramatically, however, and this chapter has identified some of the reasons why that has been so. We looked at the political dynamics of policy making that keep windows of opportunity for real change open only briefly. We reviewed the existence of intellectually incompatible paradigms of social action that cause policy advocates to shift the definition of problems and the logic of solutions to fit their preferred explanatory paradigm. And we noted, finally, that there are four fundamental policy values in a democratic society, and that policy arguments can move quite rapidly from one value to another and can also shift when the defining characteristics of one of these values shifts.

References

Bolman, L. G., & Deal, T. E. (2008). *Reframing organizations: Artistry, choice, and leadership* (4th ed.). San Francisco: Jossey-Bass.

Brown v. Board of Education of Topeka, 347 US 483 (1954).

Bushaw, W. J., & McNee, J. A. (2009). Americans speak out: Are educators and policy makers listening?—The 41st Annual Phi Delta Kappa/Gallup Poll of the Public's Attitudes toward the Public Schools. *Phi Delta Kappan, 91*(1), 8–23.

Callahan, R. E. (1962). *Education and the cult of efficiency; a study of the social forces that have shaped the administration of the public schools.* Chicago: University of Chicago Press.

Collins, R. (1994). *Four sociological traditions.* New York: Oxford University Press.

Elementary and Secondary Education Act, P.L. 89-10. 89th Congress.

Friedman, M., (1962). *Capitalism and freedom.* Chicago: University of Chicago Press.

Guttmann, A. (1987). *Democratic education.* Princeton, NJ: Princeton University Press.

House, E. R. (1998). *Schools for sale: Why free market policies won't improve America's schools, and what will.* New York: Teachers College Press.

Iannaccone, L. (1967). *Politics in education.* New York: Center for Applied Research in Education.

Kingdon, J. W. (2003). *Agendas, alternatives, and public policies* (2nd ed.). New York: Longman.

Kozol, J. (1992). *Savage inequalities: Children in America's schools.* New York: Harper Perennial.

Kuhn, T. S. (1970). *The structure of scientific revolutions* (2nd ed.). Chicago: University of Chicago Press.

Machiavelli, N. (2008). *The prince* (reproduction ed.). Fort Worth, TX: RDMc Pub.

Marshall, C., Mitchell, D. E. & Wirt, F. M. (1989). *Culture and education policy in the American states.* New York: Falmer Press.

McNeil, L. M. (2000). *Contradictions of school reform: educational costs of standardized testing.* New York: Routledge.

Mitchell, D. E. (1986). Metaphors of management: Or, how far from outcomes can you get? *Peabody Journal of Education, 63*(3), 29–45.

Mitchell, D. E., & Spady, W. G. (1983). Authority, power, and the legitimation of social control. *Educational Administration Quarterly, 19*(1), 5–33.

National Commission on Excellence in Education. (1983). *A nation at risk: The imperative for educational reform: A report to the Nation and the Secretary of Education.* United States Department of Education. Washington, DC: The National Commission on Excellence in Education.

National Defence Education Act, U.S. Code. 20 U.S.C. Chapter 17.

Schattschneider, E. E. (1960). *The semisovereign people; a realist's view of democracy in America.* New York: Holt Rinehart and Winston.

Smith-Hughes Act (1917). P.L. 347, 64th Congress, Section 18, 39 Stat. 936.

Stone, D. A. (2002). *Policy paradox: the art of political decision making* (rev. ed.). New York: Norton.

Turner, J. H. (1974). *The structure of sociological theory.* Homewood, IL: Dorsey Press.

Turner, J. H. (1978). *The structure of sociological theory* (rev. ed.). Homewood, IL: Dorsey Press.

Turner, J. H. (1982). *The structure of sociological theory* (3rd ed.). Homewood, IL: Dorsey Press.

Turner, J. H. (2003). *The structure of sociological theory* (7th ed.). Belmont, CA: Wadsworth Thomson Learning.

Turner, J. H., & Turner, P. R. (1998). *The structure of sociological theory* (6th ed.). Belmont, CA: Wadsworth .

Tyack, D. (1976). Ways of seeing: An essay on the history of compulsory education. *Harvard Educational Review, 46,* 355–388.

Tyack, D. B. (1974). *The one best system: A history of American urban education.* Cambridge, MA: Harvard University Press.

Tyack, D. B., & Cuban, L. (1995). *Tinkering toward utopia: A century of public school reform.* Cambridge, MA: Harvard University Press.

Williamson, O. E., & Masten, S. E. (1999). *The economics of transaction costs.* Northampton, MA: E. Elgar.

2

AN ENDURING ISSUE

The Relationship between Political Democracy and Educational Effectiveness

Betty Malen[1]

In the United States, the relationship between effective education and political democracy is generally viewed as "a given." Many citizens and their representatives view an effective education system as the foundation of a vibrant democracy. While educational opportunities of various sorts can support democratic purposes and strengthen democratic processes, historically, philosophers, policymakers, and publics alike have singled out the public school system as the institution that is expected to equip and inspire students to assume their civic responsibilities, become informed participants in the governance of their communities, and contribute to the creation of the good society, however that ideal may be defined. Individuals and groups disagree about how to accomplish those broad objectives; but, few citizens dispute the major premise—public schools have a critical role to play in the creation of a responsible, productive, and engaged citizenry and the development of a vital, responsive, and durable democracy (Guttman, 1999; Westheimer & Kahne 2003; McDonnell, 2000; Rothstein, Jacobson, & Wilder, 2008; Soder, 2004).

The relationship between political democracy and educational effectiveness, however, is clearly not treated as "a given." That relationship is continuously and, at times, intensely contested in debates about where in the multi-level governance system the authority for determining educational decisions should reside and how that authority should be distributed among professionals, parents, publics and policymakers (Guttman, 1999; Elmore, 1993). That relationship is further contested in debates about whether educational decisions should be determined within the political system, by market forces or through some hybrid arrangement (Carnoy, 1993; Chubb & Moe, 1987; Guttman, 1999; Mintrom, 2009).

To illustrate, historians repeatedly remind us that the "tension between local control and central authority is an endemic and perhaps dynamic characteristic of schooling in the United States" (Beadie, 2000, p. 48). They also remind us that the tension between professional and public control over key aspects of schooling is a longstanding point of contention. As McDonnell (2000) writes, "Since the advent of the Progressive era, reforms emphasizing professional expertise, democratic governance and professionalism have coexisted in an uneasy truce" (p. 8). Whether professionalism "completes rather than competes with democracy" by building capacity for democratic deliberation and instilling norms of social responsibility and client accountability is a salient but unresolved issue that fuels numerous education policy and governance disagreements (Guttman, 1999, p. 77).

Further, both supporters and critics of democratic governance reiterate that the public school system, at least on some measures, is not as responsive, equitable and productive as it ought to be. Some argue, albeit for quite different reasons, that policy elites at the federal and state level may have "little appetite for the kind of prolonged struggle needed to get to the root cause of social problems. The course of least resistance for them is a succession of visible but superficial responses to problems" that have little chance of altering established political networks and the organizational priorities and routines these powerful interests support (Stone, 1980, p. 23; see also Anyon, 1997, 2005; Stone, Henig, Jones, & Pierannunzi, 2001). For policymakers who must stand for re-election, political credits tend to be gained or lost in the adoption of "flashy" policies that can be touted on the campaign trail, not in the development and implementation of comprehensive, coherent approaches to social and educational problems (Fuhrman, 1993, p. 11).

At the local level, deeply rooted traditions of incremental decision making as well as concerns about professional and political careers, the capacity of "local cartels" (Rich, 1996) to co-opt community activists and other contingencies may prompt district-level policymakers to select and enact policies that attract attention and enhance legitimacy but do not alter, fundamentally, the orientations and operations of the school system (Hess, 1999; Ogawa, Sandholtz, Martinez-Flores, & Scribner, 2003). Even when decision-making authority is purportedly delegated to professionals and patrons at the site-level, the political processes in these more proximate and presumably improvement-oriented arenas rarely reflect the broad ideals of equal access, authentic participation, democratic deliberation and educational gains that advocates of these arrangements hope to secure (Anderson, 1998; Fuller, 2009; Handler, 1996; Malen & Cochran, 2008; Mann 1974; Whitty, Power, & Halpin, 1998).

In these and other ways, institutional structures and pluralistic bargaining may create and perpetuate a political incentive structure that makes it difficult, and, in the minds of some, virtually impossible for governments to enhance the performance of schools and to realize the array of democratic purposes they are to serve. As Chubb and Moe (1990) summarize the position, "the school's most fundamental problems are rooted in the institutions of democratic control by which they are governed" (p. 66). As others express it, the American political system is comprised of "multiple veto points that opponents can use to protect existing policy arrangements and thwart reform proposals" (McGuinn, 2006b, p. 206). For some analysts and advocates, the public school system's failure to fully realize all of its major goals, the government's inability to rectify that situation, and the presumption that democratic control is the source of school performance problems rather than an integral part of the solution to them provide grounds for an entirely different form of control that is lodged more in competitive market forces than in democratic governmental arrangements (Chubb & Moe, 1987; Plank & Boyd, 1994). Although "U.S. schools successfully educate millions of students" and provide extensive albeit inequitable access to educational programs and services (Mickelson, 2009, p. 253), the press for a greater reliance on market forces has intensified (Burch, 2009; Henig, 2009b; Mintrom, 2009), in part because a substantial number of children and youth have, indeed, been left behind by our educational institutions and our broader social support systems (Kanter & Lowe, 2006; O'Connor, Hill, & Robinson, 2009; Wells, 2009).

The press for market solutions to school performance problems is clearly evident in various types of school choice proposals (e.g., expansion of parent options to exit low-performing schools and transfer to other schools within a district, the issuance of vouchers to attend private and/or public schools, the proliferation of charter schools) as well as in the increasing use of homeschooling options and the growing number of opportunities for private companies to manage schools, prepare professionals and provide supplemental tutorial services to students. This press, in all its iterations, clearly warrants attention especially given the "increasing willingness" of policymakers and publics "to turn over popular control of the public school systems to private interests through reforms such as vouchers and other privatization efforts" that directly challenge and arguably undercut the democratic structures that characterize the U.S. public school system (Jacobson, 2009, p. 314; see also Abernathy, 2005; Fuller, 2009; Henig, 2009a; Ravitch, 2010). Despite its importance, this exit-based strategy for governing schools and for engendering improvements in them is not examined here because other chapters take up the relative merits of this approach to school governance and school improvement (see Harris & Witte, this volume). Instead, this analysis focuses on the voice-based strategy embedded in more traditional governance arrangements that afford citizens the opportunity to express their preferences indirectly, through electoral processes, and directly, through participation in the many arenas wherein education policy decisions are brokered.

Purpose and Perspective

The purpose of focusing on the voice-based strategy that undergirds democratic governance arrangements in the United States' large, diverse, tiered, and fragmented political system is to illustrate how governments have tried to reform public schools and how those efforts, in turn, have redistributed the authority for making educational decisions. The sections that follow (a) document the centralization of control over education policy decisions that occurred between 1950 and the present, and (b) discuss how this evolutionary and revolutionary shift in the balance of power across levels of the system may affect the quest for educational effectiveness. Reflecting others' appraisals, this chapter argues that one of the defining features of the politics of education during this time period is a marked and consequential redefinition of power relationships between local, state and federal levels of government (Kirst, 1988; Mazzoni, 2000) and between policymakers, professionals, parents, and the various publics who through individual participation or organized effort may seek to influence school policies and practices. Despite a strong tradition of and rhetorical commitment to local control embodied in local school boards and intermittent efforts to decentralize and democratize education by delegating authority to and redistributing authority across educators and patrons at the site level, the state and federal levels of government have acquired unprecedented control over key domains of schooling (Conley, 2003; Fusarelli & Cooper, 2009; McGuinn, 2006a, 2006b; Valli, Croninger, Chambliss, Graeber, & Buese, 2008). This new degree of centralized control holds important implications not only for who governs, but also for how the purpose and performance of public schools will be constructed and how educational programs, related services and valued outcomes will be delivered and distributed.

To be sure, both conceptual and empirical problems complicate our ability to track, assess and compare the relative power of governmental units and to link shifts in governance arrangements to educational effectiveness, variously defined. For that reason, this section highlights the analytic assumptions that undergird this analysis, acknowledges data limitations and emphasizes the provisional nature of the interpretations rendered.

Analytic Assumptions

In discussing inter-governmental relationships, this chapter makes several assumptions about the locus and distribution of that murky, multi-dimensional, and fluid phenomenon known as power.

First, an increase in power at the federal and state levels does not automatically or necessarily reduce the power of actors at the local district or the individual school levels. Indeed, policies initiated and enacted at one level may provide the political cover and currency required to advance agendas forged at other levels of the system. Whether through intricate processes of "borrowing" legitimacy and capacity from higher and lower levels of the system (Manna, 2007) or "appropriating" policies imposed from afar and using them selectively and strategically to advance local preferences and priorities (Fuhrman, Clune, & Elmore, 1988; Honig, Lorton, & Copland, 2009), players at each level of the system can capitalize on as well as be constrained by the actions taken at other levels of the system (Cohen, Moffitt & Goldin, 2007; Henig, 2009a). Further, in some instances, actors at lower levels of the system can mobilize and over-turn policies imposed on them (Grossman, 2010) and they can deflect or adapt them during implementation (Cohen et al., 2007; Cuban, 1998; Malen, 2006). While a zero-sum game is not inevitable, it is conceivable, especially if some units of the system begin to exercise control within and across key domains of decision-making in ways that sharply circumscribe the power of other units and develop policies that are difficult to duck or dilute during implementation (Malen 2003; Malen & Cochran, 2008; Sykes, O'Day, & Ford. 2009). Given the sheer volume and rapid proliferation of legislation, regulation, and litigation across various domains of education policy between 1950 and the present, it is exceedingly difficult to map in detail the manner in which the web of policies enacted at any level of the system might interact to empower or restrict other units of the system. Thus, this chapter highlights general patterns and offers provisional appraisals of apparent shifts in the balance of power between local, state, and federal levels of the system.

Second, power is not simply a function of the presence or absence of formal authority to make binding decisions in particular policy domains of education and related social policy. The power of governmental units is contingent on their capacity to meet the duties and obligations that may be attributed to or imposed upon them and to carry out whatever additional responsibilities the units may wish to assume (Malen & Muncey, 2000). Further, power at any level of the system is contingent on what Allison (1971) termed the "skill and will" with which actors convert their various sources of power into influence through highly visible strategies such as specifying rules, allocating or withholding resources and/or applying sanctions as well as through more subtle symbolic processes such as framing agendas, defining situations, and altering perceptions of problems, priorities, and possibilities (Malen & Muncey, 2000).

Third, the relative power of actors can be gauged in a variety of ways. For the reasons noted above, this chapter incorporates multiple indicators, notably formal authority arrangements, the capacity of actors to initiate as well as to react, the combination of strategies deployed and the ability to influence, for good or ill, school priorities, processes, and practices.

Finally, the relative power of actors is always an empirical question. Knowing who will be involved let alone who will be influential in particular arenas and on particular issues "cannot be delineated *a priori*" (Howett & Ramesch, 1995, p. 52). Indeed, scholars report that the roles of school boards, superintendents, teachers' unions, legislative bodies, corporations, mayors, federal courts, and state education agencies may "range from featured player to bit part in different places and in different times in the same place" (Danielson & Hochschild, 1998, p. 27).

In linking inter-governmental power relationships with indicators of educational effectiveness, this chapter assumes that the connection between forms of governance and patterns of performance is tenuous for organizations in general and for public school systems in particular (Hall, 1986; Hannaway & Carnoy, 1993). With others, Elmore (1993) observes that in the past, "the repeated cycles of centralizing and decentralizing reforms in education have had little discernible effect on the efficiency, accountability or effectiveness of public schools" (p. 34). While education policies have had various effects, governance shifts, *in and of themselves* do not appear to have had a major impact on school operations and outcomes (Croninger & Malen, 2002). The limited and often mixed evidence of governance effects on aspects of public schools may be due in part to (a) the difficulty of attributing changes in broad indicators of school effectiveness such as student attainment and public satisfaction with schools to particular reform initiatives (Jacobson, 2009; Lee, 2008), (b) the nature and duration of the governance shifts, (c) the policies advanced by different levels and units of government, (d) the scope and severity of the problems schools have been expected to address, and (e) other contingencies that shape the productivity, responsiveness and accomplishments of schools (Rothstein, 2002, 2004). Given these and other complexities, this chapter offers only provisional observations about the apparent relationship between the distribution of educational authority and various indicators of school effectiveness.

Data Limitations

Unfortunately, the empirical base for addressing questions regarding the relative power of actors within and across levels of the system and the impact of various power configurations on the governance and performance of schools is limited. We have studies of some federal education policy initiatives but not others; we have accounts of select education policy developments in some states but not all states; we have information on aspects of local governance arrangements and local responses to select state and federal initiatives in a small fraction of the more than 14,000 districts and 96,000 schools that make up the public school system (Fuhrman, Goertz, & Weinbaum, 2007). But, we do not have a complete picture of how the relative power of players within and across arenas of the system has changed across issues and overtime, how those changes have affected the governance and performance of public schools, let alone how those policy developments have affected subsequent rounds of political dynamics and power configurations (McDonnell, 2009).

While the extant literature is limited in these and arguably other ways, it is instructive. It suggests that a host of initiatives advanced to enhance public school fairness and effectiveness (variously defined) have moved critical education policy decisions away from the more proximate democratic institutions like local school boards and site-based decision-making venues and vested them in the more remote state and national policy arenas. It also suggests that the policy strategies associated with the unprecedented centralization of power may be having an unprecedented (and unintended) influence on the quality and equity of educational experiences.

too muchfocus on standardyation lost art of teaching?

The Evolutionary and Revolutionary Shift in the Locus and Balance of Power

During the 1950s and early 1960s, states were broadly viewed as the weak link in the federal-state-local chain of school governance even though some states had eliminated a sizeable number of local school districts despite local resistance to consolidation initiatives (Campbell, Cunningham, Nystrand, & Usdan, 1990; Henig, 2009a). The federal government led the call for excellence and equity in education with its post-*Sputnik* curricular initiatives in math and science, precedent-setting desegregation litigation, pioneering civil rights legislation, and compensatory education programs. Lighthouse districts generated interest in educational innovations as they disseminated information about their latest program developments and organizational changes and encouraged others to emulate their actions. In short, the federal government and select local units of the system were the visible and vocal agents of reform (Campbell et al., 1990; Malen, 2003). States helped local units fund schools, set standards for teacher certification and school facilities, and defined broad educational program requirements. However, they delegated most of the authority and responsibility for governing public schools to local districts (Campbell et al, 1990; Cohen et al., 2007; Fuhrman et al., 2007).

During this period, most districts had considerable latitude in terms of the educational revenues they could raise and the particular priorities and programs they could pursue. Although districts' capacity to finance schools varied widely, they had the operative "final say" in terms of curricular content, student services, budget and personnel (Garmes, Guthrie, & Pierce, 1978). For the most part, districts were accountable primarily to their local constituents, not to their state governments or to the federal government. Districts recognized the importance of engendering confidence in the public schools and the necessity of balancing professional views, community values, and various state and national forces (Boyd, 1976); but, they did not worry about being graded by state and federal agencies, taken over by state governments, or turned over to private management companies.

The historic reliance on local democratic governance structures and the professionals employed by them has not been a panacea. Scholars and proximate observers have questioned whether citizens were attentive and vigilant monitors of their public schools and whether their episodic involvement in formal and informal governance arenas served the public interest (Kirst & Wirt, 2009; Tucker & Ziegler, 1980; Ziegler & Jennings, 1974). They have documented stubborn signs of citizen apathy, complacency and self-interest as well as differential access to educational forums, programs and services (Burlingame, 1987, 1988; Feurstein, 2002). Often that differential access is based on citizens' income, race, and ethnicity (Brantlinger, 2003; Boyd, 1975; Cucchiara & Horvat, 2009; Fine, 1993; Horvat, Weiner, & Lareau, 2003; Wells & Serna, 1996). Scholars, educators, government officials, and constituency groups also have questioned whether local systems have been open to lay influence from any sector of society, whether they have represented the diverse constituencies in their jurisdictions and whether they have operated as efficiently, responsibly and responsively as proponents of "district-centered" governance models claimed (Beadie, 2000; Burlingame, 1987, 1988; Fantini & Weinstein, 1968; Gittell, 1967; Kirst & Wirt, 2009). Some districts may function well on broad indicators of "policy responsiveness" (Berkman & Plutzer, 2005) but on other indicators of representativeness, fairness, and effectiveness, districts have a checkered history in part because their allocations of money, time, talent and attention often mirror the patterns of privilege and neglect evident in the broader society (Burlingame, 1987, 1988; Kirst & Wirt, 2009). Studies of site level dynamics also document patterns of power that run counter to the image of open and effective democratic deliberations between professionals and lay publics in neighborhood schools (Lewis & Nakagawa, 1995; Malen & Cochran, 2008; Mann, 1974; Seitsinger & Zera, 2002; Summerfield, 1971). Perhaps that is part of the reason federal and state agencies have become, over the course of time, more actively and aggressively involved in efforts to influence the public schools. Through the consolidation of school districts and the advancement of various reform agendas, the federal and state arms of government appear to have tightened their grip on local school systems and dismantled the "historical monopoly" local districts once possessed (Henig, 2009a, p. 116).

To be sure, both federal and state efforts to exercise greater control over education policies and practices have been accompanied by repeated calls for greater parental and citizen involvement in decision-making at the local level. For instance, early efforts to provide what many termed compensatory education programs and services under the 1965 Elementary and Secondary Education Act (ESEA) also required schools to set up local advisory councils so parents could voice their concerns and influence school programs and operations. While more recent iterations grant parents/guardians an exit option if their schools do not meet state and/or federal performance standards, this law and other federal policies like the Individuals with Disabilities Education Improvement Act (IDEA) preserve, if not enforce, the formal requirement that school personnel provide parents/guardians opportunities to influence educational decisions through participation in various councils, committees and conferences. Likewise, states often call for parent representation on school improvement councils and, on occasion, enact policies like the "Chicago School Reform" that grant community residents extensive formal powers on site-based governing boards, "weaken centralized bureaucratic control of schools and replace it with locally rooted politics" (Bryk, Hill, & Shipps, 1999, p. 21). In these and other ways, federal and state efforts to exert greater control have been mediated by provisions that might enable teachers, parents and lay publics to participate in and exert significant influence on education decision making processes at the school and the district level. For a number of reasons addressed in later sections of this chapter, these recurrent but short-lived organizational decentralization initiatives have operated as a weak check on the centralization of power at the state and federal level.

The Intensification of Federal Controls

From 1950 to the present, the federal government has been intermittently but increasingly involved in efforts to influence the public schools. Some justifications for an expanded federal role in education were rooted in calls for scientific and technological advancements that would enhance national security, economic prosperity and educational productivity (Campbell et al., 1985; DeBray, McDermott, & Wohlstetter, 2005; Fuhrman et al., 2007). Other justifications were grounded in the pursuit of "the elusive ideal," equal educational opportunity (Nelson, 2005). Whatever the justification, "federal policies in the realm of education tended to expand programs already initiated at the local or state level" (Nelson, 2005, p. xiv) and to break new ground.

Although the federal courts deflected pressures to address the resource inequities embedded in state and local school finance arrangements (*San Antonio Independent School District v. Rodriguez*), the federal government did lend support to activities that informed and advanced school finance litigation in state courts (Kirst, 1979; McDermott, 2009). The Ford Foundation sponsored most of the research on school finance reform and played a major role in forging alliances that could advance the case for more equitable funding (Kirst, 1979), but the U.S. Office of Education and the National Institute of Education also sponsored research and aided the cause (Kirst, 1979; McDermott, 2009). The federal government addressed issues of access and opportunity more directly and more visibly through policies aimed initially at racial desegregation (e.g., *Brown v. Board of Education*) and later at compensatory education (e.g., Title I of the 1965 Elementary and Secondary Education Act) special education (e.g., Public law 94-142, Education for All Handicapped Children Act), bi-lingual education (e.g., *Lau v. Nichols*), and gender discrimination (e.g., Title IX). Through legislative and judicial action, the federal government expressed a strong rhetorical commitment to educational equity and developed an elaborate system of regulatory requirements to protect the rights of targeted groups, but invested rather modest financial resources in the programs designed to realize that "elusive ideal" (Nelson, 2005; see also, Rebell & Wolff, 2008).

This "relatively rapid expansion" of federal involvement in education turned into a period of "vacillation" and "reversion" (Campbell et al., 1985) even though studies of the impact of federal education policies documented some arguably impressive (as well as disappointing) results. While some communities, particularly in the Deep South had de-segregated their schools (Rebell & Wolff, 2008), others had contributed to the "quiet [and not so quiet] reversal of *Brown v. Board of Education*" (Orfield & Eaton, 1996; Rosenberg, 2004), a development that the federal government did not seek to overturn. While studies of the "cumulative effects" of federal policies for special populations indicated these initiatives had expanded and improved the services for the targeted student populations (Knapp et al., 1983), political support for a broader federal role in and greater financial support for educational and related social supports waned. But, a host of factors including what Kingdon might (1995) term a "focusing event" or, what others might term a "refocusing event"[2] operated in the 1980s and beyond, to elevate education on the governmental agenda and to emphasize efficiency rather than equity as the compelling justification for federal involvement in pre-K–12 education (Astuto & Clark, 1986; Boyd, 1988; Howe, 1991). In simplified terms, the 1983 release of *A Nation at Risk* galvanized support for a federal reform agenda that capitalized on and embellished the standards-based accountability initiatives that many states had been advancing (Mazzoni, 2000; McDermott, 2009; Bell, 1988; Fuhrman et al., 2007). More encompassing in its approach and more directive in its tactics, the standards-based accountability approach to reform laid the foundation for the ground-breaking No Child Left Behind legislation (NCLB) that dramatically altered "the means and ends" of federal education policy and the formal powers of governmental actors (McGuinn, 2006a, 2006b; see also DeBray, 2006; Manna, 2007; Vinovskis, 2009).

While federal powers had been circumscribed by a reliance on procedural safeguards, supplemental funds for "disadvantaged" student populations and routine national assessments, NCLB expanded federal powers dramatically. The law "more than doubled the amount of testing in the schools," held "all schools accountable for achieving proficiency levels in reading and math," and required all schools to "achieve the same proficiency goals for all students" by 2014 (Valli et al., 2008, pp. 1–2). The law put federal agencies "in charge of approving state standards and accountability plans" and established "a single nationwide timetable" for raising student test scores (Finn & Hess, 2004, p. 39). The law also exerted control over teacher qualifications and mandated graduated but stringent sanctions (including school reconstitution and the option to privatize school management and services) on schools that fail to make Adequate Yearly Progress. Essentially, this "results-based," high-stakes accountability system translated lofty national educational goals into "legal mandates" and insisted on test score gains and "rates of progress that no school world wide has ever achieved" (Rebell & Wolff, 2008, p. 5).

As this chapter is being written, the federal government continues to expand its powers by adding tantalizing financial grants to its slate of policy instruments to advance specific initiatives under the Teacher Incentive Fund, the School Improvement Grant, and, if predictions prevail, under Race to the Top. Ironically, despite its historically modest financial investment in public education, the federal government has managed, over the years, to create a resource-dependency relationship with states and localities that works in its favor. In essence, federal funds have spawned programs for targeted student populations that schools systems would have trouble sustaining without federal reimbursements (Kanter & Lowe, 2006; Sunderman & Kim, 2007; Sunderman & Orfield, 2006). The current move to authorize competitive grants for specified purposes may allow the federal government to create an even stronger resource-dependency relationship with states and localities given the deep budget cuts that state governments and schools systems are experiencing. Under these conditions, state governments and local systems may be eager to embrace or pressed to accede to a host of federal initiatives that purport to align, more closely, aspects of schools systems to the standards-based, high-stakes accountability agenda and the privatization provisions embedded in it (see, for example, Maxwell, 2010; McNeil & Maxwell, 2010; Robelen, 2010).

The Intensification of State Controls

Like the federal government, state governments have become increasingly, and, at times aggressively involved in efforts to influence the public schools. The signs and seeds of an intensification of state policy making activity were evident during the 1960s and early 1970s as states defined programs, developed funding systems and designed accountability provisions for K–12 schools (Campbell & Mazzoni, 1976). During the mid-1970s and early 1980s, state governments stepped up their efforts to regulate, restructure and otherwise reform schools through various "results-based" policies. Since state activism is mediated by political cultures, state economies, institutional structures, partisan alignments, competing interest, shifting coalitions and other factors, the form and degree of state activism differ across state contexts and issue areas as well as over time (Beadie 2000; James, 1991; Mazzoni, 2000). Recognizing these differences, scholars have concluded that over the past several decades, "the drive for more effective use of state authority has accelerated ... despite the countervailing rhetoric of local control ... and dispersed authority (James, 1991, pp. 1, 74; Fusarelli & Cooper, 2009; Mazzoni, 2000).

The escalation of state activism often meant that districts were not just "the forgotten player on the education reform team" (Danzberger et al., 1987); they became the maligned player. A convenient if not always deserving recipient of criticism and blame, local boards and the professional educators employed by them lost favor. But the tendency to ignore or indict local districts and to cast aspersions on professional educators was just one of many indications that traditions of local control were under siege and that states were "on the move" (Kirst, 1995b, p. 45). States enacted initiatives that tended to be more prescriptive in their tone, more comprehensive in their scope, and more punitive in their tactics. Whether acting on their own initiative or in response to federal policies, states cast education reform as largely a matter of will and relied heavily on various combinations of standards-based regulations, incentives, rewards and sanctions to exercise greater control over public schools. Under the auspices of "systemic reform" (Smith & O'Day, 1991) stronger accountability and "coherent policy" (Fuhrman, 1993), states stepped up their efforts to:

1. articulate curriculum content through various requirements, frameworks and tests;
2. define school programs through mandates that make schools select programs for at risk students from a fairly short list of state-approved options, and, in so doing, to regulate the professional development that school staffs receive; and
3. issue public sanctions ranging from public listing of "low performing schools" to focused state interventions or full-scale reconstitution, privatization or takeovers (Ladd, 1996; Malen, 2003).

While not all states have been equally active in all domains of education, generally speaking, states have coupled policy instruments in potent ways and have asserted unprecedented levels of control over schools (Conley, 2003; Malen, 2003; Neuman-Sheldon, 2006). They have tapped into the formal policymaking authority they have always held to influence aspects of education that had been previously viewed as falling within the purview of local units (Firestone, Fuhrman, & Kirst, 1991; Fowler, 2000; Fuhrman et al., 2007; Fusarelli, 2009).

A host of factors converged to make education a big ticket item for state officials. One was the professionalization of state legislatures and executive offices, a development that gave states the capacity to get involved with educational issues (Fowler, 2000; James, 1991; Mazzoni, 2000). Their longer legislative sessions, larger staffs, and expanded agency supports provided the organizational infrastructure required to secure greater influence in the education policy domain. Recurrent rounds of school finance litigation also forced states to play a more decisive role in determining how education revenues would be acquired and distributed and how schools and the educators employed in them would be held accountable for the results of those investments (Beadie, 2000; James, 1991; Mazzoni, 2000). Economic developments and caustic critiques of public schools also thrust states into the education reform frenzy. The tendency to view schools as both the cause of and cure for national and regional economic woes along with the desire to gain a competitive advantage in the global markets meant that state officials wanted the reputation, if not the actual performance, of the schools to be a draw card they could pull out to attract and retain businesses in their particular states (Mazzoni, 2000). Scathing critiques of schools, quite apart from the accuracy of their claims, created a sense of crises that state officials could not ignore (Mazzoni, 2000). Assuming that economic prosperity was contingent on "excellent" schools, state officials became "involved in educational policy making in an unprecedented way" (Boyd & Kerchner, 1988, p. 1). The federal government's decision to demand reform but devolve responsibility for it also put the spotlight on the states (Astuto & Clark, 1986; Fuhrman, 2001).

All these developments, and more, provided strong reasons for state officials, representatives of big business and other players to expand the state's role in and control over education. States were poised and pressed to act. Well before the federal government enacted NCLB, states were pushing performance based accountability policies (Kane & Staiger, 2002; Leithwood, Steinbach, & Jantzi, 2002). By 2000, 40 states were using standardized test scores to rate student achievement and school performance; 20 states had attached monetary rewards and/or sanctions to these largely student test-based performance measures (Kane & Staiger, 2002). As their policy initiatives "spread upward" (McDermott, 2009, p. 753) to shape federal policy actions and as federal preferences reinforced state initiatives, the states reaffirmed their commitment to standards-based reforms; high-stakes, test-driven accountability systems; and stringent sanctions that are now the hallmark of federal and state education reform strategies.

To be clear, between 1950 and the present, states passed and publicized various decentralization and deregulation policies (Fuhrman & Elmore, 1995); but, they also clearly intensified their efforts to control the schools. Through an "extraordinary eruption" of policy activity (Mazzoni, 1995, p. 53) states added to the volume of obligations, expectations, rules and regulations imposed on school systems. Whether they were scooping up ideas from "lighthouse districts" (Pipho, 1991), capitalizing on proposals advanced by issue networks (Mazzoni, 1995), or importing ideas from other sources, states took an active hand, and an increasingly heavy hand, in virtually every domain of education policy, including and most notably, curriculum and instruction, assessment and accountability (Airisian, 1988; Kirst, 1995a, 1995b; Fuhrman et al., 2007; Fusarelli, 2009; McDonnell & Fuhrman, 1986). States extended their reach, ratcheted-up their rhetoric, activated the formal authority they have always possessed, and fortified their strategies for getting results.

The Contraction of Local Options

The intensification of federal and state involvement in education policy does not, in and of itself, demonstrate that local actors have lost power. As earlier noted, inter-governmental power relationships are not necessarily zero sum. Units of the system may appropriate policies made at different levels of the system. Further, federal and state policies may include provisions that both tighten controls on schools and create opportunities for local voice and influence. Put differently, policies enacted at state and federal levels of the system may decentralize some aspects of education policymaking and centralize others. Moreover, even if higher levels of the system seek to exercise greater authority over parameter setting decisions that shape what local actors may and must do, local units have some recourse. Both federal and state agencies depend on local systems to implement policies enacted elsewhere. That interdependence gives local units some leverage when they seek to influence policy provisions or to protest and overturn policy decisions honed in these broader arenas (Cohen et al., 2007; Henig, 2009a; Grossman, 2010). That interdependence along with the complexities embedded in efforts to orchestrate school "reform by remote control" (Cuban, 1984) have enabled local actors to develop a long and strong history of diluting, deflecting and circumventing policies imposed from afar (Cohen et al. 2007; Cohen & Spillane, 1992; Malen, 2003, 2006).

While a loss of power at the local level is not an inevitable outcome, two lines of evidence suggest that it is a prominent outcome. First, the recurrent and varied efforts to decentralize decision making have proven to be weak checks on the centralizing tendencies described herein. Second, the standards-based, high-stakes accountability policies emanating from the federal and state governments appear to be a more durable strain of policy. This genre of initiatives is not easily ignored or rebuffed during implementation. The combination of symbols, sanctions, rules and regulations that accompany this approach to reform appear to be creating "a new set of givens" (Mazzoni, in Malen & Muncey, 2000, p. 229) that limit the latitude of local actors in visible, subtle and consequential ways.

In terms of the first line of evidence, reviews of efforts to decentralize and democratize education policymaking indicate that the scope of "new" authority delegated to schools has been modest and temporary. Save for the Chicago School Reform experiment, efforts to decentralize decision making to schools rarely expand the formal authority of site actors to make binding decisions in the critical areas of budget, personnel and programs or alter the decision-making roles of professionals, parents, publics and policymakers (Croninger & Malen, 2002; Handler, 1996; Malen & Cochran, 2009; Summers & Johnson, 1996). Further, whatever "new authority" that may have been decentralized often gets abruptly re-centralized (Leithwood & Menzies, 1998; Shipps, 1998; Shipps, Kahne, & Smylie, 1999). Consequently, educators and other local actors do not end up with more extensive or more dependable degrees of freedom. Rather, they end up with more responsibilities and obligations in part because decentralization provisions carry a price—stronger accountability for the promise of greater autonomy (Elmore, 2002). Simply put, educators take on additional assignments such as developing school improvement plans, implementing curricular frameworks, incorporating new testing procedures, adapting to various "external partners," and otherwise "demonstrating" that they are meeting the terms of more stringent "results-based" accountability systems without commensurate increases in their authority, capacity, or opportunity to influence school policy (Anagnostopoulos, 2003; Booher-Jennings, 2005; Malen & Cochran, 2009; Mintrop, 2004; Sunderman, 2001; Wong & Anagnostopoulos, 1998). Whether new rounds of local autonomy and empowerment initiatives underway in New York, Baltimore, and other cities will engender different patterns is an important but, to date, unanswered question.

In terms of the second line of evidence, a small but growing body of evidence indicates that the package of federal and state standards-based, high-stakes accountability policies may not be susceptible to the prominent patterns of ingenious evasion and creative defiance that appear in the policy implementation literature. Historically, local actors have been able to insulate themselves from and neutralize the impact of various policy directives (Cohen & Spillane, 1992; Cohen et al., 2007; Malen & Muncey, 2000). They also have been able to build-on extant policies in creative and constructive ways (Honig et al., 2009). In the current policy context, however, local actors seem less able to control the impact of standards-based, high-stakes accountability policies on their priorities and practices. Studies across settings indicate that this package of policies may be changing (for better or worse) the content of curriculum (Dorgan, 2004; Firestone, Mayrowetz, & Fairman, 1998, Firestone, Fitz, & Broadfoot, 1999; Ravitch, 2010; Rothstein et al., 2008; Sandholtz, Ogawa, & Scribner, 2004; Trujillo, 2005; Valli et al., 2008; Wilson & Floden, 2001), the pace if not the pedagogy of instruction (Dorgan, 2004; Finkelstein et al., 2000; Herman, 2004; McNeil, 2000; Swanson & Stevenson, 2002; Valli et al., 2008), and the allocation of time and personnel (Dorgan, 2004; Herman, 2004; Stetcher & Barron, 1999; Wong & Anagnostopoulos, 1998).

Although the evidence is not as extensive, these policies also appear to be changing other important aspects of schooling, such as: the nature of professional development (Fairman & Firestone, 2001; Firestone et al., 1999; Valli et al., 2008); the substance and structure of school improvement deliberations (Finkelstein et al., 2000; Maxcy & Nguyen, 2006; Valli et al., 2008); the nature, intensity, and attractiveness of teachers' work (Anagnostopoulous, 2003; Dorgan, 2004; Finkelstein et al., 2000; Swanson & Stevenson, 2002); conceptions of the primary purposes of schooling; views of the appropriate roles of governmental units (Malen & Muncey, 2000); and views of what counts as good teaching (Booher-Jennings, 2005; Valli et al., 2008). Although the effects vary depending on the severity of the stakes attached to accountability systems and, at times, the level of schooling, survey and case study data suggest that standards-based, high-stakes accountability policies are limiting the autonomy of local educators (Dorgan, 2004; Finkelstein et al., 2000; Pedulla et al., 2003), and creating a "test-driven culture" (Valli et al., 2008). This culture affects the social relations as well as the instructional practices in schools and reifies an accountability system that redefines, in fundamental and arguably troubling ways, the mission and purpose of public schools (Rothstein et al., 2008; Valli et al., 2008).

The New Balance of Power

Because education "is a state responsibility, a local function and a federal priority" (Riley, in Rorrer, 2004, p. 253), all levels of government have a vested interest in influencing education policy and practice and they all do so. While their potential and actual influence varies across aspects of the education enterprise, federal and state governments have intensified their efforts to secure more control over the core domains of public schools. In part through strategic combinations of symbols, sanctions, rules, regulations, exhortations, and resource dependencies, the broader system has exerted considerable control over the agendas of public schools and effectively rewritten the rules of the game. Federal and state governments have concentrated their efforts on "results-based" ventures and relegated local boards, district officials and site educators to a reactive, arguably subservient role in that they are required to meet the goals developed elsewhere with the resource allocations determined elsewhere or experience the sanctions set elsewhere. Although some communities, particularly those with high concentrations of high performing schools and stable sources of revenue, may be able to insulate themselves from federal and state policies, the balance of power has shifted. School systems are the clear targets and often the reluctant recipients of policies that make them assume substantial responsibility for reform outcomes but grant them little opportunity to influence reform inputs. That arrangement places local actors at a clear disadvantage. They are not powerless, but they are forced to maneuver within the relatively narrow and narrowing parameters set at the federal and state levels of the system.

How this redistribution of power across levels of government affects the distribution of power across stakeholder groups is an empirical question that warrants considerably more attention than it has received. We know, theoretically and empirically, that arenas matter, that where decisions are hammered out affects who participates and how they may (or may not) be able to influence decision processes and outcomes (Mazzoni, 1991; McDonnell, 2007). Simply put, the formal and informal arenas in which actors vie for influence are not neutral. Different arenas may be more or less open, accessible and receptive to different players and their points of view. Moreover, different arenas have their own, often tacit "rules" for participation and accommodation (Firestone, 1989; Mazzoni, 1991). In these and other ways, arenas allocate access and advantage. As Mazzoni (1991) explains,

Arenas do more than locate decisive sites for decision-making action. They legitimate a set of participants, establish the institutional and social context—including the "rules of the game"—mediate the potency of resources and strategies and encourage some means (and discourage other means) of reaching agreements.... Moving an issue to a new arena can change the key actors, relevant resources, incentives for action, influence relationship and governing rules—and hence winners and losers—in policy struggles. (p. 116)

Yet, our knowledge of how the newly constructed balance of power across levels of government affects the incentive, capacity and opportunity for policymakers, professionals, parents, and publics to influence salient dimensions of the education enterprise is remarkably limited. We know, for example, that federal, state, and local arenas have become congested. A dizzying array of interests including but not confined to corporations, businesses, text book companies, test developers, management organizations, education reform organizations and other members of "the school improvement industry" (Rowan, 2002), foundations, think tanks, issue networks, professional organizations and teacher unions, local government associations, academics, research centers, and other members of what Kingdon (1995) terms the "policy community," urban coalitions, religious organizations, and various good government groups as well mayors, county officials, state and federal legislative and executive leaders and their agencies interact to shape the ideas and the options that will be entertained as well as the provisions of the policies that will be enacted (Henig, 2009a; Malen, 2001; Mawhinney & Lugg, 2001; Miskel & Song. 2004). But whose voice counts in these arenas is not self-evident.

For example, at the federal level, Miskel and Song (2004) document that a broad slate of actors one might have expected to be prominent players on reading policy were outmaneuvered by a small circle of insiders who engineered key decisions in this arena. At the state level, the waves of state activism that characterized the 1970s, 1980s, and 1990s pushed teacher unions, the heavy hitter in the education lobby lineup, as well as other established education interest groups from the center to the margins of policymaking in many if not most states (Conley, 2003; Mazzoni, 2000; McDonnell, 2007; McDonnell & Fuhrman, 1986). Scholars documented that by the early 1980s governors and legislators "increasingly call the shots, at least those that count most" (Mazzoni, 1982, p. 170; Fuhrman, & Elmore, 1994). Throughout this period state legislatures passed initiatives despite the vocal objections and, at times, despite the active resistance of local educators, teacher unions and professional associations (Mazzoni, 1991, 1993, 1995, 2000). At the local level, the political dynamics have changed as "mayors, city councils, minority and community-based organizations" as well as "federal agencies, national foundations, private providers," professional educators, parents, and other players regularly or intermittently enter the fray (Henig, 2009a, pp. 126, 127; see also, Apple, 1996;

Mawhinney & Lugg, 2001). Whether professional educators and local officials will be able to shape policy designs in these congested arenas and/or preserve a degree of autonomy in their schools through information and impression management strategies, public relations programming, the astute use of advisory councils and shared governance structures, and other devices they have employed in the past remains an open question. What is clear, however, is that the locus of accommodation on critical education decisions shaping the purposes, priorities and practices of public school systems has shifted and that shift is one of the factors that will shape who is organized into and who is organized out of those consequential decisions.[3]

Democratic Governance as a Mechanism for Enhancing Educational Effectiveness

While the shifts in governance discussed occurred for many reasons, prominent justifications tend to pivot on claims that altering school governance arrangements will enhance school effectiveness. The available evidence casts doubt on that prominent expectation. No governmental level has a lock on engendering, let alone ensuring, improvements in the quality and fairness of the educational opportunities and experiences offered children and youth. Different governance arrangements rest on different sets of assumptions and beget markedly mixed reviews on multiple measures of educational effectiveness, including the primary, at times sole proxy, students' scores on standardized tests in the two areas (reading and mathematics) emphasized by the current accountability policies. These mixed reviews, in turn, evoke rival takes and fuel intense debates about whether and how democratic governance arrangements and the policies that emanate from them might operate to enhance the fairness as well as the effectiveness of public school systems.

Mixed Reviews of "Local Democracy" Experiments

As earlier noted, historically, local district governance structures have been the primary point of access for citizen involvement in school governance and the major mechanism for holding schools accountable to their immediate publics. Whether these institutions can operate as inclusive and effective bodies that grant perennially neglected populations more equitable access to educational programs and services and more robust opportunities to obtain the benefits of quality educational experiences remains a contested proposition. Some bodies appear to operate constructively; others struggle to create the "civic capacity," the broad-based, cross-sector coalitions required to support and sustain school improvement initiatives (Stone, Henig, Jones, & Pierannunzi, 2001).

Since public confidence in these local institutions varies across settings and over time, an array of efforts to revitalize and/or re-structure local governance arrangements surface, subside and re-surface. For example, some of these efforts focus on developing social ties and activating parents and community constituencies so they might be a more formidable force in extant local district policy arenas (Gold, Simon. & Brown, 2005; Baum, 2003; Fung, 2004; Orr, 1999); others focus on vesting authority in new arenas, notably mayors' offices (Henig & Rich, 2004; Kirst, 2000; Wong, Shen, Anagnostopoulos, & Rutledge, 2007). Given the many factors that affect political processes, policy decisions and school performance, these and other approaches to reforming local governance have not resulted in dependable improvements on measures of school effectiveness.

Another prevalent and recurrent approach to revitalizing local governance, the devolution of decision-making authority to the school site, the most proximate and presumably accessible arena for realizing meaningful citizen involvement in school affairs warrants elaboration because it provides a reasonable albeit incomplete test of the ability of decentralization experiments to engender democratic processes and enhance school effectiveness. In abbreviated terms, this approach to school reform assumes that delegating decision making authority to the site and distributing that authority across professionals and publics will break down the organizational barriers that separate schools from their surrounding communities (Tyack, 1993). Thus, these structures are advanced as mechanisms for energizing public participation in the schools, protecting the public against professional and bureaucratic indifference or incompetence, fostering stronger working relationships between professionals and publics, making better use of school and community resources and improving teaching and learning for all students (Bryk et al., 2010; Croninger & Malen, 2002). The available evidence on the ability of "local democracy" to accomplish these ambitious aims and make schools more effective is limited and mixed on several counts.

Most studies do not examine how these governance arrangements affect the quality of social relationships beyond the school walls, even though more cooperative and collaborative relationships are often part of the "promises" attached to these reforms (Bryk, Hill, & Shipps, 1999). Studies that address this aspect of local governance provide weak evidence that this promise is realized. Professionals tend to express appreciation for the support parents and community residents may provide and concerns about the time invested and stress generated when parents and community residents raise issues that challenge professionals' expertise and autonomy (Malen & Cochran, 2008). Similarly, parents and community residents express appreciation for the intrinsic rewards that can accompany participation (e.g., a sense of belonging, a sense of doing one's duty as a parent and citizen, new knowledge about school programs and operations, status as "an insider") and concerns about the time commitment and "token" involvement (Croninger & Malen, 2002; Malen & Cochran, 2008).

Assessments that go beyond the impact of decentralized governance arrangements on the participants contain encouraging "existence proofs" as well as disconcerting counter cases. Research in some settings indicates that this form of governance may foster civic engagement, enable traditionally under-represented citizens to influence school affairs, and engender meaningful improvements in neighborhood schools, especially if parents and community representatives align with civic associations and activist organizations that enhance the capacity of individuals in marginalized groups to mobilize their resources, expand their political capital and exercise influence in local decision-making forums (Fung, 2004). Other studies suggest that this form of governance may operate to co-opt community concerns, deflect criticisms of schools and diffuse the influence of parents and community activists "who wish to say something about the pattern of resource inequities [or uneven accomplishments] across schools" (Shipps, 1997, p.103) and socialize citizens into submissive roles as "trustees of the status quo" (Seitsinger & Zera, 2002, p. 4; see also Croninger & Malen, 2002; Lewis & Nakagawa, 1995). Some studies grant that citizen involvement in decentralized governance structures may stimulate marginal adjustments in school operations but these changes, alone, do little to alter school performance or the distribution of educational gains (Croninger & Malen, 2002; Hess, 1996; Leithwood & Menzies, 1998; Lewis & Nakagawa, 1995). Others point to impressive improvements, particularly in elementary schools (Bryk, Sebring, Allensworth, Leppescu, & Easton, 2010; Simmons, 2006).

Some scholars have tried to reconcile these competing assessments by looking to Chicago's experiment with "democratic localism as a lever for change" (Bryk, Sebring, Kerbow, Rollow, & Easton, 1998; Bryk et al., 2010) because it is the most thoroughly documented study of an authentic effort to delegate additional and substantial decision-making authority to local actors as a means to improve students' educational opportunities and academic accomplishments, According to Bryk and colleagues (1998), roughly one third of Chicago's underperforming elementary schools developed strong patterns of community participation and made notable changes in the organization of teachers' work, the quality of instruction, and the relationships between parents and other local actors. Despite these changes, initial analyses indicated that achievement gains were negligible across the district and modest in most schools, including those schools with active local councils in part because fiscal shortfalls meant that schools had to use their resources to maintain basic operations, not launch new initiatives (Hess, 1999b).

Subsequent efforts to sort out the "achievement effects" underscore the difficulty of linking achievement gains to governance reforms, not only because measurement is highly problematic but also because gains are unstable across years, vary by subject, and may be attributed to a host of factors that go well beyond local school council activities and influences (Hess 1999a, 1999b). Nonetheless, studies using fairly sophisticated techniques and controls for student mobility show greater gains in student achievement than earlier studies and these gains appear to be strongest in schools with active local councils and supportive principals who have adopted school improvement plans that address professional development, social relationships and student achievement (Bryk, 1999). Another analysis of the decentralization experiment maintained that "144 inner city Chicago elementary schools" all of which were low-performing in 1990 "have shown 15 years of substantial sustained achievement gains" in reading (Designs for Change, 2005, p. i). Like other studies, this analysis attributes these student achievement gains to a combination of effective practices including but not limited to local councils that carry out their formal responsibilities, organize to lobby the district for resources and principals who seek broad participation in decision making, monitor schools operations, develop faculty capacity, and foster trust among professionals, parents, and community residents (Hess 1999a). The most recent efforts to identify and explain "achievement effects" point to impressive gains in settings where local councils are actively engaged in school governance and the "essential supports for school improvement" are in place (Sebring, Allensworth, Bryk, Easton, & Luppescu, 2006; Bryk et al., 2010).

Mixed Reviews of Centralized Controls

Efforts to centralize control over public school systems through standards-based, high-stakes accountability policies provide a salient albeit partial view of how this form of governance relates to school effectiveness. In brief, the underlying assumption is that by setting high-performance standards; aligning curriculum, assessment, personnel, and professional development policies; measuring and disclosing results; and issuing rewards and sanctions based on those results, more distant governments can establish an incentive structure that functions to make schools more effective on the measures emphasized. In short, schools will realize the rational efficiencies and performance gains that robust incentive systems engender. The evidence on this approach to school governance and school effectiveness is also limited and mixed.

Given the "results-oriented" emphasis of this genre of reforms, a key question, and for some, *the* key question is whether the federal and state efforts are improving student test scores. The answer is hardly clear-cut. It depends in part on whether studies rely on national tests (e.g., National Assessment of Education Policy, NAEP) or state tests and how well they control for the numerous factors that affect those scores (Mintrop & Sunderman, 2009).

For example, studies that rely on national test data and incorporate reasonable controls find that "high accountability states" recorded significantly greater gains on the NAEP scores than did states with weaker accountability policies and intervention strategies (Carnoy & Loeb, 2002). Other studies report modest gains but no appreciable impact on reducing the achievement gap (Lee, 2008). But here again, it is difficult to know if the increase in test scores is because of, in spite of, or apart from the governance changes and the policies associated with those changes. As some scholars point out, the increases in NAEP scores "represent trends that began prior to NCLB and do not reflect any significant acceleration in the pace of improvement after NCLB" (Mintrop & Sunderman, 2009, p 355).

Some studies report that student scores on state tests are increasing but refrain from linking those increases to particular policies (Center for Education Policy, 2008); some report increases and attribute them to state and/or federal high-stakes accountability policies (Fuller & Johnson, 2001; Fusarelli & Fusarelli, 2003; U.S. Department of Education, 2007); other studies claim that the rise in test scores is a reflection of clever gaming strategies[4] such as using tests that focus on basic rather than higher-order thinking skills, manipulating who takes the tests and investing heavily in test-preparation strategies and practice sessions that may do little to enhance student learning (Haney, 2000; McNeil, 2000; Sunderman, 2001; Whitford & Jones, 2000). Still others point out that test scores were rising *before* state and federal governments began emphasizing standards-based, high-stakes accountability policies (Lee, 2008; Mintrop & Sunderman, 2009); gains may be occurring apart from or even in spite of these centralized policy strategies.

While analysts will continue to debate both the methods and results of studies designed to determine whether the current centralized controls are contributing to educational effectiveness, at this point, it seems fair to say that on the politically salient "test score" indicator, the results are not particularly compelling. As Rebell and Wolff summarized the situation, "no state is currently on track to achieve full proficiency as defined by NCLB by 2014.... Overall, progress on standardized reading and math tests has been minimal and wide achievement gaps persist between low-income and minority students and their more affluent White peers" (2008, p. 3).

As earlier noted, the standards-based, high-stakes accountability reforms are influencing many important aspects of schooling but not always in ways that enhance the quality and equity of educational experiences afforded children and youth. For example, since NCLB holds schools accountable for math and reading scores, it focuses attention on these subjects but directs attention away from other important areas of study such as history, social studies, science, art, music, character development, civic education, and physical education (Ravitch, 2010; Rothstein et al., 2008; Sirotnik, 2004; Soder, 2006). In so doing, the policy narrows the curriculum, particularly for those students in low-performing schools, the population the policy purports to help, denies students opportunities to learn other subjects, and thereby operates to expand rather than close the achievement gap (Rothstein, 2009). In some settings, the pre-occupation with improving math and reading scores has created a "basic skills frenzy" (Finn & Ravitch, 2007, p. 6) that distorts, and in some instances, displaces other important purposes of schooling (Rebell & Wolff, 2008, 2009;

Rothstein et al., 2008). The pressure to raise test scores prompts some schools and districts to "pull resources away from the most needy students.... [in order to concentrate] on students most likely to improve school-wide achievement test scores" (Sunderman, 2001, p. 526; see also, Booher-Jennings, 2005; Diamond & Spillane, 2004; Elmore, 2002; Neuman-Sheldon, 2006; Valli et al., 2008; White & Rosenbaum, 2008). Both case studies and survey data indicate that the following findings may be indicative of the "collateral damage" (Nichols & Berliner, 2007) or "corrosive effects" (Valli et al., 2008) that the centralized, high-stakes accountability policies can have on the academic and social environment of schools:

> The challenges of high-stakes testing were reshaping and driving much of what occurred in schools, from discussions at staff meetings to instruction in classrooms to interactions between students and teachers.... The direction of these changes, even in the best of schools is not encouraging.... the current emphasis on high-stakes testing, at least as manifested in the three high-poverty schools we studied, creates a test-driven culture that narrows the curriculum, weakens student-teacher relationships and undermines professional standards for teaching and learning.... High stakes testing, along with the practices promoted by it, created powerful incentives to focus exclusively on the 'bottom line'—raising test scores to make AYP... instruction became increasingly focused on narrow, sometimes disjointed tasks aligned with the fill-in-the bubble and short-constructed response items that characterized the assessments. (Valli et al., 2008, pp. vii, 3, 157; see also Pedulla et al., 2003; Rothstein et al., 2008)

In addition to producing disconcerting effects on the quality of the instructional environment and the allocation of resources dedicated to students, centralized high-stakes accountability policies may undercut school capacity for improvement. For example, some studies indicate that in settings where the threat of a severe sanction like school reconstitution is imminent, state and federal accountability policies have strained workplace relationships, made teaching and administering schools less attractive occupational choices, and jeopardized the ability of school systems to recruit and retain principals and teachers who are willing to take on the stress of "turning around" low-performing schools (Ladd & Zelli, 2002; Malen & Rice, 2009). Reports of these and other unintended consequences cast doubt on the ability of this reform strategy to improve school performance.

However, other data speak to the ability of this reform strategy to foster excellence and equity in public schools. Some studies indicate that the state and federal accountability policies may be prompting schools and schools districts to pay more attention to the students who have been under-served and to alter their views, priorities, and practices in ways that foster the success of all students in their jurisdictions. For example, Skrla, Scheurick, Johnson, and Korschoreck

(2004) point to the "substantially improved success of children of color and low-income students and the substantially improved equity in some schools and districts in some states (p. 17).

> Initially, it was largely elementary schools that were achieving this success, but now we are seeing an increasing number of secondary schools doing the same ... then ... there were whole districts that were experiencing considerable success with their low-income children of all races ... and the number is continuing to grow... [T]here is powerful evidence that in some schools and districts—including many in which we have done research—these accountability systems are driving significant improvements in academic achievement for children of color and low-income children, and thus these systems are increasing equity. (pp. 17, 18)

Given the mix of encouraging and disconcerting findings, analysts are likely to be vigorously debating the relationship between centralized controls and school effectiveness for some time to come.

Theoretically, "reforms that appear to be centralizing control over schools might well serve to promote local democratic practice" (Mintrom, 2001, p. 638). For example, standards and accountability policies have the potential to produce information that attentive publics might use to celebrate successes as well as to press for school reforms that they view as key (Cibulka, 1991; Mintrom, 2001). As public satisfaction with public schools continues to decline, it does not appear that the current bundle of centralized controls has been able to garner support for the public schools (Jacobson, 2009). Nor does it appear that professional educators, parents, and attentive publics are drawing on the information that the high-stakes accountability policies generate and publish to take the initiative and mobilize on behalf of policies that might foster improvements in their local schools (for an exception, see Grossman, 2010).

Alternative Takes on the Mixed Reviews

Scholars, analysts, and activists interpret the mixed evidence on efforts to alter governance arrangements and reform public schools in very different ways. Some suggest "the problem" of uneven and unintended results may be related to our inability to find the right division of labor and the appropriate balance of power across levels and branches of the system (Elmore, 1993; Elmore & Sykes, 1992). Simply put, we have not discovered the institutional comparative advantages that various units of the system bring to the task of enhancing school effectiveness for all students, but most notably for the students who have been under-served or left behind. Consequently, policy analysts and activists advance a variety of governance models. Some call for substantial local discretion and a concerted effort to reach out to create community partnerships and forge more collaborative relationships with social service agencies to provide "a more holistic, comprehensive and effective set of responses to children whose problems tend to be complex and multi-faceted" (White & Wehage, 1995, p. 23); some, as noted above, argue for a concerted effort to develop the cross-sector coalitions that might provide the "civic capacity" required to install and sustain major education reforms, particularly in urban areas (e.g., Stone et al., 2001; see also Henig, 2009a). Others call for substantial local discretion but vigorous moves to bring school governance into the mainstream of local politics by granting mayors and other local government officials more control over the operations of school systems and greater opportunities to coordinate school and community resources and services (Henig & Rich, 2004; Wong et al., 2007).

While the above interpretations suggest we should continue to pursue forms of democratic governance, other interpretations argue that "the problem" is related to the fragmented nature of the system, its checks and balances and the corresponding propensity to make incremental policy changes that are simply not robust enough to engender major improvements, at least in the short term (McGuinn, 2006a, 2006b). In this view, an entirely different approach is warranted. Advocates of market solutions to education problems argue that the evidence supports the argument that democratic governance, be it in the form of local democratic forums or more centralized policy systems, is fundamentally and fatally flawed. It simply cannot overcome the competing interests that can overpower the concerns of parents and students at every level of the system and every phase of the policymaking process. Hence, democratic governance must give way to market models. "Under a system of democratic control," Chubb & Moe argue, "the public schools are governed by an enormous, far-flung constituency in which the interests of parents and students carry no special status. When markets prevail, parents and students are thrust into center stage" (1990, p. 35). Whether markets mechanisms would "outperform" governmental mechanisms remains an open, empirical question (Henig, 2009b). These mechanisms may be just as undependable as the varied forms of democratic control we have relied upon (Croninger & Malen, 2002; Mintrop & Sunderman, 2009). Further, they might operate to undermine the democratic purposes and functions of public schools by draining capital from the public school system as activist parents exit and invest their resources in forging alliances that advance the institutions that serve their children rather than the institutions that must serve all children (Abernathy, 2005; Henig, 2009a). But they are the preferred solution for those who locate "the problem" in the system of democratic control.

Two additional "takes" warrant mention not only because they are both prominent and instructive but also because they direct attention to factors that may mediate the ability of any governance model to address the dual goals of advancing democratic values and improving school effectiveness.

One such take suggests that "the problem" is that we have not given governance changes a full and fair test. That is, we have not implemented them under conditions that would enable them to cultivate democratic participation in school affairs or enhance educational effectiveness (Bryk et al., 2010; Forum for Education and Democracy, 2008). In different words, we have not adequately addressed the capacity of school systems to accomplish the ambitious and important tasks assigned to them (Hatch, 2009; Malen & Rice, 2004; Sebring et al., 2006). The lack of attention to school capacity issues is a prominent theme in explanations of the uneven effects of decentralization experiments as well as in critiques of the current standards-based, high-stakes accountability version of centralized control.

For example, studies of decentralization experiments point out that these initiatives are often introduced during periods of fiscal stress, when the issue for local actors is what to cut, not how to improve (Croninger & Malen, 2002; Malen & Cochran, 2008). These studies also report that decentralization experiments in education as well as in other social service sectors rarely alter power relationships or develop the community-based infrastructures required for citizens in general and marginalized groups in particular to mobilize and influence school policies, programs, and practices (Cazenave, 2007; Malen, 2001; Malen & Cochran, 2009). Despite the pluralist perspective's prediction that those who have legitimate demands can and will organize and press the system to respond to their concerns, the available evidence demonstrates that political activism requires more than astute leaders igniting latent discontent. Sponsors, patrons, institutional rules, empowering governmental policies, and other elements of the opportunity structure are the more critical ingredients of political activism (Walker, 1991). But these key ingredients are rarely accounted for or built into policies that seek to empower local actors, cultivate civic engagement and improve the quality of life and learning in struggling schools. Moreover, decentralization initiatives rarely provide the full complement of resources that may be required for local democracies to improve social relationships, strengthen instructional programs, and enable students across the spectrum to realize the full complement of benefits that may be accrued from a stimulating and inspiring education (Bryk, 1999; Bryk et al., 1998; Bryk et al., 2010).

While critiques of the current standards-based, high-stakes accountability initiatives point to a range of reasons for the mixed reviews of this reform venture, issues regarding the capacity of schools and the governmental units that are to support them to engender instructional improvements loom large (Rebell & Wolff, 2008, 2009). Early versions of standards-based reforms paid attention to capacity issues as well as to performance targets in the "opportunity to learn" standards. These provisions recognized that educational improvements were contingent on appropriate supports as well as appropriate incentives. As scholars track the implementation and evaluate the impact of standards-based, high-accountability reform, they often discover anew that building capacity to meet high-performance standards is essential. Setting goals, measuring progress (or lack of same) and sanctioning schools becomes a futile and debilitating process if school systems and the governmental agencies that are to assist them simply lack the capacity to accomplish the tasks assigned them and realize the goals set for them (Cohen et al., 2006; Elmore, 2009; Rebell & Wolff, 2008; Sirotnik, 2004). Scholars have begun to identify the sets of resources, the "educational essentials" that may be required to transform demands for improvements in school performances into opportunities that enable all students to reap the benefits of a quality educational experience (Rebell & Wolff, 2008; see also Bryk et al., 2010; Rothstein, 2002, 2004; Rothstein et al., 2008). The obvious and critical question now is whether governments at any level of the system can muster the political will to provide whatever combination of "educational essentials" a school and its surrounding community may require to increase the likelihood that students will no longer be left behind.

The final "take" to be considered situates the "problem" in the broader socio-cultural context and calls the government up short for failing to deal with the full range of factors that affect how students perform in schools and for making schools the major social safety net for the poor. Although the federal government is often cast as the arena most attuned to the glaring and growing inequities in society and the best equipped to readdress them, the federal government has tended to rely on schools, rather than "direct intervention in society and the labor market as the fundamental mechanism for solving social and economic problems" (Kanter & Lowe, 1995, p. 5, see also, Tyack & Cuban, 1995; Wells, 2009). As a result, the social safety net has some mighty big holes that schools alone cannot fill. Health care, housing patterns, income levels, and income stability as well as other factors beyond the reach of education policy affect how students perform in schools and whether schools and their communities can muster the resources required to overcome the economic and social as well as the educational problems that are placed at the schoolhouse door (Anyon, 1997, 2005; Rothstein, 2002, 2004). To be clear, schools matter and they can do better, but however they are governed, they are still affected by the broader societal opportunity structures in which they are nested. Thus the combinations of social and educational policies we assemble will mediate the effects of whatever governance arrangements we pursue.

Closing Observations

This chapter argues that one of the defining features of the politics of education since 1950 is the evolutionary and revolutionary shift in power from local to state and federal arenas. How these institutional developments affect the ability and willingness of various policymakers, parents, professionals and publics to influence education policy warrants careful attention because institutional arrangements are never neutral (Mazzoni, 1991). While institutional arrangements do not *determine* political dynamics and policy decisions, they often shape them in consequential ways. So a major challenge facing the field is to develop the empirical base required to render thoughtful judgments regarding how the shift in power from local to state and federal arenas affects the ability and willingness of the array of elected officials, organized interests, attentive publics and "potential partisans" (Gamson, 1968) to influence the nature and purpose of public schools.

Since the relationship between governance arrangements and education effectiveness remains elusive, conceptually and empirically, another challenge facing the field is to develop a clearer understanding of how governance arrangements and the patterns of politics they engender may affect, directly and indirectly, the quality of teaching and learning and the production and distribution of valued educational outcomes. With that knowledge base fortified, we would be in a stronger position to make informed assessments of the probable consequences, if not the relative virtues of different models and modes of governance.

Perhaps the greatest challenge and the most urgent unfinished business is developing the capacity to ensure that all children have ready access to a quality education that serves the noble academic, social, and civic purposes that have been attached to the public schools. Whether as a society we seek to cultivate more "local democracy" or more centralized control, whether we work to preserve the principles and structures undergirding a political democracy or rely more heavily on market mechanisms, we have to address the transcendent capacity issues that mediate the ability of any governance arrangement to deliver on its educational promises and its public responsibilities.

Notes

1   Like so many others I am indebted to the late Bill Boyd for his leadership in and stewardship of the field. It is a privilege to author a chapter in a book he conceived but could not complete. I am also indebted to the late Tim Mazzoni, my graduate advisor and mentor for directing me to Bill's work when I was a student and for encouraging me to look to Bill as a role model worth emulating when I became a professor. I thank Robert Croninger and Bonnie and Lance Fuscarelli for engaging in lengthy conversations about the ideas presented in this chapter, Donna Muncey for her willingness to talk through issues and provide thoughtful reviews of drafts of this text; Paul Baumann and Kathleen Hoyer for their careful read of the last revision and Doug Mitchell for being an insightful, patient, and helpful editor throughout the writing process.

2   I thank Donna Muncey for making this important distinction in her review of an earlier version of this chapter.

3   Schattsneider (1960) uses similar language in his discussion of how various interests may be organized into or out of political contests.

4   As Donna Muncey pointed out, NCBL's focus on subgroups and the requirement for 95% participation could trump efforts to limit test access to students likely to perform well. Whether these features of the law serve as effective checks on the various gaming strategies that might be used to manipulate test results is an empirical question that warrants more attention than it has received.

References

Abernathy, S. F. (2005). *School choice and the future of American democracy.* Ann Arbor: The University of Michigan Press.

Anagnostopoulos, D. (2003). The new accountability, student failure, and teachers' work in urban high schools. *Educational Policy, 17*(3), 291–316.

Anderson, G. L. (1998). Toward authentic participation: Deconstructing the discourses of participatory reform in education. *American Educational Research Journal, 35*(4), 571–603.

Airisian, P. W. (1988). Symbolic validation: The case of state-mandated, high-stakes testing, *Educational Evaluation and Policy Analysis, 10,* 301–313.

Allison, G. T. (1971). *Essence of decision.* Boston, MA: Little, Brown and Company.

Anyon, J. (1997). *Ghetto schooling: A political economy of urban educational reform.* New York, NY: Teachers College Press.

Anyon, J. (2005). *Radical possibilities: Public policy, urban education, and a new social movement.* New York, NY: Routledge.

Apple, M. W. (1996). *Cultural politics and education.* New York, NY: Teachers College Press.

Astuto, T. A., & Clark D. L. (1986). *The effects of federal education policy changes on policy and program development in state agencies and local education agencies.* Bloomington, IN: Policy Studies Center.

Baum, H. S. (2003). *Community action for school reform.* Albany: State University of New York Press.

Beadie, N. (2000). The limits of standardization and the importance of constituencies: Historial tensions in the relationship between state authority and local control. In N. D. Theobald & B. Malen (Eds.), *Balancing local control and state responsibility for K-12 education* (pp. 47–91). Larchmont, NY: Eye on Education.

Bell, T. H. (1988). *The thirteenth man: A Reagan cabinet memoir.* New York, NY: The Free Press.

Berkman, M. B., & Plutzer, E. (2005). *Ten thousand democracies: Politics and public opinion in America's school districts.* Washington, DC: Georgetown University Press.

Booher-Jennings, J. (2005). Below the bubble: 'Educational triage' and the Texas accountability system. *American Educational Research Journal, 42*(2), 231–268.

Boyd, W. L. (1988). How to reform schools without half trying: Secrets of the Reagan administration. *Educational Administration Quarterly, 24,* 299–309.

Boyd, W. L. & Kerchner, C. T. (1988). Introduction and overview: Education and the politics of excellence and choice. In W. L. Boyd & C. T. Kerchner (Eds.), *The politics of education and choice in education* (pp. 1–11). Philadelphia: Falmer.

Boyd, W. L. (1976).The public, the professionals and educational policy making: Who governs? *Teachers College Record, 77*(4), 539–577.

Boyd, W. L. (1975). *Community status and conflict in suburban schools.* Beverley Hills, CA: Sage.

Brantlinger, E. (2003). *Dividing classes: How the middle class negotiates and rationalizes school advantage.* New York, NY: Routledge Falmer.

Brown v. Board of Education of Topeka, 347 U. S. 483 (1954).

Bryk, A. A., Sebring, P. B., Allensworth, E., Leppescu, S. & Easton, J. (2010). *Organizing schools for improvement: Lessons from Chicago.* Chicago, IL: University of Chicago Press.

Bryk, A. S. (1999). Policy lessons from Chicago's experience with decentralization. In D. Ravitch (Ed.), *Brookings papers on educational policy* (pp. 67–99). Washington, DC: Brookings Institute.

Bryk, A. S., Hill, P., & Shipps, D. (1999). *Improving school-community connections: Moving toward a system of community schools.* Baltimore, MD: Annie E. Casey Foundation

Bryk, A. S., Sebring, P. B., Kerbow, K., Rollow, S., & Easton, J. Q. (1998). *Charting Chicago school reform: Democratic localism as a lever for change.* Boulder, CO: Westview Press.

Burch, P. (2009) *Hidden markets: The new education privatization.* New York, NY: Routledge.

Burlingame, M. (1988). The politics of education and education policy: The local level. In N. Boyan (Ed.) *The handbook of research on educational administration* (pp. 439–450). New York, NY: Longman.

Burlingame, M. (1987). The shambles of local politics. *PEA Bulletin, 13,* 3–8.

Campbell, R. F., Cunningham, L. L. , Nystrand, R. O., & Usdan, M. D. (1985). *The organization and control of American schools.* Columbus, OH: Merrill Publishing.

Campbell, R. F., Cunningham, L. L, Nystrand, R. O., & Usdan, M. D. (1990). *The organization and control of American schools* (6th ed,). Columbus, OH: Merrill.

Campbell, R. F., & Mazzoni, T. L. (1976). *State policy making for the public schools.* Berkeley, CA: McCutchan.

Carnoy, M. (1993). School improvement: Is privatization the answer? In J. Hannaway & M. Carnoy (Eds.), *Decentralization and school improvement: Can we fufill the promise?* (pp. 163–201). San Francisco, CA: Jossey-Bass.

Carnoy, M., & Loeb, S. (2002). Does external accountability affect student outcomes? A cross-state analysis. *Education Evaluation and Policy Anlaysis, 24,* 305–331.

Cazenave, N. A. (2007). *Impossible democracy: The unlikely success of the War on Poverty Community Action programs.* Albany, NY: State University Press of New York.

Center for Education Policy. (2008). *Has student achievement increased since 2002? State test score trends through 2002–2006.* Washington, DC: Author.

Chubb, J. E., & Moe, T. M. (1990). *Politics, markets and America's schools.* Washington, DC: Brookings Institute.

Chubb, J. E., & Moe, T. M. (1987). Politics, markets and the organization of schools. *American Political Science Review, 2*(4), 1065–1087.

Cibulka, J. G. (1991). Educational reforms: Performance information and political power In S. H. Fuhrman & B. Malen (Eds.), *The politics of curriculum and testing: The 1990 yearbook of the Politics of Education Association* (pp. 181–201). London: The Falmer Press.

Cohen, D. K., Moffitt, S. L. & Goldin, S. (2007). Policy and practice. In D. K. Cohen, S. H. Fuhrman & F. Mosher (Eds.) *The state of education policy research* (pp. 63–85). Mahwah, NJ: Erlbaum.

Cohen, D. K. & Spillane, J. P. (1992). Policy and practice: The relationship between governance and instruction, *Review of Research in Education, 18* 3–49.

Conley, D. T. (2003). *Who governs our schools? Changing roles and responsibilities.* New York, NY: Teachers College Press

Croninger, R., & Malen, B. (2002). The role of school governance in the creation of school community. In K. Leithwood & P. Hallinger (Eds.), *Second international handbook of educational leadership and administration* (pp. 281–320). Dordrecht, the Netherlands: Kluwer.

Cuban, L. (1984). School reform by remote control: SB 813 in California. *Phi Delta Kappan, 66,* 213–215.

Cuban, L. (1998). How schools change reforms: Redefining reform success and failure, *Teachers College Record, 99,* 453–377.

Cucchiara, M. B., & Horvat, E. M. (2009). Perils and promises: Middle-class parental involvement in urban schools, *American Educational Research Journal, 46*(4), 974–1004.

Danielson, N. M., & Hochschild, J. (1998). Changing urban education: Lessons, cautions, prospects. In C. N. Stone (Ed.), *Changing urban education* (pp. 277–295). Lawrence: University Press of Kansas.

Danzberger, J. P., Carol, L. N., Cunningham, L. L., Kirst, M. W., McCloud, B. A., & Usdan, M. D. (1987). School boards: The forgotten player on the education team. *Phi Delta Kappan, 69,* 53–59.

DeBray, E. (2006). *Politics, ideology and education: Federal policy during the Clinton and Bush administrations.* New York, NY: Teachers College Press.

DeBray, E., McDermott, K., & Wohlstetter, P. (2005). Introduction to the special issue on federalism reconsidered: The case of the No Child Left Behind Act. *Peabody Journal of Education, 80*(2), 1–18.

Designs for Change. (2005). *The big picture: School-initiated reforms, centrally initiated reforms and elementary school achievement in Chicago (1990 to 2005).* Chicago, IL: Designs for Change.

Diamond, J. B., & Spillane, J. P. (2004). High-stakes accountability in urban elementary schools: Challenging or reproducing inequality? *Teachers College Record, 106*(6), 1145–1176.

Dorgan, K. (2004). A year in the life of an elementary school: One school's experiences in meeting new mathematics standards. *Teachers College Record, 106*(6), 1203–1228.

Education for All Handicapped Children Act of 1975, Public Law 94-142. 89 Stat. 773 (1975).

Elementary and Secondary Education Act of 1965, Public Law 89-10. 79 Stat. 27 (1965).

Elmore, R. F. (2009). The problem of capacity in the re(design) of education accountability systems. In M. A. Rebell & J. R. Woll (Eds.), *NCLB at the crossroads: Reexamining the federal effort to close the achievement gap* (pp. 230–261). New York, NY: Teachers College Press.

Elmore, R. F. (1993). School decentralization: Who gains? Who loses? In J. Hannaway & M. Carnoy, (Eds.), *Decentralization and school improvement: Can we fulfill the promise?* (pp. 33–54). San Francisco, CA: Jossey-Bass.

Elmore, R. F. (2002). *Bridging the gap between standards and achievement: The imperative for professional development in education.* Washington, DC: Albert Shanker Institute.

Elmore, R. C., & Sykes, G. (1992). Curriculum policy. In P. W. Jackson (Ed), *Handbook of research on curriculum* (pp. 185–195). New York: MacMillan.

Fairman, J. C., & Firestone, W. F. (2001). The district role in state assessment policy: An exploratory study. In S. H. Fuhrman (Ed.), *From the capital to the classroom: Standards-based reform in the states* (pp. 124–147). Chicago, IL: National Society for the Study of Education.

Fantini, M., & Weinstein, G. (1968). *Making urban schools work.* New York, NY: Holt, Rinehart & Winston.

Feurstein, A. (2002). Elections, voting, and democracy in local school district governance. *Educational Policy, 16,* 15–36.

Forum for Education and Democracy. (2008, April). *Democracy at risk: The need for a new federal policy in education.* Washington, DC: Author.

Fine, M. (1993). Parent involvement: Reflections on parents, power, and urban public schools *Teachers College Record, 94*(4), 682–729.

Firestone, W.. A. (1989). Educational policy as an ecology of games. *Educational Researcher, 18*(7), 18–24.

Firestone, W. A., Fuhrman, S., & Kirst, M. W. (1991). State education reform since 1983: Appraisal and the future. *Educational Policy, 5*(3), 233–250.

Firestone, W. F., Fitz, J., & Broadfoot, P. (1999). Power, learning and legitimation: Assessment implementation across levels in the United States and the United Kingdom. *American Educational Research Journal, 36*(4), 759–793.

Firestone, W. A., Mayrowetz, D., & Fairman, J. (1998). Performance-based assessment and instructional change: The effects of testing in Maine and Maryland. *Educational Evaluation and Policy Analysis, 20,* 95–113.

Finkelstein, B., Malen, B., Muncey, D. E., Rice, J. K., Croninger, R. G., Briggs, L., et al. (2000). *Caught in contradictions: The first two years of a school reconstitution initiative.* College Park, MD: Department of Education Policy and Leadership, University of Maryland.

Finn, C. E., Jr., & Hess, F. M. (2004). On leaving no child behind. *The Public Interest, 157,* 35–56.

Finn, C. E., & Ravitch, D. (Eds.). (2007). *Beyond the basics: Achieving a liberal education for all children.* Washington, DC: Thomas B. Fordham Institute.

Fowler, F. C. (2000). Converging forces: Understanding the growth of state authority over education. In N. D. Theobald & B. Malen (Eds.), *Balancing local control and state responsibility for K-12 education* (pp. 123–146). Larchmont, NY: Eye on Education.

Fuhrman, S. H. (1993). The politics of coherence. In S. H. Fuhrman (Ed.), *Designing coherent education policy* (pp. 1–34). San Francisco, CA: Jossey-Bass.

Fuhrman, S. H. (2001) Introduction. In S. H. Fuhrman (Ed.), *From the capital to the classroom: Standards-based reform in the states* (pp. 1–12). Chicago, IL: National Society for the Study of Education.

Fuhrman, S. H., Clune, W., & Elmore, R.F. (1988). Research on education reform: Lessons on the implementation of policy. *Teachers College Record, 90*(2), 237–258.

Fuhrman, S. H., & Elmore, R. F. (1994). Governors and education policy in the 1990s. In S. H. Fuhrman & R. F. Elmore (Eds.), *The governance of curriculum* (pp. 30–55). Alexandria, VA: Association for Supervision and Curriculum Development.

Fuhrman, S. H., & Elmore, R. F. (1995). Ruling out rules: The evolution of deregulation in state education policy. *Teachers College Record, 97,* 279–209.

Fuhrman, S. H., Goertz, M. E., & Weinbaum, E. H. (2007). Educational governance in the United States: Where are we? How did we get here? Why should we care? In D. K. Cohen, S. H. Fuhrman, & F. Mosher (Ed.), *The state of education policy research* (pp. 1–61). Mahwah, NJ: Erlbaum.

Fuller, B. (2009). Policy and place--Learning from decentralized reforms. In G. Sykes, B. Schneider, & D. N. Plank (Eds.), *Handbook on education policy research* (pp. 855–875). New York, NY: Routledge.

Fuller, E. J., & Johnson, J. F. (2001). Can state accountability systems drive improvements in school performance for children of color and children from low-income homes? *Education and Urban Society, 33*(3), 260–283.

Fusarelli, L. D. (2009). Improvement or interference? Re-envisioning the "state" in education reform. In B. C. Fusarelli & B. S. Cooper (Eds.), *The rising state: How state power is transforming our nation's schools* (pp. 243–270). Albany, NY: State University of New York Press.

Fusarelli, B. C., & Cooper, B. S. (Eds.). (2009). *The rising state: How state power is transforming our nation's schools.* Albany, NY: State University Press of New York.

Fusarelli, B. C., & Fusarelli, L. D. (2003). Systemic reform and organizational change. *Planning and Changing, 34*(3&4), 169–177.

Fung, A. (2004). *Empowered participation: Reinventing urban democracy.* Princeton, NJ: Princeton University Press

Gamson, W. A. (1968). *Power and discontent.* Homewood, IL: Dorsey Press.

Garmes, W. I., Guthrie, J. W., & Pierce, L. C. (1978). *School finance: The economics and politics of public education.* Englewood Cliffs, NJ: Prentice-Hall.

Gold, E., Simon, E. with Brown, C. (2005). A new conception of parent engagement: Community organizing for school reform. In F. English (Ed.) *The Sage handbook of educational leadership* (pp. 237–268). Thousand Oaks, CA: Sage.

Gittell, M. (1967). *Participants and participation.* New York, NY: Praeger.

Grossman, F. D. (2010). Dissent from within: How educational insiders use protest to create policy change. *Educational Policy, 24*(4), 655–686.

Guttman, A. (1999). *Democratic education,* revised edition. Princeton, NJ: Princeton University Press.

Hall, R. H. (1986). *Dimensions of work.* Beverley Hills, CA: Sage

Handler, J. (1996). *Down from bureaucracy: The ambiguity of privatization and empowerment.* Princeton, NJ: Princeton University Press.

Hannaway, J., & Carnoy, M. (Eds.). (1993). *Decentralization and school improvement: Can we fulfill the promise?* San Francisco, CA: Jossey-Bass.

Haney, W. M. (2000). The myth of the Texas miracle in education, *Education Policy Analysis Archives, 8* (41). Retrieved August 22, 2006, from http://epaa.asu.edu/epaa/v8n41/

Hatch, T. (2009). *Managing to change: How schools can survive (and sometimes thrive) in turbulent times.* New York, NY: Teachers College Press.

Henig, J. R. (2009a). The politics of localism in an era of centralization, privatization and choice. In R. L. Crowson & E. B. Goldring (Eds.), *The new localism in American education* (pp. 112–129). Walden, MA: Wiley-Blackwell.

Henig, J. R. (2009b). *Spin cycle: How research is used in policy debates: The case of charter schools.* New York, NY: The Russell Sage Foundation and the Century Foundation.

Henig, J. R., & Rich, W. C. (2004). Mayor-centrism in context. In J. R. Henig & W. C. Rich (Eds.), *Mayors in the middle: Politics, race and mayoral control of urban schools* (pp. 3–24). Princeton, NJ: Princeton University Press.

Herman, J. L. (2004). The effects of testing on instruction. In S. H. Fuhrman & R. F. Elmore (Eds.), *Designing accountability systems for education* (pp. 141–166). New York, NY: Teachers College Press.

Hess, F. M. (1999). *Spinning wheels: The politics of urban school reform.* Washington, DC: Brookings Institute.

Hess, G. A. (1996). *Implementing reform: Stories of stability and change in 14 schools.* Chicago, IL: The Chicago Panel on School Policy.

Hess, G. A. (1999a). Expectations, opportunity, capacity, and will: The four essential components of Chicago school reform. *Educational Policy, 13*(4), 494–517.

Hess, G. A. (1999b). Understanding achievement (and other) changes under Chicago school reform. *Educational Evaluation and Policy Analysis, 21*(1), 67–83.

Honig, M. I., Lorton, J. S., & Copland, M. A. (2009). Urban district central office transformation for teaching and learning improvement: Beyond a zero-sum game. In R. L. Crowson & E. B. Goldring (Eds.), *The new localism in American education* (pp. 21–40). Walden, MA: Wiley-Blackwell.

Horvat, E. M., Weininger, E. B., & Lareau, A. (2003). From social ties to social capital: Class differences in the relations between schools and parent networks. *American Educational Research Journal, 40*(2), 319-352.

Howe, H. III. (1991). America 2000: A bumpy ride on four trains. *Phi Delta Kappan, 73*(3), 192–203.

Howlett, M., & Ramesch, M. (1995). *Studying public policy.* Oxford, UK: Oxford University Press.

Jacobson, R. (2009). The voice of the people in education policy. In G. Sykes, B. Schneider, & D. N. Plank (Eds.), *Handbook on education policy research* (pp. 307–318). New York, NY: Routledge.

James, T. J. (1991). State authority and the politics of educational change. In G. Grant (Ed.), *Review of research in education, vol. 17* (pp. 169–224). Washington, D.C.: American Educational Research Association.

Kane, T. J., & Staiger, D. O. (2002). Volatility in school test scores: Implications for test-based accountability systems. *Brookings Papers on Education Policy, 5*, 235–283. Retrieved May 26, 2009, from http://www.jstor.org

Kingdon, J. (1995) *Agendas, alternatives and public policies,* second edition. New York, NY: Longman.

Kanter, H., & Lowe, R. (1995). Class, race and the emergence of federal education policy: From the New Deal to the Great Society, *Educational Researcher, 24*(3), 4–11, 21.

Kanter, H., & Lowe, R. (2006). From New Deal to no deal: No Child Left Behind and the devolution of responsibility for equal opportunity. *Harvard Educational Review, 76*(4), 474–502.

Kirst, M. (2000). New "improved" mayors take over city schools. *Phi Delta Kappan, 81*(7), 538–546.

Kirst, M. W. (1995a). Recent research on intergovernmental relations in education policy. *Educational Researcher, 24*(9), 18–22.

Kirst, M. W. (1995b). Who's in charge? Federal, state and local control. In D. Ravitch & M. A. Vinovskis (Eds.), *Learning from the past* (pp, 25–56). Baltimore, MD: The Johns Hopkins University Press.

Kirst, M. W. (1988). Recent state education reform in the United States: Looking backward and forward. *Educational Administration Quarterly, 24*, 319–328.

Kirst, M. W. (1979). The new politics of state education finance. *Phi Delta Kappan, 60*, 427–432.

Kirst, M. W., & Wirt, F. (2009). *The political dynamics of American education* (4th ed.). Richmond, CA: McCutchan.

Knapp, M. S., Sterns, M., David, J., Turnbull, B., & Peterson, S. (1983, January). *Cumulative effects of federal educational policies on schools and districts.* SRI Project 3590. Menlo Park, CA: SRI International.

Ladd, H. (1996). *Holding schools accountable: Performance-based reform in education.* Washington, DC: Brookings Institute.

Ladd, H., & Zelli, A. (2002). School-based accountability in North Carolina: The responses of school principals. *Educational Administration Quarterly, 38*(4), 494–529.

Lau v. Nichols, 414 U. S. 563 (1974).

Lee, J. (2008). Is test-driven external accountability effective? Synthesizing the evidence from cross-state causal-comparative and correlational studies. *Review of Educational Research, 78,* 608–644.

Leithwood, K., & Menzies, T. (1998). Forms and effects of school-based management: A review. *Educational Policy, 12,* 325–346.

Leithwood, K., Steinbach, R., & Jantzi, D. (2002). School leadership and teachers' motivation to implement accountability policies. *Educational Administration Quarterly, 38*(1), 94–119.

Lewis, D. A., & Nakagawa, K. (1995). *Race and educational reform in the American metropolis: A study of school decentralization.* Albany: State University of New York Press.

Malen, B. (2001). Generating interest in interest groups. In H. Mawhinney & C. Lugg (Eds.), The 2000 Politics of Education Association special issue on interest groups in United States education. *Educational Policy, 15,* 168–186.

Malen, B. (2003). Tightening their grip? *Educational Policy, 17*(2), 195–216.

Malen, B. (2006). Revising policy implementation as a political phenomenon: The case of school reconstitution. In M. I. Honig (Ed.), *New directions in education policy implementation: Confronting complexity* (pp. 83–104). Albany: State University of New York Press.

Malen B., & Cochran, M. V. (2008). Beyond pluralistic patterns of power: A review of research on the micropolitics of schools. In B. S. Cooper, J. G. Cibulka, & L. D. Fusarelli (Eds.), *Handbook of education politics and policy* (pp. 148–178). New York, NY: Routledge.

Malen, B., & Muncey, D. (2000). Creating a "new set of givens?" The impact of state activism on school autonomy. In N. D. Theobard & B. Malen (Eds.), *Balancing local control and state responsibility for k-12 education* (pp. 199–244). Larchmont, NY: Eye on Education.

Malen, B., & Rice, J. K. (2004). A framework for assessing the impact of education reforms on school capacity: Insights from studies of high-stakes accountability initiatives. *Educational Policy, 18*(5), 631–660.

Malen, B., & Rice, J. K. (2009). School reconstitution and school improvement. In G. Sykes, B. Schneider, & D. N. Plank (Eds.), *Handbook on education policy research* (pp. 464–477). New York, NY: Routledge.

Mann, D. (1974). Political representation and the urban school advisory councils. *Teachers College Record, 75,* 251–270.

Manna, P. (2007). *School's in: Federalism and the national education agenda.* Washington, DC: Georgetown University Press.

Mawhinney, H., & Lugg. C. (Eds.). (2001),.The 2000 Politics of Education Association special issue on interest groups in United States education. *Educational Policy, 15.*

Maxcy, B. D., & Nguyen, T. S. (2006). The politics of distributing leadership: Reconsidering leadership distribution in two Texas elementary schools. *Educational Policy, 20*(1), 163–196.

Maxwell, L. A. (2010, February 10). State lawmakers warn of federal instrusion. *Education Week,* pp. 15, 17.

Mazzoni, T. L. (1982). Education interest groups and state school policymaking. *Planning and Changing,* 158–171.

Mazzoni, T. L. (1991). Analyzing state school policymaking: An arena model. *Educational Evaluation and Policy Analysis, 13,* 115–138.

Mazzoni, T. L. (1993). The changing nature of state education policy making. *Educational Evaluation and Policy Analysis, 15*(4), 357–379.

Mazzoni, T. L. (1995). State policy-making and school reform: Influences and influentials. In J. D. Scriebner & D. H. Layton (Eds.), *The study of educational politics* (pp. 53–73). New York: Falmer Press.

Mazzoni, T. L. (2000). State politics and school reform: The first decade of the "educational excellence" movement. In N. D. Theobard & B. Malen (Eds.), *Balancing local control and state responsibility for k-12 education* (pp. 147–196). Larchmont, NY: Eye on Education.

McDonnell, L. M. (2000). Redefining democratic purposes. In L. M. McDonnell, P. M. Timpane & R. Benjamin (Eds.), *Rediscovering the democratic purposes of education* (pp. 1–18). Lawrence: University Press of Kansas.

McDonnell, L. M. (2007). The politics of education: Influencing policy and beyond. In S. H. Fuhrman, D. K. Cohen, & F. Mosher (Eds.), *The state of education policy research* (pp. 19–40). Mahwah, NJ: Erlbaum.

McDermott, K. A. (2009). The expansion of state policy research. In G. Sykes, B. Schneider, & D. N. Plank (Eds.), *Handbook on education policy research* (pp. 749–766). New York, NY: Routledge.

McDonnell, L. M. (2009). Repositioning politics in education's circle of knowledge. *Educational Research, 38*(6), 417–427.

McDonnell, L. M., & Fuhrman, S. H. (1986). The political context of school reform. In V. D. Mueller & M. P. McKeown (Eds.), *The fiscal, legal and political aspects of state reform of elementary and secondary education* (pp. 43–64). Cambridge, MA: Ballinger.

McGuinn, P. (2006a). *No Child Left behind and the transformation of federal education policy, 1965–2005.* Lawrence: University of Kansas Press.

McGuinn, P. (2006b). Swing issues and policy regimes: Federal education policy and the politics of policy change. *The Journal of Policy History, 18*(2), 205–240.

McNeil, L. M. (2000). *Contradictions of school reform: Educational costs of standardized testing.* New York, NY: Routledge.

McNeil, M. & Maxwell, L. A. (2010, June 9). States up ante on applications for race to top, *Education Week, 29* (33), 1, 27.

Mickelson, R. (2009). Race, ethnicity and education. In G. Sykes, B. Schneider, & D. N. Plank (Eds.), *Handbook on education policy research* (pp. 240–253). New York: Routledge.

Mintrom, M. (2001). Educational governance and democratic practice. *Educational Policy, 15*(5), 615–643,

Mintrom, M. (2009). Local democracy in education. In G. Sykes, B. Schneider, & D. N. Plank (Eds.), *Handbook on education policy research* (pp. 793–804). New York: Routledge.

Mintrop, H. (2004). *Schools on probation: How accountability works (and doesn't work).* New York, NY: Teachers College Press

Mintrop, H., & Sunderman, G. L. (2009). Predictable failure of federal sanctions-driven accountability for school improvement—and why we may retain it anyway, *Educational Researcher, 38*(5), 353–364.

Miskel, C., & Song, M. (2004). Passing reading first: Prominence and processes in an elite policy network, *Educational Evaluation and Policy Analysis, 26*(2), 89–109.

Nelson, A. (2005). *The elusive ideal: Equal educational opportunity and the federal role in Boston's public schools 1950–1985.* Chicago, IL: The University of Chicago Press.

Neuman-Sheldon, B. (2006). *Building on state reform: Maryland school restructuring.* Washington, DC: Center on Education Policy.

Nichols, S. L., & Berliner, D. C. (2007). *Collateral damage: How high-stakes testing corrupts America's schools.* Cambridge, MA: Harvard Education Press.

O'Connor, C., Hill, L. D., & Robinson, S. R. (2009). Who's at risk and what's race got to do with it? In V. L. Gladsen, J. L. Davis, & A. J. Artiles (Eds.), *Review of educational research in education, vol. 33* (pp. 1-34). Washington, DC: American Educational Research Association and Thousand Oaks, CA: Sage.

Ogawa, R. T., Sandholtz, J. H., Martinez-Flores, M., & Scribner, S. P. (2003). The substantive and symbolic consequences of a district's standards-based curriculum. *American Educational Research Journal, 40*(1), 147–187.

Orfield, G., & Eaton, S. E. (1996). *Dismantling desegregation: The quiet reversal of Brown v. Board of Education.,* New York, NY: The New Press.

Orr, M. (1999). *Black social capital: The politics of school reform in Baltimore, 1986–1998.* Lawrence: University of Kansas Press.

Pedulla, J. J., Abrams, L. M., Madaus, G. F., Russell, M. K., Ramos, M. A., & Miao, J. (2003). *Perceived effects of state-mandated testing programs on teaching and learning: Findings from a national survey of teachers.* Boston, MA: Lynch School of Education, Boston College.

Pipho, C. (1991). Centralizing curriculum at the state level. In M. F. Klein (Ed.), *The politics of cur-*

riculum decision-making: Issues in centralizing the curriculum (pp. 67–96). Albany: State University of New York Press.

Plank, D., & Boyd, W. L. (1994). Antipolitics, education, and institutional choice: The flight from democracy. *American Educational Research Journal, 31*(2), 263–281.

Ravitch, D. (2010). *The death and life of the great American school system: How testing and choice are undermining education.* New York, NY: Basic Books.

Rebell, M. A., & Wolff, J. R. (2008). *Moving every child ahead: From NCBL hype to meaningful educational opportunity.* New York, NY: Teachers College Press.

Rebell, M. A., & Wolff, J. R. (Eds.). (2009). *NCBL at the crossroads: Reexamining the federal effort to close the achievement gap.* New York, NY: Teachers College Press.

Rich, W. C. (1996). *Black mayors and school politics: The failure of reform in Detroit, Gary and Newark.* New York, NY: Garland.

Robelen, E. W. (2010, January 6). Stimulus is spurring legislation: States position themselves to win competitive grants, *Education Week, 29*(18), 1, 21.

Rorrer, A. (2004). Intersections in accountability reform: Complexity, local actors, legitimacy and agendas. In L. Skrla & J. J. Scheurich (Eds.), *Educational equity and accountability: paradigms, policies, and politics* (pp. 251–266). New York, NY: Taylor & Francis Books.

Rosenberg, G. (2004). Substituting symbol for substance: What did Brown really accomplish? *Political Science and Politics, 37*(2), 205–209.

Rothstein, R. (2002). *Out of balance: Our understanding of how schools affect society and how society affects schools.* Chicago, IL: Spencer Foundation.

Rothstein, R. (2004). *Class and schools: Using social, economic, and education reform to close the black-white achievement gap.* Washington, D C: Economic Policy Institute.

Rothstein, R. (2009, January 28). Getting accountability right. *Education Week,* pp. 36, 26.

Rothstein, R., Jacobson, R., & Wilder, T. (2008). *Grading education: Getting accountability right.* Washington, DC & New York, NY: Economic Policy Institute and Teachers College Press.

Rowan, B. (2002). The ecology of school improvement: Notes on the school improvement industry in the United States. *Journal of Educational Change, 3,* 283–314.

San Antonio Independent School District v. Rodriguez, 411 U. S. 1 (1973).

Sandholtz, J. H., Ogawa, R. T., & Scribner, S. P. (2004). Standards gaps: Unintended consequences of local standards-based reform. *Teachers College Record, 106*(6), 1177–1202.

Schattsneider, E. E. (1960). *The semi-sovereign people.* New York, NY: Holt, Rhinehart and Winston.

Scheurich, J. J., Skrla, L. & Johnson, J. F., Jr. (2004). Thinking carefully about equity and accountability. In L. Skrla & J. J. Scheurick (Eds.), *Educational equity and accountability: Paradigms, policies, and politics* (pp. 13–27). New York: RoutledgeFalmer.

Sebring, P. B., Allensworth, E., Bryk, A. S., Easton, J. Q., & Luppescu, S. (2006). *The essential supports for school improvement.* Chicago, IL: Consotium on Chicago School Research at the University of Chicago.

Seitsinger, R. M., & Zera, D. A. (2002). The demise of parent involvement in school governance *Journal of School Leadership, 12*(4), 340–367.

Shipps, D. (1998). Corporate influence on Chicago school reform. In C. N. Stone (Ed.), *Changing urban education* (pp. 161–183). Lawrence: University Press of Kansas.

Shipps, D. (1997). The invisible hand: Big business and Chicago school reform. *Teachers College Record, 99*(1), 73–116.

Shipps, D., Kahne, J., & Smylie, M. A. (1999). The politics of urban school reform: Legitimacy, city growth, and school improvement in Chicago. *Educational Policy, 13*(4), 518–545.

Simmons, J. (2006). *Breaking through: Transforming urban school districts.* New York, NY: Teachers College Press.

Sirotnik, K. A. (2004). Introduction: Critical concerns about accountability concepts and practices. In K. A. Sirotnik (Ed.), *Holding accountability accountable: What ought to matter in public education* (pp. 1–17). New York, NY: Teachers College Press.

Skrla, L., Scheurich, J. J., Johnson, J. F., Jr., & Korschoreck, J. W. (2004). Accountability for equity: Can state policy leverage social justice? In L. Skrla & J. J. Scheurick (Eds.), *Educational equity and accountability: Paradigms, policies, and politics*, pp. 51-78. New York: RoutledgeFalmer.

Smith, M. S., & O'Day, J. (1991). Systemic school reform. In S. H. Fuhrman & B. Malen (Eds.), *The politics of curriculum and testing* (pp. 233–267). London: Taylor and Francis.

Soder, R. (2004). The double bind of civic education assessment and accountability. In K. A. Sirotnik (Ed.), *Holding accountability accountable: What ought to matter in public education* (pp. 100–115). New York, NY: Teachers College Press.

Stetcher, B. M., & Barron, S. (1999, April). *Test-based accountability: The perverse consequences of milepost testing.* Paper presented at the Annual Conference of the American Educational Research Association, Montreal, Canada.

Stone, C. N. (1980). The implementation of social programs: Two perspectives, *Journal of Social Issues, 36*(4), 13–34.

Stone, C. N. (2009). Who is governed? Local citizens and the political order of cities. InJ.S. Davies & D. L. Imbroscio (Eds.), *Theories of urban politics*, Los Angeles, CA: Sage.

Stone, C. N., Henig, J. R., Jones, B. O., & Pierannunzi, C. (2001). *Building civic capacity: The politics of reforming urban schools.* Lawrence: University Press of Kansas.

Summerfield, H. L. (1971). *The neighborhood-based politics of education,* Columbus, OH: Charles E. Merrill.

Summers, A. A., & Johnson, A. W. (1996). The effects of school-based management plans. In E. A. Hanushek & D. W. Jorgenson (Eds.), *Improving America's schools: The role of incentives* (pp. 75–96). Washington, DC: National Academy Press.

Sunderman, G. L. (2001). Accountability mandates and the implementation of Title I schoolwide programs: A comparison of three urban districts. *Educational Administration Quarterly, 37*(4), 503–532.

Sunderman, G. L., & Orfield, G. (2006). Domesticating a revolution: No Child Left Behind reforms and state administrative response. *Harvard Educational Review, 76*(4), 526–556.

Sunderman, G. L., & Kim, J. (2007). The expansion of federal power and the politics of implementing the No Child Left Behind Act. *Teachers College Record, 109*(5), 1057–1085.

Swanson, C. B., & Stevenson, D. L. (2002). Standards-based reform in practice: Evidence on state policy and classroom instruction from the NAEP state assessments. *Educational Evaluation and Policy Analysis, 24*(1), 1–27.

Sykes, G., O'Day, J., & Ford, T. G. (2009). The district role in instructional improvement. In G. Sykes, B. Schneider, & D. N. Plank (Eds.), *Handbook of education policy research* (pp. 767–784). New York: Routledge.

Trujillo, A. (2005). Politics, school philosophy, and language policy: The case of Crystal City schools. *Educational Policy, 19*(4), 621–654.

Tucker, H., & Ziegler, H. L. (1980). Professionals versus the public. New York, NY: Longman.

Tyack, D. (1993). School governance in the United States: Historical puzzles and anomalies. In J. Hannaway & M. Carnoy (Eds.), *Decentralization and school improvement: Can we fulfill the promise?* (pp. 1–32). San Francisco, CA: Jossey-Bass.

Tyack, D., & Cuban, L. (1995). *Tinkering toward utopia.* Cambridge, MA: Harvard University Press.

U.S. Department of Education. (2007). *No Child Left Behind: Performance and accountability report, fiscal year 2007.* Washington, DC: U.S. Government Printing Office.

Valli, L., Croninger, R. G., Chambliss, M, J., Graeber, A. O., & Buese, D. (2008). *Test-driven: High-stakes accountability in elementary schools.* New York, NY: Teachers College Press.

Vinovskis, M. A. (2009). *From A Nation at Risk to No Child Left Behind: National goals and the creation of federal education policy.* New York, NY: Teachers College Press.

Walker, J. L., Jr. (1991). *Mobilizing interest groups in America: Patrons, professions, and social movements.* Ann Arbor: University of Michigan Press.

Wells, A. S. (2009). "Our children's burden": A history of federal education policies that ask (now require) our public schools to solve societal inequality. In M. A. Rebell & J. R. Wolff (Eds.), *NCBL at the crossroads: Reexamining the federal effort to close the achievement gap* (pp. 1–42). New York: Teachers College Press.

Wells, A. S., & Serna, I. (1996). The politics of culture: Understanding local political resistance to detracking in racially mixed schools. *Harvard Educational Review, 66*(1), 93–118.

Westheimer, J., & Kahne, J. (2003). What kind of citizen? Political choices and educational goals, *Encounters on Education, 4,* 47–64.

White, J. A., & Wehage, G. (1995). Community collaboration: If it is such a good idea, why is it so hard to do? *Educational Evaluation and Policy Analysis, 17,* 23–38.

White, K. W., & Rosenbaum, J. E. (2008). Inside the black box of accountability" How high-stakes accountability alters school culture and the classification and treatment of students and teachers. In A. R. Sadovnik, J. A. O'Day, G. W. Bohrnstedt, & K. M. Borman (Eds.), *No Child Left Behind and the reduction of the achievement gap: Sociological perspectives on federal educational policy* (pp. 97–114). New York, NY: Routledge.

Whitford, B. L., & Jones, K. (Eds.). (2000). *Accountability, assessment and teacher commitment: Lessons from Kentucky's reform efforts.* Albany: State University of New York Press.

Whitty, G., Power, S., & Halpin, D. (1998). *Devolution & choice in education: The school, the state and the market.* Bristol, PA: Open University Press.

Wilson, S. M., & Floden, R. E. (2001). Hedging bets: Standards-based reform in classrooms. In S. H. Fuhrman (Ed.), *From the capitol to the classroom: Standards-based reform in the state* (pp. 193–216). Chicago, IL: National Society for the Study of Education.

Wong, K. W., & Anagnostopoulos, D. (1998). Can integrated governance reconstruct teaching? Lessons learned from two low-performing Chicago high schools. *Educational Policy, 12*(1), 31–47.

Wong, K. W., Shen, F. X., Anagnostopoulos, D., & Rutledge, S. (2007). *The education mayor: Improving America's schools.* Washington, DC: Georgetown University Press,

Ziegler, L. H., & Jennings, M. K. (1974). *Governing American schools.* North Scituate, MA: Duxbury Press.

PART II

The Fundamental Issues

Structure, Governance, and Market Forces

Douglas E. Mitchell

The three chapters of Part II present three strikingly different perspectives on the dynamics of education policy shifts during the last six decades. David Cohen and Susan Moffitt argue persuasively that powerful policy initiatives coming from centralized policy making agencies have overreached the capacity of schools to accommodate or comply with their demands. They argue that local school systems lack the instructional infrastructure needed to effectively implement recent federal and state policy initiatives. As a result, escalating policy demands are stimulating reverberating political conflicts as the inability to implement new policies stimulates resistance, pro forma compliance, deflection and subversion. Escalating concern over inadequate school performance followed by centralization of policy-making powers cannot guarantee adequate implementation in the absence of the institutional capacity to appropriate policy goals and mount the programs needed to reach them.

Jane Hannaway and Joel Mittleman focus their analysis on the emergence of powerful national teachers unions. As teacher unions have negotiated typical industrial unionist job and worker rights protections (including limiting administrative rights to evaluate teachers and maintenance of the single salary schedule based on educational degrees and years of teaching experience), these authors note a counterbalancing pressure arising from the availability of new information and data management technologies that now make it possible to link teacher work performance directly to the student achievement test scores. They note that the Obama administration is pressing hard for the inclusion of student testing data in the evaluation and compensation of teachers. This initiative has gained a lot of support from economists and other research scholars and appears to be gaining traction with union leaders, particularly in the American Federation of Teachers.

Douglas Harris and John Witte lift up the "Economics 101" theory of how market place competition is expected to produce competition and innovation in school programs and practices. Competitive innovations are, in turn, expected to increase both the efficiency and the overall performance levels of the public schools. They see growing support for the application of market mechanisms in education as springing from a growing belief that schools operating as public service bureaucracies are inherently inefficient and lack the motivation to aggressively pursue alternative approaches to curriculum, instruction and utilization of student assessment data to guide school program designs.

Taken together, these three chapters highlight some of the reasons why school policy has been changing rapidly and yet not developing a broad consensus regarding how best to reach world-class school performance. The contrasting perspectives found in these chapters reveal why education policy debates remain energized and multifaceted. With such divergent views about how educational performance is shaped by educational structures it is not surprising that each new wave of school reform policies seems to ignore or even contradict the last ones.

3

THE INFLUENCE OF PRACTICE ON POLICY[1]

David K. Cohen and Susan L. Moffitt

As study of the politics of education developed after WWII, researchers investigated the play of influence in federal, state, and local education matters, the influence of interest groups on policy, the politics of teaching and curriculum, and even political influence in classrooms. Some probed the ways in which teaching and curriculum became occasions for political dispute, while others explored how interest groups and government decisions influenced teaching and curriculum. In all of these studies, researchers probed how teaching and other aspects of schools were shaped by state and local school systems and other agencies; they did little to probe the influence that teaching, curriculum, and other elements of education might exert on politics.

Governments and interest groups do influence practice, including teaching, management, curriculum and learning, but it also works the other way: practice affects governance, politics, and policy. We discuss these relationships in two areas: the relations between policy and practice, and the relations between the formal structure of governance on the one hand, and teaching, learning, and curriculum on the other. Title I of the 1965 Elementary and Secondary Education Act (ESEA) is the chief case we use to illustrate how politics and policy can be a consequence as well as a cause of what some sociologists term the "core technology" of education.

Policy and Practice

The relations between social policy and practice present a dilemma: public and private agencies identify problems and offer solutions, whether for welfare, drug use, or weak schools, yet the key problem solvers are the offending, needy, or damaged people and organizations that policy aims to correct. Governments typically have more power than those at whom social policy is directed and they devise instruments— incentives, ideas, money, leadership, rules, and more— to encourage the desired responses from practice. Yet these help only if they are used well by those who are said to be the problem, whose capability therefore is likely to be modest, and others who may assist. Though policymakers define problems and devise remedies, they are rarely the ultimate problem solvers; that falls to the people and organizations that have the problem. Policymakers therefore depend on those that are the problem to solve it. The latter depend on policymakers for some resources—incentives, ideas, money, and more—if they decide to solve the problem, and want help.[2] Practitioners and policymakers often are at odds; yet the success of policy, and perhaps practice, depend on finding mutually agreeable ways to manage this dilemma. Their mutual dependence creates opportunities for reciprocal political influence.

The dilemma can be difficult to manage even in seemingly simple situations, as when teachers try to help students improve weak compositions. Teachers may see students as the problem, but students are the key problem solvers, for only they can learn to improve their compositions. Teachers can offer examples, assign exercises, coax, help, and insist, but they depend on students to use these things. Teachers have more power and knowledge, but students' will and ability are their own. Like others in authority, teachers depend on the people with problems to solve them. Teachers who set tasks which students are unprepared to perform risk resistance, revolt, or loss of authority. If students will not do as teachers say, teachers must settle for what students will do.[3]

Most discussions of policy and practice in education took a different tack: for decades they focused on governmental position. Policy that was made in central agencies and left little room for local autonomy was identified as "top-down," as were studies that adopted such a perspective; policies that encouraged local autonomy and adaptation were identified as "bottom up," as were studies that considered policy implementation from a local perspective.[4] Centralized, top down, policies tend to emphasize compliance, while localized, bottom up, policies emphasize adaptation. By moving beyond position, the dilemma seems to encompass aspects of both: mutual influence can afford some measure of compliance and some measure of adaptation. The point is that the arrow works in both directions.

Position in government can be important, but it is not the only or even the primary consideration for, especially in the United States, top and bottom are rubbery terms. Title I of the 1965 ESEA is a federal program, so a top-down view of its implementation should begin in Washington. Yet the program devolves extensive authority to the states, which allocate funds, screen local applications, and assist and evaluate local programs. The federal government is the top agency for states, and states are the federal agency's bottom of first resort. But those agencies in Albany and Sacramento are the top for local districts, even as the school principals' top is the local central office, and the teachers' top is the principal. State Title I offices' problems of control and compliance vis-à-vis local education authority (LEA) central offices thus closely resemble the problems of control and compliance that LEA central offices have with schools. The problems that researchers have associated with the top of policy also are found at the bottom: Tension between policy and practice pervades the same agencies and individuals, rather than being aligned only with top and bottom. LEA central office workers who set direction concerning Title I for principals, teachers, and students also work as "street-level" bureaucrats in relation to those who set direction for Title I in state agencies. These public managers are both central controllers and street-level bureaucrats, workers at both top and bottom who try to influence those for whom they make or interpret policy while also trying to cope with those who make or interpret policy for them. In such cases, top and bottom converge in the same person and office.

A focus on governmental position obscures this paradoxical situation, but the dilemma illuminates it, by highlighting tension between those who set the direction for action and those who interpret and carry it out, whatever their position in formal organizations. The tension is found in the relations between government policy and practice, but it arises at all levels of government and in public and private agencies. The terms *policy* and *practice* refer here to the difference between direction setting actions and implementation activities, whether they occur in government or outside it.

The dilemma helps to illuminate the ways in which influence flows both ways between politics and policy on the one hand, and practice on the other. Policies are created politically, but they can create or change politics by providing resources and benefits to practitioners who form constituencies that then use the resources to shape politics and policy. For example, state passage of charter school legislation was helped along by a small band of advocates, but the legislation enabled the growth of charter schools and associated organizations, which have become a formidable political force in states and nationally, pressing for more charter schools among other things. Policies can promote or discourage incentives, motivation, and resources for political participation by individuals or groups, and that participation can shape politics and policy.[5]

Practice also can influence politics and policy by way of policies' fate in implementation.[6] The further policies press practice to depart from whatever its current form may be, the more difficult are the entailed changes in practice; the more difficult those changes are, the more likely that policy creates incompetence in practice (Bardach, 1977). To avoid that, more new capability would have to be acquired in practice, and more existing capability would have to be abandoned or unlearned. Yet the more ambitious a policy, and the more incompetence it creates, the more difficult it is to mobilize the resources that could forestall incompetence in practice, for the further policy presses practice into the unknown, the more difficult is to know what the required new capability might be, and the more likely is practice failure. Failure can erode trust in practitioners, but since the problem can be traced to policy, contagion can threaten policy as well. In short, policy implementation influences politics by realigning interests and reshaping the policies themselves as they are adapted to local settings and stimulate support or opposition.

For example, shortly after Title I began in 1965, evidence that it had failed in practice threatened the program. One study reported that Title I was badly and perhaps illegally managed, and another reported that the program did not improve student performance.[7] The program soon seemed to be at risk politically; organized interests capitalized on the evidence of practice failure to advance their political agendas. Some pressed to turn the program into unrestricted grants while others urged more targeted instructional assistance rather than unrestricted grants. The reports of practice failure shaped politics, which shaped policy and program operations; those changes helped to change practice in the 1970s. Four decades later, evidence that No Child Left Behind (NCLB) had not had the expected effect on achievement—owing to a collision between rigidly ambitious federal policy goals and weakness in practice— opened the program to intense criticism. The reports of practice failure changed the politics around NCLB, creating doubt and opposition among former supporters, in and out of government. That increased pressure for the central government to weaken several of the bill's key provisions.[8] Practice failure was contagious in both cases, and political influence spread swiftly from classrooms to politics and policy.

The dilemma highlights the two-way flow of political influence in education because it calls attention to tension and mutual dependence in the relations between policy and practice. Mutual dependence arises in incentives to collaborate, to mobilize resources, to improve practice, and to make policy succeed, while tension arises, among other ways, in the risks associated with policy efforts to change practice. Such things sometimes play out in anticipated action and adjustment before policy spills into public view; if so, practice influences policy as it is made. Often they play out later, as efforts to implement policy are under way. Either way, the more policy puts practice at risk of failure, the more it can damage the interests and legitimacy not only of practitioners but also of policymakers. The potential contagion from practice failure to policy and politics is a key feature of their mutual dependence; it also is a potential source of change in policy and politics, since the prospect of failure can concentrate policymakers' minds and energies. Thus we see implementation not only as an effort to turn policy into practice, but also a continuing interaction about how practice may influence policy and politics by way of political feedback from practice to policy and politics.

Infrastructure and Politics

The political structure of U.S. government gives a distinctive form to the relations between politics and education, and to policy formation and implementation. On one level our story is a relatively familiar one, about how a fragmented political system and weak government affect decision making for education. That fragmented system enabled public schools to develop in ways that tended to insulate them from state and federal political influence, while opening them to many local influences, and non-governmental influences of many sorts. The politics of education were mostly local for most of U.S. history. State politics had a relatively narrow focus, in which funds for local schools and a few course requirements were two of the chief elements. The political structure of schooling shaped the sites and content of politics. On another level, however, our story is an unfamiliar one about how the fragmented system led to very weak educational infrastructure supporting educational practice, which in turn shaped the politics of education and education policy.

The familiar story begins with the sources of fragmented governance in federalism, the separation of powers, and decentralization. State governments were the formal constitutional center of U.S. education, but most states delegated most authority to localities, for most of their history. Local districts are the fundamental governance unit. There are some 14,000-odd districts, and their influence is extraordinary in world perspective. Despite the recent growth of state and national power, these districts make a great range of decisions, including finance, educational program, and nearly all human resource matters. There has been some variability in states' influence in education: Hawaii has no local districts, and southeastern state agencies were stronger than most other states (Wirt, 1982). But until recently the general pattern was extensive delegation of power. State governments began to exercise more influence in the last few decades, but most are still far from what, in world perspective, could be called central control (Cohen & Spillane, 1992).

Financial support for most U.S. schools depends partly on local taxes, which creates large and often enormous inequality in educational resources among districts. It also depends partly on state aid, which contributes to often great inequality in educational resources among states. Intensifying residential segregation by race and class through the late 19th and 20th centuries turned many neighborhood schools and school districts into racial and economic enclaves, and district finance and teacher assignment practices created large inequality among schools' educational resources, within districts (Massey & Denton, 1993). The growing congruence of race and social class with wealth differences in state and local jurisdictions compounds unequal fiscal and educational capability.

Governments also are divided internally by the separation of powers. Federal, state, and most local general governments have three branches, and state and local school governments are divided into executive and legislative branches, which are subordinate to the three branches of state general government and in some cases to local general governments. The result is a remarkably dispersed governance system, in which what appears to be a single decision often must be made, modified, re-made, and re-modified by several branches of government at several levels.

This fragmented political structure led to another sort of fragmentation, as state and federal policies tried to solve problems of educational practice. Since the policies had to work across political boundaries among and within governments, federal agencies sought to build bridges to states and localities, within the fragmented governance system. Added general governance authority in education was unthinkable, so each program was outfitted with its own administration: budget, personnel, evaluation, and the like. That was true of Headstart and ESEA Title I, of programs to reform the education of disabled students, to provide bilingual education for non-English speaking students, and to insure sex equity in schools across the nation, among others (Cohen & Spillane, 1992).

The result was policy and program specific political and managerial silos, ingenious devices that coped with fragmented and weak government by creating managerial systems and political support that bridged the fragmentation of federalism. That enabled coordination of operations across levels of government in the absence of much general administrative capability. The silos enabled policies and programs to mobilize tens, hundreds, or thousands of managers and educators, in hundreds or thousands of jurisdictions, at several levels of government. But it multiplied fragmentation within federal, state, and local education governments, for the silos created independent policy sectors at each level of government; they enabled coordination within programs or policies across levels of the federal system, but they impeded coherent action across sectors, among programs, and between programs and mainstream operations, within governments. Though the design of American government incarnates a deep mistrust of state power, the design of most education policy expressed an abiding hope for the power of government, and a wish to harness it to solve social problems. The policy and program silos are evidence of the clash; they enable problem solving in a fragmented system, but at the price of even more fragmentation, and more complex administration (Bankston, 1982; Cohen, 1982; Rogers & Whetten, 1982; Meyer, 1983).

This pattern has parallels in private sector agencies concerned with education. Networks of advocacy organizations, professional groups, and special purpose R&D agencies grew up around single purpose policies or programs. One helped to build support for PL 94-142, The Education for All Handicapped Children Act, and another coalesced around Title I of the 1965 ESEA. Such networks can help to coordinate and stabilize program operations, as well as to mobilize support for programs across governments and among many sorts of agencies (Peterson, Rabe, & Wong, 1986; Cohen, 1982). The networks are ingenious, for they help to support problem-solving policies and programs in a political system that was designed to impede such work, but because they mirror the fractures that policies and programs create within governments, they also support that fragmentation.

Weak government is the other distinctive feature of education politics in the United States. Hostility to strong domestic government was built into the political design of the U.S. in the late 18th century; combined with economic liberalism in the next century, it led states to delegate core educational functions like tests, curricula, and textbooks to private firms. States outsourced the technical and professional capability that most national systems retain, so that the capability of state and local agencies that operate school systems and schools remained quite limited. Very few agencies had much capability to govern, to manage, or to mobilize strong education programs. Most state agencies were small and weakly staffed (McDonnell & McLaughlin, 1982; Murphy, 1974). In fact, most state education department managers are paid with federal funds. State and local school agencies have few staffers with expertise in curricula, learning, teaching, and teacher education. Most states delegated most instructional decisions to localities, most localities delegated them to schools, and most school principals delegated them to teachers. Even most large city districts had modest managerial and educational capability. Though states and localities have grown more active, their weakness persists in somewhat lessened form into the present (Minnici & Hill, 2007).

Effects of Weak Governance

One manifestation of this situation can be found in the location of political decisions and disputes. The outsourcing of most core capability meant, for instance, that state decisions and debates about curriculum tended to be limited to text adoption and topic inclusion. And these divisions occurred chiefly in states with state-adopted texts, for text adoption was the chief decision that states made about curriculum. Most disputes about what students studied and what books they read were local. Weak governance was also manifested in the sharp disproportion between the ambitious policies and programs that states began to launch in the last decades of the twentieth century, and the human resources that states deployed to support the initiatives. In the 1980s, California, a state that had more people and a larger economy than most nations in the world, launched a major statewide reform of mathematics teaching and learning, yet the state education agency employed fewer than three professionals to advise and assist hundreds of school districts, thousands of schools, and tens of thousands of teachers (Wilson, 2003).

These were only the surface evidence of the underlying problem: public education never developed the infrastructure of practice—the common instruments and related capability—that guide and undergird practice, and mediate between practice and policy in most nations. That was no oversight; it was a central feature in the design of U.S. public education (Reese, 2005). The three most important infrastructure elements are: common curricula, linked examinations, and teacher education that enables their use. A critical part of educational infrastructure is common curricula. In the United States, there was no such thing; decisions about curriculum adoption were left to local schools or districts: each school or school system chose its texts, subject to some state regulation, and most left instruction to teachers. But most texts were the province of national publishers. Each district, in many districts each school, and in many schools each classroom, had its own texts, which teachers used quite differently (Floden, Porter, Schmidt, Freeman, & Schwille, 1981). Practitioners lacked a common course of study in which teachers and students could work, and, absent that, neither the central government nor states, nor many local districts could use that common course of study to influence practice, should they wish to.

Another element of the infrastructure of practice is examinations that are tied to curricula. Such examinations can link assessment of students' academic progress to what they study; that was impossible in the United States, because tests could not be linked to a non-existent common curricula. Examinations also can be useful in diagnosis, for they make it possible for practitioners to determine how well students are learning the curriculum and where they need more work. In the absence of common curricula and related examinations, psychologists devised norm-referenced tests, which rated students' performance relative to others who took the test. Norms for achievement were created from the population of test-takers, rather than from the curriculum students were to learn. Norm-referenced tests were designed to screen out curriculum effects; local, state, and federal authorities had no way to determine whether students were learning what they were supposed to learn.

Teacher education is a third important element of the infrastructure of practice. In many national school systems it centers on the curricula that intending teachers will teach; professional education is tied to the instructional content on which teachers and students will work. Because teacher education in the U.S. could be grounded in no common curriculum, teacher educators tried to teach intending teachers how to teach no particular curriculum, an educational anomaly if ever there was one. For that reason among others, teacher education was weak preparation for classroom practice, and remains so.

The elements of educational infrastructure sketched here are common in many national school systems, but they did not develop in the United States with the exception, for a time, of the New York State Regents and the Advanced Placement (AP) program.[9] The existence of such an infrastructure does not assure quality education; that depends on how well it is designed, how educators use it, and how the design and use interact with culture and society. But if designed and used reasonably well, and decently supported by society and culture, infrastructure can enable other things. Chief among them is a common language concerning teaching, learning, and academic content. Teachers who work with such an infrastructure have common instruments that enable them to set academic tasks that are referenced to curriculum and assessment. They have a common framework that helps to define valid evidence of students' work. They have a common vocabulary with which to identify, investigate, discuss and solve problems of teaching and learning, and thus the elements of common professional knowledge and skill. Practitioners therefore have a common language to use in communication with each other. More to the point for our story, they therefore also have a common language to use in communication with policymakers, the public, and politicians.

Our less familiar story—about practice shaping politics and policy—begins here. The absence of an infrastructure of practice in the United States is a technical and professional effect of weak and fragmented governance for public education, but it reacts back on politics and policy. Though quite important, it has been little noticed by scholars, policymakers, and practitioners. One consequence of the weakness has been that if policymakers or others sought to improve teaching and learning, they had to either devise infrastructure themselves or find other means to influence practice. If state or local policymakers or educators wanted to adopt an innovative instructional program and increase the probability that it would be used well, they had to invent or purchase it, invent or purchase means to help practitioners learn how to use it, and then try to sustain it through changes in staff, policies, and local circumstances. Much more often than not, they left it at adoption, because to do more would have been a major stretch in imagination and operations (McLaughlin, 1991). Similarly, if federal officials sought to influence instruction with new policies or programs, they had to either invent or purchase some elements of the missing infrastructure or leave it to locals to invent what they could. Very few federal programs chose the former course.[10] In such cases the feature of practice that influenced policy was the lack of infrastructure, which required either heroic efforts by policymakers and managers to invent or otherwise acquire elements of infrastructure that might influence practice, or to use instruments that were unlikely to have much influence owing to the absence of those that might.

In most cases policymakers devised or adapted instruments that left a great deal to local invention. Since WWII the instruments were money (with Title I of the 1965 ESEA and Individuals with Disabilities Education Act (IDEA), procedural mandates (with Title I of the 1965 ESEA and IDEA), accountability for outcomes (as with minimum competency testing, state systemic reform, Improving America's Schools Act [IASA] and NCLB), standards (with state systemic reform, IASA and NCLB), and tests (with state systemic reform, IASA and NCLB). None of these had any direct bearing on teaching and learning, so the work of devising the teaching, learning, and educational management that might turn these policies and programs into practice was left almost entirely to practice. Only one federal program, Reading First, ever required particular curriculum, and no state systemic reform pressed that far (Cohen & Moffitt, 2009, chapter 6). The absent infrastructure of practice shaped policy by pressing it away from some instruments that could have constructively linked policy and practice and toward others that could make only weak links at best.

This approach was politically appealing because the instruments did not obviously intrude on classroom work, they did not require particular curricula, and they did not entail large investments in building or rebuilding education. These things had appeal because federal intrusion on classroom work was the Death Valley of U.S. politics, a place that few politicians wanted to visit. But these political strengths were an educational weakness, for the instruments were neither salient to classroom practice nor strong influences on it. The lack of infrastructure not only impeded central influence, but as policymakers recently took a more aggressive interest in improved instruction, also led them to instruments that were strong but only weakly connected with practice. NCLB's accountability regime is the chief current case in point. It provoked a storm of political and educational activity, but there is no evidence of any substantial influence on learning (Cohen & Moffitt, 2009, chapters 6 & 7).

Hence another feature of the influence of practice on policy was pervasive weakness in the design of federal and state policies and programs. The late 1950s and early 1960s curriculum reforms had weak and transient effects, in large part because they used a single instrument—textbooks—in an effort to fundamentally change complex practices of teaching and learning in schools across the nation (Powell, Farrar, & Cohen, 1985, chapter 5). Title I had modest effects on practice, in large part because the only instrument available was money and a few procedural requirements for its use; federal policymakers and program managers had no leverage on the educational resources, including the quality of teaching, that federal money bought; this was another case of using very weak instruments to solve a very complex and deeply-rooted problem (Cohen & Moffitt, 2009, chapter 4).

More recently, state and federal standards-based reforms sought to shape teaching and learning by building an exoskeleton of standards, tests, and accountability around schools, districts, and governance. Standards, tests, and accountability were unprecedented state and federal actions, but they did not translate into common purposes, common professional norms, common curricula, a common language for diagnosing and solving educational problems, let alone common practices of teaching, learning, and instructional leadership. Even if we assume that high quality standards and assessments could be useful parts of some infrastructure, they are very far from practice, and have proved to be a poor guide to improve it (Cohen & Moffitt, 2009, chapters 6 & 7). Yet those instruments had political appeal, for they were thought to shape practice without violating the political taboos on federal interference in classrooms. The policies could seem educationally aggressive without venturing deeply into education. Operating in a system that lacked anything remotely approaching infrastructure, policymakers and those who sought to shape policy could imagine that weak schools could repair themselves with guidance from tests, standards, and accountability (Smith & O'Day, 1991). Such ideas could only flourish in a system of weak government, in which policymakers had little experience with the instruments that could affect teaching and learning. Standards-based reform deployed instruments that were historically aggressive and politically innovative, but peripheral to practice; this is the most recent and most consequential example of how the structure of practice can shape policy and politics.

Another feature of the influence of practice on policy therefore was policies and programs whose implementation yielded weak and sometimes counterproductive effects in schools and classrooms. With a few exceptions, researchers, evaluators, and journalists reported that federal policy and programs did not deliver on their promises, a tradition that began with the curriculum reforms of the late 1950s and continued through several studies of Title I, evaluations of federal professional development programs, and the Clinton and Bush policies.[11] Those reports fed a growing sense that schools were not performing well, and that contributed to still another effect of practice on politics: the erosion of public confidence in and support for public education through the 1980s and 1990s. In response, beginning with state standards-based reforms in the mid and late 1980s, state and federal politicians devised increasingly aggressive measures to change what they saw as a recalcitrant enterprise (Cohen & Moffitt, 2009, chapter 5).

As federal and state policies grew more ambitious, they opened up a growing gap between program aims and practitioners' capability; that was still another result of the influence of practice on policy and politics. The history of Title I of the 1965 ESEA is the chief case in point. It began as a program that sent money to schools so that they could decide how to improve education for disadvantaged students; it required only accountability for how the money was spent. But by the end of the 1980s, it began to become a program that required schools to boost students' achievement: Title I would no longer improve education for disadvantaged students by adding money, but it would hold schools accountable for students' test scores. For its first several decades Title I's aim was vague—to improve education for disadvantaged students—and that vagueness was suitable for a federal program that had little leverage on states and localities. That changed in the 1980s, as the problem Title I would solve came to be achievement gaps between advantaged and disadvantaged and black and white students. Yet if the aims grew more precise and vastly more ambitious, Title I did not deploy instruments that were even close to commensurate with those aims.

One reason for the change in Title I focus was mounting evidence of the achievement gap. It had not been part of the origin of Title I, for in 1965 there was no public evidence of it, in part because school administrators closely guarded data on students' performance. Just a year later James Coleman's *Equality of Educational Opportunity Survey* (EEOS) reported social class and racial inequality in scores on national tests (Coleman, United States Office of Education, & National Center for Education Statistics, 1966). It was the first national study to report such things, but hardly the last. In the 1970s and early 1980s evidence from the National Assessment of Educational Progress (NAEP), the Sustaining Effects Study (SES), and other studies highlighted large differences in average achievement by race and class (Carter, 1983).[12] Evidence on the achievement gap presented a vivid picture of unequal education, and an appealing target.

That evidence also was taken to mean that the schools were failing disadvantaged students, and that Title I had not succeeded. Both ideas gained traction despite contrary evidence: several studies showed that achievement gaps began before students entered school, and remained roughly constant over the years of school. Few commentators or politicians pointed out that the achievement gap was caused not by schools but by enormous social and economic inequality that came to school with students, and that schools prevented the gaps from growing (Downey, Hippel, & Broh, 2004). Additionally, a large and well-designed study reported that Title I students made modest gains in achievement over similarly situated students who were not in Title I, and that what seemed a large program in Washington was very modest in the schools (Carter, 1983). For example, a 1970s National Institute of Education study had reported that "compensatory education students spend an average of five and one-half hours per week in special instruction," which was between 15% and 20% of the time students spend in school, and the SES further scaled down that estimate (Carter, 1983). The boost in student achievement that was associated with Title I was roughly what one would expect from the program's modest scale and scope. These points were made in small type in thick copies of technical reports that resided in analysts' and researchers' offices, far from practice and practitioners' organizations. Practice was not organized to learn from experience, to review practice in light of that learning, or to communicate about it, another consequence of the absent infrastructure. That helped to open the way to claims about education that were not grounded in evidence, and to unexamined ideas about what Title I might or should accomplish.

Title I was a modest program that was modestly effective, but the gains were small when viewed in light of the gap in achievement; as that gap gained visibility in research and debates about schools during the 1980s Title I seemed less effective. The school reform movement that began with *A Nation At Risk* reinforced that view, for its advocates held that schools allowed most students to do pallid work and that the solution was to raise academic challenge. The problems with Title I began to seem only a special case of deeper problems with the entire system of public education (Cohen & Moffitt, 2009, chapter 5).

The first result was a late-1980s revision of the program's guiding ideas. In 1965 the education deficit was thought to reside with the children of poor families and resource shortages in their schools: poor children came to school with less knowledge and skill than their more advantaged peers, and their schools had fewer educational resources than schools attended by advantaged students. Title I addressed these deficiencies by adding funds that schools could use as they chose, as long as they used them to offer remedial instruction of some sort. By the end of the 1980s that view was being replaced by the idea that the key deficit lay not with students nor with funds alone, but with schools that did not do nearly enough to improve instruction. The shift was momentous, for it meant that schools would have to make deep changes. Educators would have to turn from indifferent efforts to teach basic skills to more ambitious work, which could only be done with much improved capability. That would take considerable learning and unlearning, and if schools were half as deficient as the new ideas implied, educators would need help. The mere addition of funds was unlikely to work, for money alone teaches nothing; educators would need new knowledge and know-how. That would require policy instruments that were strong and salient enough to change teaching and learning in thousands of schools, and those would add up to elements of an educational infrastructure. Yet the federal government was not in a position to offer the required assistance, to build infrastructure, or to require schools' compliance.

How were schools to acquire the capability to realize the new aims in practice? How could schools close the achievement gap if Title I did not directly require them to change instruction and help them do it? No one answered these questions; indeed, no one seems to have asked them. The 1988 Hawkins-Stafford amendments to the 1965 ESEA declared that the program was to reduce the achievement gap, and that schools would be held accountable for student outcomes. That pushed the limits of political feasibility but avoided dealing with the absent educational infrastructure; the amendments dealt with the central government's very weak position by setting very modest criteria for compliance (Cohen & Moffitt, 2009, chapter 5). Title I was a modest program that contributed modestly to very unequal schools, and the federal government did not have the political moxie to seriously enforce schools' accountability for student outcomes. With the incongruence between very ambitious aims and very weak instruments, Hawkins-Stafford began to fundamentally change Title I; the increasing disproportion between aims and instruments culminated in No Child Left Behind. Federal and state policies more aggressively sought to correct a long history of inequality, but they sought to do so with instruments that were politically viable but educationally weak (Cohen & Moffitt, 2009, chapter 7). This too was an effect that practice has had on policy and politics.

Paradoxes of Policy, Politics, and Practice

For several decades after W W II, the unique design of U.S. education governance enabled policymakers to initiate or change federal policies without seriously negative consequences to themselves. The Education For All Handicapped Children Act, for example, effectively delegated complex new operations and substantial costs to local schools, with serious consequences for budget and management. Local educators complained, but federal policy was not seriously threatened; the legislation stayed in place, as did the local effects. The lack of strong infrastructure and fragmented government meant that relations between governments and schools, and among governments and public and private agencies, were quite loose. Policies and programs could identify problems for which practitioners were the ultimate problem solvers without close communication or tight connections between policy and practice, for they were largely separate worlds. Policy design left much to be desired, but the ensuing problems in practice only led to painful consequences for policymakers when there were visible reports of practice failure; mere problems were not sufficient to provoke political or policy change.

That began to change late in the 20th century, as policymakers devised more aggressive schemes to affect practice, and attached consequences to noncompliance. Standards–based reform reduced the distance between policy and practice, for state and federal agencies' more aggressive stance meant that they became more embroiled in solving the deepest problems of public education. The policies also assigned more responsibility for students' performance to states, localities, and schools, and did so in dramatic, public fashion. This meant that policymakers no longer simply defined problems, offered remedies and assigned the rest to schools, but rather sought to decide how the schools would solve their deepest problems, when they would solve them, and what would count for success.

That extraordinary assertion of federal and state involvement tightened the relationships defined by the dilemma. Policymakers still set problems and proposed solutions, and practitioners still were the ultimate problem–solvers, but policy and practice grew much more closely and visibly linked. In part that was because the policies were so aggressive, and in part because responsibility for results was assigned to schools and state and local governments. On both counts, failures in practice could much more easily be traced to policy. As the new policies proved difficult to implement because ambitious policies encountered weak capability in practice and the environment, the dynamics described by the dilemma played out. Signs of practice failure and controversy grew, and began to flow back, visibly and strongly, onto policy and politics.

The situation can be summarized in three paradoxes.[13] One concerns government. IASA, Goals 2000, and NCLB were to bring coherence to education by creating rational relationships among academic standards, educational processes, and outcomes: academic standards would express educational content and outcomes; owing to their accountability, educators would orient schools to those outcomes; and tests would check on performance and provide targets for improvement. Yet this system was to be put into practice in many thousands of state and local jurisdictions and individual schools that had long been fragmented and weak, in which there was no common professional knowledge of school improvement, and in which schools, teachers, and districts had great autonomy. State and federal politicians tried to use policy to do what politics could not, so government fragmentation persisted through the new policies.

There was, as a result, considerable inconsistency between the states' standards and tests. In many cases there also was considerable inconsistency between the standards and tests that each state requires. There often was considerable inconsistency between each state's standards and tests on the one hand, and school curricula on the other. These inconsistencies have been the basis for continuing controversy about the design of the policies, the extent of their implementation, and the reasons for implementation problems. U.S. public education was not meant to be coherent, and its fragmented structure suffused implementation of IASA and NCLB with symptoms of the disease that the policies were supposed to cure. Since the policies were designed in ways that enabled them to work politically, they addressed neither the structural basis of incoherence in government nor the absence of infrastructure, but sought to eliminate the problems that these things caused with tests and standards. IASA and NCLB were expected to turn an extraordinarily fragmented educational non-system into fifty coherent state systems in which teaching and learning followed standards and tests. Yet they would do this by changing policy alone, with no change either in the structure of governance or the infrastructure of education. The policies presumed that the governments that caused the incoherence would effectively implement policies demanding coherence.

panacea

A second paradox concerns capability. The new policies required extensive capability to improve teaching and learning, but it was precisely the absence of that capability that was an important cause of the schools' uneven and often weak performance. Advocates of reform argued that this was because schools had not been accountable for student learning with appropriate penalties and rewards, and had no common standards for what should be taught and learned. If schools had such standards and were accountable, educators would know what to teach, they would have incentives to teach what standards and tests called for, and students would learn more.

Yet if educators were to make effective use of the new policies, they would require much more than standards, tests and accountability. They would require infrastructure that could connect policy with practice, and the knowledge to use it effectively. Those could make it possible for educators to know why some classrooms and schools did well when others, similarly situated, did not. It could provide guidance for effective teaching and the improvement of ineffective teaching. Yet these were the very things that educators had not known when the reforms were adopted; that was said to be why so many teachers and schools were ineffective, and why students had not learned more. The new policies required much more professional and scientific knowledge than their predecessors, otherwise schools, states, and districts could not deliver on the outcomes for which they were now accountable. Yet that knowledge did not exist; if it had, schools would have been much better, yet the new policies did not attempt to build the educational infrastructure that could have helped to build such knowledge. The policies presumed that a system that lacked capability and had failed millions of children could, on its own, quickly acquire the capability to make them succeed.

A third paradox concerns excellence and equality. IASA and NCLB require states to set high standards for academic performance, and to use tests and accountability to insure that performance. At the same time, IASA and NCLB require states to make average school outcomes equal among races and social classes. How could schools eliminate average race and class achievement differences by holding everyone to high standards, when the schools and students in question suffer from large and sometimes huge social class and racial inequality in educational resources? The policies proposed that tests, standards and accountability would reverse the educational effects of the economic, social, and educational inequalities that mark U.S. students and schools. The new policies would assure that average performance for poor or minority group students was equal to that for advantaged and Caucasian students, and they would accomplish this even though great inequality in social, racial, and educational resources remained.

Each paradox points to fundamental difficulties that arose as the dilemma played out in a system of fragmented government and weak infrastructure. The absent infrastructure of practice deprived practitioners of instruments that would enable common problem solving and close communication, and it deprived policymakers and others of means to learn about and shape teaching and learning. Weak and fragmented education governance has been a central feature of the politics of education, but no less important are the ways in which the absence of infrastructure has shaped education policy and politics. The politics of education has potent sources at the very heart of education, just as clearly as in state legislatures and local school boards.

Notes

1 Parts of this chapter are based on our book (Cohen & Moffitt, 2009). Thanks to Lorraine McDonnell for helpful comments.
2 Although this dilemma has not been central to most analyses of the relations between policy and practice, several scholars have called attention to aspects of it. Elmore (1979) wrote that "unless the initiators of a policy can galvanize the energy, attention, and skills of those affected by it ... the effects of policy are unlikely to be anything but weak and diffuse" (p. 611). McLaughlin (1987) wrote that policy implementation is a "problem of the smallest unit" (p. 189). Elmore and McLaughlin (1988) wrote that the fate of reforms ultimately depends on those who are the object of distrust Lin (2000) wrote that "every grand idea and good wish that policymakers have lies in the hands of others who implement them" (p. 14).
3 For an account of how the dilemma has played out in U.S. high schools, see Powell, Farrar, and Cohen (1985).
4 Berman and McLaughlin (1978) reviewed these ideas in the RAND Change Agent Study, in the late 1970s.

5 Political science terms this policy feedback (Campbell, 2003; McDonnell, 2009; Mettler, 2005; Pierson, 1993; Soss, 1999).

6 See also Lowi (1969) for an argument that policy adoption mobilizes interests; he argues that many people don't know that their interests are being affected until after a policy has been adopted and hence are politically mobilized by the adoption of the policy.

7 The first study was by Martin and McClure (1960). The second by Mosbaek (1968).

8 For analysis of these developments, see Cohen and Moffitt (2009), chapters 3 and 7.

9 The Regents exams implied a curriculum, and students who sought a Regents degree studied things that were likely to prepare them for the exams. Similarly, in the AP, students in schools across the country studied common curricula in mathematics, history, and other subjects. The curricula were referenced to AP examinations that were used to determine whether they could be exempted from university courses. Teachers who taught AP courses, along with college professors who taught the same subjects judged and graded students' exams each year, and devised the next year's exams.

10 For a relatively recent case in point, see the analysis in (Cohen & Moffitt, 2009, chapter 5), of the Hawkins-Stafford Amendments to the 1965 ESEA, of 1988.

11 On the curriculum reforms, see Powell et al. (1985) and Dow (1991); on Title I ESEA and several related matters see Cohen and Moffitt (2009, chapters 3, 4, 5).

12 For the NAEP data, see Cohen and Moffitt (2009, chapter 6).

13 The next several paragraphs are adapted from Cohen and Moffitt (2009).

References

Bankston, M. (1982). *Organizational reporting in a school district: State and federal programs.* Stanford, CA: Institute for Research on Educational Finance and Governance School of Education Stanford University.

Bardach, E. (1977). *The implementation game.* Cambridge, MA: MIT Press.

Berman, P., & McLaughlin, M. W. (1978). *Implementing and sustaining innovations.* Prepared for the U. S. Office of Education, Dept. of Health, Education, and Welfare. Santa Monica, CA: Rand Corporation.

Campbell, A. L. (2003). *How policies make citizens: Senior political activism and the American welfare state.* Princeton, NJ: Princeton University Press.

Carter, L. F. (1983). *A study of compensatory and elementary education: The sustaining effects study. Final report.* Santa Monica, CA: Systems Development Corporation.

Cohen, D. K. (1982). Policy and organization: The impact of state and federal educational policy on school governance, *Harvard Educational Review, 52*(4), 474–499.

Cohen, D. K., & Moffitt, S. L. (2009). *The ordeal of equality: Can federal regulation fix the schools?* Cambridge, MA: Harvard University Press.

Cohen, D. K., & Spillane, J. P. (1992). Policy and practice: The relations between governance and instruction. In G. Grant (Ed.), *Review of research in education* (pp. 3–49). Washington, DC: American Educational Research Association.

Coleman, J. S., United States. Office of Education & National Center for Education Statistics. (1966). *Equality of educational opportunity.* Washington: U.S. Dept. of Health Education and Welfare Office of Education.

Dow, P. B. (1991). *Schoolhouse politics: lessons from the Sputnik era.* Cambridge, MA: Harvard University Press.

Downey, D. B., Hippel, P. T. V., & Broh, B. A. (2004). Are schools the great equalizer? Cognitive inequality during the summer months and the school year. *American Sociological Review, 79*(5), 613–635.

Education for All Handicapped Children Act (EHA) (Pub. L. No. 94-142).

Elementary and Scondary Education Act (1965). (Pub. L. 89-10, 79) Stat. 27, 20 U.S.C. ch. 70

Elmore, R. F. (1979). Backward mapping: Implementation research and policy decisions. *Political Science Quarterly, 94*(4), 601–616.

Elmore, R. F., & McLaughlin, M. W. (1988). *Steady work: Policy, practice and the reform of American education*. Santa Monica, CA: Rand Corporation.

Floden, R. E., Porter, A. C., Schmidt, W. H., Freeman, D. J., & Schwille, J. R. (1981). Responses to curriculum pressures: A policy-capturing study of teacher decisions about content. *Journal of Educational Psychology, 73*, 129–141.

Hawkins-Stafford Amendments to the 1965 ESEA (1988). P.L. 100-297, Hawkins Stafford amendments (sec. 1015 (c)(2)(B)).

Individuals with Disabilities Education Act 20 U.S.C. §1432(1).

Lin, A. C. (2000). *Reform in the making: the implementation of social policy in prison*. Princeton, NJ: Princeton University Press.

Lowi, T. J. (1969). *The end of liberalism; ideology, policy, and the crisis of public authority*. New York: Norton.

Martin, R., & McClure, P. (1969). *Title 1 of ESEA: Is it helping poor children?* Washington, DC: Washington Research project of the Southern Center for Studies in Public Policy and The NAACP legal Defense and Education Fund.

Massey, D. S., & Denton, N. A. (1993). *American apartheid*. Cambridge, MA: Harvard University Press.

McDonnell, L. (2009). Repositioning politics in education's circle of knowledge. *Educational Researcher, 38*(6), 417–427.

McDonnell, L., & McLaughlin, M. W. (1982). *Education policy and the role of the states*. Santa Monica, CA: Rand Corporation.

McLaughlin, M. (1991). The RAND change agent study: Ten years later. In A. Odden (Ed.), *Education policy implementation* (pp. 143-156). Albany: State University of New York Press.

McLaughlin, M. W. (1987). Learning from experience: Lessons from policy implementation. *Eucational Evaluation and Policy Analysis, 9*(2), 171-178.

Mettler, S. (2005). *Soldiers to Citizens: The G.I. Bill and the making of the greatest generation*. New York: Oxford University Press.

Meyer, J. (1983). Centralization of funding and control in educational governance. In J. W. Meyer & W. R. Scott (Eds.), *Organizational environments: Ritual and rationality* (pp. 178–198). Beverly Hills, CA: Sage.

Minnici, A., & Hill, D. D. (2007). Educational architects: Do state education agencies have the tools necessary to implement NCLB? Washington, DC: Center on Education Policy.

Mosbaek, E. J. (1968). Analysis of compensatory education in five school districts. Washington DC: D.E. Tempo.

Murphy, J. T. (1974). State education agencies and discretionary funds; grease the squeaky wheel. Lexington, MA: Lexington Books.

National Commission on Excellence in Education. (1983). *A nation at risk: The imperative for educational reform: A report to the Nation and the Secretary of Education, United States Department of Education*. Washington, DC: The National Commission on Excellence in Education.

No Child Left Behind. Pub. L 107-110, 115 Stat. 1425, enacted January 8, 2002.

Peterson, P. E., Rabe, B. G., & Wong, K. K. (1986). When federalism works. Washington, DC: Brookings Institution.

Pierson, P. (1993, July). When effect becomes cause: Policy feedback and political change. World Politics, 45, 595-628.

Powell, A., Farrar, E., & Cohen, D. K. (1985). The shopping mall high school. Boston: Houghton Mifflin.

Reese, W. J. (2005). *America's public schools*. Baltimore: Johns Hopkins University Press.

Rogers, D. L., & Whetten, D. A. (1982). *Interorganizational coordination: Theory, research, and implementation*. Ames: Iowa State University Press.

Smith, M. S., & O'Day, J. (1991). Systemic school reform. In S. H. Fuhrman & B. Malen (Eds.), *The politics of curriculum and testing* (pp. 233-267). London: Taylor & Francis.

Soss, J. (1999). Lessons from welfare: Policy design, political learning, and political action. *American Political Science Review, 93*(2), 363-380.

Wilson, S. (2003). *California dreaming*. New Haven, CT: Yale University Press.

Wirt, F. (1982). *Schools in conflict: The politics of education*. Berkeley, CA: McCutchan.

4

EDUCATION POLITICS AND POLICY IN AN ERA OF EVIDENCE

Jane Hannaway and Joel Mittleman

Introduction

This chapter attempts to make the case that politics of education is undergoing a fundamental shift. The shift is due to the increasing availability of information not only about the performance of education systems but, more importantly, about the determinants of that performance. As a consequence, issues once sacrosanct are now on the table and actors once dominant are looking for new grounds of legitimacy.

The Way It Was

The last half of the 20th century witnessed tremendous policy change in education, as described in this volume. Despite widespread effects on critical aspects of education, such as financing, governance, and administrative oversight, policies had little effect on what went on behind the classroom door. There, individual teachers largely determined what was taught with little institutional oversight over what was taught and how much students learned.

Well-known theorists, including James G. March, Karl Weick, John Meyer, and Brian Rowan, constructed theories to explain what were apparent anomalies in education relative to other types of organizations. In most organizations, some mechanism of formal control directs, to some significant effect, the technical work of the organization. Detailed procedural directives, for example, guide the work of medical professionals as well as airline pilots. Craft work is often monitored or supervised by masters of the craft. And still other types of work, say, sales, are managed through examining volume. Indeed, even the work of professors is at least partly evaluated on publication output.

Why was the productive part of the K–12 education system—the teaching and learning activity—so disjointed from the structure? Why were attempts to coordinate and control the central production tasks in education continuously thwarted? Theoretical ideas developed about the "loose-coupling" of education systems (March & Olsen, 1976; Weick, 1976); and related ideas in institutional theory (Meyer & Rowan, 1983) described the structure and governance patterns of education systems as "myths" that legitimized the organization to the outside and protected its technical tasks from close scrutiny.

Underlying the theories were assumptions about goal ambiguity and information. The extent to which schools should pursue specific learning objectives was largely open to debate and differences of opinion were tolerated. Individual teachers, even within the same school, commonly had the discretion to choose textbooks and other materials for their classrooms and emphasize subjects and skills as they saw fit. Indeed, in a 1989 study, Andrew Porter reported that the fourth- and fifth-grade teachers in Michigan differed by a full 23 weeks in the amount of time they spent on math instruction.

In addition, little was known with much certainty about the technology of teaching. What worked and what didn't in terms of instructional strategy was simply not clear. The work was complex and, perhaps, idiosyncratic to the individual teacher. Moreover, many saw effective pedagogy as dependent on the unique characteristics of the students. A 1972 report commissioned by the Presidential Commission on School Finance concluded: Research has found no public expenditure that "consistently and unambiguously makes a difference in student outcomes" (cited in Whitehurst, 2008, p. 1). As late as 1999, a National Academies of Science report on the state of education research reported, "In no other field is the research base so inadequate and little used" (cited in Whitehurst, 2008, p. 1). Without agreement on objectives or processes, legitimate bases for establishing mechanisms of coordination and control were lacking in education.

Many of the legitimating myths were not unreasonable. Indeed, that's why they held up. Teachers were trained in state-approved programs and, as a consequence, they were certified officially by the state as teachers. It did not matter that the programs of study varied tremendously across training institutions and across individuals. Teacher pay structures, often also determined by the state, also made sense. They rewarded teachers for more training, e.g., advanced degrees, and experience. Presumably more training is better than less; and practice makes perfect, or at least better.

No doubt the decentralized nature of education in the United States—where the Constitution reserves authority over education for the states, and states traditionally have delegated operational responsibility to local jurisdictions—contributed to the lack of development of the more central controls, e.g., national testing and national teacher training and certification that developed among many industrialized countries with national education ministries

(Goldhaber, 2010). But, even in a decentralized education system, one would expect known effective practices to spread and take hold in a formal way. But they didn't. Fads passed through the system regularly, often with great hype and hope, but little was systematically connected to performance and little stuck. In short, the system learned little, but it operated steadily and was commonly accepted as working.

Though the tasks of teaching and learning remained fairly stable, the last half of the 20th century witnessed significant changes in the politics of education. The teachers unions and the federal government both ascended as power players in education. The growth in both their influence and the convergence, or divergence, in their interests set the stage for policy.

The National Education Association (NEA) and American Federation of Teachers (AFT) were founded in 1857 and 1916, respectively, but it was not until the 1960s that the unions transformed "from somewhat sleepy organizations to institutions widely regarded today as the most powerful political forces in education" (Kahlenberg, 2006, p. 7). Together they now command more than 4.6 million members (90% of all public schoolteachers) and over $1 billion in annual revenue (Kahlenberg, p. 7).

Teacher union power emerged as a direct result of the unions' successful fight to collectively bargain over wages, benefits and working conditions. Prior to collective bargaining, teacher working conditions were arbitrary and uncertain. Teachers were responsible for tasks like shoveling snow on school grounds; and they could be fired or promoted at the whim of administrators. The conditions were in sharp contrast to what private-sector organized labor had won in salaries and conditions for its members. Despite having a college degree, the average teacher in 1952 made $400 *less* than the average factory worker (Kahlenberg, 2006). Change was written on the wall.

The pivotal moment in the teacher labor movement came on November 7, 1960, in New York City. After the city's mayor prevented teachers from having a vote on collective bargaining, the newly formed United Federation of Teachers (UFT) staged a risky walkout. Led by Albert Shanker and David Selden, about 5,000 teachers—only 10% of the city's teaching force—went on strike. It worked. Collective bargaining was put to a vote and won in June 1961: 27,000 to 7,000 votes (Kahlenberg, 2006).

The decision sent shockwaves around the country. "As a direct consequence of collective bargaining," Kahlenberg writes, "union membership skyrocketed" (2006, p. 15). State legislators around the country began passing laws allowing collective bargaining by public employees. Recognizing the changing times, President Kennedy issued Executive Order 10988 in January 1962, allowing federal employees to bargain collectively for the first time. Given their successes, teacher unions sought a broader mandate on the policies governing American education, fighting to get policy "written into their contracts" (Kahlenberg, 2006, p. 14). In 1967, for example, the UFT staged a 14-day strike over nonwage issues: strengthened school discipline policies, reduced class sizes, and expanded of supplementary programs for disadvantaged schools (Kahlenberg, 2006, p. 14).

The power of the unions goes beyond the bargaining table. "States lacking the right to collectively bargain … substituted (lobbying) the state legislature for the local bargaining table" (Cohen, Walsh, & Biddle, 2008, p. 2). State legislation could set "the most critical issues of the teaching profession … how often teachers must be evaluated, when teachers can earn tenure, the benefits they'll receive, and even the rules for firing a teacher" (Cohen et al., p. 1). The hands of local management were largely tied when it came to evaluating and rewarding employee performance, a key management function in most organizations.

The unions also command broad based influence by leveraging their large memberships into grass roots political operations. Today, the NEA boasts a 3.2 million member bloc of potential voters, donors and lobbyists. Since 1990, it has given over $30 million to political candidates, 93% of whom were Democrats (Center for Responsive Politics, 2010a). The AFT, with 1.4 million members, has given over $27 million, 99% going to Democrats (Center for Responsive Politics, 2010b). Beyond dollars, however, union members are what *Politico*'s Jonathan Martin called "key foot soldiers" for the Democratic party. "In 2004," he explained, "one out of every ten delegates to the Democratic convention was a member of a teacher's union" (Brookings Institution, 2009).

The unions and the congressional Democrats worked hand in hand for decades establishing policies and funding programs that increased federal aid to schools, especially for disadvantaged students. It was a win–win situation and one that presumably held the moral high ground. Additional funds were made available for the most needy students. And while there was little solid evidence that the programs made a difference in student outcomes, there were good reasons to suggest it was a solid investment. After all, schools had highly elaborated structures that made sense despite poorly developed technical systems. Teachers were trained professionals paid based on reasonable indicators of skill and competence. The emphasis was placed on inputs, and for understandable reasons. "Efforts to actually inspect educational outputs—to coordinate the specifics of what is taught to individual students by particular teachers—would invariably increase conflicts with parents and students, cause dissatisfaction among teachers, and vastly increase the burdens of administrators" (Meyer, Scott, & and Deal, 1983, p. 59). The system worked smoothly as it was. And the United States was long #1 in high school and college graduation rates and in economic prowess. Why worry?

Challenges and Changes

By the end of the century, the consensus was beginning to crumble. The economic malaise of the 1970s and 1980s gave way to a generalized anxiety

Could this have been attributed to other factors? [handwritten margin note]

about the failure of American education. International tests showed U. S. students performing poorly relative to students in other countries, and the United States was losing its top ranking as having the most educated workforce.

Initially called to arms by *A Nation At Risk* in 1983, reform moved slowly, but the conversation changed. Measured performance was emphasized over documented inputs. President George H.W. Bush convened an education summit in 1989, assembling governors from all 50 states and established national goals for education for 2000. With tremendous bipartisan support, Congress passed Goals 2000 in 1994, the framework for the reauthorization of the Elementary and Secondary Education Act (ESEA) proposed by President Clinton who, as governor of Arkansas, chaired the 1989 Goals Panel. A national state-driven standards movement was born. Importantly, the standards were to apply to *all* students in a state. Classroom, school and district control over curriculum was curtailed; and states were directed to develop systemic reforms that linked curriculum, assessment and teacher training. Presumably, "loose-coupling" was tightening up.

Later, with the 2001 passage of No Child Left Behind (NCLB) under President George W. Bush, outcomes became tied to accountability. States could develop their own standards and assessments, but NCLB required them to hold schools accountable for learning outcomes. The federal government had instituted another chink in the armor of local discretion.

These new pressures created unprecedented urgency for discovering best practices. "The proliferation of standards-based reforms and high-stakes accountability regimes ... built demand for research on 'proven' strategies among educators" (Towne, Wise, & Winters, 2004, p. 10). The U.S. Department of Education (2002) announced a new priority to "transform education into an evidence-based field." "We will accomplish this goal," the Department explained in its *Strategic Plan: 2002–2007,*

> by dramatically improving the quality and relevance of research funded or conducted by the Department. Also, we will provide policymakers, educators, parents, and other concerned citizens with ready access to syntheses of research and objective information that allow more informed and effective decisions, and we will encourage the use of this knowledge. (p. 51)

This transformation is being enabled by another important consequence of the accountability movement: the emergence of large data bases containing measures of student performance. Once started, progress was swift. Investment began in states that had led the adoption of test-based accountability systems and had a need to track progress. Texas, Florida, and North Carolina, for example, each began tracking annual student performance on state tests in 1995, well before NCLB requirements.

By 2002, spurred by NCLB, almost every state had some kind of assessment program, and 30 states rated the performance of their schools, up from 19 states in 1998 ... "almost a 60% increase in just four years" (Hannaway, 2003, pp. 21–22). In short, where testing went, data and analysis followed. The federal government supported the data development effort with grants to states to develop longitudinal data systems. By 2009, fully 50 states were able to track individual student achievement over time and, thereby, measure learning *growth*, not just level.

Figure 4.1 shows the fast pace of development of state data systems in the 10 key data elements identified by the Data Quality Campaign. "In 2005, no state had all 10 Essential Elements of a high-quality longitudinal data system in place," the non-partisan Data Quality Campaign reported in 2009. "This year 12 states have all 10 elements; 34 states have eight or more elements; and only two states have fewer than five elements" (Data Quality Campaign, 2010, p. 4).

Unlike earlier reforms and elaborations to the education system, the primary contribution of data systems may be to institutionalize change in practices. In short, data systems may have real value rather than serving as another legitimizing myth. Indeed, we argue that it is the basis for undermining many of the myths. State data capacity—providing information on performance and progress—is a key part of the Obama administration's education reform agenda. According to one education reporter, "Long relegated to back offices in school districts and states, [education data systems] are now...the backbone of education improvement efforts" (McNeil, 2009, p. 13). As Obama (2009) put it: "... we are making a major investment in (data systems) ... (to) cultivate a new culture of accountability in America's schools."

There may be no going back.

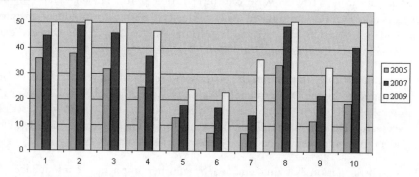

1. Unique statewide student IDs	4. Info on untested students	7. Student-level college readiness scores
2. Student-level enrollment, demographic, and program participation	5. Teachers matched to students	8. Student-level graduation / dropout
3. Matching student-level test records year to year	6. Student-level transcript data	9. K-12 and post-sec matching
10. Data quality audit system		

Source: Data Quality Campaign, Inaugural Overview of States' Actions to Leverage Data to Improve Student Success, p. 5

Figure 4.1 Number of states with longitudinal data elements, 2005-2009.

Reckoning, Realignment, and Resistance

In a remarkably short lag time the effects of the new information were felt. Enabled by unprecedented amounts of data on school processes and outcomes, researchers could now inform education policy by "pars[ing] student achievement in ways they never had before." "A new generation of economists," explained Green in a *New York Times Magazine* cover story, "devised statistical methods to measure the 'value added' to a student's performance by almost every factor imaginable." The results were clear: "When researchers ran the numbers in dozens of different studies, every factor under a school's control produced just a tiny impact, except for one: which teacher the student had been assigned to" (Green, 2010, MM30).

The single salary schedule, perhaps the most sacred feature of teacher contracts, provides a useful indicator or emerging changes. The schedule, as noted earlier, is largely determined by years of experience and degrees/credits earned, and it is near universally applied across the country with the support of the unions. It has long been recognized as a possible source of inefficiency in the education system; but it has always had the advantage of being simple and also providing protection for teachers from arbitrary treatment by administrators. *A Nation At Risk*, for example, criticized the system:

> Salaries for the teaching profession should be increased and should be professionally competitive, market-sensitive, and performance-based. Salary, promotion, tenure, and retention decisions should be tied to an effective evaluation system that includes peer review so that superior teachers can be rewarded, average ones encouraged, and poor ones either improved or terminated. (National Commission on Education, 1983)

But to no effect. Acceptable alternatives were not readily available. There was little agreement about grounded bases for personnel evaluation.

Alternatives are now emerging. The long hold of the single salary schedule is being threatened. Research enabled by the last decade's data revolution is challenging the very basis of the single salary schedule. Teachers are now widely recognized as not only the most important within school factor determining student achievement, but also widely varied in their contributions to student success. Indeed, the difference in having a top ranked teacher and a bottom ranked teacher can result in a year's worth of student achievement. Despite the great variation, teacher quality cannot be predicted well by observable characteristics, such as years of experience or degrees, the very characteristics that largely determine salary differences. The differences researchers find are in student results and are not strongly related to imputed teacher characteristics. Study after study by different researchers, in different states, using different test scores reaches the same conclusion. As a result, the political consensus protecting the single salary schedule is cracking under the weight of the evidence.

President Obama's campaign reflected the changing terms of the debate. "New evidence shows that from the moment our children step into a classroom," he asserted in a frequent campaign refrain, "the single most important factor in determining their achievement is not ... [their background], it's who their teacher is" (Organizing for America, 2007). This recognition led Obama, addressing the NEA's annual meeting in 2007, to sound what the *Philadelphia Inquirer* called "the first note deviating from the promise-anything tenor of visits by several presidential candidates to the union this week" (Fitzgerald, 2007). "It's time we rewarded, and supported, and honored the professional excellence you show every day," Obama declared, adding a line that drew boos from the crowd: "If you excel at helping your students achieve success, your success will be valued and rewarded" (Organizing for America, 2007). The words were not what union members who had worked so hard for his election wanted to hear.

Despite opposition, Obama has long maintained his position. In his first major education address as president, Obama repeated his call for performance pay. Performance pay, Brill argues, in a *New York Times Magazine* cover story, has "become a litmus test for seriousness about improving schools" (2010, MM32). As proof of its commitment, the Obama administration expanded the federal Teacher Incentive Fund from $97 to $400 million. More consequentially, it also made participation in the $4.3 billion Race to the Top competition contingent on states "chang[ing] their laws to give principals and superintendents the right to judge teachers based on their students' academic performance" (MM32).

The unions have taken note. A March 2008 article in *NEA Today* addressed this new reality: "Republicans, Democrats, governors, legislators, presidential candidates, and school board members all are advocating for changes in teacher pay... This is an issue that simply can't be ignored" (Flannery & Jehlen, 2010). Alternative compensation systems, it explained, are already in place in 36 states, "And more are certainly on their way" (Flannery & Jehlen, 2010). Union members, it concluded, would need to take a stand: "It's important for all NEA members to arm themselves with information and resources on the subject. Know what to embrace. Know what to avoid" (Rosales, 2010).

Though both traditionally opposed to changes in the single salary schedule, the two unions have recently taken divergent paths. Defying the mounting pressure to align teacher pay with student outcomes, the NEA's director of Collective Bargaining and Member Benefits argues, "We all must be wary of any system that creates a climate where students are viewed as part of the pay equation" (Rosales, 2010). As such, the NEA urges its members to resist compensation based on student test scores, subjective evaluations, or teaching in a hard-to-fill subject. This resistance is "more than purely institutional rhetoric... Small districts in Nebraska and Missouri, for instance, were sued for attempting to pay signing bonuses to teachers in shortage areas" (Goldhaber, 2009, p. 21).

The AFT has taken a different path. In a recent speech, AFT president Randi Weingarten (2010) flatly declared "Our system of evaluating teachers has never been adequate." Instead, "we must use good and meaningful data … to transform teacher evaluation from a perfunctory waste of time into a powerful catalyst for student achievement." The union's recent actions reflect this commitment. High profile negotiations in New York City, New Haven, and Detroit have all yielded contracts that incorporate new teacher evaluations and bonuses based on student achievement data. To build on these efforts, the union has also partnered with private foundations to invest in a 10-year Innovation Fund, which will "develop, test and refine" innovative systems for measuring, improving and rewarding teacher quality (AFT, 2010).

The story is far from over. But the game has changed.

A New Day?

Union reform is not new. Long before the pressures imposed by today's data realities informed union leaders worked to change the tenor of union management deliberations. Over 20 years ago Albert Shanker, head of the AFT, led new thinking on teacher unionism based on ideals of teacher professionalism, even arguing that there was merit in thinking about pay for performance:

> Most people in this country believe hard work and better work ought to be rewarded, and opposing this makes us look like we are not interested in quality. So, we ought to think about ways of handling the issue while avoiding the pitfalls…. (cited in Kahlenberg, 2006, p. 21)

Shanker had envisioned unions as a major player in education reform. Efforts were made by union locals across the country to institute reforms, such as teacher peer review, to deal with criticisms about teacher evaluation, teacher incompetence and inadequate teacher professionalism (Kerchner & Koppich, 2000; Kerchner, Koppich, & Weeres, 1997). The idea was to work collaboratively and cooperatively with management to improve education. But reform unionism never really spread (Koppich, 2006). And a number of local union reformers lost elections to competitors more concerned with traditional bread and butter issues than issues of professional reform.

The situation today is in some ways similar and in some ways different. If anything, the stakes are higher and the facts clearer. On the one hand, issues of bread and butter and job security are paramount for most local public employees. Issues of tenure, evaluation, dismissal, hiring and firing, and seniority are front and center. Given the economic reality, for individual teachers it is probably personal, more than professional, and they expect protection from their union.

On the other hand, our future national well-being in a global economy is directly dependent on the productivity of our education system. And current indicators of low teacher performance among many teachers and weak teacher oversight have created an imperative for action, at both the national and local levels. Much of the showdown is happening locally in New York City, Washington, DC, and Los Angeles, where mayors, who took on schools as their key mission, are centrally involved for their own political survival.

For the first time since their ascendance onto the political scene, the teachers' unions' are finding their relationship with the Democratic party to be strained. The challenge on the table, and it is a formidable one, is for union leaders and public officials to craft policies and practices that are fair in evaluating teachers and that still recognize the central economic importance and credibility of the emerging findings about teacher effectiveness. "Education," President Obama asserted in a recent speech, "is the economic issue of our time" (Marr, 2010). Fortunately, leaders on both sides recognize the urgency of the challenge. "No issue should be off the table, provided it is good for children and fair to teachers" AFT president Randi Weingarten declared in her first major address as union president (AFT, 2008). Moving forward, all sides will have the benefit—and burden—of an emerging research base that is disrupting the traditional system even as it informs what will follow.

References

American Federation of Teachers (AFT). (2008). *'Reinvest, don't disinvest,' Weingarten urges in major speech.* Retrieved from http://www.aft.org/newspubs/news/2008/111708.cfm

American Federation of Teachers (AFT). (2010). *AFT Innovation Fund Mission.* Retrieved from http://www.aft.org/about/innovate/mission.cfm

Brill, S. (2010, May 17). The Teachers' unions' last stand. *The New York Times Magazine.* Retrieved from http://www.nytimes.com/2010/05/23/magazine/23Race-t.html

The Brookings Institution. (2009). *Obama's education policy.* Retrieved June 9, 2010, from http://www.brookings.edu/interviews/2009/0313_education_whitehurst.aspx

The Center for Responsive Politics. (2010a). *National Education Association: Summary.* Retrieved from http://www.opensecrets.org/orgs/summary.php?%20id=D000000064

The Center for Responsive Politics. (2010b). *American Federation of Teachers: summary.* Retrieved from http://www.opensecrets.org/orgs/summary.php?%20cycle= A&type=P&id=D000000083

Cohen, E., Walsh, K., & Biddle, R. (2008). *Invisible ink in collective bargaining: Why key issues are not addressed.* Retrieved from http://www.nctq.org/p/publications/docs/ nctq_invisible_ink_20080801115950.pdf

Data Quality Campaign. (2010). *Inaugural overview of states' actions to leverage data to improve student success.* Retrieved from http://www.dataqualitycampaign.org/files/ DQC_survey_report_JAN_2010_3.11.10_singles.pdf

Fitzgerald, T. (2007, July 5). Obama tells teachers he supports merit pay. *The Philadelphia Inquirer.* Retrieved June 9, 2010, from http://www. Philly.com/philly/news/8335627.html Flannery, M. E., Jehlen, A. (2010). *NEA: Where is your pay heading?* Retrieved June 9, 2010, from http://www.nea.org/home/4221.htm

Goldhaber, D. (2009). *Teacher pay reforms: The political implications of recent research.* Washington, DC: The Center for American Progress. Retrieved from http://www.americanprogress.org/issues/2006/12/pdf/teacher_pay_report.pdf

Goldhaber, D. (2010). Lessons from abroad: Exploring cross-country differences in teacher development systems and what they mean for U.S. policy. In J. Hannaway & D. Goldhaber (Eds.), *Creating a new teaching profession* (pp. 81–114). Washington, DC: Urban Institute Press.

Green, E. (2010, March 2). Building a better teacher. *The New York Times Magazine*. Retrieved from http://www.nytimes.com/2010/03/07/magazine/07Teachers-t.html

Hannaway, J. (2003). Accountability, assessment, and performance issues: We've come a long way ... or have we? *Yearbook of the National Society for the Study of Education, 102*(1), 20–36.

Kahlenberg, R. D. (2006). The history of collective bargaining among teachers. In J. Hannaway & A. J. Rotherham (Eds.), *Collective bargaining in education: Negotiating change in today's schools* (pp. 7–25). Cambridge, MA: Harvard Education Press.

Kerchner, C. T., Koppich, J., & Weeres, J. (1997). *United mind workers: Unions and teaching in the knowledge society.* San Francisco: Jossey-Bass.

Kerchner, C. T., & Koppich, J. (2000). Organizing around quality: The frontiers of teacher unionism. In T. Loveless (Ed.), *Conflicting missions? Teacher unions and education reform* (pp. 281–316). Washington, DC: Brookings Institution Press.

Koppich, J. E. (2006). The as-yet-unfulfilled promise of reform bargaining. In J. Hannaway & A. J. Rotherham (Eds.), *Collective bargaining in education: Negotiating change in today's schools* (pp. 203–229). Cambridge, MA: Harvard Education Press.

March, J. G., & Olsen, J. P. (1976). *Ambiguity and choice in organizations.* Universitetsforlaget.

Marr, K. (2010, Aug 22). Obama's truce with teachers. *Politico*. Retrieved August 22, 2010, from http://www.politico.com/news/storied/0810/41306.html

McNeil, M. (2009, March 18). Data systems set for critical fund infusion. *Education Week,* pp. 13, 15.

Meyer, J.W. & Rowan, B. (1983). Institutionalized organizations: Formal structure as myth and ceremony. In J. W. Meyer & W. R. Scott (Eds.), *Organizational Environments: Ritual and Rationality* (pp. 21–44). Beverly Hill, CA: Sage Publications.

Meyer, J. W., Scott, W. R., & Deal, T. E. (1983). Institutional and technical sources of organizational structure: Explaining the structure of education organizations. In J. W. Meyer & W. R. Scott (Eds.), *Organizational environments: Ritual and rationality* (pp. 45–70). Beverly Hill, CA: Sage.

The National Commission on Education. (1983). *A nation at risk: The imperative for educational reform.* Retrieved from http://www2.ed.gov/pubs/NatAtRisk/index.html

Obama, B. (2009, March 10). Speech on education to U.S. Hispanic Chamber of Commerce. Retrieved from http://blogs.wsj.com/washwire/2009/03/10/obamas-remarks-on-education-2/tab/article/

Organizing for America. (2007). *Remarks of Senator Barack Obama to the National Education Association annual meeting.* Retrieved from http://www.barackobama.com/2007/07/05/ remarks_of_senator_barack_obam_18.php

Porter, A. (1989). External standards and good teaching: The pro's and con's of telling teachers what to do. *Education Evaluation and Policy Analysis***,** *11*(4), 343–356.

Rosales, J. (2010). *NEA: Examining merit pay.* Retrieved from http://www.nea.org/home/36780. htm

Towne, L., Wise, L. L., & Winters, T. M. (2004). *Advancing scientific research in education.* Washington, DC: The National Academies Press. Retrieved from http://books.nap.edu/openbook. php?record_id=11112&page=R1

United States Department of Education. (2002). *Strategic plan: 2002–2007.* Retrieved from http:// www2.ed.gov/about/reports/strat/plan2002-07/plan.pdf

Weingarten, R. A. (2010, January 12). *New path forward: Four approaches to quality teaching and better schools.* Retrieved from http://aft.3cdn.net/227d12e668432ca48e_twm6b90k1.pdf

Weick, K. (1976). Educational organizations as loosely coupled systems. *Administrative Science Quarterly, 21,* 1–9.

Whitehurst, G. J. (2008). *Rigor and relevance redux: Director's biennial report to Congress.* Retrieved from http://ies.ed.gov/director/pdf/20096010.pdf

5

THE MARKET FOR SCHOOLING

Douglas N. Harris and John F. Witte

Introduction

Education in the United States has radically evolved over the 250 years of our existence as a nation state. It has progressed from an almost exclusively private system, open primarily to the wealthy, to one of the earliest and most vibrant systems of universal public education, with a relatively modest private school sector. However in the last 20 years, that public sector system has undergone considerable change. While it is yet based primarily on residential assignment to traditional public schools, the role of the individual through private decisions is resurgent and the education system is currently headed toward a more equal partnership of state and market control.

This chapter describes the evolution of educational governance in America, especially the significant changes that have occurred over the last two decades, and considers prospects for the future. We include the creation of the first voucher programs to allow students to attend private schools with public funding, the ascendance of magnet and charter schools within the public sector, and the possibility of open enrollment between public school districts. These options are captured in Table 5.1, which illustrates the various educational options, including which schools students attend and the institutional structure of the schools themselves. The institutional structure relates to both the funding of schools and their governance and management. Children can attend public or public-sponsored schools, or independent private schools, the vast majority being religiously affiliated. What is of most interest in Table 5.1 is the distinction in the public institutional context between traditional residential zoning of children to schools and the recognition of broad publicly funded choice that, while still perhaps constrained by school district and state policies, has non-traditional public governance (i.e., other than school boards) and/or private management. Thirty years ago that analytical distinction would not be relevant because publicly funded choice options were almost non-existent. Today, as indicated, those options consist of magnet and charter schools, publically funded private schools (through either tuition tax credits, vouchers, or tax credit supported scholarships), and open enrollment that allows students to attend public schools of their choice in districts other than their district of residence.

We continue below with the early history and evolution of markets, followed by a discussion of the reasons or "drivers" behind that evolution. One of those drivers is the increased support for markets not only in education but in society at large. We, therefore, provide a brief introduction to the economic theory supporting this general movement and how the theory applies to schooling. Economic theory suggests several specific mechanisms through which markets might affect schooling and we discuss the evidence on each. Based on this analysis—historical, theoretical, and empirical—we discuss the uncertain future of the market for schooling.

The Historical Evolution of Educational Choice

Parental choice in education began before the founding of the nation. With some modest exceptions in Massachusetts and some other colonies,[1] early education in America was usually home-based, with teachers providing instruction in exchange for modest fees and often room and board (Protsik, 1994; Reese, 2005). It was also the province of the wealthy and usually restricted to males. To give some idea of how removed early America was from 20th-century public education, Thomas Jefferson, in his legislative role in the Virginia legislature, introduced a radical public education proposal in which all children would receive a free education through the third grade, with many fewer students, selected on merit, proceeding to intermediate grades and very

Table 5.1 A Typology of Educational Choice Options

Institutional Options	School Enrollment Options		
	Residential Zoning	District-Constrained Choice	Broad Choice
Public	Traditional public schools	Magnets; ESEA choice	Open enrollments
Hybrid	EMO-managed public schools	District-run charters	Privately run charters; Vouchers and tuition tax credits
Private	Schools led by community based organizations	—	Unsubsidized Private schooling

few on to university (Tozer, Violas, & Senese, 1995, pp. 30–33). The proposal was not enacted in his lifetime. He died in 1824.

The provision of universal public education arose primarily in the second half of the 19th century and the early 20th century, spurred by education policy entrepreneurs such as Horace Mann. However, structural factors, such as the needs of the industrial revolution and the influx of immigrants were also critical. These forces spurred codification in state constitutions and statutes providing for school districts and their taxing powers, state grants to these districts (often for buildings), and compulsory education laws. The education systems were quite bifurcated by city and rural areas. In the rural areas, one-room, multi-graded schools predominated and room and board was part of teacher compensation (Protsik, 1994). In the later 19th century, single-graded, multi-room elementary schools and high schools developed in the cities.

The Anglican and Protestant tone of the public schools also led to the first significant exodus from the public schools when Catholics rebelled. Following the edicts of Third Plenary Council of Catholic Bishops held in Baltimore in 1884, Catholic parishes were required to create private Catholic schools and parishioners were compelled to send their children to the schools (Buetow 1970; Gleason, 1985). Those edicts generally held through Vatican II in 1962. Catholic enrollment peaked in 1965, accounting for over 90% of all private school enrollment (*Catholic Schools in America*, 1995, chapter 3). Even after four decades of steady decline since, Catholic schools still teach 42.5% of private school students, with another 38.1% in other religiously affiliated schools (National Center for Education Statistics, 2009, Table 1, p. 6).

Public school choice also has a long history, but until the 1970s it was limited to a few very elite and special schools that would today be termed magnet schools. These are publicly funded and governed in a manner similar to traditional public schools, but differ in lacking the usual attendance boundaries and, occasionally, in using entry requirements. The famous Bronx School of Science, the University of Chicago Lab School created by John Dewey, and the Boston Latin School (which also was the first U.S. public school in 1635) are all prominent examples. Public school choice became a much more serious issue with the institution of forced busing used for racial desegregation in the late 1970s and 1980s. The magnet school concept was utilized in many large, urban school districts as an attempt to hold White, middle-class families who were fleeing to the suburbs and to attract their enrollment to schools serving minorities. Although defining magnet schools was not easy, a national survey by Rolf Blank in 1983 found that 138 of the 350 largest school districts had magnet schools. By 1990 he wrote that "…today it would be difficult to find an urban school district without a magnet school program" (p. 77). Magnet schools continue today, but the range of other forms of choice developed from the late 1980s on has diminished their visibility.

Beginning in the late 1980s, in the state of Minnesota, two critical forms of modern education choice were created by state statutes. Minnesota pioneered public support for private schools in the form of tuition tax credits enacted in 1967, and given constitutional approval in the famous *Mueller v Allen* decision in 1983.[2] Charter schools were first authorized in Minnesota 1991. Since the opening of City Academy in St. Paul, Minnesota, in the fall of 1992, charter schools have expanded rapidly across the country, and currently educate over 1.4 million students in 4,600 schools across 40 states and the District of Columbia (Center for Education Reform, 2009). There is a very clear pattern in the way state charter laws have been amended over time. The amendments almost universally relax restrictions on the creation, number, and type of charter schools allowed (Shober, Manna, & Witte, 2006). Charter schools come in a wide range of forms and with widely varying statutory provisions across states. However, the common elements are: (a) they are publicly funded; (b) they require a charter that contains provisions for the organization, management, and goals of the school; and (c) they are subject to lessened forms of school district regulation than traditional schools.

An earlier entry in public school choice, but later to be recognized, is inter-district open enrollment. Although voluntary inter-district transfer programs existed as early as 1980, the nation's first mandatory inter-district open enrollment program was passed into law by the Minnesota state legislature in 1988 (Boyd, Hare, & Nathan 2002). Under open enrollment laws, students are allowed to attend public schools in districts other than their district of residence. As with charter school options, state laws vary dramatically. Some policies place considerable restrictions on sending and receiving districts, some programs are voluntary, meaning potential sending and receiving districts can refuse student requests, and most have some exemptions for districts that are at school building capacity.

As with charter schools, open enrollment has grown dramatically, and created competition for students, especially in enrollment declining districts. Open enrollment could, in the end, be the most significant and contested education choice option. Since the first open enrollment law in 1988, 42 states had passed open enrollment laws by 2008, with 19 having mandatory laws (Education Commission of the States, 2008).

While the precise details of open enrollment policies vary, there are several features of these programs common across states. First, open enrollment programs are designed in a manner such that state funding follows students across district lines. That is, if a student transfers from one district to another, the receiving district will usually receive funds close to the state aid per pupil, and the residential district will lose the equivalent amount. The precise amount of aid accompanying students varies across states, but it is generally greater than the additional cost of educating one additional student (Reback, 2008).[3]

Second, open enrollment laws generally specify a select number of reasons that districts may invoke when refusing transfer applicants from entry into their districts. The most common reason for rejection is capacity; administrators may reject applicants if they feel the district, or specific schools within a district, do not possess sufficient space to serve additional students. Many states also allow rejection for behavioral problems, such as suspension, expulsion, or a history of drug or alcohol use. Finally, until recently many states were allowed to reject applicants if their admission was not in compliance with an established desegregation plan or would otherwise upset the racial balance in the district. The current legal standing of such provisions is in doubt, however, given the 2008 Supreme Court decision in *Parents Involved in Community Schools Inc. v. Seattle School District*. While open enrollment programs generally allow districts some leeway to reject transfer applicants, they are not permitted to selectively accept applicants. If the number of applicants exceeds capacity, then districts are usually statutorily required to accept students by lottery process.

Intra-district choice is similar to open enrollment except that the choices are designed by school districts and limited to individual district schools. The restrictions on intra-district choice are similar to open enrollment as is the weakening this entails in residential zoning requirements. Intra-district choice has been the response in many districts trying to meet the increased competition from charter schools and other forms of publicly funded choice.

Finally, publicly funded vouchers to send students to private schools first came to America in 1990 in Milwaukee, Wisconsin. The first cohort of students receiving vouchers that year numbered 341. Twenty years later, approximately 20,000 students received vouchers to go to 120 private schools in Milwaukee. And other voucher or "scholarship" programs exist in Ohio, Florida, Arizona, and the District of Columbia.[4] The Milwaukee program began as a highly targeted pilot program that was limited to low-income students in the city who had not attended a private school in the prior year. It was also limited to secular private schools in an effort to avoid a First Amendment court challenge. It was initially capped at 1,500 students. Many of those restrictions ended in 1996 when the legislature dramatically expanded the program, most importantly to include religious private schools. The Milwaukee program was challenged in federal court but the U.S. Supreme Court did not take the case, opting later to decide on a similar program enacted in Ohio. In that case, the court decided in favor of the constitutionality of the Cleveland voucher program in *Zelman v. Simmons* (2002).

Florida has gone further than any other state with vouchers with three current voucher programs (Harris, Herrington, & Albee, 2007). The first is a very popular voucher program for students with disabilities entitling them to receive services from any public or private provider in the state. The second, which is popular among businesses and has spread to many states, is a "scholarship" program funded by credits on state taxes owed by the businesses. The third is a pre-school voucher program that is typical of ones that for many years have used state and federal monies to subsidize pre-school education in private, often religious settings. The state had a fourth voucher program targeted to students in failing public schools, but this law was struck down by the courts for reasons

Table 5.2 Percent of All Students in Non-Assigned Public (Choice) Schools, 1993 and 2007

Year	1993	2007
Total % in Choice Schools:	20	27
Public:	11	16
Magnet	—	2.3
Charter	—	2.0
Home Schooled	—	2.9
Inter- or Intra-District Choice[1]	—	8.8
Private	10	12
Religious	8	9
Non-Religious	2	3

[1]Derived estimate subtracting magnet, charter, and home-schooled from the total public. "Home-schooled" arguably belongs in the "private section"; however, we have left it in the public because this is how the original report did it and the original categories are necessary to estimate the amount of inter- and intra-district choice.
Source: National Center for Education Statistics, *Trends in the Use of School Choice: 1993 – 2007*, 2010.

explained later. State law has had a significant role to play in the development of market plans and will affect the future as well.

In summary, while vouchers receive the lion's share of attention and are flashpoints of bitter controversy over educational choice, many more students have non-traditional school assignments through charter, schools, open enrollment, other within-district options, and home-schooling. A recently released report based on a continuation of a household survey on education begun in 1993 provides the most definitive picture available on school choice attendance and trends. Table 5.2 indicates that from 1993 to 2007, the number of students *not* in assigned public schools has increased from 20% to 27%, with most of the growth occurring in public non-assigned school options. Unfortunately, the report does not provide a complete breakdown of public school options, but it was possible to calculate the percent home schooled (2.9%), in charter schools (2%) and in magnet schools (2.3%). The remaining 8.8% must be in some form of inter- or intra-district choice options (National Center for Education Statistics, 2010, p. 4). The report also indicates that in 2007, those in assigned public schools are more likely to be Hispanic, poorer, from less well-educated families, or from rural areas (National Center for Education Statistics, 2010, Table 1, p. 11).

Drivers of Marketization

Clearly, much has changed in the role of markets in schooling over the past 30 years. But why? We identify and, following work by Harris and colleagues (2007), discuss seven main reasons for the shift:

1. The increased role of state and federal governments in financing and regulating public education;
2. Shifts in the racial politics of schooling;
3. Changes in the perceived need to instill common language, culture, and values;
4. Alignment of parent and child interests and expanded parental education levels;
5. Redefinition of community;
6. Perceived failures of public education; and
7. National and international trends toward marketization and privatization in society in general.

Increased role of state governments.   While not about choice per se, *Brown v. Board of Education* in 1954 was a significant stepping stone in the evolution of market policies because it represented the first major threat to local control over public education. From the 1970s through early 1990s, local control was further diminished as states were subject to lawsuits threatening to overturn local funding systems that generated tremendous inequalities across districts. Plaintiffs were frequently successful in their efforts, and this forced states to centralize school funding to reduce cross-district inequity. Even states not subject to lawsuits moved to centralize funding simply to preempt legal action. Funding centralization was significant because entrenched local interests made it virtually impossible to open up the market for schooling with school district funds. The politics were different, and more open to choice, at the state level and state funding allowed students to move out of district-assigned schools.

Racial politics.   *Brown v. Board of Education* and funding equity lawsuits also reduced resource inequities across racial groups. The 42% Black-White gap in salaries paid in 1946 was nearly eliminated by 1965. Likewise, the average pupil-teacher in predominantly Black schools was 22% greater than that in White schools in 1946, but only 8% in 1965, and the gap has now been essentially eliminated (Harris & Herrington, 2006). But desegregation was not without controversy in the Black community. Many Black teachers lost their jobs as Black children moved into formerly White schools that continued to hire White teachers. This was a significant blow to the social and economic fabric of the Black community, but one that was generally accepted at the time because of the larger civil rights victory it represented and, more practically speaking, because it meant greater resources for Black children. The offsetting problem was the acceleration of White flight to the suburbs, which affects many aspects of urban education today.

The politics of choice in the Black community are now quite different. On the one hand, *Brown* and state funding lawsuits made education funding more equitable. But there remain very large achievement gaps, largely unchanged since 1990 (Harris & Herrington, 2006), creating widespread discontent in the Black community. Also, *Brown* eventually created an even more capable pool of Black teachers, making the Black community feel more inclined to educate Black children "on their own" with Black teachers in schools located in Black communities. Choice was a way to do just that. The traditional public education system therefore began to lose what was previously one of its most ardent supporters. One recent poll shows that 57% of Black adults favor vouchers—and the number increases to 74% when the sample is limited to Black families with children (Cooper, 2005). There have also been numerous Black leaders strongly and actively supporting vouchers. Racial segregation is no longer their primary concern.

Common language, culture, and values.   One reason for the emergence and endurance of the uniform state delivery model has been the unique position of the United States as a country of immigrants and the perceived need to unify a country diverse in ethnicity, language, and national origin (Coleman, 1990). This was one of the purposes of public education well into the 1950s. But gradually the percentage of the U.S. population born in other countries began to decline and the immigrants who came often had some knowledge of the English language and American values. While school choice is most popular in states like Florida and Arizona with large immigrant populations, today's immigration is predominantly Hispanic, a group that is more enthusiastic about choice on religious grounds (Harris et al., 2007). Also, the electorates in these two states have more socially conservative and business-friendly political ideologies, which also work in favor of choice. Finally, language skills can be gained through television and other public media in ways not possible in the past.

The need for schools to instill common values was also seen as less important with the fall of the nation's primary opponent, the Soviet Union. The Cold War with the Soviets was a clash in values, and that battle was seen as won.

Alignment of parent and child interests and parent education levels.   During the 19th century, most people lived on farms and families had many children in part because they needed them to work and make the farms successful. Parents in these situations had little interest in sending their children to school, which not only took time away from farm work but increased the odds that the children would leave farm life altogether. In cities, too, parents often expected older children to contribute to family income, child-rearing, and other household work. This is partly why some of the earliest state actions in education were compulsory schooling laws that required parents to send their children to school.

Many parents were also illiterate or, at best, had only rudimentary academic skills. Given that informed choice is a basic principle of markets (more on this below), it was harder in those days to justify turning these decisions over to parents. In this regard, the public education system has perhaps become a victim of its own success, creating widespread advanced learning so that parents might now be able to make decisions that the government has been making for them. Over time, therefore, parents have become both more willing and more able to make schooling decisions for their children.

Redefinition of community. Coleman (1990) argues that the meaning of community has gradually become less rooted in geography. A child's community is no longer the children next door, but those on the soccer team. Likewise, parental communities are oriented more around work, especially with the increasing number of households where both parents work outside the home. The Internet has only accelerated this trend as children and their parents interact via text messages and email. In this new world, parents and children alike are less connected to their physical neighborhoods and therefore perhaps to their neighborhood public schools as well. While it is reasonable to argue that this redefinition of community makes local neighborhood schools even more important (Ravitch, 2010), such arguments have clearly lost out in actual policy debates.

Perceived failures of public education. At about the same time as *Brown*, the Soviet Union launched the *Sputnik* spacecraft in 1957, a technological achievement that raised concerns over U.S. scientific competency and the adequacy of its educational system. Additional pressures began to develop by the late 1970s and early 1980s. As noted by Harris and Herrington (2006), average scores on the SAT were apparently (though not actually) plummeting, and there was widespread belief that schools had lowered academic standards and shifted away from rigorous academic content. This apparent decline in educational quality was then blamed, in A Nation at Risk (National Commission on Excellence in Education, 1983), for the problems of the U.S. economy—high inflation, high unemployment, and heavy competition from Asian nations, where, coincidentally or not, achievement test scores were higher. This combination of factors created strong pressure for change and "reform" of the traditional public school system.

Trend toward marketization and privation in society. While there was pressure to reform, there are many directions policymakers might have chosen. Why markets? As the country was reeling from economic challenges, particularly from Japan and other Asian countries in the 1980s, popular management analyses suggested that companies that seemed to be faring the best in the United States were ones that had adopted the principles of decentralization and entrepreneurialism. On a political level, just as the rise of *Sputnik* had signaled a challenge to U.S. power, the fall of the Soviet Union signaled a victory not only over communism and the defeat of the model of strong, centralized government control. Thus, in both the public and private spheres, new ways of thinking about government and public delivery of service helped usher in expanded use of markets and privatization into the provision of government services. These concepts received support from both Republicans, and conservative foundations and think tanks, who have traditionally supported free markets, and from some Democrats such as President Clinton, whose "third way" was very much in line with this part of the Republican tradition. It is therefore no surprise that the country's long-standing public educational system also came under the scrutiny of market reasoning.

These drivers of choice are closely intertwined and rooted in larger social and economic forces. *Brown v. Board* changed both the role of state and federal governments and racial politics. The economic changes that led to marketization are the same ones that led to international competition in both economic activity and test scores. The technology that has driven economic growth has also created the technology that has disconnected children and parents from their neighborhoods. We explore later how future social and economic forces may affect the future of the market for schooling. But first we explore further the last driver of markets—the trend toward marketization in education and the theory underlying this.

Economic Theory and Markets

Underpinning any major shift in policy is a set of theories and arguments put forth by advocates and often rooted in broader academic and ideological traditions. The growth of marketization is no exception. We have already explained how the ideology of markets became reinforced by a larger societal shift toward markets, but it is so central to understanding the potential advantages and disadvantages of markets that a fuller theoretical explication is necessary. After explaining some of the early intellectual history of the market for schooling, we continue with a discussion of contemporary theory on the subject. While it will come as no surprise that the theories about markets come from economics, the specifics of theory are often not well understood.

 Some trace the intellectual origins of educational choice to a section in Thomas Paine's *The Rights of Man* (part 2, chapter 5; Wheeler, 1908) in which he proposes a parental stipend to pay a child's tuition. However, he only proposes this for children in rural areas, not in "corporate towns" where provision could be made by public schools. The modern intellectual origin of education choice is more often attributed to a voucher proposal by Milton Friedman originally published in 1955, but more widely circulated in *Capitalism and Freedom* in 1962. That article highlights the government monopoly over public education, with its attendant inefficiencies and high costs. Friedman's answer was to create a market through generally unregulated state-funded vouchers to parents to purchase any form of education they desired.

An elaboration of the details of possible voucher programs, as well as advocacy, was later provided by Coons and Sugarman (1978). Leading up to unsuccessful California referenda on vouchers, they also offered a detailed statute. Interestingly, in an effort to make it politically more acceptable, they provided for set aside seats for the poor, and provisions limiting what add-ons parents could provide—neither of which was included in Friedman's initial writings, nor ever accepted by Friedman or the referenda proponents (Coons & Sugarman, 1991). At about the same time, John Chubb and Terry Moe, in a very widely read book, *Politics, Markets and American Schools* (1990), carried that argument forward but more through an attack on the bureaucratic paralysis of public education than on the economic efficiencies to be gained from vouchers or other choice reforms.

Economics 101. We discussed earlier the problems that these reformers sought to address. But why were markets considered the solution? Partly because they had demonstrated success in other sectors of the economy, and that success was backed up by basic economic theory. We elaborate on that theory below, discussing the circumstances under which markets are most likely to be successful and the goals markets do and do not help to achieve.

For economists, markets are simply interactions among producers of goods and services (supply) and the consumers of those services (demand). The two groups negotiate over two things: price and quantity (as well as quality; more on this later). Eventually, the market for all goods settles down to an "equilibrium" price and quantity—the prices we see advertised in newspapers and on store shelves.

A crucial insight of market theory is that, under certain assumptions, the market equilibrium is efficient, in the sense markets facilitate trades that make both parties to transactions better off. The assumption is that, in equilibrium, all of these mutually beneficial trades have already occurred so that the only way to make anyone better off is through redistribution that makes someone else worse off. Redistribution can therefore improve equity, but it cannot improve efficiency. There is little question that markets can and do generate enormous wealth and this is typically interpreted as a gain in utility or overall well-being—and, yes, efficiency.

But markets are only efficient under certain conditions. Starting with the basic motives driving the key actors, consumers are assumed to be rational, self-interested decision-makers. They have complete information and the goods and services exchanged must be identical. As Henry Ford once quipped, "Any customer can have a car painted any color that he wants so long as it is black" (Ford & Crowther, 1922, p. 72). Moreover, it must be possible for producers to enter the market without barriers such as large fixed costs, and the market must be structured so that no producer can influence the market single-handedly (no monopolies). When these assumptions hold, there is "perfect competition" and nothing to stand in the way of mutually beneficial—and efficient—exchanges among producers and consumers. This basic logic can be found in any basic economics textbook.

The assumptions of perfect competition are obviously unrealistic and this is a constant source of criticism of the economics profession in general, and even more so its application to education. The criticism is in some ways exaggerated because these assumptions reflect the analytic approach of economists more than it does what economists believe about how the world really works. Strict assumptions greatly aid in creating formal mathematical models that can be tested using real data. So, on the one hand, criticizing economists for the assumption of perfect competition is akin to criticizing physicists for assuming that there are "frictionless planes." On the other hand, physicists do not make value judgments in the way economists do with their focus on efficiency; and from a rhetorical standpoint, the fact that perfect competition is the starting point also implicitly suggests that we should assume perfect competition holds unless proven otherwise. This tends to focus attention on efficiency over other values like equity and, in this sense, economic theory is not value-free.

We could discuss at length the ways in which people are irrational and not self-interested, but this gets us too far into a broad critique of economics when in fact we are most concerned here with a critique within the specific context of schooling. One of the key distinguishing features of schooling is that the primary consumers are children and there is little dispute that the government must play a role in ensuring child well being, even beyond the state's own self-interest. It is not so much that children are irrational (though as parents, the authors can both attest that this is the case), but that children are dependent and heavily influenced by their environments. In no nation is the well-being of children left to parents alone. We can still view parents as consumers, but only partially because of these broader child welfare concerns and because parents never really experience the schooling their children receive, except in indirect ways, through teacher-parent conferences, what their children tell them, and what homework assignments are sent home.

Neither parents nor students are well informed consumers. They know better than anyone else their own preferences regarding which academic programs and long-term personal goals to which education can be directed. But, just as they know relatively little about health and medicine in making their choices about doctors, parents and children know little about how human development occurs or how education might help them reach their goals and satisfy their preferences. This lack of complete information means that, even if parents and students were rational, they might still make bad decisions.

Education also comes in diverse forms, increasingly so as markets become more common. In the past, the governance of public education was designed to, and did quite successfully, create similar systems across broad categories of schools (e.g., rural and urban). Course standards created by state governments and school districts ensure that all students have a similar basic core of content, consistent with the nation's longstanding goal of public education: creating a common core of knowledge and values. There are options (e.g., electives), but all students have the same menu to choose from. The diversity of options means that, in a market environment, schools can compete not based on price and quality, but instead create "niche markets" in which they alone operate. Economists refer to this as "horizontal product differentiation," by which they mean aspects of education about which people disagree (Glomm, Harris, & Lo, 2005). Religion and values are the clearest examples. In contrast, "vertical product differentiation" (quality) is difficult to achieve if state control prevents schools from charging tuition on top of state subsidies. There is evidence of competition on quality (Witte, 2000), but still there is almost certainly less than there would be in a completely free market. In higher education, for example, student loans can be used at almost any college, but colleges (especially private ones) can charge any tuition they choose. This yields at least a perception of considerable vertical differentiation between, say, Harvard and regional public colleges that have only a fraction of the resources. Like private colleges, private schools are not subject to tuition restraints and it is therefore no surprise that private schools still primarily serve the wealthy. So, there is a trade-off here. Diversity of educational services increases efficiency when preferences are diverse by allowing for a better match between preferences and school services, but this comes at a cost in terms of reduced competition within each individual niche, reducing competition and efficiency with respect to quality.

The scope for competition becomes even smaller when considering the local nature of the market and the structure of costs. Education is a service that, almost by definition, has to be provided locally. (The growth and potential of distance learning is beginning to call this into question, but even those programs typically require students to have some local, in-person interaction with teachers.) Also, schools have to reach a minimum size in order to be viable—e.g., providing a wide enough breadth of courses, each attended by enough students to generate sufficient revenue to cover costs. What this means is that every geographic area will have some schools, but not many. If each of those schools secures a niche, then there may be little direct competition.

Clearly, competition in the education marketplace will never be perfect, and therefore the result will not be perfectly efficient. But this does not mean this imperfect marketplace can be improved on through state intervention. The real question is, given the inherent nature and limitations of the schooling market, what is the best approach? Markets or state control? Or something in between?

To even begin to examine these questions, we need to consider at least briefly the strengths and weaknesses of these two broad options. Government control is typically considered appropriate, even according to economic theory when the benefits of a good or service are received by people other than the producer or consumer. Education is such a good. Certainly, the individuals who receive education benefit from it, but there is also evidence that society as a whole benefits, too. Educated adults are more engaged citizens, rely less on government welfare payments, commit fewer violent crimes, and develop healthier children, just to name a few (Wolfe & Haveman, 2002). These "positive externalities" for society are estimated to be perhaps as large as the private benefits to individuals. But markets ignore social benefits. Therefore, in education, government action through subsidies increases the efficiency of schooling by making sure that the public benefits are obtained, on top of the private ones. In other words, to address externalities, the government has to become one of the consumers, in order to obtain the social benefits that parent- and student-driven choice would ignore.

But these external benefits alone only justify government *subsidies* for education, such as those used in a growing number of states to fund charter schools and private school vouchers. There is no theoretical requirement that government agencies that subsidize schools also have to govern and manage them. Public funding does not mean schools have to be governed by school boards, subject to content standards and standardized tests, and otherwise tightly regulated through state and federal law. Justifying these additional state controls requires some additional rationale and this usually comes in the form of a goal other than efficiency.

Friedman (1962) and Coleman (1990) discuss the role of markets as a trade-off between efficiency (a strength of markets) and social cohesion (a strength of the state). This is why changes in immigration and race have played such a major role in the evolution of choice policies. Levin (2002) outlines a more comprehensive framework with four central values: (a) efficiency; (b) equity; (c) social cohesion; and (d) freedom of choice. Although he discusses these values directly relative to vouchers versus public schools, he also utilizes this theoretical framework to compare vouchers to charter schools, open enrollment plans and other forms of choice. There is widespread public support for the idea that education should be made available to all free of charge and education has long been viewed as an equalizing force in society. If this pursuit of equity means providing students with a common educational experience, then regulation is perhaps a reasonable approach. Regulations do not guarantee equal or equitable outcomes, but they do restrict the educational *process* and help ensure that students are treated in similar ways. Regulation of the process could also increase efficiency if there were one educational process known to be the best for the vast majority of students (what Tyack, 1974, calls the "one best system"), though it is not clear even in that case that the government has to be the one to implement it. Similarly, regulation could increase efficiency by preventing ineffective schools from opening up, although this may come at a cost if the regulatory process also prevents effective schools from opening. The final element of Levin's framework—freedom of choice—has played a growing role in the market debate. Wealthier families already have choices, it is said, because they can afford to move to new neighborhoods, while lower income families (often racial minorities) have fewer housing opportunities and therefore less freedom. This moral argument needs to be considered alongside the theories and evidence of effects.

State-markets hybrids. While we have discussed so far the advantages of states and markets overall, most of the actual policy options on the table are hybrid market–state models. What we call traditional residential zoning is in fact not a strict state–only model because, while it includes nearly full government funding and government production, there is some limited consumer choice. Overall, this is obviously closer to state control than free markets, but parents still have a say in where their children attend school by choosing where they live. While students living in any given catchment area or attendance zone have typically been required to attend a specific school, parents and prospective parents, realizing the importance of schools, have long included school quality as one of the most important factors in their choice of residence. There is clear evidence, for example, that school quality affects housing prices (Figlio, 2004). This is sometimes called "Tiebout" choice after the economist who first postulated a model of choice built around housing decisions (Tiebout, 1956). As we might expect, the assumptions under which this form of choice results in efficiency are even more unrealistic than the assumptions underlying perfectly competitive markets, but it could be that this provides the best balance of efficiency, equity, and other criteria.

Other hybrid options are suggested in Table 5.1. First, the state might decide to control production, but leave consumption choices to markets. For example, it might be better for the government to allow parents to have choice, but for all schools to be government-run schools. Alternatively, perhaps it is better for parents to have few choices, but educational services could be provided by private (for-profit or non-profit) organizations. While we do not focus on it in this chapter, privatization of production is one way to partially utilize markets while giving parents choices (what we might call the privatization of consumption) is another approach.

While economic theory has played a central role, it is clear from this discussion that this approach has real limits. The assumptions of the theory rarely hold, especially in education, and the local in-person nature of education means that competition will always be limited. Even to the degree that economic theory is useful for understanding the efficiency of schooling, there are other important criteria that have to be considered, about which economics has little to say. But economic theory is a useful starting point and, at the very least, explains why the market concept is a powerful and popular one. It also provides a useful structure for discussing the ways in which markets might be beneficial.

Effects of Markets

We have so far largely asserted that competitive markets are efficient without really explaining why. Below, we discuss each mechanism through which markets might improve schooling and discuss what research shows. We also consider the ways in which markets might have unintended consequences.

Possible Advantages of Markets

There are four main mechanisms through which markets can potentially improve schooling: (a) developing innovative instructional and administrative techniques, (b) matching students to teachers and teachers to colleagues, (c) creating better schools, and (d) inducing schools to compete with one another thereby "lifting all boats."

Innovation. Going back to the early roots of the current shift to marketization in the 1980s and early 1990s, this was the most common argument as critics argued that public schools were over-regulated and bureaucratic (Chubb & Moe, 1990). Teachers were seen as hamstrung by district rules and union contracts that prevented them from trying new things. If this is the problem, then it stands to reason that one of the main advantages of markets would be to innovate, in the sense of creating new approaches to instruction and administration. One natural solution to this problem is privatization because, in theory, this loosens the rules and regulations and contracts between government agencies and providers can focus more on the outcomes of education rather than the process. Markets are known for innovation.

There is little to suggest that the shift to markets has created instructional or curricular innovation, however. In fact, charter and voucher schools tend to use the very same textbooks and instructional methods as public schools. One study observed a sample of private, charter, and public schools and found few observable differences (Benveniste, Carnoy, & Rothstein, 2003). Exceptions to this rule include home schools and virtual schools which operate on completely different models. Curriculum and instruction in those cases are indeed very different (and, in the case of home schooling, highly varied).

Administration is a different matter. Charter and private schools are more likely to use alternative compensation plans for teachers (Ballou & Podgursky, 1997), less likely to offer tenure or equivalent job protections, and more likely to hire teachers from alternative routes such as Teach for America. Another "innovation" is that charter schools hire mainly young teachers who also require lower salaries (Carnoy, Jacobsen, Mishel, & Rothstein, 2006). If the goal were innovation, then hiring younger teachers might make sense, but the practice appears to be driven mainly by necessity. Charter schools spend less overall compared with public schools, and experienced teachers in public schools are reluctant to give up their pensions and tenure protections to move to a charter school. On the other hand, while there is debate about whether teacher education and credentials improve teaching, experience is essentially the only measureable trait of teachers that can be clearly demonstrated to improve performance (Harris & Sass, forthcoming). There may be a trade-off between innovation and effectiveness in the basics of instruction, unless, of course, the innovation really does create transformative improvement.

Matching.   Since parents and students have different preferences, we can increase efficiency simply by doing a better job of giving these consumers what they want. This is reflected in the economic concept for horizontal product differentiation (Glomm et al., 2005) and evidence that across a range of voucher programs that parental satisfaction increases more in private, voucher schools than former public schools (Witte, 2000; Howell, Peterson, Wolf, & Campbell, 2002; Witte, Cowen, Fleming, Wolf, & Lucas-McLean, 2009). Teachers also have diverse preferences. Some teachers think students' academic skills are more important, while others think that students should be prepared for jobs. Some espouse whole language approaches while others use phonics. Some rely on lecture and others use more group work and differentiated instruction. In the traditional education model, it is difficult for teachers (and administrators) in a given school to come together toward a common model because the traditional model is supposed to provide a "cafeteria" of options to students.

One way that improved matching of students and teachers might improve education is through a stronger sense of mission. While there is a broad mission to public education writ large in the past, it was rare for a school to have a mission beyond vague generalizations like educating the whole child or meeting the needs of all students. Private schools, in contrast, usually have distinct missions. Religious private schools (mostly Catholic) and some charter schools (e.g., National Heritage Academies) focus on values. Other charter schools, while having academic curricula very similar to public schools, differ in offering social studies programs targeted to specific ethnic groups, with school names like Cesar Chavez Elementary, Malcolm X, and El Shabbaz. If the creation of a sense of mission, distinct from the public school cafeteria mission, is positive, then the move to markets appears to have been a success.

Better schools.   Differences in administration and policy suggest that some innovation may have occurred, perhaps addressing the public school bureaucratic puzzle described by Chubb and Moe (1990). But even if we could not identify a specific change in practice (the sense of mission, for example, might hard to observe by walking into a school), private/charter schools may use their resources more efficiently and do more with less.

Studies of the impacts of various free market reforms on student achievement are decidedly mixed. Extensive reviews of charter schools (Bifulco & Bulkley, 2008) and vouchers (Zimmer & Bettinger, 2008) find that some portion of studies find positive effects, many find no effect, and some even find negative effects on student achievement. A simple average of the estimates would probably be slightly positive. This is offset, however, by a finding by some of the same researchers that there was no difference between voucher and non-voucher students in reading or math growth over 3 years in Milwaukee (Witte et al., 2010).

There is very little evidence of the effects on non-achievement student outcomes. Bettinger and Slonim (2006) gave $10 to different groups of students and suggested they give it to charity. Students using vouchers gave more of the money to charity, suggesting that even though they are making a "private" schooling choice, they are maintaining a sense of civic engagement. Also, one recent study presents some evidence that charter schools may increase high school graduation and college-going rates (Zimmer et al., 2009). Given the conflicting values held by different stakeholders, and clear importance of non-achievement outcomes, additional studies of this sort will no doubt play an important role in future debates.

Competition: Lifting all boats.   Even if private/charter schools are not better than public schools, the increased choices for parents may create competition that improves all schools. The process of "creative destruction," in theory, induces lower-performing schools to lose students and shut their doors, while high-performing schools expand and thrive. In this environment, every school and its leaders are under pressure to attract students and help them succeed—more so than in traditional public schools where students are essentially captive audiences.

The evidence on competition effects is also mixed. In a summary by Gill and Booker (2008), three of six main studies find positive competition effects. Other extensive reviews come to similar conclusions (Carnoy, Adamson, Chudgar, Luschei, & Witte, 2007; Zimmer et al., 2009). To further highlight the ambiguity, two papers apparently using the same data come to almost opposite conclusions about whether competition among school districts increases student achievement (Hoxby, 2000; Rothstein, 2005).

It is not hard to see why competitive effects in education might be less than in a typical private marketplace, even in cities like Washington, DC, Detroit, and Milwaukee where choice is pervasive and where almost every parent has many options to choose from. Hess (2007) argues that even in these competitive contexts, the jobs of school leaders and personnel rarely ride on how many students they attract and keep. Few charters ever close because of low student performance as the market theory would suggest (Hassel & Batdorff, 2004; Bulkley, 2001; Hill et al., 2001). Also, one effect of the charter schooling movement has been to reduce attendance in Catholic schools—one choice option crowding out another.

Other scholars, too, are exploring some of the practical realities of hybrid state-market models. Open enrollment and chartering of schools may work together to foster competition over students. This combination could be extremely important in the future as enrollments decline in many districts. It will also undoubtedly create tension and hostility as districts fight over dwindling numbers of students. Witte and Carlson (2007) have begun to study these competitive pressures across a number of states. It is also possible that competition might be thwarted by the actions of school districts. Witte has proposed a spatial theory of education choice at the school district level that parallels spatial economic theory used in research on firm location, among other economic decisions. That theory is based on an assumption that school districts will maximize the acquisition of state aid through an ideal level of student enrollment and they will do this through the creation and location of charter schools, the judicious use of open enrollment, and a combination of the two (Witte & Carlson, 2007).

Possible Disadvantages of Markets

Eliminating the "common" in common schools. While some see innovation and niche markets as a good thing, others see this as a weakness, and one antithetical to the democratic ideal in which people of all creeds and backgrounds come together and to learn common language, culture, and values. The elimination of the common school also reinforces concerns that society will continue to "pull apart," with the more advantaged and privileged groups in society having little interaction with others. Critics of this argument are quick to respond by pointing out the significant inequalities and separation that the existing system of public education has engendered, in terms of funding as well as separation of students, the topic we turn to next.

Resegregation. Ironically, one of the first widespread moves toward school choice occurred in the aftermath of the *Brown v. Board of Education* decision when new private schools emerged to serve Whites (Blacks could not afford them) and school districts created "open-enrollment" that, on the face of it, allowed Blacks to enroll anywhere but in practice meant that Blacks would stay in the schools they had always attended. The idea that they did so "by choice" was intended to keep the status quo intact while being consistent with the letter of the new desegregation law.

Despite early resistance, desegregation did eventually occur across the country (schools in the North were also segregated, though not usually by law as in the South). This accomplishment was one of the pillars of the Civil Rights movement and widely considered to be key in the declining achievement and economic gaps since then (Harris & Herrington, 2006). This is why some express concern that choice might lead to resegregation. Indeed, there is evidence that choice does lead to greater segregation (Bifulco & Ladd, 2008).[5] While this form of voluntary segregation might be less pernicious than its earlier de jure form (Viteretti, 1999), it still does conflict with the notion of common schooling. Given the extensive segregation that remained under the traditional public education model, and the increasing legal impediments to state-driven desegregation, it is not yet clear how much worse markets might be in this regard.

Leaving more disadvantaged students behind. Early in the charter school movement, there was concern that charter schools would essentially become publicly funded prep schools, siphoning off the best and brightest students. This in turn could hurt the students remaining in public schools through peer influences (Harris, 2010) and reduced parental accountability (because parents of less advantaged students tend to be less educated and less active in school). There is some evidence supporting the fact that more disadvantaged students are left behind. While charter schools do tend to locate in neighborhoods serving disadvantaged families (Glomm et al., 2005), they tend to attract the most well off families in those neighborhoods (Carnoy, Jacobsen, Mishel, and Rothstein, 2005). It is not clear whether this amounts to leaving those students "behind" because these students, in theory, could benefit from the pressures of innovation and competition.

Conflicting priorities among stakeholders. Recall that one of the driving forces behind markets in schooling is dissatisfaction with U.S. test scores compared with other countries. But parents may not see the needs of their children in quite the same way. While all parental groups say they value academic quality (Armor & Peiser, 1998), their decisions also show that they pay close attention to school racial composition (e.g., Lankford & Wyckoff, 2005) and safety (Armor & Pesier, 1998). Safety might translate into achievement, but this will at best be in small and indirect ways.

If we take this theory and evidence as a whole, there is good reason to think that both the advocates and opponents of choice and privatization are correct. Utilizing markets for schooling probably improves student outcomes a little on the average and it certainly improves parent satisfaction. But it also increases racial and ethnic segregation, and some of the perceived benefits, such as parent satisfaction are viewed as problems in terms of common schooling. Opponents are also correct that the market of schooling is different from other services and this is partly why it has not unleashed the torrent of school improvement that some of the debates have suggested. Since both sides appear to have legitimate points regarding the facts of markets in schooling, the final resolution may come down to how society resolves conflicting social and educational values.

Prospects for the Future

The future of markets in schooling is uncertain. First, from the standpoint of research, most of the studies only focus on short-term effects and the main benefits may occur through larger systemic shifts. Decades from now, if the schooling market continues to becomes more consumer driven, it could alter perceptions of education in ways that alter the willingness to provide funding. This could go either way. On the one hand, parents and citizens alike might be more satisfied with a market system and be willing to provide more money for it. On the other hand, as in higher education, education may increasingly be seen as a private good and one that consumers themselves should pay for without public support.

A schooling market could also change perceptions about the teaching profession. Today it is seen by many as lacking prestige and dominated by unions; and therefore associated with blue collar and other low-paying jobs where unionization is more common. A schooling market could change that if innovative administrative practices continue and these changes are seen as attractive to potential teachers. On the other hand, if decreased unionization means less job security, then the job may be less attractive to even effective teachers. Given the widespread agreement that teachers represent the most important school resource, who enters the profession is no small matter.

Online learning could also transform the market for schooling, depending on how online instruction evolves and improves and how much value parents and policymakers assign to this new approach. If online learning remains piecemeal, so that students take individual courses online but continue to be educated primarily within the walls of a nearby school, then it is likely to remain a separate matter from the larger debates over charters, vouchers, and tuition tax credits (Peterson, 2010). However, if the demand for completely online education grows, then the market and online debates will be increasingly intertwined. Given that in-person schooling also allows parents to work outside the home, and that the effective practice of online learning seems to involve a blend of in-person and online learning, there are limits to how far online learning can replace brick-and-mortar schools. But to the degree that online learning does become part of schooling, it will be difficult to argue against a marketplace for online learning when there are so many options easily available—expanding the cafeteria.

Yet, there are legal and political impediments to markets. A number of commentators and proponents of vouchers believed the *Zelman* decision would open a flood gate of voucher programs across the United States. That has not occurred partly because of significant barriers in state constitutions. Ironically, these barriers have nothing to do with modern voucher programs—they were designed to prevent pubic money from aiding Catholic schools at the turn of the last century. These "Blaine Amendments" passed more than a half-century ago in 37 states and, along with the constitutional requirements for provisions of "free and uniform" education, present significant legal barriers to voucher programs that are challenged in court. The Florida voucher program that was over-turned was decided on the basis of that state's own "free and uniform" clause, which may spell trouble for voucher efforts in other states.

Tuition tax credits remain a viable option for avoiding legal impediments. Although it could be argued that this is largely a difference in accounting, the courts have indicated that there are important legal differences (*Lemon v. Kurtzman*, 1971; *Rosenberger v. Regents*, 1995). By keeping the money out of government hands, tuition tax credits further distance the government from religion and therefore avoid some legal issues surrounding the separation of church and state (see further legal discussion below). In addition to this legal difference, there is a political difference between vouchers and tax credits—tax credits can be promoted as tax cuts, whereas vouchers require the collection of revenue.

There may also be limits to the level of political support. While the opinions of Blacks and other minorities are trending in favor, teacher unions remain strongly opposed to markets, so much so that the president of the American Federation of Teachers recently said "no issue should be off the table, with the single exception of vouchers" (Weingarten, 2010). Also, there is only modest support from wealthier suburban voters, a powerful voting bloc that believes the current system is in their own interests. Political support will likely remain stronger in states like Arizona, Florida, and Texas that have weak unions and that have large Hispanic populations (Harris et al., 2007). Hispanics are important because, while they share a "minority" status with Blacks, they are also more socially conservative and Catholic, and therefore more interested in the type of religious private schooling that long been the main exception to the traditional public school model. Also, there is enough tension about Hispanic immigration in Florida and the Southwest that it is easy to imagine strong support among non-Hispanics to provide alternative schooling options, in the same way that "choice" became a way of avoiding integration in the wake of *Brown v. Board of Education.*

Neither the overall direction nor the ever-important details is easy to forecast, though all the drivers that have led to greater support for markets and modification of the traditional system seem firmly in place. Immigration and state and federal control over schools continue to grow. Minority support for markets in education, as well as the larger moral argument in favor of parental choice, will likely to continue. The "good old days"—when communities were seen as geographic places, the public schools were considered great, and the United States was *the* world economic power—are unlikely to return.

If we had been writing this article 25 years ago, we probably would not have forecast the kind of change we have seen and documented here. Whenever there is talk of major changes in a key governmental program, the odds are against it. But given the major changes we have seen, it is only reasonable to think that this might be an exception. The market for schooling and the role of the state are likely to look very different decades from now.

Notes

1. A form of compulsory education was first introduced in 1642 in the Massachusetts Bay Colony. Although it provided for public schools in larger towns, its main focus was on parents' responsibility to see that their children were educated.

2 *Mueller v. Allen*, 463 U.S. 388, 103 S. Ct. 3062, 77 I. Ed. 721 (11 Ed. Law Rep. [763]) (1983). Writing for the 5 to 4 majority was Justice Thurgood Marshall. Tuition tax credits allow parents of private school students to recoup some of their tuition payments in terms of tax credits on state income taxes. Various limits and forms of credits apply in different states.

3 In most states, for each transfer student receiving districts gain (and districts of residence lose) an amount of funding equal to the non-compensatory aid per pupil provided by the

state. In the case of students with special needs, the district of residence must also compensate the receiving district for the costs of fulfilling those needs (Reback, 2008).
4 The Washington, DC, program is currently being allowed to "die" in that no new students have been given vouchers since fall of 2009. That, of course, could change with a new Congress in 2011.
5 Some studies only look at the percentage of students in a district or region who are minority, but these studies mask the fact that educational markets are highly localized, and the only way to really understand the effects on segregation is to analyze student- and school-level data. The Bifulco and Ladd study is one of the few to conduct the analysis this way.

References

Armor, D. L., & Pesier, B.A. (1998). Interdistrict choice in Massachusetts. In P. E. Peterson & B. C. Hassel (Eds.), *Learning from school choice* (pp. 157–186). Washington, DC. Brookings Institution Press.

Ballou, D., & Podgursky, M. (1997). *Teacher pay and teacher quality* (pp. 129–162). Kalamazoo, MI: W.E. Upjohn Institute.

Benveniste, L., Carnoy, M., & Rothstein, R. (2003). *All else equal: Are public and private schools different?* New York: Routledge.

Bettinger, E. P., & Slonim, R. (2006). Using experimental economics to measure the effects of an educational experiment on altruism. *Journal of Public Economics*, *90*(8–9), 1625–1648.

Bifulco, B., & Bulkley, K. (2008) Charter schools. In H. Ladd & E. Fiske (Eds.), *Handbook of research in education finance and policy* (pp. 425–446). New York: Routledge.

Bifulco, R., & Ladd, H. F. (2004, August). *The Impacts of Charter Schools on Student Achievement: Evidence From North Carolina*. Working Papers Series No. SAN04-01. Durham, NC: Terry Sanford Institute of Public Policy, Duke University.

Blank, R. K. (1990). Educational effects of magnet high schools. In W. H. Clune & J. F. Witte (Eds.), *Choice and control in American education* (pp. 77–110). New York: Falmer Press.

Boyd, W. L., Hare, D., & Nathan, J. (2002). *What really happened? Minnesota's experience with statewide public school choice programs: Center for School Change*. Minneapolis: Humphrey Institute of Public Affairs, University of Minnesota.

Buetow, H. A. (1970). *Of singular benefit: The history of U.S. Catholic education*. New York: Macmillan.

Bulkley, K E. (2001). Educational performance and charter school authorizers: The accountability bind. *Educational Policy Analysis Archives, 9*. Retrieved August 1, 2010, from http://epaa.asu.edu/epaa/v9n37.html

Carnoy, M., Jacobsen, R., Mishel, L., & Rothstein, R. (2006). Worth the price? Weighing the evidence on charter school achievement. *Education Finance and Policy, 1,* 151–161.

Carnoy, M., Adamson, F., Chudgar, A., Luschei T, & Witte, J. (2007). Vouchers and public school performance: A case study of the Milwaukee Parental Choice Program. Washington, DC: Economic Policy Institute.

Catholic Schools in America. (1995). Montrose, CA: Fischer.

Center for Education Reform. (2009). *National charter school data*. Retrieved August 5, 2009, from http://www.edreform.com/_upload/CER_charter_numbers.pdf

Chubb, J. E., & Moe, T. M. (1990). *Politics, markets, and schools*. Washington, DC: Brookings Institution.

Coleman, J. (1990). Preface: Choice, community, and future schools. In W. Clune & J. Witte (Eds.), *Choice and control in American education* (Vol. 1, pp. ix–xxi). Philadelphia: Farmer Press.

Coons, J. E., & Sugarman, S. D. (1978). *Education by choice: The case for family control*. Berkeley: University of California Press.

Coons, J. E., & Sugarman, S. D. (1991). *Scholarships for children*. Berkeley, CA: Institute for Governmental Policy Studies.

Cooper, S. (2005). School vouchers: An educational conundrum for Black America. *Journal of Blacks in Higher Education, 35,* 79–80.

Education Commission of the States. (2008). State policies for open enrollment database. Retrieved October 17, 2008, from http://www.ecs.org/html/educationissues/OpenEnrollment/OEDB_intro.asp

Figlio, D. N., & Lucas, M. E. (2004). What's in a grade? School report cards and the housing market. *American Economic Review, 94*(3), 591–604.

Ford, H., & Crowther, S. (1922). *My life and work.* New York: Doubleday.

Friedman, M. (1962). *Capitalism and freedom.* Chicago: University of Chicago Press.

Gill, B., & Booker, K. (2008). School competition and outcomes. In H. Ladd & E. Fiske (Eds.), *Handbook of research in education finance and policy* (pp. 183–202). New York: Routledge.

Gleason, P. (1985). Baltimore III and education. *U.S. Catholic Historian, 4,* 273–306.

Glomm, G., Harris, D., & Lo, T. (2005). Charter school location. *Economics of Education Review, 24*(4), 451–457.

Harris, D. (2010). How do school peers influence student educational outcomes? Theory and evidence from economics and other social sciences. *Teachers College Record, 112*(4), 1163–1197.

Harris, D., & Herrington, C. (2006). Accountability, standards, and the growing achievement gap: Lessons from the past half-century. *American Journal of Education, 112*(2), 209–238.

Harris, D., Herrington, C., & Albee, A. (2007). The future of vouchers: Lessons from the adoption, design, and court challenges of Florida's three voucher programs. *Educational Policy, 21*(1), 215–244.

Harris, D., & Sass, T. (2007). *Teacher training, teacher quality, and student achievement. National Center for the Analysis of Longitudinal Data in Education Research (CALDER).* Working Paper #3. Washington, DC: Urban Institute.

Hassel, B. C., & Batdorff, M. (2004). *High-stakes: Findings from a national study of life-or-death decisions by charter school authorizers.* Chapel Hill, NC: Public Impact.

Hess, F. (2007). A market for knowledge? Competition in American education. In M. Landy, M. Levin, & M. Shapiro (Eds.), *Creating competitive markets.* Washington, DC: Brookings Institution Press.

Hill, P., Lake, R., Celio, M.B., Campbell, C., Herdman, P., & Bulkley, K. (2001). *A study of charter school accountability.* Seattle: Center on Reinventing Public Education. University of Washington.

Howell, W.G., & Peterson, P. E. (with P. J. Wolf. & D. E. Campbell). (2002). *The education gap: Vouchers and urban schools.* Washington, DC: The Brookings Institution.

Hoxby, C. M. (2000) Does competition among public schools benefit students and taxpayers? *American Economic Review, 90*(5), 1209–1238.

Lankford, H., & Wyckoff, J. (2005). Why are schools racially segregated? Implications for school choice policies. In J. T. Scott (Ed.), *School choice and diversity: What the evidence say* (pp. 9–26). New York: Teachers College Press.

Lemon v. Kurtzman, 403 U.S. 602 (1971).

Levin, H. (2002). A comprehensive framework for the evaluation of educational vouchers. *Educational Evaluation and Policy Analysis, 24*(3), 159–174.

National Center for Education Statistics. (2009). *Characteristics of private schools in the United States: Results from the 2007–08 Private School Universe Survey.* Washington, DC: U.S. Department of Education.

National Center for Education Statistics. (2010). *Trends in the use of school choice: 1993–2007.* Washington, DC. U.S. Department of Education.

National Commission on Excellence in Education. (1983). *A nation at risk.* Washington, DC: Author.

Parents Involved in Community Schools Inc. v. Seattle School District No. 1, 127 S.Ct. 2738 (2007).

Peterson, P. (2010). *Saving schools: From Horace Mann to virtual learning.* Cambridge, MA: Harvard University Press.

Protsik, J. (1994, November). *History of teacher pay and incentive reforms*. Paper presented at the Consortium for Policy Research in Education Conference, Washington DC.

Ravitch, D. (2010). *The death and life of the great American school system*. New York: Basic Books.

Reback, R. (2008). Demand (and supply) in an inter-district public school choice program. *Economics of Education Review*, 27(4), 402–416.

Reese, W. J. (2005). America's public schools: From the common schol to "No Child Left Behind." Baltimore, MD: Johns Hopkins University Press.

Rosenberger v. Regents, 515 U.S. 819 (1995).

Rothstein, J. (2005). *Does competition among public schools benefit students and taxpayers? A comment on Hoxby (2000)*. NBER Working Paper #11215. Cambridge, MA: National Bureau of Economic Research.

Shober, A., Manna, P., & Witte, J. (2006). Flexibility meets accountability: State charter school laws and their influence on the formation of charter school in the United States. *Policy Studies Journal, 34*(4), 563–585.

Tiebout, C. M. (1956). A pure theory of local expenditures. *The Journal of Political Economy. 64*(5), 416–424.

Tozer, S. E., Violas, P. C., & Senese, G. B. (1995). *School and society: Historical and contemporary perspectives*. New York: McGraw-Hill.

Tyack, D. B. (1974). *The one best system: A history of American urban education*. Cambridge MA: Harvard University Press.

Viteretti, J. P. (1999). *Choosing equality: School choice, the Constitution, and civil society*. Washington, DC: Brookings Institution Press.

Weingarten, R. (2010). *A new path forward: Four approaches to quality teaching and better schools*. American Federation of Teachers. Retrieved August 26, 2010, from http://aft.3cdn. net/227d12e668432ca48e_twm6b90k1.pdf

Wheeler, D. E. (Ed.), (1908). *Life and writings of Thomas Paine, Vol. 5*. New York: Vincent Parke and Company.

Witte, J. (2000). *The market approach to education: An analysis of America's first voucher program*. Princeton, NJ: Princeton University Press.

Witte, J., & Carlson, D. (2007). *Competition for students in public schools: A multi-state study*. Washington, DC: Association of Public Policy Analysis and Management Meetings.

Witte, J. F., Cowen, J. M., Fleming, D. J, Wolf, P. J., & Lucas-McLean, J. (2009). *The MPCP Longitudinal Educational Growth Study: Second year report*. Fayetteville: Department of Education Reform, University of Arkansas.

Witte, J. F., Cowen, J. M., Fleming, D. J, Wolf, P. J., Condon, M. R., & Lucas-McLean, J. (2010). *The MPCP Longitudinal Educational Growth Study: Third Year Report*. Fayetteville: Department of Education Reform, University of Arkansas.

Wolfe, B. L., & Haveman, R. H. (2002). Social and nonmarket benefits from education in an advanced economy. In Y. K. Kodrzycki (Ed.), *Education in the 21st century: Meeting the challenges of a changing world* (pp. 97–142). Boston: Federal Reserve Bank of Boston.

Zelman v. Simmons Harris. 536 U.S. 639 (2002), 234 F .3rd 945, reversed.

Zimmer, R., & Bettinger, E. P. (2008). Beyond the Rhetoric: Surveying the evidence on vouchers and tax credits. In H. Ladd & E. Fiske (Eds.), *Handbook of research in education finance and policy* (pp. 447–465). New York: Routledge.

Zimmer, R., Gill, B., Booker, K., Lavertu, S., Sass, T. R., & Witte, J. (2009). *Charter schools in eight states: Effects on achievement, attainment, integration, and competition*. Santa Monica, CA: Rand Corporation.

PART III

The Foundations of Educational Equity

Douglas E. Mitchell

divide an area into political districts to give special advantage to one group

When it comes to the protection of the constitutional rights of individuals and groups of Americans, the judiciary stands out as the most important branch of government. Our national record of constitutional rights abuses is long and depressing. It includes endorsement of slavery, creation of apartheid school systems, gerrymandering of representational districts, the internment of peaceful citizens, and the use of referenda and statutes to strip individuals or groups of constitutional protections. When efforts have been made to redress these abuses, elected legislatures, executive administrations and rank and file voters have shown a ready willingness to violate the Constitution in pursuit of private privilege or pandering to group biases. Though their performance over the last two decades has been disappointing, for much of the second half of the 20th century the American courts displayed remarkable courage and commitment to the protection of constitutional rights.

The two chapters of Part III review the last half-century of student due process and freedom of expression rights, and the judicial and political history of efforts to secure racial and ethnic equality in matters of education. Tedi and Douglas Mitchell detail the judicial history from the sweeping support of student freedoms pronounced in *Tinker v. Des Moines Independent Community School District* (1969) and the equally profound declaration of equal rights in *Brown v. Board of Education* (1954) through the gradual retrenchment in both domains. The authors conclude that current judicial guidelines in both student rights and racial equity are not much different today than they were in 1950 before the period of aggressive judicial enforcement of constitutional guarantees.

Carolyn Brown and Bruce Cooper examine major developments in the struggle for racial and ethnic equality in the schools. They attend more closely to the legislative and administrative history, but paint a similar picture of the evolution from sweeping rhetoric to modest gains. They end their analysis with a look at how, particularly through the provisions of the No Child Left Behind the 2001 reauthorization of the Elementary and Secondary Education Act, equality of educational access and opportunity have morphed into standards based accountability policies aimed at holding schools responsible for overcoming enormous achievement gaps. This is an admirable aspiration, of course, but this and other chapters in this volume leave us far from confident that the goals are anywhere within reach.

References

Brown v. Board of Education of Topeka, 347 U.S. 483 (1954).
Tinker v. Des Moines Independent Community School District, 89 S.Ct. 733 (1969).

6

CIVIL RIGHTS FOR INDIVIDUALS AND GROUPS

Tedi K. Mitchell and Douglas E. Mitchell

Among the most hard-fought and controversial educational policy issues agonizing public education in the United States over the past 60 years has been securing equal rights and equal educational opportunities for individuals and social groups. The pursuit of equality of social and educational opportunities has required sustained, sometimes aggressive action over a very long period. The struggle has involved community actions, legislative mandates, executive enforcement and, above all, persistent litigation in the courts. Nevertheless, the legacy of slavery, bigotry, and abuse of basic constitutional rights remains, to this day, deeply embedded in the American civic culture. While the predicament of African Americans has been the most visible manifestation of the nation's failure to treat all citizens fairly, the mistreatment of other groups, and of individual students deprived of their constitutional due process and freedom of expression rights, have been just as serious if not always as clearly displayed. The courts of the United States, particularly the Supreme Court, have been playing a major role in defining the constitutional rights of students as individuals, and the civil rights of families and students who, because of their color, ethnicity, physical or mental limitations, or gender, have been denied educational opportunities or have experienced limited/segregated educational access.

This chapter first reviews the issue of individual students' constitutional rights and then addresses the broader issue of civil rights of families and students as they relate to education.

School Governance and Individual Students' Rights

American public school education was born and developed in Puritan New England. Initially, the primary purposes for founding and maintaining public schools were twofold: first, "to guard religion and virtue and correct the innately wayward young" (Ladd, 1970, p. 220) and second, to provide them with the necessary skills to be economically self-sufficient. With the passage of time and an increased school population, educators also became responsible for politically socializing their students—"taming and civilizing the anarchic instinct of the populace, inculcating social and moral values," and "establishing a uniform national character" (Berkman, 1970, p. 569). Coercion and force were used by some educators if students could not be persuaded to voluntarily participate in this process and, when such actions were challenged in court, educators claimed that such methods were necessary if education was to go forward. Students were considered wards who were afforded privileges, not persons with substantive rights and, therefore, must learn to conform to the roles carved out for them by adults.

To help achieve the educational purposes of instruction and political socialization state legislatures granted school boards, administrators and teachers the authority to control students' actions during the school day. As a result of that authority, two models of school governance developed—the first labeled the Puritan model and the second, the Professional model. These two models were support by five educational-legal doctrines.

The legal doctrines, *in loco parentis* (the legal power of the male parent given to the tutor or school master—traceable from the Code of Hammurabi, through Roman law and English common law [Manley-Casimir, 1978, p. 103]) and *parens patriae* (originating from English common law, encompassing the "legal infant theory" in which the State does not act "in place of parents" but is itself a guardian" [Yudof, 1974, p. 221]), have supported the Puritan model. The educational doctrines of efficiency and order, expertise, and commonality of interest (which began to develop at the end of the 19th century) have supported the Professional model. One or more of these doctrines were invoked by school authorities when challenged in court for they claimed that (a) students were not "fully protectable 'persons'" under the Constitution and (b) the educational interests of the State took precedence over the interest of individual students. And, unless an educator's challenged behavior was demonstratively egregious, the courts deferred without serious question.

The judiciary's policy of deferring to educators, giving no more than a cursory review to the actions of school authorities, continued until the 1940s and 50s when two United State Supreme Court decisions—*West Virginia State Board of Education v. Barnette* (1943) and *Brown v. Board of Education* (1954)—redirected judicial review of education action. These two decisions ushered in an era of judicial reform in education that continued for approximately three decades.

The *Barnette* case, decided in 1943, challenged the political socialization methods used by educators to foster patriotism in students. In handing down its decision, the Court began to alter the political socialization process and also undermine the Puritan governance model which holds that students lack constitutional rights. The Court freed students, on grounds of conscience, from having to salute the flag, declared they do possess some constitutional rights, and established the duty of the courts to prevent school officials from abridging those rights. While school boards have "important, delicate, and highly discretionary functions," all of them must be performed "within the limits of the Bill of Rights" (1943, p. 637). In making this statement, the Court began to develop an alternative model of school governance which has been called the "Legalistic" model (Yudof, 1974). Despite the affirmation of Legalistic decision making, however, the Court continued to endorse the idea that school officials might exercise their Puritanical and Professional prerogatives within the bounds of the Bill Rights' legalistic framework.

Brown v. Board of Education, the second case, was decided by the Supreme Court in 1954. It declared racially segregated public education facilities to be a violation of the Fourteenth Amendment's equal protection clause, underlined the constitutional rights of students, and raised serious questions about the credibility of both the Puritan and Professional models of school governance. The evidence reviewed by the Court revealed that the actions of state and local authorities materially violated all five educational-legal doctrines. The State, in its role as *parens patriae*, had not acted to protect the well-being of the African American students and local school districts had misused their *in loco parentis* authority. It was made abundantly clear that dual school systems are not an efficient use of educational resources or talents and educational policies based on racial bigotry or ignorance are not expressions of expert knowledge or understanding. Finally, the evidence proved a segregated educational system was clearly not in the best interest of all students.

The Court asserted that "Today, education is perhaps the most important function of state and local government." It is the foundation of good citizenship, "a principal instrument in awakening the child to cultural values, in preparing him for later professional training ... helping him to adjust normally to his environment." Moreover, "it is doubtful that any child may reasonably be expected to succeed in life if he is denied that opportunity of an education." Thus, "such an opportunity, where the state has undertaken to provide it, is a right which must be made available to all on equal terms" (*Brown*, 1954, p. 493).

Although the *Barnette* decision clearly stated that students have constitutional rights, a number of educators chose to interpret that decision very narrowly. Unless an educator's challenged behavior was demonstratively egregious, many courts still deferred without serious question. Not saluting the American flag was the *only* right supported by the decision as far as they were concerned. Other expression rights were not recognized—at least while students were attending school. Moreover, while the *Brown* decision identified education as a *right*, most educators still considered it to be a privilege which could be denied without violating any due process requirements. In the aftermath of the 1954

Brown decision (and its companion 1955 decision), school administrators in some Southern communities expressly used the power to suspend and expel students to thwart school desegregation and civil rights protest activities.[1]

While many educators continued to view the Court's decision narrowly and to deny students due process in school proceedings, some members of the legal scholarly community took a much broader view. They embraced the legalistic model of school governance[2] and argued that the Court had declared constitutional protections for students in *Barnette*, even while they were in school. In reading *Brown*, they believed the Court was declaring education to be a fundamental right—a right protected by the Fourteenth Amendment's due process clause.[3] That being the case, before abridging a student's access to education by suspension or expulsion, the student should be entitled to some form of due process. Procedural due process, therefore, is the starting point of most legal scholars' analysis of the issue of student rights.

In 1957, the *Harvard Law Review* published Warren Seavey's article, "Dismissal of Students: 'Due Process,'" that addressed issues of constitutional due process rights for students. Instead of reaffirming the traditional view of school personnel being *in loco parentis*, Seavey stated that educators should view themselves as "fiduciaries for their students and … afford to their students every protection" (p. 1407). While the primary focus was the rights of university students, those enrolled in K–12 public institutions were not ignored. This article was cited by the Fifth Circuit Court of Appeals in its *Dixon v. Alabama State Board of Education* (1961) decision.[4] In this case, the circuit court declared that the State could not "condition the granting of even a privilege upon the renunciation" (p. 156) of a student's constitutional rights.

William Van Alstyne, another legal scholar, challenged the treatment that college students received from administrators and courts and questioned the soundness of the school governance Puritan model of *in loco parentis* and *parens patriae* and Professional model of efficiency (Van Alstyne, 1963).

In 1963, for the second time, the federal judiciary dealt with the issue of college students' procedural rights (*Due v. Florida A. & M. University*, 1963), the district court, in this case, upholding the university's disciplinary committee's decision to suspend a group of students. In doing so, however, the court noted that the students' Fourteenth Amendment rights were not violated because the students had been given a formal notice of the charges and a proper hearing.

The question of whether high school students might also have procedural due process rights was raised in the 1964 *Woods v. Wright* case. Without notice or hearing a group of students were expelled by the school board and the decision was appealed to the federal court system because one of the students claimed both that her due process rights had been violated and that her First Amendment right of liberty of expression had been restrained. This case, like *Dixon*, was reviewed by the Fifth Circuit Court of Appeals, and the court found for the students, reversing and remanding the case. Although the court made no decision about the denial of freedom of expression and due process, they determined that when a denial of "a constitutionally guaranteed right" had been charged then the district court should have issued a temporary restraining order "to protect against the loss of the asserted right" (*Woods*, 1964, pp. 374, 375).

The *University of Kansas Law Review* (1965) was the first journal to publish an article on the emerging rights of secondary students, its primary focus being due process. From that point on, the constitutional rights of K–12 public school students were addressed in both legal journals and educational journals. Legal scholars believed "the formality of decision making is grounded in the supposition that the values of fairness, liberty, dignity, and participation require promulgating general roles and applying them in a uniform fashion" (Yudof, 1974, p. 305). Many educational writers, particularly those critical of the legalistic model, focused on the "need to maintain authority relationships and a sense of shared community purpose in public schools" and perceived "legalization as a threat to those values" (Yudof, 1974, p. 305). It was recognized that the inevitable result of the legalist model would be "a diminution or channeling of official discretion to make decisions affecting teachers and students" (Yudof, 1974, p. 305).

First Amendment Expression Rights

Students' First Amendment freedom of expression and the civil rights movement became entwined when the Fifth Circuit Court of Appeals was asked to resolve the issue raised in two cases involving African American high school students, *Burnside v. Byars* (1966) and *Blackwell v. Issaquena County Board of Education* (1966). Students at both schools wore "freedom buttons" on their campuses after school authorities banned those specific buttons and the students were suspended from school. Although the cases were similar, the Fifth Circuit's decisions were not the same. The court adopted a case-by-case approach to determine the merits of each school's regulation. The court asked if it was an unreasonable rule which abridged a student's expression rights or a reasonable regulation imposed to maintain proper disciple in the school. The court stated it "must ask whether the gravity of the 'evil,' discounted by it improbability, justified such invasion of free speech as is necessary to avoid the danger" (*Blackwell*, 1966, p. 754).

In ruling in favor of the students in *Burnside*, the court declared the "freedom buttons the students wore were "a means of silently communicating an idea" which they hoped would encourage the members of their community to exercise their civil rights (*Burnside*, 1966, p. 747). Because school personnel are officers of the state[5] any abridgement of a student's First Amendment right to freedom of speech is constitutionally acceptable only when such rules and regulations "*measurably* contribute to the maintenance of order and decorum within the educational system" (*Burnside*, 1966, p. 748, emphasis added).

The wearing of the buttons did not disrupt the school's order and decorum, the students had been expelled for violating the regulation—not causing a commotion or disruption. Because students had worn buttons in the past, with no banning or disciplinary action taken, the court concluded "the regulation forbidding the wearing of 'freedom buttons' on school grounds (was) arbitrary and unreasonable, an unnecessary infringement on the students' protected right of free expression" (*Burnside*, 1966, p. 749). In balancing students' First Amendment rights with the duty of school officials to "further and protect the public school system," the court stated,

> We wish to make it quite clear that we do not applaud any attempt to undermine the authority of the school. We support all efforts made by the school to fashion reasonable regulations for the conduct of their students and enforcement of the punishment incurred when such regulations are violated. Obedience to duly constituted authority is a valuable tool, and respect for those in authority must be instilled in our young people.
>
> But ... we must also emphasize that school officials cannot ignore expression of feelings with which they do not wish to contend. They cannot infringe on their students' right to free and unrestricted expression as guaranteed to them under the First Amendment to the Constitution, where the exercise of such rights in the school buildings and schoolrooms does not materially and substantially interfere with the requirement of appropriate discipline in the operation of the school. (*Burnside*, 1966, p. 749)

In *Blackwell* the court upheld the actions of the school authorities because the "students conducted themselves in a disorderly manner, disrupted classroom procedure, interfered with the proper decorum and discipline of the school and disturbed other students who did not wish to participate in the wearing of the buttons" (1966 p. 753). In balancing the rights of the appellant students with those of the school system the federal court, citing an earlier Supreme Court decision, wrote:

> The constitutional guarantee of freedom of speech "does not confer an absolute right to speak" and the law recognized that there can be an abuse of such freedom. The Constitution does not confer "unrestricted and unbridled license giving immunity for every possible use of language and prevent the punishment of those who abuse this freedom." *Whitney v. People of State of California* 274 U.S. 357, 47 S.Ct. 641, 71 L.Ed. 1095 (1927). (*Blackwell*, 1966, pp. 753, 754)

These cases are significant because this was the first time a court ruled a K–12 public school student's right to freedom of expression to be a protected right. And the reasonability of a school regulation abridging a constitutional right was subjected to a stricter standard of scrutiny than had generally been done in the past. The *Burnside* decision, however, did more than just affect the control function of the school and the standard of judicial review used by the courts. One of the primary educational functions of schools, political socialization, an area the courts had rarely touched, was also altered by this decision, although that was probably not fully realized at the time.

As was mentioned earlier, schools have always had two primary educational functions—political socialization and instruction. The first function, the cultural transmission of the political customs that regulate and direct political life, happens by incorporating a variety of formal and informal activities within the school's curriculum (Dawson & Prewitt, 1968). Some educators believe that in order to successfully socialize students it is necessary to suppress viewpoints or sentiments that are not officially approved. Some also believe that any form of controversy is out of place in the schools. These educators easily support regulating student speech and conduct. If students espouse alternative viewpoints, they are held to be guilty of defying authority or disrupting the education enterprise and, therefore, in need of discipline. The second function, instruction, is generally accomplished through the transmission of knowledge— the teaching of specific courses—and except for religious instruction, this area, though politically very controversial, remains largely untouched by judicial decisions.

By affirming a student's right to express alternative, dissenting, or controversial opinions, the Fifth Circuit altered the school's political socialization function. This court made it clear that, within its jurisdiction, a state does not have an absolute right to control the cultural messages students shall receive. Further, school personnel do not have the right to suppress controversial expressions by the students, unless they explicitly violate the *Burnside* standard.

Although students had constitutionally protected speech rights in the Fifth Circuit it was not until 1969, when the United States Supreme Court handed down *Tinker v. Des Moines Independent Community School District* (1969), that it was clear that all students have such rights. Knowing that students were planning to protest the Viet Nam war by wearing black armbands to school, Des Moines school administrators enacted a regulation banning the wearing of such bands and suspended the students who violated the ban. Reversing the District and Eighth Court of Appeals decisions affirming the school administrators' actions (and denying the students' right to express themselves in this manner) the majority of the Court ruled in favor of the students. They stated that the armbands were a "silent, passive expression of opinion" akin to "pure speech" and thus protect by the First Amendment. The Court wrote,

> In our system, state-operated schools may not be enclaves of totalitarian-ism. School officials do not possess absolute authority over their students. Students in school as well as out of school are "persons" under our Constitution. They are possessed of fundamental rights which the State must

respect, as they themselves must respect their obligations to the State. In our system, students may not be regarded as closed-circuit recipients of only that which the State chooses to communicate. They may not be confined to the expression of those sentiments that are officially approved. In the absence of a specific showing of constitutionally valid reasons to regulate their speech, students are entitled to freedom of expression of their views… (S)chool officials cannot suppress "expressions of feeling with which they do not wish to contend. (*Tinker*, 1969, p. 737)

The Court affirmed the "material and substantial interference" standard that the Fifth Circuit had announced in the *Burnside* decision and went on to say "undifferentiated fear or apprehension of disturbance is not enough to overcome the right to freedom of expression." In order to "justify prohibition of a particular expression of opinion" school officials would now have to show that such action "was caused by something more than a mere desire to avoid the discomfort and unpleasantness that always accompany an unpopular viewpoint" (*Tinker*, 1969, p. 737).

This decision further affirmed the legalistic model for governing schools – a model including both the traditional democratic principles of constitutionally protected liberty for all citizens and elements of progressivism. If they had not done it before, educators would now be expected to acknowledge the First Amendment's presence in the educational scene and the political socializations methods used in the classroom and on campus would have to take that fact into account.

Fourteenth Amendment Due Process Rights

The question of whether K–12 students had procedural due process rights continued to be raised in the legal and educational literature and in the courts. In 1970 two scholars provided comprehensive reviews of student discipline cases. One of them, Higgins (1970), concluded that the seriousness of the disciplinary measure should determine which due process procedures should be afforded students. The other scholar, Katz (1970), found that courts "in different jurisdictions have demonstrated three distinct and in many ways, contradictory attitudes in dealing with challenges to school hearing proceedings" (p. 293). One group of court cases only required that the school have a reason for expelling a student but the reason didn't need to be disclosed and the "manner in which the sufficiency of the reason is determined is unimportant." The second group required "a full-dress adversary proceeding with all the emoluments of a criminal trial…." The third group, the majority of state court decisions, however, required "some sort of hearing be afforded in which the student has an opportunity to present his [sic] case to an impartial tribunal" (Katz, 1970, p. 293).

The Center for Law and Education reported that they were besieged with requests for help from students who had been suspended without any form of hearing (Mitchell, 1989). Investigations revealed that errors were being made, students were being suspended for constitutionally protected First Amendment activities, and suspensions were being used by teachers and principals as a weapon in the battle to desegregate schools, in the North as well as in the South. Moreover, some school officials were using the short-term suspension because it was "faster and less troublesome than detention ... [or] counseling, which requires specially trained personnel and having to run the risk of being vetoed by another school official" (Lines, 1972, p. 39).

The issue was finally resolved when the Supreme Court agreed to review a case that addressed the issue of students' constitutional rights focused on the procedural due process component of the Fourteenth Amendment. A group of students in the Columbus, Ohio, school district claimed that public school administrators deprived them of their education without a hearing of any kind and such action was unconstitutional. A three-judge federal court held for the students (*Lopez v. Williams*, 1973, renamed *Goss v. Lopez* at Supreme Court), and the district appealed directly to the Supreme Court. The school board and school officials refused to admit "their autonomy might be limited by constitutional requirements" and "were not going to give up until the United States Supreme Court told them they were wrong" (Zimring & Solomon, 1975, p. 474, quoting from an interview with two of the original attorneys for the plaintiffs). In deciding *Goss v. Lopez* (1975), the Supreme Court told them that they were, indeed, wrong, thus affirming, once again, the Legalistic model of governance.

The Court determined a student's interest in his/her continuing access to education is protected by both the property and liberty clauses of the Fourteenth Amendment. In the instant case, the Ohio education code created and defined the property interest. The liberty interest is the student's right to maintain his/her "good name, reputation, honor, or integrity." Charges of misconduct, if sustained and recorded, could seriously damage a student's "standing with ... fellow students ... and ... teachers as well as interfere with later opportunities for higher education and employment" (*Goss*, 1975, p. 736).

After weighing the interests of both the State and the students, the Court declared all students facing suspension "must be giving some kind of notice and afforded some kind of hearing" *before* being suspended unless the student's presence "poses a continuing danger to persons or property or an ongoing threat of disrupting the academic process" (*Goss*, 1975, pp. 739, 740). Such a student may be removed immediately but due process procedures must follow as soon as it is practical. Claims that the school district could not operate efficiently if required to provide some form of "notice and hearing" were rejected by the Court in stating, "We have imposed ... requirements which are, if anything, less than a fair minded school principal would impose upon himself in order to avoid unfair suspension" (*Goss*, 1975, p. 740).

Eighth Amendment and Corporal Punishment

In the 1970s some states permitted school personnel to administer corporal punishment to students as a means of maintaining discipline as "school authorities viewed corporal punishment as a less drastic means of discipline than suspension or expulsion...." (*Ingraham*, 1977, p. 657). The use of such punishment in a Florida junior high school, where the severity of the punishment caused physical injury to two students, prompted a lawsuit claiming that: (1) the paddling constituted "cruel and unusual punishment in violation of the Eighth Amendment and (2) to the extent that paddling is constitutionally permissible, the Due Process Clause of the Fourteenth Amendment requires prior notice and an opportunity to be heard" (*Ingraham*, 1977, p. 654). The students lost, however, as the Supreme Court, in a five to four decision, stated that the history of the Eighth Amendment and prior Court decisions confirmed that "it was designed to protect those convicted of crimes" and held that it "does not apply to the paddling of children as a means of maintaining discipline in public schools" (*Ingraham*, 1977, p. 665). The Court also found that due process procedures are not necessary prior to administering corporal punishment as its "practice is authorized and limited by the common law" (*Ingraham*, 1977, p. 683).

Fourth Amendment Search and Seizure

In 1985, the question of whether the Fourth Amendment was applicable to schools was answered when the Supreme Court decided *New Jersey v. T.L.O.* (1986). It was a search and seizure case, a school administrator having cause to search a student's purse and, in so doing, discovering drugs and evidence that the student was dealing. The administrator turned the items over to the police who filed charged against the student. While the issue before the Court was whether evidence seized in an unlawful school search could be excluded from juvenile court proceeding, the Court decided to consider the broader issue of whether the Fourth Amendment applies to searches by school officials.

The Court ruled that the Amendment's prohibition on unreasonable searches and seizures did apply to searches done by public school officials but the search of *T.L.O.'s* was not a Fourteenth Amendment violation. They chose not to address the exclusionary issue but discussed the appropriate standard for searches by school people instead. The probable cause standard that applies to searches of adults is not appropriate in the school setting, according to the Court, and so formulated a "reasonable suspicion" standard for the schools. According to Zirkel (2009), this decision served as an approximate turning point in the judicial activism of the Court. "While it continued the *Tinker* majority's movement of individual constitutional rights across the schoolhouse gate, *T.L.O.* also echoed the *Tinker* dissent's emphasis on giving school officials latitude when facing threats to the safety and security of public schools" (p. 706).

In his concurring opinion, Justice Powell articulated a view that the Court came to embrace more and more fully when addressing subsequent cases involving students' constitutional rights—that the Professional model, rather than the Legalistic model, is the more appropriate school governance model. He wrote, "I would place greater emphasis ... on the special characteristics of elementary and secondary schools that make it unnecessary to afford students the same constitutional protections granted adults and juveniles in a nonschool setting" (*T.L.O.*, 1986, p. 349). In addition, he believed that an adversarial relationship (such as law enforcement officers have with criminal suspects) rarely existed between school authorities and pupils. "Instead, there is a commonality of interests between teachers and their students" (*T.L.O.*, 1986, p. 351).

Expression and Search and Seizure Cases from the 1980s Onward

The Court has heard three additional freedom of expressions cases since 1985, *Bethel School District #403 v.* Fraser (1986), *Hazelwood School District v. Kuhlman* (1988), and *Morse v. Frederick* (2007). In the two 1980s decisions, the Court gave school authorities greater leeway to limit student expression on the school campus. In the *Bethel* case, a speech made by student *Fraser* was deemed to be lewd and indecent by school authorities and the Court agreed. Further, because the speech was not political, the school officials "can determine what speech is appropriate in the school setting" (Cambron-McCabe, 2009, p. 710). The speech rights of students in school "are not automatically coextensive with the rights of adults in other settings" and "a school need not tolerate student speech that is inconsistent with its 'basic educational mission' ... even though the government could not censor similar speech outside the school" (*Hazelwood*, 1988, p. 267).[6] And it was in this context that the Court considered the First Amendment claims of the students in *Hazelwood*. While the Court did not fully reverse *Tinker* in this case, it did rule that educators have final control over the contents of the student newspaper because it is (a) a part of the school's journalism curriculum and (b) the majority of costs for the paper are borne by the school district. A new category, school sponsored expression, was established by the *Hazelwood* decision making it permissible to censor student expression rights even when they did not "materially and substantially" interfere with the requirements of appropriate discipline, and were not lewd, indecent or libelous.

Two years after *Bethel* and *Hazelwood* legal scholar Chemerinsky wrote,

> Over the three decades of the Burger and Rehnquist Courts, there have been virtually no decisions protecting rights of students in schools. Indeed, there have been remarkably few rulings concerning students' speech, despite hundreds of lower court decisions on the topic. There have been only two Supreme Court cases concerning student speech in elementary,

middle school, and high schools, excluding cases concerning religious expression.... In both, the Court rejected the students' First Amendments claims and sided with the schools. (quoted in Yudof, Kirp, & Levin, 2002, p. 225)

The most recent expression case, *Morse v. Frederick*, handed down in 2007, further marginalized the *Tinker* conception of constitutionally protected freedom of expression. Ruling that a high school principal did not violate a student's speech rights when she confiscated his banner, a 6–3 Court majority rationalized its decision by, "distilling from *Frazer* two basic principles." The first was "the special characteristics of the school environment circumscribe students' First Amendment rights," the second that "*Tinker*'s mandate that school authorities must demonstrate 'substantial disruption' before regulating student speech during school-sponsored activities should no longer apply" (Conn, 2007, p. 160).

Also prominent on the Supreme Court docket since *T.L.O.* have been three additional Fourth Amendment search and seizure cases. Concerns about drug use by students have prompted school districts to adopt drug-testing programs in schools. The first drug policy challenge to reach the Court was *Vernonia School District 47J v. Acton* (1995). The policy required random testing of all students involved school athletics. In its decision, the Court ruled students' Fourth Amendment rights were not violated. Summing up the holding, Cambron-McCabe (2009) wrote, "The Court found the policy was narrowly tailored to athletes, where risk of harm was significant; was minimally intrusive; and furthered the school officials' responsibility to care for students." Blanket drug testing of all students was not permitted but, "when individualized suspicion exists, specific students can be tested without violating their constitutional rights" (p. 711).

The second case, *Board of Education v. Earls* (2002), also challenged a drug policy—one that required all students who wished to participate in any extracurricular activities to take a drug test and, further, to agree to submit to additional random testing if requested. The Court upheld this policy also, deciding even the individualized reasonable suspicion standard does not apply in this area.

The final case, *Safford Unified School District v. Redding* (2009), addressed the issue of whether a student strip search ordered by a vice principal was a violation of the student's Fourth Amendment rights. The Supreme Court declared that strip searches are suspect, and applied *T.L.O.*'s two-part reasonableness test—reasonable at inception and reasonable in scope—to determine whether Constitutional protection has been breached. While the search was reasonable at inception, the scope was not reasonable. The search of belongings and outer clothing falls within the reasonableness standard but a strip search requires "'distinct elements of justification' for school officials to conduct such a search."

It must not be "excessively intrusive in light the age and sex of the student and the nature of the infraction" and the Court found "that the degree of the assistant principal's suspicion did not 'match the degree of intrusion'" (Thompson, 2009, p. 167).

Thompson (2009) summarizes that the Court no longer fully embraces the Legalistic model of school governance but the judicial majority is still rejecting a conservative minority justice's call for a "full return to the doctrine of *in loco parentis*." He believes that the result gives "school officials the discretion they need to administer their schools, while subjecting the limits of their power to state and local school officials elected by their constituents" (p. 168).

The Civil Rights of Social Groups

Growth and contraction in support for the constitutional rights of individual students is just one facet of a sweeping civil rights movement that flourished during the middle years of the twentieth century. Aggressive grassroots action, belatedly supported by the courts, also tackled the segregation and denial of opportunity affecting children of various racial, ethnic and social groups. The Supreme Court's *Plessey v. Ferguson* decision in 1896 created the widely utilized "separate but equal" doctrine used to justify clearly separate but definitely not equal rights for those Americans, children and adults, who were not White. While the decision dealt with a commerce issue, it was quickly applied to all aspects of life. In the field of education, in many states, students from kindergarten through graduate school were segregated on the basis on color and ethnicity, attending schools and institutions that the Court, in 1954, would find to be not only inadequate but, in principle, a violation of the Fourteenth Amendment's equal protection clause.

Prior to 1954, efforts to overturn "separate but equal" education, in the federal court system, were focused on institutions of higher education. *Missouri ex rel. Gaines v. Canada* (1938), *Sipuel v. Board of Regents of the University of Oklahoma* (1948), *Sweatt v. Painter* (1950), and *McLaurin v. Oklahoma State Regents* (1950) all required the Supreme Court to focus on the "equal" provision and, in addition, "to determine whether separateness might carry with it subtle and unquantifiable inequalities" (Yudof et al., 2002, p. 368). Having successfully opened access to higher education, attention shifted to elementary and secondary schools. As early as 1946, in California, the federal district court ruled on K–12 ethnic segregation in *Mendez v. Westminster* (1946).

Mendez struck the first blow at *de jure* school segregation. Mitchell and Mitchell (in press) wrote, "In *Mendez*, the early twentieth-century tradition of local school districts establishing separate 'Mexican schools' was ruled illegal since the State of California, which had laws permitting racial separation, had not identified people of Mexican ancestry as a separate 'race.'" The decision was appealed but was affirmed by the Ninth Circuit Court of Appeals. The then Governor Earl Warren, prompted by the litigation, "backed the successful 1947 repeal of California Education Code provisions providing for segregation of Chinese, Japanese, Mongolian, or American Indian public school students."

Brown v. Board of Education (1954) and *Bolling v. Sharpe* (1954), its companion case, concerned elementary and secondary education students in four states and the District of Colombia. The decisions handed down found that "in the field of education the doctrine of 'separate but equal' has no place" (*Brown*, 1954, p. 484), that it was unconstitutional based on the Fourteenth Amendment (*Brown*) and the Fifth Amendment (*Sharpe*). Although *Brown* declared segregation unconstitutional, it provided no remedy, the formulation of a remedy framework came in the decision known as *Brown II,* in 1955.

The Supreme Court, in *Brown v. Board of Education* (1955), placed responsibility for desegregating the schools in the hands of the lower federal courts and the local school boards, the parties to act with "all deliberate speed" (*Brown II*, p. 310). It was a standard that "describes an unspecified remedy that would take effect in an undefined interval of time" (Yudof et al., 2002, p. 372). As a result, delay in implementing *Brown* was inevitable. According to Crump by putting "the defendants in charge of the remedy," the Court was "plac[ing] the fox in charge of bringing the hen house into compliance with law," while at the same time, the failure to provide clear rules "disadvantaged the honest politician who sincerely desired to achieve compliance" (Yudof et al., 2002, p. 373).

From 1955 until 1964 "all deliberate speed" was akin to the speed of a snail— moving in reverse. Or as Horowitz and Karst wrote, "[T]he desegregation of southern school districts was not characterized by speed, deliberate or otherwise" (Yudof et al., 2002, p. 373). Southern politicians and school boards employed all manner of resistance, and the Court, having no army to enforce its decisions, could do very little to stop it. It required the combined powers of the legislative, executive and judicial branches to force the desegregation of schools in the recalcitrant southern states. In what Rogers and Bullock characterized as the "administrative–judicial era" (Yudof et al., 2002, p. 375) did significant progress toward desegregation in the South finally come about.

In 1963, before he was assassinated, President John F. Kennedy sent a civil rights bill to the Congress. It was the political savvy and leadership of his successor, President Lyndon B. Johnson, however, that persuaded a foot dragging Congress to enact the Civil Rights Act of 1964. "This legislation empowered the Department of Health, Education, and Welfare (HEW) to withhold federal funds from school districts that discriminated against blacks and gave the Attorney General authority to file desegregation suits on the complaint of private citizens." To do this, "HEW promulgated guidelines requiring school districts to make a good faith start toward desegregation" (Yudof et al., 2002, p. 375). Kluger wrote in *Simple Justice* that during the next 10 years, in the area of education, "the federal government put the 1964 rights bill to a great deal of use. The Justice Department would bring legal actions against more than 500 school districts during the decade." And, HEW, "charged in 1965 with suspending federal education aid to school districts that discriminated racially, would file more than 600 actions" (Kluger, 1977, p. 759). In addition, the Elementary and Secondary Education Act was passed, "making sizable federal funds available to local school districts and providing the government with a mighty financial club to enforce compliance with the desegregation orders of federal courts" (Kluger, 1977, p. 760).

Following *Brown II* and prior to the 1964 Civil Rights Act, the Supreme Court rarely intervened in desegregation litigation pursued in the lower courts. *Cooper v. Aaron* in 1958, and *Goss v. Board of Education* in 1963 were the two exceptions. The first concerned the desegregation of the Little Rock, Arkansas, schools. In response to a court order, the school district was prepared to integrate Central High School but the state's governor ordered the posting of the National Guard at the front entrance to prevent the Black students from entering the building. Unable to persuade the governor to change his stand, President Eisenhower ordered military paratroopers to the city to protect the Black students as they attended classes. As a result of these activities, the school board petitioned the district court to suspend the implementation of the desegregation program for two and a half years. They claimed that a sound education program could not be maintained because of the disruption. The district court granted the petition, the ruling was appealed to the Eighth Circuit Court of Appeals who reversed the ruling, and then appealed to the Supreme Court. The Court declared that desegregation must continue.

In the second case, a number of school districts used pupil assignment laws to perpetuate one-race schools. One variation, which was at issue in *Goss*, was the use of a "minority to majority" student transfer plan which involved formally desegregating a district but then granting students who found themselves part of a racial minority in their new school permission to transfer back to their old school, the school where they would be once again in the majority. The Court said of this procedure, "the right of transfer, which operates solely on the basis of a racial classification, is a one-way ticket leading to but one destination, i.e. the majority race of the transferee and continued segregation" (*Goss*, 1963, p. 687).

After 1964, the Court granted *certiorari* to a number of appeals, the decisions of which caused a major change in the nature and pace of school desegregation in the South. The first was *Green v. County School Board* (1968). The Court, in rejecting the "freedom of choice" plan the New Kent County, Virginia, school district had adopted, told the district a "unitary, nonracial system of public education" (*Green*, p. 440) was what they needed to establish, and that delaying doing so was no longer tolerable. The burden on the school board was "to come forward with a plan that promises realistically to work and promises realistically to work now" (*Green*, p. 439). It also developed what became known as the *Green* factors—factors that might make a school racially identifiable. In addition to the student bodies, schools could also be racially identifiable with regard to faculty, staff, extracurricular activities, physical facilities, and transportation.

"The Court didn't further define what it meant when it said a plan had to 'work' and what 'effects" had to be undone and how, nor what it meant by a 'unitary system'" (Yudof et al., 2002, p. 380). It did, however, make clear what it meant by "now" when it decided *Alexander v. Holmes County Board of Education* (1969) and *Carter v. West Feliciana Parish School Board* (1970). It held that even a "few month's delay in desegregation to avoid disruption during the school year was impermissible and peremptorily ordered immediate desegregation" (Yudof et al., 2002, p. 380).

Civil Rights—the 1970s and Onward

Swann v. Charlotte-Mecklenburg Board of Education, handed down in 1971, was significant for two reasons. First the Court defined "with more particularity the responsibilities of school authorities in desegregating a state-enforced dual school system...." (*Swann*, p. 19). The Court informed school authorities that district courts could use any of the following, as deemed necessary, to achieve a unitary school system : (a) the closing of old schools and/or the location new school construction so that a duel system is either not perpetuated or reestablished; (b) the desegregation of school faculty and staff; (c) the rearrangement of school attendance zones; (d) the integration of extra-curricular activities; and (e) the transporting—bussing—of students to integrate formerly segregated schools. Second, since Charlotte-Mecklenburg was a large metropolitan school system that included urban, suburban, and rural areas, the Court acknowledged that a "metropolitan area with dense and shifting population, numerous schools, [and] congested and complex traffic patterns" would have more difficulty making adjustments but they, nevertheless, would have to be made (*Swann*, p. 15).

This decision came down in a time of political change at the national level as Republican Richard Nixon moved into the White House. The Center for National Policy Review, in its "Justice Delayed and Denied" report, concluded that "there is little question that the Nixon administration's negative policy declarations have impaired enforcement action and demoralized the HEW civil rights staff" (Kluger, 1977, p. 765). In addition, bussing, one of the ways mentioned in *Swann* to achieve integration, was publicly opposed by Nixon and that placed him in opposition to the Supreme Court. Indeed, "he instructed Justice Department officials to start drafting a constitutional amendment against bussing to nullify the Court's decision" (Kluger, p. 768). Such an amendment did not succeed, but his efforts provided him political capital with those who may not have objected to bussing Black students, but were enraged that White students should be transported to achieve integration. And yet by the 1972–73 school year, "46.3 percent of the black children in the eleven Southern states were attending schools in which the majority of children were white. No other sector of the nation had achieved anything near that degree of desegregation" (Kluger, p. 768).

Special Education

Non-White students in the South were not the only ones who faced school access problems. Many young people who were physically or mentally disabled were totally excluded from the public schools and parent coalitions were formed to politically and legally challenge the situation. In addition to lobbying various politicians they, too, brought the issue to the courts. *Mills v. Board of Education* (1972) and *Pennsylvania Association for Retarded Children (PARC) v. Commonwealth* (1972) were the two important cases and both decided in favor of the children.

PARC, a consent order handed down by the federal district court of Pennsylvania in 1971, is regarded as the first "right to education" case concerning disabled children. The order stated that "Having undertaken to provide a free public education to all of its children, including its exceptional children, the Commonwealth of Pennsylvania may not deny any mentally retarded child access to a free public program of education and training" (*PARC*, p. 1260).

Mills (1972), heard in the federal district court of the District of Columbia, was broader than PARC because it included all children excluded from publicly supported education. The court decreed that "no child eligible for a publicly supported education in the District of Columbia public school shall be excluded from a regular public school assignment … unless such child is provided (a) adequate alternative educational services suited to the child's needs, which may include special education or tuition grants…" The District was ordered to provide such an education "regardless of the degree of the child's mental, physical or emotional disability or impairment. Furthermore, defendants shall not exclude any child resident in the District of Columbia from such publicly supported education on the basis of a claim of insufficient resources" (*Mills*, p. 878).

As a result of winning these two cases, parents filed similar lawsuits in more than 30 states. Since it was clearly a national issue, political pressure was brought to bear on Congress and the legislative body enacted the Rehabilitation Act (Section 504), 29 U.S.C. sections 701-796.1 in 1973 and the Education for All Handicapped Children Act (also referred to as Public Law 94-142), now known as the Individuals with Disabilities in Education Act, 20 U.S.C. sections 1400-1490. Whereas Section 504 is an avowedly civil rights statute, Yudof (1984) notes that the handicapped children's act "was both a civil rights statute and a federal assistance statute all rolled into one" (p. 172). Moreover, while Congress established program responsibility, minimal funding has been provided by the federal government. The real financial burden is borne by state and local governments and state legislatures and local school districts are still struggling with this problem. A 1997 law review note stated a search of an "on-line database revealed that nearly 1,000 cases had been brought under the IDEA since it was first enacted" (Yudof et al., 2002, p. 703). They are still the single largest number of education cases heard by lower federal or state courts.

The Supreme Court's entry into the fray occurred when it was asked to rule that an instructional program provided to a deaf student must enable her to reach her highest potential in order to meet statute's "free appropriate public education" standard. In response the Court demurred, writing in *Board of Education v. Rowley* (1982) that

> Noticeably absent from the language of the statue is any substantive standard prescribing the level of education to be accorded handicapped children. By passing the Act, Congress sought primarily to make public education available to handicapped children.... Congress did not impose upon the States any greater substantive education standard than would be necessary to make such access meaningful. Thus, the intent of the Act was more to open the door of public education (to these children) on appropriate terms than to guarantee any particular level of education once inside. (quoted in Yudof et al., 2002, p. 705)

The Court viewed the statute as a civil rights act, providing students equal access to public schooling rather an "educational statute guaranteeing an optimal learning experience for handicapped youngsters" (Yudof, 1984, p. 171).

Western and Northern Desegregation

The plight of non-White students in the West was heard by the Supreme Court in 1973 when the jurists heard arguments in *Keyes v. School District No. 1* (1973). The school district of Denver, Colorado, had never been under a constitutional or statutory requirement that mandated or permitted racial segregation in its schools. However, parents of non-White students charged the school board with using methods that created or maintained racially or ethnically segregated schools throughout the district. The Court found that in some areas that segregation did exist, that it was maintained by state action, and that the "segregated core city schools were educationally inferior to the predominately 'white' ... school in other parts of the district—that is, 'separate facilities ... unequal to the quality of education provided'" (Keyes, 1973 p. 194).

However, in the first northern case, *Milliken v. Bradley* (1974), a majority of the Court began to limit commitment to fully desegregating schools by overturning a lower court order that had sought to bring about metropolitan integration in the greater Detroit area. While it was a large urban district like *Swann*, the area to be desegregated was made up of many school districts rather than one. Although schools within the city of Detroit were victims of *de jure* segregation (produced by governmental actions), the surrounding districts were not overt parties to this policy, so the Court found that rearranging their residential patterns, which had evolved from housing market choices, would be too complicated. Hence, the Court ignored both the role the state of Michigan had played, and the restrictive covenants and other actions some communities had taken to promote segregation.

Two large northern cities in Ohio that had continued to operate dual school systems were challenged to desegregate in *Columbus Board of Education v. Penick* (1979) and *Dayton Board of Education v. Brinkman* (1979). In these cases, the Court held that the districts' actions "had the effect of increasing or perpetuating segregation" (Dayton, 1979, p. 538). While other decisions continued defining the reach and limits of the various school district desegregation plans during the 1970s and 80s, the concerted effort on the part of the executive branch and the Supreme Court to provide all students with unitary school systems came to an end in 1991. As re-segregation of schools became substantial, the Court stepped back from its historic role as desegregation monitor and advocate.

In 1991, the Court in *Board of Education of Oklahoma City Public Schools v. Dowell* (1991) agreed with a district court's dissolution of a 1972 school desegregation decree "on the ground that the school board had complied in good faith for a sufficient amount of time" (Yudof et al., 2002, p. 418). Although a number of schools had been allowed to return to their one-race status, the Court's majority were of the belief that local control should govern the system, that the length of time a district was under court supervision should be considered in permitting a dissolution decree and practicality should play a significant role in determining the unitariness of the district.

The Oklahoma decision marks the death of the *Brown* decision as some of the lower courts in the South have since declared districts to be unitary whether they were or not, and holdings such as *Freeman v. Pitts* (1992; DeKalb County Alabama) and *Missouri v. Jenkins* (1995; Kansas City) have shoveled dirt upon its grave. Indeed, a number of the districts have made administrative decisions which have permitted their schools to become re-segregated. Moreover, in 2007, even voluntary plans to use race "when assigning some students to schools in an effort to end racial isolation and represent re-segregation" in Seattle, Washington, and Louisville, Kentucky, was rejected by the Court in its *Parents involved in Community Schools v. Seattle School District. No. 1 et al.* (2007).

Rights of Language Minorities in Schools

The Bilingual Education Act was passed by Congress in 1968; its purpose to "promote research and experimentation on how best to meet the needs of" non-English proficient (NEP) and limited-English proficient (LEP) students. The Office of Civil Rights (OCR), in 1970, extended "the nondiscrimination provisions of Title VI of the Civil Rights Act of 1964 to NEP and LEP students." However, little enforcement was undertaken by OCR.

Chinese-speaking students filed suit seeking "relief against the unequal educational opportunities" afforded them by the San Francisco School District and in 1974 the Supreme Court handed down the *Lau v. Nichols* decision. Basing its decision on Title VI of the Civil Rights Act, the San Francisco school district was found to have provided its Chinese-speaking minority with "fewer benefits than the English-speaking majority … which denies them a meaningful opportunity to participate in the educational program" (*Lau*, 1974 p. 569). The district was ordered to correct the situation.

The education of limited–English–proficient students has been highly controversial, both educationally and politically. This has been particularly true in regards to Spanish speaking students. This language group is the largest minority in the United States (and is growing rapidly). For example, California, whose schools now enroll a majority of non-White students, has the largest linguistic minority student population in the country, could not enact a new bilingual education law in 1987. Indeed, in 1998 California voters passed Proposition 227, an initiative that mandated English only instruction unless parents specifically request otherwise.

Sex Discrimination

Public schools, in general, are co-educational institutions. The differential treatment of male and female students, however, has long been commonplace. For example, for years girls were excluded from team sports. Textbooks defined male and female roles differently and teachers responded differently to the two genders. Once again, a substantial body of litigation and policy, focusing on discrimination emerged—this time based on gender rather than race. Congress addressed the issue, enacting Title IX of the Education Amendments of 1972, modeling that law on Title VI of the 1964 Civil Rights Act. Since its passage "the nonjudicial branches have become [the] primary definers and enforcers of equal educational opportunity with respect to gender" (Yudof et al., 2002, p. 541). Problems still exist but progress is being made. Title IX has also been used in cases of school districts failing to take appropriate action when students sexually harass another student such as in *Davis v. Monroe County Board of Education* 526 U.S. 629 (1999), for example. Initially, when a student faced harassment because of sexual orientation, as was the case in *Nabozny v. Podlesny* 92 F. 3d 446 (7th Cir. 1996), the issue of equal protection, rather than Title IX, was raised in trying the case. Most recently, *Education Week* (*Education Week*, 2010) reported that the Justice Department intervened in a harassment case—one involving gender stereotypes—invoking the protection of Title IX.

Undocumented Students

Education is seen as a basic social good but a majority in the Supreme Court has refused to affirm that it is a constitutionally "fundamental" interest or right.

It, however, is not "merely some governmental 'benefit' indistinguishable from other forms of social welfare legislation" (*Plyler v. Doe*, 1982). In 1975, Texas' state legislature voted "to withhold from local school districts any state funds for the education of children who were not 'legally admitted' into the United States." It also "authorized local school districts to deny enrollment in their public school to children not 'legally admitted' to the country" (p. 206). A class action was filed, the question being raised was whether, "consistent with the Equal protection Clause of the Fourteenth Amendment, Texas may deny to undocumented school age children the free public education that it provides to children who are citizen of the United Sates or legally admitted aliens" (p. 206). *Plyler v. Doe* answered the question. These children do have the same right to a free public education that all other children have.

To summarize, during the last 60 years individual students' constitutional rights and the civil rights of families and students as they relate to education were initially rather dramatically expanded but then substantially retracted. The 1969 *Tinker v. Des Moines* case identifies the high water mark for individual students' expression rights. In this decision, the Supreme Court affirmed that while one of the school's functions is the political socialization of students, young people may not to be confined to expressing only those sentiments that are officially approved. They have constitutionally protected First Amendment speech rights that they do not leave at the schoolhouse door. As the Court repeatedly addressed student expression rights in 1986, 1988, and 2007, however, each new decision granted school authorities broader powers to limit student expression on the school campus. By 2007, the *Morse v. Frederick* decision so marginalized student expression rights that "substantial disruption" no longer needed to be demonstrated for administrators to halt student expressions— making it clear that the *Tinker* ruling no longer applies.

Brown v. Board of Education of 1954 marked the high point in establishing the civil rights of social groups when it declared unconstitutional the doctrine of "separate but equal" in the public schools and mandated desegregation of dual race schools. Almost immediately, beginning with the imprecise remedy presented in *Brown II* (1955), this high ground began to slip away. Court guidance was so imprecise that resistant state and local school officials could stall implementing desegregation/integration plans for years. Through years of "all deliberate foot dragging" litigation, district after district hassled their way through the lower courts gradually chipping away at the *Brown* principle. Some districts actually did develop unitary school systems, but by 1991, the Supreme Court was no longer willing to act as the advocate for and monitor of integration. It was decided that instead of insuring results, simply spending an extended time was under court supervision was sufficient to justify releasing a district from court desegregation orders. By 2007, even voluntary plans using race as a factor in structuring the composition of student school attendance was rejected in the *Parents involved in Community Schools v. Seattle School District*.

Current judicial guidelines do as much to protect the privileges of advantaged citizens and the powers of public officials as to advance the constitutional and civil rights of the weak and the disadvantaged.

Notes

1 A number of the school desegregation cases make reference to the suspension and expulsion of Black students who attempted to desegregate White schools. The Wilcox County decision (*United States v. Wilcox County Board of Education*, 454 F.2d 1144 91972) handed down by the Fifth Circuit Court of Appeals is an excellent example.
2 Legalistic or legalization refers to the tendency "to discover, construct, and follow rules" as a method for settling disputes and to adhere to prescribed procedures in their formulation and application (Yudof, et al., 2002, p. 305).
3 Those who argued that education was a fundamental right protected by the federal Constitution lost the argument when the Court handed down its *San Antonio School District v. Rodriguez* (1973). The majority ruled that education was not among the rights explicitly or implicitly guaranteed by that document.
4 A group of African American students had been expelled from an Alabama state college because of their participation in civil rights demonstrations off campus. They filed in federal district court claiming a violation of their Fourteenth Amendment due process rights and then appealed the decision of the district judge who upheld the actions of the administration.
5 In *Thornhill v. State of Alabama* (1940) the Court ruled that "the right to communicate a matter of vital public concern is embraced in the First Amendment right to freedom of speech and therefore is clearly protected against infringement by state officials" (1966, p. 754) and so by including school authorities in the "state officials" category their actions, rules and regulations must also pass constitutional muster.
6 It is necessary to use *Hazelwood* because, while the Court cites *Bethel* as having stated that on pages 682 and 685, neither of those lines are found on said pages. The Court actually paraphrased its 1986 decision in *Hazelwood*.

References

Court Cases

Alexander v. Holmes County Board of Education, 396 U.S. 19 (1969).
Bethel School District No. 403 v. Fraser, 478 U.S. 675 (1986).
Blackwell v. Issaquena County Board of Education, 363 F.2d 749 (1966).
Board of Education of Independent School District #92 of Pottawatomie County et al. v. Earls et al., 536 U.S. 822 (2002).
Board of Education of Oklahoma City Public Schools v. Dowell, 498 U.S. 237 (1991).
Bolling v. Sharpe, 347 U.S. 497 (1954).
Brown v. Board of Education, 349 U.S. 294 (1955).
Brown v. Board of Education of Topeka, 347 U.S. 483 (1954).
Burnside v. Byars, 363 F.2d 744 (1966).
Carter v. West Feliciana Parish School Board, 396 U.S. 290 (1970).
Columbus Board of Education v. Penick, 443 U.S. 449 (1979).
Cooper v. Aaron, 358 U.S. 1 (1958).
Dayton Board of Education, 443 U.S. 526 (1979).
Dixon v. Alabama State Board of Education, 294 F.2d 150 (1961).
Due v. Florida A. & M. University, 233 F. Supp. 396 (1963).
Freeman v. Pitts, 503 U.S. 467 (1992).
Goss v. Board of Education, 373 U.S. 683 (1963).

Goss v. Lopez, 95 U.S. 565 (1975).

Green v. County School Board, 391 U.S. 430 (1968).

Hazelwood School District v. Kuhlman, 484 U.S. 260 (1988).

Hendrick Hudson District Board of Education v. Rowley, 458 U.S. 176 (1982).

Ingraham v. Wright, 430 U.S. 651 (1977).

Keyes v. School District No. 1, Denver Colorado, 413 U.S. 189 (1973).

Lau v. Nichols, 414 U.S. 563 (1974).

Lopez v. Williams, 372 F. Supp. 1279 (1973).

McLaurin v. Oaklahoma State Regents, 339 U.S. 637 (1950).

Mendez v. Westminster, 64 F. Supp. 544 (1946).

Milliken v. Bradley, 418 U.S. 717 (1974).

Mills v. Board of Education, 348 F. Supp. 866 (D.D.C., 1972).

Missouri ex rel Gaines v. Canada, 305 U.S. 337 (1938).

Missouri v. Jenkins, 515 U.S. 70 (1995).

Morse v. Frederick, 551 U.S. 393 (2007).

New Jersey v. T.L.O., 469 U.S. 325 (1986).

Parents Involved in Community Schools v. Seattle School District No. 1 et al., 551 U.S. 701 (2007).

Pennsylvania Association for Retarded Children (PARC) v. Commonwealth, 343 F. Supp. 279 (E.D.Pa., 1972).

Plessy v. Ferguson, 163 U.S. 537 (1896).

Plyler v. Doe, 457 U.S. 202 (1982).

Safford Unified School #1 v. Redding, 129 S.Ct. 2663 (2009).

San Antonio Independent School District v. Rodriguez, 411 U.S. 1 (1973).

Sipuel v. Board of Regents of the University of Oklahoma, 332 U.S. 631 (1948).

Swann v. Charlotte-Mecklenburg Board of Education, 402 U.S. 1 (1971).

Sweatt v. Painter, 339 U.S. 629 (1950).

Thornhill v. State of Alabama, 310 U.S. 88 (1940).

Tinker v. Des Moines Independent Community School District, 89 S.Ct. 733 (1969).

Vernonia School District 47J v. Acton, 515 U.S. 646 (1995).

West Virginia State Board of Education v. Barnette, 319 U.S. 624 (1943).

Woods v. Wright, 334 F.2d 369 (1964).

Published Works

Berkman, R. L. (1970). Students in court: Free speech and the functions of schooling in America. *Harvard Educational Review, 40*(4), 567–595.

Cambron-McCabe. (2009, June). Balancing students constitutional rights. *Phi Delta Kappan, 90*, 709–713.

Conn, K. (2007). Rights of public school officials to regulate student speech. *School Law Reporter, 49*(8), 159–161.

Dawson, R. E., & Prewitt, K. (1968). *Political socialization: an analytic study.* Boston: Little.

Education Week. (2010, April 7). Bullying incidents raise questions about role of school officials. *Education Week, 29*(28), 4.

Higgins, J. H. C. (1970). The discipline of secondary school students and procedural due process: A standard. *Wake Forest Law Review, 7.*

Katz, J. W. (1970). The opportunity to be heard in public school disciplinary hearings. *Urban Education, 4*(4), 292–309.

Kluger, R. (1977). *Simple justice.* New York: Vintage Books.

Ladd, E. T. (1970). Allegedly disruptive student behavior and the legal authority of school officials. *Journal of Public Law, 19*(2), 209–249.

Lines, P. (1972, July). The case against short suspension. *Inequality in Education, 12*, 39–46.

Manley-Casimir, M. E. (1978). The Supreme Court, students' rights and school discipline. *Journal of Research and Development in Education, 11*(4), 101–115.

Mitchell, T. K. (1989). *The role of state legislatures and state board of education in mediating the impact of the Tinker and Goss decision.* Unpublished doctoral dissertation, University of California, Riverside.

Mitchell, R., & Mitchell, D. (in press). The limits of desegregation accountability. In K. Simms, D. Brewer, R. Goodyear, & E. Bensimon (Eds.), *An introduction to urban education.* New York: Routledge, Taylor & Francis Group.

Seavey, W. (1957). Dismissal of students: 'Due process'. *Harvard Law Review, 70*(8), 1406–1410.

Thompson, D. P. (2009, September). Speaking of strip searches: Safford Unified Sch. Dist. v. Redding, 129 S.Ct. 2633 (2009). *School Law Reporter, 51,* 165–168.

Wuester, T. J. (1965). School expulsions and due process. *University of Kansas Law Review, 14,* 108–116.

Van Alstyne, W. (1963). Procedural due process and state university students. *UCLA Law Review, 10,* 368–389.

Yudof, M. (1974). Some aspects of discipline in Texas schools. *Journal of Law and Education, 3*(2), 221-231.

Yudof, M. (1984). Education for the handicapped: Rowley in perspective. *American Journal of Education, 163*(2), 163–177.

Yudof, M., Kirp, D., Levin, B., & Moran, R. (2002). *Educational policy and the law* (4th ed.): Australia/Belmont, CA: West/Thompson Learning.

Zimring , F. E., & Solomon, R. L. (1975). Goss v. Lopez: The Principle of the Thing. In R. Mnookin (Ed.), *In the interest of children* (pp. 449–508). New York: W.H. Freeman.

Zirkel, P. A. (2009). School law all stars: Two successive constellations. *Phi Delta Kappan, 90*(10), 704–708.

7

EDUCATION POLITICS AND EQUITY POLICY SINCE 1950

From Rights to Accountability

Carolyn A. Brown and Bruce S. Cooper

Introduction

The year was 1950, an important starting point in educational policy in the United States, thus providing an excellent turning point for an analysis of the dynamics between politics and public policy in education. In some ways, the year was a mid-20th century nadir for fair and just public education politics and policy in the United States. Schools were local, segregated in multiple ways, and inequitably funded. De jure racial segregation was in full sway in the schools, while de facto discrimination by race along with ethnicity, gender, and linguistic and academic capacity operated nearly everywhere. School funding policies that were largely dependent on local property taxes, resulting in an imbalance in school district wealth, were accepted as the status quo.

Children with limited English-speaking skills, and special educational and physical needs, for example, were ignored, shunted away, and thus hardly visible in public schools. In 1950, arguably, America's students were inequitably educated, and schools operated with few requirements to serve the needs of all children. Local districts, much less state and national governments, poorly evaluated schools.

At mid-century, K–12 education reform and improvement were barely on the national agenda. Education was primarily a local effort; the states' role was secondary and the federal involvement was limited to promoting better vocational, technical, and agricultural education (e.g., the Smith-Lever Act, 1914, and Smith-Hughes Act, 1917), and providing for the education of Native Americans (Johnson-O'Malley Act, 1934). Private schools, primarily operated by the Roman Catholic Church, served only about 8% of the student population and were hardly noticed on the national education agenda (Cooper, 1987).

Purpose of the Chapter

This chapter analyzes five education policy efforts between 1950 and 2000 that gave rise to a national focus on equality of educational opportunity for all children, regardless of their race, background, income, needs or locations. We argue that the politics of education changed as new interest groups emerged to fight for education support (Cooper, 2009; Boyd, 2002). These groups formed coalitions and moved education to the national agenda—from the Eisenhower era, through the liberal shift under presidents John F. Kennedy and Lyndon B. Johnson, through the conservative movement of the 1980s, right up to the Obama regime.

These 50-plus years of education politics led to important policy outcomes that brought educational equity to center stage and shifted education politics from the local and state arenas to the national levels. This growing nationalization of education politics began with a drive toward a social equity agenda and moved to a focus on academic equity. Since 1950, national politics have led to the formation of national policies; and the United States is, arguably, moving toward a unified system of education with common standards, curricula, and tests.

This chapter focuses on the relationship between political movements and public policy formation in education, highlighting five major movements between 1950 and 2000. Boyd (1998) made the point that to understand reforms in education, we need to relate the politics to the policies, to see the "entanglement of policy and political knowledge in the domains of organizational administration..." as "policy is designed to influence or control public and private behaviors" (p. 129).

Five Political Challenges, Five Education Policies

Five major policy initiatives have shifted the centers of power for education politics since 1950. Education politics and resulting policy have grown more fully national and "nationalized", as education moves to the U.S. agenda. President Obama is continuing the drive toward a stronger federal role in assuring equity in education, which has developed around five key policies resulting from five major political movements that are the basis of this chapter:

1. *Racial De-Segregation Politics:* In 1954, in the *Brown v. Board of Education of Topeka* decision, the U.S. Supreme Court determined that racial segregation of public schools was a violation of the Fourteenth Amendment "Equal Protection" clause of the Constitution.
2. *Federal Funding for Poor and Non-English Speaking Students:* Eleven years later, in 1965, under pressure from the liberal presidential administration of Lyndon Johnson, Congress passed the Elementary & Secondary Education Act (ESEA) to provide direct federal funding to schools serving disadvan-

taged children, including those in poverty and those who entered school with limited proficiency in English.

3. *State Funding Equity:* In 1971, the California Supreme Court in *Serrano v. Priest* extended the right to an equal education to children affected by school district poverty, declaring that district funding inequities were unconstitutional. Similar equity lawsuits have been filed in an additional 45 states.

4. *Special Education Equity:* Congress passed the landmark PL 94–142 law in 1975 that required a free, public education that met the unique needs of children with disabilities.

5. *No Child Left Behind and National Standards:* In 2001, a Republican Congress reauthorized the ESEA as No Child Left Behind, which substantially expanded the authority of the federal government in enforcing accountability standards for student performance and teacher quality. The Obama administration is continuing the federal involvement with his active support of the Common Core (national) standards and its increasingly rigorous requirements for federal "Race to the Top" funds.

A Framework for Analysis

The three P's of education reform are politics, policy, and progress, where social progress can only occur when politics and policy are closely aligned. This chapter asserts that the major policy changes in education between 1950 and 2010 can be viewed as attempts to redress inequity through the influence of either interest group participation or the use of power resources by specific key policy actors.

Interest Group Participation

One approach starts with the "who" of education policy making—examining the political leaders, those policy entrepreneurs who originate, advocate, enact or block policy initiatives. An impressive "who's who" of education policy influence can be developed for each of the large and surprising policies of the last 60 years. This "who's who" includes individuals who through topical expertise, social or organizational position, political acumen, and/or personal charisma have been able to articulate ideas, inspire loyalty, negotiate agreements, and/or coerce compliance. In some policy areas the key actors are insiders to the educational establishment; in other cases, they have been community organizers and activists; and in still others they have been based in universities, industry or government.

Power Resources

Many observers analyze policy making by examining the distribution and exercise of political power among key actors and groups. These analyses sometimes emphasize the distinctions between executive, legislative and judicial roles and authority. It is equally popular to differentiate power resources found at various levels of policy making and governance. More often, analysts try to map the utilization of power resources available to various stakeholders who are promoting or resisting policy change.

We now discuss how each of these five major policy developments in education was formed through political actions and activism. Three of the five policies were the result of interest group participation: integration, fiscal equity, and special education. The remaining two were influenced by the power resources of major inside political actors, leading to the Elementary and Secondary Education Act, and the passage of the No Child Left Behind Act and the accountability movement.

1. Schools and Racial Desegregation

We see a complicated mix of politics and policy around the issues of racial equity and quality education for all. When Congress and presidents could not (or did not) act, school reformers turned to the federal or state courts, depending on the issues and whether the rights of students were protected by the U.S. or state constitutions. The emerging politics of race in education in the 1950s were deeply controversial, which restrained legislative action and forced reformers to use community activism and, ultimately, the courts to gain changes.

A key trigger for new policies in U.S. education was the all-important *Brown v. Board of Education of Topeka* (1954) case before the U.S. Supreme Court, which ruled that racial segregation of schools was a violation of the Fourteenth Amendment of the U.S. Constitution, guaranteeing "equal project under the law." This decision went off like a skyrocket, emerging from and supporting the national civil rights movement and similar efforts to desegregate public and private services and institutions.

So, while the executive and the legislative branches were unable to end the discrimination policies in local education, the judiciary took strong action, using the Constitution's guarantee of equal rights. Green (2008) captured the need for government policy intervention concerning issues of racial (de) segregation when he explained that "the existing racial hierarchies made it difficult for communities of color to self-determine and shape their collective selves and participate fully in a democratic society" (p. 388).

Recent census data show that 47% of all Americans are persons of color, making racial equity in education—both its politics and its policy—a critical issue in this analysis. Once the *Brown* decision was handed down by the high court, states and localities had to deal with issues of integration (or at least "desegregation"), which hardly eliminated racial separation as the policies followed the politics. But new policies and programs did begin to offer opportunities in cities, while the suburbs remained more White than Black. As Wells (1991) so well explained,

Although the degree of racial insensitivity appeared to be diminishing over time, the prejudice found in the white suburbs forced many transfer students to make difficult choices. They could either suppress their anger and frustration, re-create their own racial attitudes and distance themselves from people of color, or search for a difficult balance between their critique of white racism and their need to survive in a predominantly white society. (p. 239)

Thus, legally mandated integration did not immediately lead to acceptance; and the civil rights movement, civil disobedience, and protests in the 1960s took the principles of equality and civil rights of the *Brown* decision and moved them from the courts to the community, city councils, local school boards, and Congress, as described more fully below. But without the civil rights mandates, as affirmed by the courts, the politics might have remained unfocused; and the devices for changing school policies and practices might well have gone untested and unchanged. In addition, protest groups were willing to return to court again and again to push for civil rights. As late as 2001, in *Alexander v. Sandoval,* special interest groups sued school districts for the use of federal funding (Title VI dollars) for obvious discrimination—but not for unintentional or non-legal treatment of people of color.

Applying the dual focus of politics and policy, as related to school desegregation, we see that the political groups were often unable, using democratic institutions (Congress, state legislatures, local school boards), to force integration. Perhaps the elected officials were unwilling or uninterested in making new policies to increase school integration, as many White voters were not in favor in the early 1950s of admitting Black children to their schools. The civil rights movement was just starting, which initially hardened the lines between integrationists and the well-entrenched mainstream segregationists.

By the 1960s, the politics shifted from the democratic arenas to the courts to the "streets" and to the courts, where more liberal judges, appointed by presidents Kennedy and Johnson, and even Eisenhower, acted to interpret the Equal Protection clause of the Fourteenth Amendment—and ruled that segregation by race was not legal. Thus, the *Brown* decision gave courage to local groups to protest, picket, and press communities to close all-Black schools or to pair up Black and White schools for racial integration. Thus, the politics were initially limited, but the policy changes were dramatic.

The courts were unable to act alone; but they stimulated special interest groups and the politics began to change the policy—town by town, school district by district. Picketing, sit-ins, and boycotts were systematically arranged through organizations such as the NAACP under the leadership of Dr. Martin Luther King, Jr. the Urban League, the Student Non-violent Coordinating Committee (SNCC), and others. These politics led to policy changes encouraged by the leadership of the Supreme Court under Chief Justice Earl Warren. The civil rights movement, the courts, civil action, and racial upheavals of the 1960s moved the policy agenda ahead and gave courage to various political advocacy groups.

The legislative process alone did not help to desegregate or improve education for poor children of color. It took strong direct action and aggressive court decisions. Active, visible, grass-roots organizing helped move the racial desegregation issues to the courts, where constitutional provisions sometimes overcame the shortcomings of the voting process, and started the movement to integrate public schools.

By 1964, however, the Democrats had control of Congress and the White House under Lyndon Johnson and were able to pass major legislation: most notably the Civil Rights Act of 1964 and the Elementary and Secondary Education Act (ESEA) of 1965. The Civil Rights Act and ESEA are central to the education politics and policies in the late 1960s and through the 1970s. Green (2008) states that "Education remains the most important crucible for remedying disparities, enhancing life opportunities, developing citizens, and promoting a genuine democracy" (pp. 405–406).

Progress in improving education for children of color has come slowly, as society itself has struggled to define the role of race in education. Today, desegregation in schools is far from complete, and a seemingly intractable achievement gap between racial groups persists. As Boger (2000) observed, "We risk a rapid return to a time when each school child could and did identify 'white schools' and 'black schools' simply by reference to the predominant race of the children attending" (p. 1794).

2. Federal Educational Programs for the Poor and Limited English Proficient

The *Brown* ruling brought attention to the quality of education for African American students and fueled a larger national discourse about the nature of education for all children. First, President Kennedy and then President Johnson were concerned about the number of American children growing up in poverty, based on data on child poverty that became available with the 1950 and 1960 census (Bailey & Mosher, 1968). According to U.S. Census data, 16% of America's children were living in poverty, largely in rural and inner-city, urban areas. This new awareness of child poverty—and its potential impact on education—converged with the political unrest brought about by the civil rights movement.

African Americans, who constituted 13% of the population and saw 65% of their children living in poverty (Snyder & Shafer, 1996), wanted an education for their children equal to what many White children were receiving. School integration was only part of the answer. How were the schools going to find the resources to educate children coming to school from poor families? President Johnson's War on Poverty stimulated the development of legislation to meet the needs of poor children both in and out of school.

The politics behind the War on Poverty, of which ESEA was part, flowed from the pinnacle of political power—part of the emerging interest in education by the executive branch of the federal government. The politics of ESEA in 1965 was top down—from the president to Congress to states and localities. And arguably, the federal involvement in education has continued as an executive branch initiative through the No Child Left Behind Act, which was developed by a committee appointed by the Bush administration to promote George W. Bush's campaign promise to "leave no child behind" (*Fact Sheet*, 2003). The Obama administration's current proposed ESEA reauthorization, *Blueprint for Education,* continues the executive leadership to increase involvement in public education.

Although President Kennedy had introduced legislation during his brief term of office, not until President Johnson took office after Kennedy's assassination did pressure from the administration, exerted on Congress, lead to passage of legislation aimed at providing federal resources to local schools explicitly for the education of poor children (Jennings, 2001). Early school funding legislation under the Kennedy administration had "run aground because of resistance from advocates of aid to private schools… [who] wanted their schools to be included in any federal programs" (Jennings, 2001, p. 3). Largely, this resistance came from the U.S. Catholic Conference, which operated approximately 85% of American private schools (NCES, 2004). Advocates for "separation of church and state," led by the National Education Association (NEA), opposed any federal aid to private and religious schools (Jennings, 2001).

Aside from the private school issues, two other groups rose up in opposition to federal aid to education. Southern congressional representatives opposed federal funds to education because they feared those funds would be followed by federal mandates—specifically, requirements for greater racial integration. In addition, Republican members of Congress and their conservative constituents suspected that federal funding would lead to federal regulatory involvement in and control of K–12 schools (Jennings, 2001).

Localism in school government was also deeply entrenched in the institution of American education. State-level involvement in regulating and funding schools was just beginning to grow in the 1950s. Direct federal funding of K–12 schools for instructional programs was a new concept. Objections by Southerners, if not removed, were rendered irrelevant in 1964 when Johnson signed the Civil Rights Act, which ended the legal barriers to full access to, and participation in, all U.S. institutions—including schools (Bailey & Mosher, 1968).

Johnson responded to the conflict between the U.S. Catholic Conference and the NEA by appointing the Gardner Commission, charged with developing a compromise (Bailey & Mosher, 1968). Although, the Gardner Commission worked to develop solutions, Johnson, himself, is credited with much of the political effort that eventually resulted in the passage of the first national school equity legislation, the Elementary and Secondary Education Act of 1965 (ESEA) (Jennings, 2001).

The final ESEA legislation required that the funds be distributed directly to schools, according to the number of poor children in each school—public or private (or religious). School districts were designated to act as the public trustee for the funds for schools (ESEA, 1965). The effect was that the districts allocated units (teachers, instructional assistants, and supplies) to impoverished public and private schools, so no money was directly received by private schools. Both the U.S. Catholic Conference and the NEA were satisfied and withdrew their objections, clearing the way for ESEA's passage (Bailey & Mosher, 1968).

Johnson managed to remove the final obstacle, including conservatives' fear of federal regulatory interference in local schools, by including a clause in the legislation assuring that the federal government could not "exercise any direction, supervision, or control over the curriculum, program of instruction, administration or personnel or over the selection of any instructional materials in any educational institution or school system" (Jennings, 2001, p. 4). This legislative compromise assured that the Democratic majority in Congress wouldn't meet with enough resistance from Republicans to kill the bill, and ESEA was passed in 1965.

As the political climate of education has shifted and re-shifted since 1965, ESEA has changed. Throughout the 1970s media attention and public opinion focused increasingly on the failure of American schools to provide students with sufficient skills and knowledge to allow them to contribute to business and industry for Americans to remain economically competitive in global markets. Levin (1999) frames the education reform movement as an international (and largely conservative) political movement during the Reagan-Thatcher years. Others have pointed to a real decline in educational quality as the result of social inequities (Kozol, 1967, 1995; Rebell, 2005). Whatever the reasons, American education throughout the 1970s became increasing perceived as lagging behind other developed countries. In 1981 the Reagan administration appointed the National Commission on Excellence in Education to explore these concerns.

The release of *A Nation at Risk* in 1983 was a seminal event in the denigration of American schools, which has been cited repeatedly since its release as evidence that schools needed greater institutional oversight and higher standards for accountability. Tracing the social and political conditions that created a belief in the failure of American schools is beyond the scope of this paper; but these factors, arguably, have led to a greater federal involvement in schooling; and ESEA and its subsequent reauthorizations have been vehicles for this increasing federalization of education.

ESEA's 1988 reauthorization, the Hawkins-Stafford Act, liberalized how funds could be spent at the school level—adding the school-wide project provision that allowed schools to use ESEA Title I funds for "whole school reform" without having to account for eligibility of individual students by poverty (Wong & Meyer, 2001). By liberalizing Title I spending, the school-wide project model expanded discretionary spending of Title I dollars by school principals and local school boards. This new direction also increased flexibility in how Title I dollars were spent, eliminating the requirements to test just Title I eligible students each year and, thus, called into question how schools were being held accountable for the achievement of all students (Wong & Meyer, 2001). By 1994, over half of Title I schools were qualified for school-wide project funding. As a result, the 1994 reauthorization tightened accountability standards for school-wide project schools (Taylor & Piche, 1990).

Over the next decade, the standards and accountability movement would change the political environment in which schools functioned and would open the doors for increasing federal involvement. The 2001 ESEA reauthorization, entitled No Child Left Behind (NCLB)—and the volumes of regulations that have grown from it—have made significant changes in the original legislation. NCLB essentially rendered the 1965 compromise with Republicans null and void by using the ESEA reauthorization as a vehicle for imposing unprecedented levels of federal accountability standards on all schools.

The politics of federal involvement in education has changed dramatically since ESEA was first authorized in 1965. A plethora of research has shown that poverty does, indeed, affect a child's opportunity and even their ability to learn, and that additional resources are required to meet the needs of these poor children (Coleman, 1966; Anderson, 1992). When we examine 44 years of federal compensatory programs for children living in poverty, we find increases in the of role of federal politics of school equity, but the effects of these education policies over the years are not entirely clear across the states and localities.

First, how do we define progress when it comes to educating poor children? We certainly have made changes in holding schools, districts, and states accountable for the learning outcomes of all students—even (and especially) marginalized populations of poor and minority students; however, a substantial gap still remains between achievement of students from various racial and class groups. (Whites and Asians consistently outperform African Americans and Latinos, and children from affluent homes outperform students living in poverty on standardized tests.) (*Nation's Report Card*, 2005).

We have seen a larger federal presence in education as the nation is moving toward a more standardized, and some would argue, a more equalized education for all. But, if progress were to be measured—according to President Johnson's vision in 1965 that extra funding would lead to better education which would pull poor children out of the cycle of poverty (Bailey & Mosher, 1968)—the policies of ESEA have clearly not succeeded. In 1965, for example, 16% of America's children were living in poverty; today 18% live in poverty.

Throughout the 1960s, the movement toward equal educational opportunity for all children that had begun with the *Brown* decision also rippled through the populations of students who came to school without proficiency in English. In 1968, Congress added Title VII to ESEA under the Bilingual Education Act, which provided federal funds as competitive grants directly to school districts to be used for educational programs, teacher training, instructional assistants, development and dissemination of materials, and implementation of parent involvement projects for students whose native language was not English (*Bilingual Act: Twenty Years Later*, 1988). The law did not require provision of bilingual education; and in line with ESEA goals, the Bilingual Education Act placed emphasis on low-income students by disallowing the participation of students from moderate-income families (*Bilingual Act: Twenty Years Later*, 1988).

Implementation of bilingual education, and the requirements to provide instruction in a student's native language as well as English, remained firmly at the local level with Massachusetts being the first state to institute extensive bilingual education in 1971 with several other states following.

In 1974, interest group pressure through the use of the judiciary was successful when the Supreme Court ruled in *Lau v. Nichols* (1974) that "San Francisco's failure to develop an appropriate program for Chinese-speaking students prevented the students from participating and achieving in school because of the limitations placed on them by the language barrier" (Ryan, 2002, p. 3). The U.S. Department of Education reacted to *Lau* with the "*Lau* Guidelines" to provide specific guidance to school districts that were failing to comply with ESEA Title VII. And Congress responded to the *Lau* decision by including "national origin" in the language of the Equal Educational Opportunities Act of 1974, which prohibited states from denying equal educational opportunities to students based on "race, color, sex, or national origin" (Ryan, 2002, p. 4).

Advocates for bilingual education continued to use the courts to clarify how bilingual services should be provided. The debate continued over whether non-English speaking students should be educated in a bilingual or English-only immersion environment. Federal courts—especially the Fifth and Ninth circuits—in areas with high populations of Spanish-speaking students maintained the *Lau* position that "school are not free to ignore the needs of limited English speaking children for language assistance to enable them to participate in the instructional program" (*Lau v. Nichols*, 1974), but the courts did not specifically require bilingual education.

In 1998, the referendum system in California took center-stage in how the politics of bilingual education would play out. Ron Unz, a wealthy Republican and former gubernatorial candidate, used California's referendum system—and his own money—to initiate and promote Proposition 227, which passed in 1998 and specifically prohibits public school teachers from using a language other than English for instruction. Under Proposition 227, children with limited English proficiency spend one year in a sheltered English classroom, and thereafter they are immersed in the English-only mainstream (Ryan,

2002). Additionally, the law allows parents to choose to "opt in" to bilingual education programs (Crawford, 2000).

The politics of language in education has not yet settled into policy. Initiatives to outlaw bilingual education have been instituted in several other states. The debate over how best to educate limited-English-proficiency students has continued to rage, and has found new momentum after the passage of NCLB, which requires these students to pass English-language based standardized tests. Advocacy groups keep leading the charge for legislation that recognizes the special needs of children who do not speak English as a first language.

3. Politics of Fiscal Equity

Much as the *Brown* decision attempted to remove discrimination based on students' race, the next key political struggle in education was to reduce the effects of inequities in property-based school tax resources, which were the major sources of school funds. As King, Swanson, and Sweetland (2003) explained, "Courts are the formal mechanisms created by society for evaluating social policies with parameters established by constitutional and statutory authority...; furthermore, judicial interpretations often stimulate (even compel) legislatures to alter school finance policy" (p. 272).

The school financial equity movement began when the California high court in *Serrano v. Priest* (1971) found that the state's public schools were inequitably funded, based on inequalities in local property wealth and tax base and ordered the state to provide more funding to poorer districts and use other methods of reducing the differences in per-pupil expenditures in property rich and property-poor communities. Like *Brown,* the *Serrano* decision involved poor families being discriminated against in education, this time based on income rather than race or ethnicity.

As James Guthrie (2004) explained:

> In 1964, John Serrano spoke with his son Anthony's middle school principal. He inquired if there was some way in which the caliber of his son's schooling could be enhanced. In candor, the principal counseled Mr. Serrano to move, for as long as the family resided in Baldwin Park [a poor section of Los Angeles County], his children would be unlikely to receive the quality education they preferred. (p. 3)

Baldwin Park, California, raised less money for education per student when compared to, say, fancier Beverly Hills or Santa Barbara, because Baldwin Park required twice the millage (property tax) rate, as compared to the richer nearby communities, just to raise half the per pupil amount. When the Serrano family took their equity case to the California high court, experts reported dozens of such stories among California's almost 1,200 local school districts. "The wealthiest [districts] … had 15 times the level of assessed value per student as the poorest" (Guthrie, 2004, p. 4).

For the first time, in the *Serrano* case, economic discrimination based on the mal distribution of property wealth (i.e., assessed valuation of land, homes, and commercial-industrial buildings), which caused schools in poor areas to have fewer resources than those in wealthy property areas, was found by California's Supreme Court to be in violation of the equal protection provisions of the California Constitution. For example, Brimley and Garfield (2008) explain that the California high court also cited the Fourteenth Amendment of the U.S. Constitution as a basis for their decision.

As Odden (1992) explained, "Using both the equal protection clause of the 14th Amendment of the U.S. Constitution and state constitution education clauses, cases argued that it was unconstitutional for local property wealth to be linked with revenues per pupil" (p. 3).

In 1973, The U.S. Supreme Court ruled, however, in *Rodriguez v. San Antonio Independent School District* that income was not a protected category like race, gender, and religion. Thus, state-level lawsuits have confirmed that many state constitutions do protect the rights of citizens under their equal protection and state education clauses, using mainly the state constitutional provisions, not the U.S. Constitution. Thus, the politics of financial equity echoed the politics of racial equality (*Brown*), and gradually between 1974 and the present, the funding of schools has shifted from the less equal local property tax sources, to broaden state funding sources to provide somewhat greater equity district-by-district.

As a matter of federal policy, this equity principle was overturned in the Texas school finance case, *San Antonio v. Rodriguez* (1974), which declared that fiscal equity was not a federal right under the U.S. Constitution, and that each state now was required, if it chose to pursue equity, to rely on provisions of its own State constitution. To date 45 states have filed some kind of lawsuit seeking redress for in equitable funding of districts. Again, the politics of education, and the resulting policies, were triggered by an inequity in resources and forced states to take a more active political role in education funding. For example, New Jersey was forced by the state court to pass a state income tax law to raise money to equalize property-poor districts.

The key political actors in the politics of equity were local school leaders, working closely with lawyers and other policy experts in a state-after-state struggle. While policies allowed discrimination based on wealth and income, politics as in *Brown* made it difficult to impossible for residents in low-income communities to muster the political clout to change state regulations. So, going to state court has been the strategy used for fiscal equity claims, since the Fourteenth Amendment of the U.S. Constitution protects traditional categories (race, gender, age groups) but does not consider poverty as a protected group. Of the 45 states that have filed some form of state equity lawsuits, 23 states have been successful at overturning the funding policies and requiring greater state funding to balance lower local tax income.

After the court actions in these states, the political process shifted to the state legislatures and governors, who must raise the funds to provide greater equity. For example, New Jersey had its *Serrano*-type decision in 1973 with *Robinson v. Cahill,* wherein a poor Jersey City family, the Robinsons, sued New Jersey Governor Cahill and won (Lehne, 1978). But the Rutgers Law Center that organized the suit has returned to court 14 times (in seven *Robinson* cases) and then seven new ones, called *Abbott v. Burke,* to force the New Jersey legislature to ante up more funding for the 31 poorest "Abbott districts" (*Progress Toward* …, 2009).

New Jersey is interesting because it is one of the richest, highest spending states in the nation, with some of the most impoverished communities in Newark, Jersey City, Paterson, Camden, Passaic, and other areas. We see powerful examples of just how key education improvements, like funding equity, can start in the judiciary, then the courts can force the governor and legislature to provide greater financial equity. Recently, the high court in New Jersey acknowledged that the poor districts under the *Abbott* decisions, are now spending as much as the richer districts, and discontinued the case (*Progress Toward*, 2009).

So, as we've seen in this section, the politics of funding equity has been focused initially in the courts; voter organization and turnout in the nation's poorest districts tend to be low and to lack state level influence. Thus, the courts have both forced and empowered governors and legislative leaders to provide financial equity policies that provide greater financial equity in states like California in *Serrano* and New Jersey in *Robinson* and then *Abbott.*

4. Federal Legislation for Children with Special Needs

Legislation to establish policies that entitled handicapped children to a free public education was the result of years of activism by advocacy groups—first through the courts and later through direct lobbying in Congress. The landmark policies in the early 1970s, were set by two laws. First, Congress passed Section 504 of the Rehabilitation Act (1973), stating that "No otherwise qualified individual with a disability in the United States, shall solely by reason of his or her disability, be excluded from the participation in, be denied the benefits of, or be subjected to discrimination under any program or activity receiving Federal financial assistance."

And then in 1975, the enactment of the Education of All Handicapped Children Act (1975) took important steps to guarantee children with special needs a quality education in the "least restrictive" classroom environment, based on clinical assessments by a team of specialists and the creation of an Individualized Education Plan (IEP) for each "classified" child.

The Council for Exceptional Children—founded in 1922 at Teachers College, Columbia University to advocate for the education of children with special needs—along with two groups founded by parents of handicapped children to provide support for and advocate for the needs of their children—formed the core of the interest group activism that led to the policy requiring free, public education for handicapped children. Before 1975, handicapped children were educated in institutions, separate facilities, or not at all. These groups fought their battle in court and used the "equal educational opportunity" argument that was used in *Brown* (1954).

The Civil Rights Movement … provided the initial impetus for the efforts to secure educational rights for students with disabilities. In *Brown* … the Supreme Court unknowingly laid the foundation for future right to education cases on behalf of students with disability. (Russo & Osbourne, 2008, p. 7)

In 1972, two additional state court cases (*Pennsylvania Association for Retarded Children v. Commonwealth of Pennsylvania* and *Mills v. Board of Education of the District of Columbia*) provided seminal rulings in favor of groups of parents advocating for public school access for their disabled children (Itkonen, 2009).

Not only did these courts agree that handicapped children were entitled to a free, appropriate public education, but they added that "no mentally retarded child, or child thought be mentally retarded could be assigned to a special education program or be excluded from the public schools without due process" (Russo & Osbourne, 2008, p. 9). The right to due process would become a cornerstone of special education legislation.

With cases pending in 21 states by 1973, advocacy groups for special needs children began to change strategy when the U.S. Supreme Court ruled against the plaintiff in the school finance case, *San Antonio v. Rodriquez*, claiming that an equal education "is not within the limited category of rights … as guaranteed by the Constitution" (*San Antonio v. Rodriguez*, 1973). Concerned that they might lose, if appeals were brought before the U.S. Supreme Court, advocacy groups took their appeals to Congress relying on a lobbying rather than a litigious strategy.

Through consistent activism and lobbying, the movement for education for handicapped children found two powerful advocates in Senator Harrison Williams (D-NJ) and Senator Jennings Randolph (D-WVA). These men had been active in disability rights and together introduced a bill in Congress to provide incentives to states to provide public school services to children with disabilities.

School districts across the country began to view inclusion of special needs children in public schools as inevitable and were concerned that further legislation might not provide adequate funding. They also feared the impact of parents' right to due process on districts' decisions about student placement. To ensure that their interests were considered, districts joined forces with parent groups to advocate for legislation for the education of handicapped children (Itkonen, 2009).

Representative George Miller (D-CA) negotiated an agreement between parent advocacy groups and the National School Boards Association, and which the Education for All Handicapped Children Act (PL 94-142) was passed in 1975. This law spelled out a "Bill of Rights" for children with special needs. This law included a free, and appropriate to their unique needs, public education for all children, regardless of the severity of the disability. The education is to be conducted in "the least restrictive environment", based on an individualized education program, and developed respecting parents/guardians procedural due process rights, utilizing nondiscriminatory assessments, and inviting parental participation (Itkonen, 2009).

The politics of interest group advocacy through the judiciary and then the legislative branch of government moved equality of educational opportunity forward. Today, over 100 parent advocacy groups form the Consortium of Citizens with Disabilities (CCD, 2009), which continues to advocate for the needs of disabled children in school districts, state legislatures, Congress, and the courts. In 1994, the PL 94-142 reauthorization incorporated much of the case law that has accumulated since 1975 and significantly expanded the law as the Individuals with Disabilities Education Act (IDEA). Though still underfunded and struggling with issues of implementation and accountability, IDEA is, inarguably, an institution in American schools.

5. No Child Left Behind and National Standards

In 2001, the political movements toward academic standards and student test score accountability that had begun in 1983 with a scathing indictment of American public schools in *A Nation at Risk*, culminated in the passage of the reauthorization of ESEA renamed NCLB. NCLB build on the momentum that had been gained throughout the previous two decades. This time period included the passage of Goals 2000, a set of non-binding and very general educational standards meant to establish a national baseline for education, and an increasing interest in federal involvement in education.

These efforts to move American education toward federal control have been driven largely by political actors within presidential administrations and Congress from both side of the political spectrum. *A Nation at Risk* was contracted by the Reagan administration to examine public schools; a set of national standards were first drafted by the first Bush administration and then formally adopted, renamed, and promoted under the Clinton administration. While NCLB was drafted by a committee appointed by the executive branch under the Bush administration, it was Senator Ted Kennedy, a Democrat, who provided the powerful impetus for its passage in Congress.

NCLB is mandating unprecedented federal requirements for student and teacher accountability with the stated goal of forcing states and districts to provide the educational services needed to bring every child up to the state standards by the year 2014. Adequate yearly progress measures were based on standardized test scores, and systems were implemented to assure that all teachers were highly qualified. While these requirements have met with resistance, it is notable that even though NCLB funds amount to only 7%–8% of school budgets, few states have formally opted out— Arizona, Hawaii, Minnesota, New Mexico, and Virginia. Other states, i.e., Vermont and Utah, are picking and choosing requirements within NCLB to apply to their schools (Pusey, 2010).

While the U.S. Constitution gives the federal government no explicit involvement in education, little challenge has been levied against the national mandates. Connecticut challenged the law as an unfunded mandate, but not as an unconstitutional encroachment (Archer, 2005)

Although standards and the tests that measure them continue as state-level policy, the mandates of NCLB and increasing pressure from the Obama administration are pushing these increasingly under federal control. For example, the Obama administration's Race to the Top funds are being offered to only a few states (12 total) on a very competitive basis. Rules for eligibility incorporate a commitment to innovation including the use of charter schools and at least a tacit acceptance of federal control in the form of the national Common Core Standards, which have, to date, been adopted by 34 states. These standards will effectively raise, if not usurp, the state-level standards (Common Core Standards Adoption, 2010), moving us closer to national standards, curricula, and assessments.

The politics of national standards and testing may be the trickiest area in the big educational picture, since these efforts cut across all students, districts, and states, creating for the first time a press for a "one best system" (Tyack, 1975). As Fuhrman, Resnick, and Shepard (2009) recently explained: "Now it's time to take what's been learned from that experience [standards movement] and make sure that this time around, the standards actually matter for teachers, students, and the country" (p. 28).

Currently, the National Assessment of Educational Progress (NAEP) is the only reliable national assessment of American students' learning, with the limitation of being a periodic, randomized, and anonymous set of tests—thus preventing local families, students, and educators from knowing and acting on their individual student's scores. NAEP involves only a limited, random sample of American students and is primarily used for interstate educational comparisons. And, thus, NAEP data act as a gauge for how effective the state-level tests are. While NAEP may be helpful as a summative assessment of American education, it is less useful as a formative tool for directing and improving school pedagogy, curriculum, and policies. Currently, however, states struggle to meet the demands of required standardized test under NCLB. As Robelen (2009) reports:

> States reported recent cuts in their testing budgets because of fiscal constraints.... And states face a variety of hurdles in ensuring the validity and reliability of those tests, such as staff capacity, assessment security, and developing alternate assessments for students with disabilities. (p. 19)

One year before the *Brown* case was settled (1953), Congress established the U.S. Department of Health, Education, and Welfare (HEW) to oversee a wide range of social service programs. Up to that time, education had not been a formal part of the federal government administration (U.S. Department of Education, 2010). HEW expanded in 1965 to encompass and administer the Johnson administrations War on Poverty. By 1979, federal involvement in education had reached a point where the Carter administration organized a separate U.S. Department of Education, which has expanded to a cabinet position, a range of mandates and programs, and a total annual budget of $160 billion (U.S. Department of Education, 2010).

Politics and Policy: Changes and Developments

Looking across the six decades between 1950 and 2010, we note three major national trends in U.S. education politics and policy: (a) convergence and centralization of control; (b) greater equity and access for all; and (c) a tightening of the standards, testing, and relations between methods and outcomes.

First, the politics of education have moved from scattered and diffused centers, converging in the courts, Congress, and the White House. Education went from being a rather mixed local matter, to being a national priority, often related to the competitiveness and productivity of the U.S. economy. When times were tough, the public would often blame the schools for failing to turn out innovative productive workers and innovative corporate leaders.

Candidates for the presidency, governorship, Congress, and the Supreme Court have often been called upon to comment on their perceptions of education and to provide remedies for the nation's education problems. Barak Obama, for example, in his first speech on education as president in 2009, was no different. As the *Washington Post* reported, "President Obama sharply criticized the nation's public schools yesterday, calling for changes that would reward good teachers and replace bad ones, increase spending, and establish uniform academic achievement standards in American education" (Wilson, 2009, p. 1). Here the president is calling for standards, adjustment of pay and "uniform" outcomes, illustrating the new role of national leaders in education.

Second, education moved in the last 60 years from sometimes operating as places of discrimination based on race, gender, economic disadvantages, language limitations, and physical, emotional, and intellectual handicaps to being designed and funded to help children most in need. Schools have come to reflect the needs of all children, from all backgrounds and with a range of abilities. Many U.S. children are found to be in need of extra assistance, and schools are enabled and funded to provide this assistance. The politics has changed, as leaders were called upon to help the children not benefitting from their schools. And policies changed to include programs for the poor, the limited English speaking, the child of color, and those with limitations—around key issues like racial segregation, financial inequities, and the poor treatment of special needs and limited-English proficient children, e.g., from civil rights to legal decisions, to laws and then to education policies that seek to improve the education of all children.

Third, in these six decades, education policies have begun to put the means and ends together, testing students, assessing progress, and demanding a stronger connection between teaching and learning, curriculum and outcomes. While in the 1950s, politicians hardly knew or cared what students were learning or to what levels they were learning, today politicians are calling upon schools to produce, giving them the resources, and holding them more accountable. We see a move from a concentration on process to more concern about "outcomes," and then attempts to adjust the policies to the results. As Elmore, Abelmann, and Fuhrman and colleagues (1996) explain:

> A new model of state and local school governance is evolving that we call "the new educational accountability" … with a primary emphasis on measured student performance as the basis for school accountability, the creation of a relatively complex set of standards by which students are compared by school and locality, and the creation of a system of rewards and penalties and intervention strategies to introduce incentives for improvement. (p. 65)

Thus, the politics has shifted from diffuse to central, and the role of national and state leaders has increased, and education policies are seeking greater equity for all students, linking process to outcomes as never before.

Conclusion

The processes and politics have significantly changed, from agitation to litigation to lobbying, to voting, to implementing, and then to reviewing results; and the process begins again. Thus, the key actors have grown and changed. The main arenas have expanded from being small and local to larger and national; and the policies, which once mainly dealt with local children and schools, now affect whole categories of students across the nation.

The future may hold that education will become a federally regulated, publicly supported national service—controlled and governed in Washington, DC, working with state capitals that relate to communities and schools. Standards, curriculum, and assessment are becoming more highly centralized and nationalized and, in the future, all children may be held to national standards, and to take national tests based on national criteria. So, as the politics grows and expands, the policies become focused, regulated, and universal.

As the current U.S. Secretary of Education, Arne Duncan, recently stated in a news conference about the growing federal role, the universal nature of such legislation, and the federal expectations about influencing state and local levels in policy making:

> Today, I am calling on all of you to join with us to build a transformative education law that guarantees every child the education they want and need—a law that recognizes and reinforces the proper role of the federal government to support and drive reform at the state and local levels. (Duncan, on-line, October 10, 2009)

(handwritten margin note: "Yikes!")

References

Abbott v. Burke, 477 A. 2d 1278, NJ: Superior Court, Appellant Division (1984).

Alexander v. Sandoval, 532 U.S. 275 (2001)

Anderson, J. (1992, April). *Poverty and achievement: Re-examining the relationship between school poverty and student achievement: An examination of eighth grade student achievement using the National Education Longitudinal Study of 1988.* Paper presented at the Annual Meeting of the American Educational Research Association. San Francisco, CA.

Archer, J. (2005, April 13). Connecticut pledges first state legal challenge to NCLB law. *Education Week, 24*(31), 4.

Bailey, S. K., & Mosher, E. K. (1968). *ESEA: The U.S. office of education administers a law.* Syracuse, NY: Syracuse University Press.

Bilingual Education Act of 1968, Title VII, Elementary and Secondary Education Act. 89th Congress. 10. (1965).

Bilingual Education Act: Twenty Years Later. (1988). Occasional Papers in Bilingual Education, 6. Washington, DC: National Clearinghouse for Bilingual Education, U.S. Department of Education.

Boger, J. C. (2000). Willful color-blindness: The new racial piety and the re-segregation of public schools. *North Carolina Civil Law Review, 78*, 1719–1725.

Boyd, W. L., Kerchner, C. T., & Blyth, M. (Eds.). (2008). *The transformation of great American school districts: How big cities are reshaping the institution of public education.* Cambridge, MA: Harvard Education Pres.

Brimley, V., & Garfield, R. R. (2008) *Financing education in a climate of change* (10th ed.). Boston: Allyn and Bacon.

Brown v. Board of Education of Topeka. 47 U.S. 483 (1954).

Civil Rights Act of 1964 (Pub.L. 88-352, 78 Stat. 241), enacted July 2, 1964

Coleman, J. S. (1966). *Equality of educational opportunity study.* Washington, DC: .S. Department of Health, Education, and Welfare.

Consortium of Citizens with Disabilities (CCD). (2009). Retrieved from http://www.c-c-d.org/

Common Core Standards Adoption by State (2010). Association of Supervision and Curriculum Development. Retrieved from http://www.ascd.org/public-policy/common-core-standards.aspx

Cooper, B. S. (1987). The changing universe of U.S. private schools. In H. Ha & T. James, (Eds.), *Private schools and the public interest* (pp. 33–62). London: Falmer Press.

Cooper, B. S. (January 21, 2009). "Beyond Bricks and Mortar," Commentary, *Education Week,* p. 27, in Pres. Obama's Inaugural Issue.

Crawford, J. (2000). *At war with diversity.* Bristol, UK: Multilingual Matters.

Duncan, Arne. (October 10, 2009). "One good move," 2009. onegoodorg/1gm/1gmarchive/2009/10/arne_duncan_-_s.html.

Elmore, R. F., Abelmann, C. H., & Fuhrman, S. H. (1996). The new accountability in state education reform: From process to performance. In H. F. Ladd (Ed.), *Holding schools accountable: Performance-based reform in education* (pp. 65–98). Washington, DC: Brookings Institution.

Education of All Handicapped Children Act. 94th Congress. 142 (1975).

Elementary and Secondary Education Act. 89th Congress. 10. (1965).

Equal Educational Opportunities Act of 1974. 20th U.S.C. § 1703.

Green, P. (2008). The politics of (de)segregation. In B. S. Cooper, J. G. Cibulka, & L. D. Fusarelli (Eds.), *Handbook of education politics and policy* (pp. 388–410). New York: Routledge-Taylor & Francis.

Guthrie, J. W. (2004). Twenty-first century education finance: Equity, adequacy, and the merging challenge of linking resources to performance. In K. DeMoss, & K. K. Wong (Eds.), *Money, politics and law: Intersections and conflicts in the provision of education opportunity. Yearbook of the American Education Finance Association* (pp. 1–16). Larchmont, NY: Eye on Education.

Fact Sheet on the Major Provisions of the Conference Report to H.R. 1, the No Child Left Behind Act (2003). U.S. Department of Education. Retrieved from http://www.ed.gov/nclb/overview/intro/factsheet.html

Fuhrman, S. H., Resnick, L., & Shepard, L. (2009, October 14). Standards aren't enough. *Education Week Commentary*, 28.

Hawkins-Stafford Amendment of 1988, Elementary and Secondary Education Act. 89th Congress. 10. (1965).

Individuals with Disabilities Education Act (IDEA) 20 U.S.C. § 1400.

Itkonen, T. (2009). Stories of hope and decline. *Educational Policy, 23*(1), 43–65.

Jennings, J. (2001). Title I: Its legislative history and its promise. In Borman, G. D., Stringfield, S. C., & Slavin, R. E. (Eds.), *Title I: Compensatory education at the crossroads* (pp. 1–24). Mahwah, NJ: Erlbaum.

Johnson-O'Malley Act of 1934. Pub. L. 93–638, 88 Stat. 2203, 2213–2214 (25 U.S.C. 455–457)

King, R. A., Swanson, A. D., & Sweetland, S. R. (2003). *School finance: Achieving high standards with equity and efficiency* (3rd ed.). Boston: Allyn & Bacon.

Kozol, J. (1967). *Death at an early age*. New York: Houghton-Mifflin.

Kozol, J. (1995). *Amazing grace*. New York: Harper Perennial.

Lau v Nichols. 414 U.S. 565 (1974).

Levin, B. (1999). *Reforming education: From origins to outcomes*. New York: Routledge-Falmer.

Lehne, R. (1978). *The quest for justice: The politics of school finance reform*. New York: Longman.

Mills v. Board of Education of the District of Columbia, 348 F. Supp 866 (D. DC 1972)

Mitchell, D. E., & Boyd, W. L. (1998). Knowledge utilization in education policy and politics: Conceptualizing and mapping the domain. *Educational Administration Quarterly, 34*(1), 126–140.

National Center for Education Statistics. (2004). U.S. Department of Education. www.nces.ed.gov.

National Center for Education Statistics (NCES). (2010). *Common core data*. U.S. Department of Education website. Retrieved from http://www.nces.ed.gov

Nation's Report Card. (2005). U.S. Department of Education, National Center for Education Statistics. Retrieved from http://nationsreportcard.gov/reading_math_2005/

No Child Left Behind (NCLB) Act of 2001. Pub. L. No. 107-110, § 115, Stat. 1425 (2002).

Odden, A. R. (Ed.). (1992). *Rethinking school finance: An agenda for the 1990s*. San Francisco: Jossey-Bass.

Pennsylvania Association for Retarded Children v. Pennsylvania, 334 F.Supp. 1257 (E.D. PA 1972)

Progress Toward Equal Educational Opportunity for Urban Students in New Jersey. (2009). Education Law Center. Rutgers University. New Brunswick, NJ. Retrieved from http://www.edlaw-center.org/ELCPublic/AbbottvBurke/AbbottHistory.htm

Pusey, S. (2010). *States opt out of NCLB*. AEP Online. Retrieved from http://www.aepweb.org/industryinfo/newsletter/legarchives/NCLB3-2-04.htm

Rebell, M. (2005). Adequacy litigations: A new path to equity. In J. Petrovich, & J. S. Wells (Eds.), *Bringing equity back* (pp. 75–87). New York: Teachers College Press.

Rehabilitation Act of 1973. 93rd U.S.C § 504.

Robelen, E. W. (2009, October 14). Budget woes putting squeeze on state testing, GAO Reports. *Education Week, 29*(7), 19.

Robinson v. Cahill, 62 N.J. 473 (1972).

Russo, C. J., & Osbourne, A. G. (2008). *Essential concepts and school-based cases in special education law.* Thousand Oaks, CA: Sage.

Ryan, W. (2002) The Unz initiative and the abolition of bilingual education. *Boston College Law Review 43*(2), 487–519.

San Antonio Independent School District v. Rodriguez, 411 U.S. 1 (1973).

Serrano v. Priest, 5 Cal.3d 584 (1971).

Smith-Hughes Act. 65th Congress. 347. (1917).

Smith-Lever Act. Public Law 95. (1914).

Snyder, T. D. & Shafer, L. L. (1996) *Youth indicators, 1996.* Washington, DC: U.S. Department of Education, National Center for Education Statistics.

Taylor, W. L., & Piche, D. M. (1990). *A Report on shortchanging children: The impact of fiscal inequity on the education of students at risk.* Washington, DC: Congress of the U.S. House Committee on Education and Labor.

Tyack, D. B. (1975). *The one best system: History of American urban education.* Cambridge, MA: Harvard University Press.

Wells, A. S. (1991). *The sociology of school choice: A study of black students' participation in a voluntary transfer program.* Unpublished dissertation, Teachers College, Columbia University, New York.

Wilson, S. (2009). Obama says public schools must improve. *Washington Post*, March 11, p. 1.

Wong, K. K., & Meyer, S. J. (2001). Title I school wide programs as an alternative to categorical practices: An organizational analysis of surveys from the Prospects Study. In G. D. Borman, S. C. Stringfield, & R. E. Slavin (Eds.), *Title I: Compensatory education at the crossroads* (pp. 1–24). Mahwah, NJ: Erlbaum.

PART IV

Globalization

Its Power and Limitations

Douglas E. Mitchell

The two chapters of Part IV offer bookend perspectives on the nature and impact of economic, political, and information technology globalization as they have unfolded in the last six decades. David Plank and Bob Johnson see global economic and political competition as powerfully reshaping educational curricula—forcing mathematics, science and technology to center stage. They see global economic and political pressures as so powerful that they "make algebra the new Latin," and turn traditional "curriculum wars" over reading methods, religion, and other curriculum components into mere sideshows that preoccupy local citizen groups but cannot compete with the homogenizing, standards-driven march toward the new economy's curricular necessities. Global geo-political and economic competition, they insist, has forced centralization of education policy making and usurped local curriculum prerogatives.

Heinz-Dieter Meyer paints a very different picture of global dynamics. He sees national cultures as robust and highly dependent on their unique historical evolutionary development. Historical "path dependency," Meyer insists, has enabled national (and possibly even regional and local) cultures to blunt even the most intensive reform and the most powerful reformers from substantially changing the basic social goals and organizational structures of established school systems. Meyer recounts the failure of U.S. reformers to reconstitute German secondary schools following the Allied victory in World War II. Even though Germany was defeated in war and was the target of a massive rebuilding program with clear international priorities for transforming their schools, the traditional German culture kept their schools focused on preparing elites rather than moving them to the mass educational system preferred in the United States.

Reading these two chapters together raises fascinating and important questions about the nature and limits of globalized economics and international competition as sources of educational change and cultural transformation. Are national policy makers being driven by globalization of their environments to adopt new school designs, new goals and new curricula? Or are national policy makers utilizing the symbols of globalization to pursue cultural and political preferences long embedded in the nation's public school cultural presuppositions and legitimated policies and structures? No doubt, both globalization as pressure and globalization as opportunity are at work, but it is important to discern when the global agenda is unavoidable and when it is being opportunistically used to pursue other goals.

8

CURRICULUM POLICY AND EDUCATIONAL PRODUCTIVITY

David N. Plank and Bob L. Johnson, Jr.

Once upon a time the U.S. education system was a sleepy backwater on the disciplinary map for students of politics. Relatively few students aspired to enroll in college, many dropped out before completing high school, and the rest were tracked into courses that satisfied the generally modest academic demands of employers. African Americans and Latinos attended separate schools. Boys took shop classes, and girls took home economics. Superintendents ran their schools with little interference from boards, unions, or outside interests. Despite these relatively modest aspirations and accomplishments, the U.S. outperformed virtually all other countries on most indicators of educational performance and attainment (Goldin & Katz, 2008).

The apparent calm that prevailed in the education system represented an extended but nevertheless transitory hiatus in the political storms that have swirled around public schools from their inception. Michael Katz and others have portrayed the riotous conflicts that surrounded public education in the 19th century, many of them originating in the diverse linguistic and cultural preferences of recent immigrants (Katz, 1975; Bowles & Gintis, 1977; Katznelson & Weir, 1988). These were for the most part put to rest by the triumph of the administrative professionals, who governed the U.S. education system for half a century with only limited and occasional opposition. The "one best system" that they established sought to define schooling as a managerial task, to be accomplished by professionally trained administrators with increasing efficiency and minimal interference from outsiders (Callahan, 1962; Ravitch, 2001; Tyack, 1974). Their success for most of 50 years led political scientists to characterize the governance of the education system as a "closed system," only minimally influenced by external political interests and trends (Wirt & Kirst, 1972).

The "one best system" came under increasing challenge as the importance assigned to educational opportunity and educational success began to rise, both for individual students and for the accomplishment of large public purposes. On the one hand, the Supreme Court's decision in *Brown v Board of Education of Topeka* placed educational opportunity at the center of the intensifying national struggle over questions of race, equity, and social justice. On the other hand, the launch of *Sputnik* stoked widespread anxieties as to whether the U.S. education system was good enough to keep up with the U.S.S.R. and other competitors, both in space and back on Earth.

Over the course of the past half-century, the view that increasing educational performance and attainment is necessary to the accomplishment of critical national objectives has become deeply institutionalized, in the United States and in countries around the world (Plank & Davis, 2009). The stakes attached to educational performance have risen ever higher, both from the point of view of society as a whole and from the point of view of individual students, as have expectations about what each can and should accomplish. The education system has consequently moved to the center of public policy debate, at both state and national levels.

As public concern with educational issues has grown, the curriculum has moved inexorably into the political spotlight, in two distinct ways. The more visible and entertaining of these features periodic skirmishes in the increasingly open and acrimonious "culture wars," in which disagreements about the appropriate role of sex education, evolution, and Harry Potter in classrooms summon up profound and persistent value conflicts in American society. These conflicts are a sideshow, however, to the seemingly less controversial but ultimately more consequential changes that have been adopted in response to the growing weight of economic and political importance assigned to the public school system.

In this chapter we present an overview and analysis of the politics of curriculum in the American education system in the past half-century. Our primary focus is on long-term trends in the curriculum that have gathered steam in the wake of the *Brown* decision and the launch of *Sputnik*, but we give some attention to the curriculum wars as well.

The Logic of Expansion and the Contest for Position

In countries around the world, the pace of educational expansion accelerated steadily over the course of the 20th century, as basic educational attainments came to be seen as a necessary condition for effective and productive citizenship (Meyer & Hannan, 1979). This expansion occurred along two dimensions. On the one hand, national governments strove to extend educational opportunities to previously marginalized groups including girls, rural residents, ethnic and linguistic minorities, and children with disabilities. Governments relied on the education system to ensure that citizens were literate in the national language, armed with canonical knowledge, and appropriately socialized to civic values and norms (e.g., Weber, 1976). On the other hand, the level of education deemed necessary for economic productivity and civic success continually rose. Where 4 years of schooling was initially viewed as sufficient to acquire the rudiments of literacy and civic competence, governments have more recently encouraged and ultimately required young people to remain in school for 6 years, 8 years, 12 years, or even longer (Bruns, Mingat, & Rakomotalala, 2005). Education has become the largest item of public expenditure in most countries, as more and more young people spend more and more years in school. The press to keep young people in classrooms (and out of the labor market) for longer and longer periods has been further strengthened by international rivalries that require the United States to "keep up" with educational advances in other nations.

From the point of view of students and households, the steady evolution of the economy toward industries and occupations relying on the accumulation and exchange of knowledge and information has focused attention on education as the single most important determinant of individual success (Schultz, 1975; Reich, 1992). The wage premium for highly educated workers has increased dramatically, while real wages for those with less than a high-school education have declined (Goldin & Katz, 2008). As a result, the contest for positional advantage in educational attainment has intensified, as young people find themselves obliged to acquire more and better educational credentials to keep up with their peers.

At one level these pressures reinforce one another, as public efforts to increase educational performance and attainment for all raise the levels of performance and attainment necessary to ensure individual positional advantage, driving average educational attainments ever higher. At the same time, however, these pressures exacerbate conflicts within the education system, as public efforts to guarantee civic minima, equalize educational opportunities, and close achievement gaps enter into conflict with individual efforts to ensure privileged access to the scarce social rewards that are allocated through the system. These conflicts have come into the open in the past half-century.

Civil Rights Revolution and the Legacy
of *Brown v. Board of Education*

In the United States, the civic and economic importance of education was powerfully affirmed by the Supreme Court's decision in *Brown v. Board of Education*. Before 1954, the education provided by the public school system for children from stigmatized groups was inferior by design, intended to prepare them for their assigned "place" in the social order. Latinos and African Americans were often educated in separate, inferior schools. Girls were prevented from taking shop classes and advanced mathematics. Students with handicaps were educated in "special" schools, or excluded from school altogether. The *Brown* decision challenged these arrangements, affirming the principle that African American (and by implication all) children should be given an equal opportunity for educational success.

The *Brown* decision brought about a dramatic intensification in the competition for educational resources and rewards, as members of previously disadvantaged groups sought to win a fairer share for themselves and their children, while those who benefited from prevailing arrangements sought to protect their prior claims. The stakes assigned to educational success consequently rose, and the political salience of the proposed redistribution of educational resources—both material and symbolic—likewise increased.

By identifying educational opportunity and attainment as the keys to individual mobility and prosperity, and as the most powerful available lever to shift the distribution of power and resources, *Brown* raised the practical question of how children from previously marginalized groups were to be assured of equal educational opportunities. The most direct answers to this question proved to be politically explosive. The prospect of integrated schools set off violent confrontations in many parts of the country, and efforts to open new opportunities to members of previously disadvantaged groups through various forms of affirmative action quickly foundered on white resistance and claims of reverse discrimination.

In recent years, partly by default, the curriculum has emerged as a principal focus of the struggle to equalize educational opportunities, in two very different ways. On the one hand, educators and policy-makers have sought to broaden opportunities for educational success by incorporating new content aimed at making the curriculum more inclusive and more responsive to the experiences and values of diverse groups of students. On the other hand, they have sought to ensure at least minimal educational success for all students by intensifying the accountability pressure on schools and teachers, focused on reducing or eliminating the gaps in achievement between designated subgroups of students on standardized assessments of performance in core academic subjects.

The Quest for Inclusion

The curriculum offers an explicit statement about what knowledge and skills are most highly valued. As efforts to equalize educational opportunities by integrating schools foundered, educators and others sought to broaden the curriculum to acknowledge the experiences and contributions of African Americans, Latinos, Native Americans, Asian Americans, and women in social studies and literature courses, and to make schools more respectful of and responsive to the diverse cultural and linguistic backgrounds of their students. The struggle to make curricula more inclusive and "multicultural" brought about visible changes in many schools, but it simultaneously aroused vigorous resistance from those who regarded the incorporation of new voices and new perspectives as an intrusion on the sacred space of their own traditions and values, mocking attention to previously neglected authors and historical figures as a curtsey to "political correctness" and a retreat from prevailing standards of rigor and quality.

Efforts to adapt the curriculum in the direction of inclusion and responsiveness to the needs and concerns of marginalized groups (African Americans, Latinos, women) have consequently triggered vociferous conflicts. One arena for these conflicts has been the process for adopting new textbooks, especially in large-market states including Texas and California. Efforts to shift textbooks away from a celebrationist account of American history and government toward a more inclusive and critical view have encountered powerful resistance from those who perceive such a shift as inimical to national unity and hostile to the prevailing social order (Schlesinger, 1992). The incorporation of literature produced by non-White, non-male authors into the English curriculum has met with similar protests. At one level this is simply another front in the ongoing "culture wars" (see below), but at a deeper level it represents a powerful rearguard action to counter efforts to enlist schools in the service of equal educational opportunity, now that more direct strategies to achieve this goal have been foreclosed.

A critical flashpoint for these conflicts has been language of instruction. The growing number of students arriving at school speaking languages other than English (or non-standard dialects of English) encouraged efforts in states and school districts across the country to develop instructional approaches and curriculum materials that would support their educational success (Smitherman, Villanueva, & Caragajah, 2003). These efforts set off intense battles, culminating in the adoption by many states of policies that strictly limit or even forbid schools to teach children in any language other than standard English (Gándara & Hopkins, 2010).

Some communities have organized charter schools that offer curricula directly focused upon the experiences and values of particular groups (although schooling offered in languages other than English continues to be barred in many states). Charter schools featuring Africa-centered or Native American instructional materials and cultural traditions are increasingly common, as are charter schools offering the standard curriculum to students drawn entirely from these groups. As scholars from the Civil Rights Project have recently argued, however, these schools can be regarded as a reaffirmation of the doctrine of "separate but equal" that *Brown v. Board* was meant to overturn (Frankenberg, Siegel-Hawley, & Wang, 2010).

The End of Tracking

As Diane Ravitch (2001) has documented, the legacy of John Dewey dominated the American education system through the middle years of the 20th century, though hardly in a manner that Dewey endorsed. "Progressive" educators developed child-centered curricula that responded to children's diverse interests and aptitudes largely by assigning them to specific curricular tracks, ostensibly on the basis of their diverse talents and interests. In fact, however, assignment to different tracks often reflected evaluations of what was realistic or appropriate for particular groups of students, which in turn reflected social prejudices and stereotypes. Poor and minority students were steered toward vocational and remedial tracks, and girls were assigned to home economics and discouraged from enrolling in advanced courses in mathematics and science.

The potentially damaging effects of tracking provided the foundation for the 1967 decision in *Hobson v. Hansen* that ruled that curricular assignment based on culturally biased "intelligence tests" was inherently discriminatory. In the years since, the compromised history of tracking has led to its stigmatization and to the virtual abandonment of the term, if not the practice, in schools across the country (Oakes, 2005).

The end of tracking poses a variety of policy challenges, however, including how to respond to the irrefutable fact that children have different interests and aptitudes. On the one hand, this has led to a variety of efforts to diversify the curriculum through the development of diverse "pathways," often focused on specific employment sectors (Oakes & Saunders, 2008.). All of these pathways are expected to give children the skills and knowledge they need for both college and careers. On the other hand, there is an increasingly explicit counter-attack underway that seeks to rehabilitate tracking based on academic aptitude (Loveless, 2009), on the twin arguments that ability grouping benefits high-ability children more than has previously been acknowledged and that the neglect of vocational subjects imposes costs on employers and career-minded students.

The dilemma posed by seeking to provide curricula that respond to the diverse needs and interests of different students without perpetuating inequities in educational opportunities and attainment has for the time being been resolved in favor of standardizing expectations and curricula, with the notional goal of preparing all students for success in college. This defuses a political problem, but leaves unanswered the question whether treating all students "alike" (at least in terms of curriculum) will in fact improve the performance of previously disadvantaged students or provide them with opportunities equal in any meaningful sense to the opportunities available to their more privileged peers.

Standards, Assessments, and Accountability

The political storms generated by efforts to integrate schools or develop inclusive curricula ultimately led to the virtual abandonment of both strategies in favor of an approach to "equalizing" opportunity that relies neither on school integration nor on curriculum revision. Instead, educators are to be held strictly accountable for measurable progress on standardized assessments of basic skills in English, mathematics, and to a lesser extent science (Smith & O'Day, 1991). The prevailing argument is that all children should be expected to perform at the same high level, with "no excuses" accepted from their schools or teachers. This strategy has the dual political advantage of demanding little or no sacrifice from the white middle class—who increasingly refuse even to pay the taxes that would make "equal opportunity" a reality, much less to share their schools with needier children—and shifting the burden of responsibility for educational success or failure to local educators and, ultimately, to the students themselves.

This strategy emerged in its full glory with the adoption of the No Child Left Behind Act (NCLB) in 2001, which required schools to ensure proficiency in tested subjects (i.e., English, mathematics, and eventually science) for all students by 2014. More recent versions include initiatives by the federal government and the Gates Foundation, among others, which demand that all students be prepared for college and careers.

The quest to ensure that all schools and students perform at satisfactory levels has in turn produced inevitable and increasingly inexorable pressure toward centralized control of the curriculum, in order to ensure that all students are being measured against the same standards. Over the past 30 years, states have asserted ever-greater authority over previously local decisions about curriculum; the logic of standardization via centralization has produced growing pressure to adopt national standards and assessments as well. The first Bush administration launched an initial sortie toward national standards in the final decade of the 20th century; a second, notionally "bottom-up" campaign to develop "common core" standards has been led by the National Governors Association and the Council of Chief State School Officers, with strong support from the Obama administration.

Fifty years after *Brown*, the challenge of responding to demands for equality of educational opportunity legitimated and affirmed by the Supreme Court is increasingly being answered with progress toward an education system in which all children are expected to perform at high levels on standardized assessments in basic subjects that are increasingly tied to state and ultimately national standards. The forces unleashed by *Brown* have been greatly strengthened by their confluence with concerns about American competitiveness in the global economy, which originated in their modern form with the launch of *Sputnik* in 1957.

Sputnik and International Competitiveness

The idea that more and better education is critical to the challenge of keeping up with international competitors dates back in the United States at least to the 19th century, when universities including Johns Hopkins and the University of Chicago, organized themselves along lines suggested by the great German universities and recommended by the economic and military successes of Prussia. The new model included a greatly expanded focus on science and scientific research as key criteria for institutional excellence (Geiger, 1993, 273).[1]

In the half-century since the launch of *Sputnik,* the idea that education matters for national security and economic competitiveness, and the ancillary claim that American prosperity is imperiled by falling behind its international rivals, has increasingly come to be taken for granted by policy-makers. This view achieved its apotheosis with the publication of *A Nation at Risk* in 1983. Energized by martial metaphors and apocalyptic rhetoric, *A Nation at Risk* asserted that the security and prosperity of the United States were threatened by a "rising tide of mediocrity" emanating from the schools, and that dramatic improvements in educational performance would be required to enable the United States to maintain its global pre-eminence (Ginsberg & Plank, 1995).

The United States is not the only country striving to excel through education, however. Nations around the world have committed themselves to improving educational performance as a strategy for achieving or sustaining international competitiveness. International assessments including the Trends in International Mathematics and Science Study (TIMSS) and the Programme for International Student Assessment (PISA) offer handy measures of who's up and who's down in the academic league table, and study tours seek insight into the secrets of Japan's (or Singapore's, or Korea's, or Finland's) educational success. The consequence is a permanent educational arms race, as the United States strives to meet or exceed the performance of rivals who are themselves seeking to maintain a competitive advantage through education.

The New Latin

Throughout Europe for most of a millennium, fluency in Latin was the mark of an educated person, and a prerequisite for many kinds of employment. Proficiency in Latin was hard to acquire, easy to measure, and relevant to performance in some important occupations including diplomacy and the priesthood. Increasingly, however, it came to serve mainly as an adornment and a marker of social status, useful for distinguishing those with the resources and leisure to acquire it from everyone else.[2] Mathematics is in many key respects the new Latin, useful as a marker of an educated person and relevant to performance in some important occupations, but of uncertain economic or social value otherwise.

One key consequence of the stress placed on education as the key to international competitiveness has been a steadily increasing focus on mathematics as the key indicator of educational success, accompanied by growing concern with the place of mathematics in the U.S. curriculum. This may be attributed in the first instance to the widespread conviction that economic and military success depends disproportionately or even decisively on a sufficient supply of highly qualified graduates in the so-called STEM (Science, Technology, Engineering, and Mathematics) fields. After the launch of *Sputnik*, it was widely feared that Russian engineers had proven their superiority to American ones, and that focused investment in mathematics and science education would be required to enable the United States to catch up. More recently, the fact that China and India train many more engineers than the United States is regularly cited as evidence that the nation is falling behind key international competitors, which will ipso facto have dire consequences for the American economy at some point in the future (e.g., NCEE, 2007).

The focus on mathematics may also be attributed to the fact that comparing performance in mathematics across countries is relatively straightforward, while comparing performance in other subject matters (literacy, history, science) is necessarily complicated by cross-national differences in language, culture, and curriculum (e.g., do students study biology in the first year of the secondary school science curriculum, or in the last?). Mathematics thus provides a ready yardstick for international comparisons, and improving performance in mathematics emerges as a critical national priority. The relatively poor mathematics performance of American students on international assessments thus provides a convenient basis for claims that the entire education system is in need of dramatic improvement.

Efforts to increase mathematics performance have been a virtually constant theme in U.S. education policy for half a century. The National Defense Education Act (NDEA) supported the development and dissemination of new mathematics curricula that emphasized the understanding of key mathematical concepts and, in the view of critics, devalued facility in calculation (Kline, 1973). Following the publication of *A Nation at Risk* (NCEE, 1983), virtually all states acted to increase the number of mathematics courses required for high school graduation. Current policy initiatives that seek to guarantee college readiness for all students focus much of their energy on getting all students through 2 years of Algebra, including (as in California) policies that require youngsters to enroll in Algebra I in the eighth grade. Completion of high school calculus is effectively prerequisite to admission in selective colleges.

What's Measured Matters Most

The other key consequence of the policy focus on mathematics and STEM is the neglect of other subjects that are of less apparent importance for national competitiveness, including the arts, social studies, foreign languages, and other "soft skills." The narrowing of the curriculum to focus on subjects that are readily measured and presumed essential has nevertheless proceeded apace, with some students in low-performing schools doing little work outside of intensive (and typically remedial) English and mathematics (Oakes, Muir, & Joseph, 2000). Whether this kind of curricular intensification is wise remains an open question. There is a strong case to be made that productive adult citizenship requires at least minimal competence in literacy and mathematics, but it does not necessarily follow that requiring more and more of these "basic" subjects (and correspondingly less of other subjects) will yield commensurate gains in individual or national productivity, particularly for students whose interests and aptitudes lie elsewhere.

There is particular irony in the current neglect of foreign language education in the United States, as this was an essential complement to the focus on mathematics and science in the NDEA. The combined focus on what might be characterized as the educational bases for "hard" and "soft" power (Nye, 2004) has given way to a nearly exclusive focus on mathematics and science as the keys to international power and prestige.

The Push for National Standards

The assertion that steady improvement in educational performance is essential to the nation's economic and military security leads inevitably toward the articulation of national standards and ultimately toward a national curriculum, by way of an expanding federal role in the education system. If education is a critical national security interest, it defies logic that decisions about what children should learn should be left to the whims of 50 states or 15,000 school districts. The push toward national standards has inspired a vigorous defense of local control, as states and school districts have responded to federal challenges to traditionally local prerogatives, but the policy trend is clearly moving toward increased standardization.

As some recognized at the time, the NDEA marked an essential first step toward a greatly expanded federal role in the education system (Featherman & Vinovskis, 2001). The new resources and curricular materials that the federal government made available to local school districts in the late 1950s have given way over the succeeding decades to a series of increasingly direct interventions in the curriculum. These included multiple initiatives brought into being by successive renewals of the Elementary and Secondary Education Act, along with the creation of the National Assessment of Educational Progress (NAEP). These initiatives were initially deferential to local control, with participation in NAEP remaining optional for states until 2001. Nevertheless, the press toward national standards and a national curriculum continued apace.

The publication of *A Nation at Risk* advanced the process even further, as did the subsequent rise of strong business advocacy for stronger (and implicitly national) standards in the "excellence" and accountability movements (NCEE, 1990). A serious move to design and implement national standards was launched at the end of the 1980s (Ravitch, 1995), prematurely as it turned out. This effort crashed and burned fairly quickly, but the twin logics of equal opportunity and national security surrendered none of their ideological or rhetorical power, and it was only a matter of time before the issue would have to be confronted again.

The 2001 renewal of the ESEA (known as No Child Left Behind) soon revived the push for national standards. NCLB greatly intensified the press of accountability on schools and school districts to improve the performance of their students. One direct consequence was the introduction of mandatory state participation in NAEP, necessary to support cross-state comparisons of student achievement.

The final triumph of the half-century-long press for national standards and assessments may now be at hand. The Obama administration has clearly learned from the failed initiative of the late 1980s, in which the federal government sought to design and implement national standards with very limited local involvement. In concert with external partners including business-led Achieve and the Gates Foundation, the administration is encouraging the development of "common core" standards and associated assessments under the auspices of the National Governors Association and the Council of Chief State School Officers, for subsequent adoption by the states.

Who Decides?

As the competition for educational resources has intensified, and as the stakes of educational success have risen both for individuals and for the nation as a whole, the logic of confidence that sustained traditional governance arrangements has steadily eroded. One consequence, as Plank and Boyd (1994) have argued, is that the critical conflicts in American education policy are increasingly located in the "anti-politics" of institutional choice, in which apparently procedural disagreements about where decisions should be made stand in for fundamental disagreements about the distribution of material and symbolic resources in the education system.

The Trend toward Centralization

In the past half-century, the struggle to equalize educational opportunities and the simultaneous campaign to ensure American economic and military competitiveness have tipped the scales decisively toward more centralized governance in the U.S. education system. The politics of redistribution argue on behalf of an expanded role for federal and state authorities (Peterson, 1981), while the affirmation of a national interest in educational performance argues for the adoption of national standards and assessments in order to ensure that all students are performing at acceptable levels. The virtues of local control retain their defenders, but the power to determine what happens in American schools and classrooms has steadily moved away from local actors toward centralized agencies, as state and federal authorities mobilize resources and assert their authority to turn previously local education systems toward the service of state and national goals.

The convening of the nation's governors at the Education Summit of 1989 by the Republican President George H. W. Bush marked a critical shift in inter-governmental relations in education. The president's decision to convene the meeting and the willingness of governors to attend signaled a shift in policy leadership in education away from districts and states to the federal level. For the first time in history, a U. S. president, in conjunction with state executives, met to discuss the creation of national educational goals. The content of the goals themselves was secondary to the fact that they were developed and endorsed by meeting participants. This highly symbolic yet historic meeting to discuss curriculum goals widened the opening of the door for an increased federal role in education policy. Succeeding presidents have since seized this opportunity to expand the federal role in education far beyond the agenda of the Summit attendees.

These developments have had particularly dramatic consequences for the curriculum, responding to and reinforcing powerful and perhaps inexorable momentum toward national standards and assessments. The launch of *Sputnik* and the passage of the NDEA sparked a continuing struggle to wrest control of math and science curricula away from school-based professionals in favor of disciplinary specialists based in universities and research organizations, while the struggle to equalize educational opportunities spurred a variety of federally funded activities aimed at developing standardized curricula and instructional strategies to improve the educational performance of previously disadvantaged children.

The passage of NCLB in 2002 marked a dramatic escalation of efforts to assert central control over curricular decisions, as the Elementary and Secondary Education Act evolved from its original goal of providing additional resources to schools serving poor students toward the far more ambitious goal of ensuring that all students meet state standards for academic performance. Current debates over the renewal of ESEA portend further moves toward national standards and assessments. Policy-makers have targeted the putative weakness of state standards as a fatal flaw in NCLB, as highly variable standards of "proficiency" across states undermine efforts to ensure that all students achieve at acceptable levels. The Obama administration is consequently encouraging states to adopt "common core" standards and assessments that will establish uniform expectations for students and schools. Adoption is notionally voluntary, to avoid the stigma of federal usurpation of state prerogatives, but access to a growing array of federal resources (potentially including ESEA) is increasingly dependent on states' participation in the "common core" initiative.

Accountability for Educators

Over the past 50 years, the logic of confidence that traditionally governed the education system has given way to a logic of accountability, in which students, teachers, administrators, and schools are increasingly held responsible for accomplishing specific outcomes, most often reckoned in terms of scores on standardized tests. This has undermined the authority and legitimacy accorded to local teachers, administrators, and school boards, as their performance has been subjected to external (and rarely flattering) scrutiny. De facto authority has shifted to state governments and private sector actors who set the standards, produce the assessments, and determine what level of performance that represents "success."

The federal report, *A Nation At Risk* (NCEE, 1983), played a prominent role in setting this tone, particularly in regards to teachers. While the report fell short of laying explicit blame at the feet of educators, it did much to raise questions concerning the legitimacy of the current educational system and those working in it, by deploying the rhetoric of bellicose nationalism to insist that educational performance was a key determinant of economic and military competitiveness.

> Our Nation is at risk ... the educational foundations of our society are presently being eroded by a rising tide of mediocrity that threatens our very future as a Nation and a people. What was unimaginable a generation ago has begun to occur—others are matching and surpassing our educational attainments.... If an unfriendly foreign power had attempted to impose on America the mediocre educational performance that exists today, we might well have viewed it as an act of war. As it stands, we have allowed this to happen to ourselves. (NCEE, 1983, p. 7)

Such rhetoric has created legitimacy issues for educators with various publics at all levels of government. Chief among these are the business and legislative communities, which have emerged as loud and powerful voices in curriculum debates. Recent decades have witnessed an aggressive and unprecedented effort by these and other groups to centralize the curriculum at the state and national levels using multiple policy levers.

The politics of curriculum and instruction in this venue focus on a set of conflicts that have as their flashpoint issues of teacher professionalism and autonomy. With the move toward a hyper-rational, standards-driven, no-nonsense approach to instruction across the states, recent reforms represent a threat to the professionalism and autonomy of teachers as members of the educational community (Johnson, 2003). Add to these conditions an increasingly prescribed and narrow curriculum, the development of "teacher-proof" curriculum, high-stakes testing and sanctions for school failure and it is easy to understand why teachers might feel as if they are indeed under siege from educational leaders and policy-makers.

Policy moves that standardize and centralize the curriculum run counter to the ambiguities that define the teaching-learning process (McNeil, 2000). Today's teachers find themselves caught between the conflicting demands of a centralized curriculum and the need for autonomy dictated by the realities of teaching. It is a dilemma that places them squarely in the crossfire of criticism and makes them increasingly vulnerable to public scrutiny.

Unions and the Business Lobby

The centralization of authority in the education system has fostered the growth of powerful national lobbies seeking to influence the policy debate. On the one hand, since the publication of *A Nation at Risk* (NCEE, 1983) business interests have involved themselves far more actively in education issues, arguing for rigorous standards and assessments and increased accountability for educators, along with increased efficiency in the use of educational resources. Partly in response, teachers unions have emerged as powerful political actors at both the state and national levels, protecting and affirming the professional rights of teachers and the claims of the education system on public resources.

As the American education system has increasingly come to be identified with national security and national competitiveness, a number of high-profile business leaders have assumed a vocal role in education policy debates, demanding reform and improved performance. In 1984, for example, Ross Perot led the charge for educational reform in Texas, calling for a new focus on academic excellence and reduced emphasis on football and other distractions (Plank, 1986). In the succeeding decade a variety of business organizations published reports bemoaning the state of American schools (Ginsberg & Plank, 1995); business-led organizations including Achieve and Just for the Kids continue to set the reform agenda, emphasizing the importance of ambitious standards, regular assessments, and accountability for results.

The expanded engagement of the business community with educational issues has also led to a reaffirmation of the venerable goal of increased efficiency in schools and school operations, including both resistance to spending more money on education and an intensified focus on essential knowledge and skills and the depreciation or elimination of "fads and frills" in the curriculum (Callahan, 1962). In recent years the familiar demands of business leaders for increased efficiency and improved performance have been accompanied by the growth of direct engagement by for-profit actors in the core business of schooling, as charter management organizations, tutoring companies, and on-line entrepreneurs join textbook and test publishers in the development and delivery of curriculum and instruction (Rowan, 2006; Burch, 2009). The expanded role of private sector organizations in the educational system has further strengthened the press toward the development of common standards, curricula, and assessments.

Teachers unions and other professional associations remain the key source of resistance to the reform agenda articulated by business leaders. They have mobilized to protect the rights and prerogatives of their members, arguing that teacher autonomy and professionalism are essential to children's educational success (Darling-Hammond & Baratz-Snowden, 2005). In this effort they have disputed the claim that everything that matters can be measured or that only what can be measured matters, and argued instead that only professional teachers can respond effectively to the unique interests and talents of individual children. Much current reform rhetoric portrays teachers unions as reactionary and indifferent to issues of efficiency and performance, but in fact the confidence of business reformers in the promise of fashionable reform strategies—choice, accountability, national standards and assessments—lacks much in the way of empirical justification. The unions' argument in support of traditional institutions and arrangements along with increased resources is at least an equally plausible account of how to improve the performance of American schools (Ravitch, 2010). At present, however, the arguments put forward by business leaders define the reform agenda.

Summary

The seemingly inexorable progress toward centralization and a strengthened federal role in the American education system has emerged in response to powerful developments in the economy and the broader society. At the same time, however, the loss of local autonomy taps deep fears of political control and indoctrination, which has had two sorts of consequences. On the one hand, it has led to an increasingly standardized and impoverished curriculum, as policy-makers and textbook publishers have sought to avoid the taint of politicization by focusing single-mindedly on essential knowledge and basic skills that can be readily evaluated on standardized assessments. On the other hand, though, it has paradoxically ignited the series of frequently picturesque battles over what remains of the local curriculum that are known as the curriculum wars.

Curriculum Wars

The increased focus on curriculum that followed the *Brown* decision and the launch of *Sputnik* has reanimated deep conflicts in American society. These conflicts have generally gravitated around three poles, though specific curriculum issues reflect complex interactions among all three. The first of these concerns the respective rights and responsibilities of parents and the State, reflecting anxieties about values, tradition, and the prospect of indoctrination. The second concerns conflicting views of science and religion, which have typically manifested themselves in conflicts over the teaching of evolution and more recently in disputes over instruction about climate change. The third originates in uncertainty about the character of American society, in worries about language of instruction, "multicultural" curricula, and competing definitions of patriotism. These conflicts remained largely but not entirely submerged in the era of the "one best system," when the Anglo-Protestant establishment had pretty much everything their own way, but they have been restored to life as the individual and collective stakes attached to educational performance have increased. The result is the familiar and ongoing curriculum wars that burst out with increasing frequency in states and school districts across the United States.

Traditional and Reform Pedagogy

One of the perennial hot spots in the curriculum wars is the continuing struggle between advocates of "progressive" and "traditional" approaches to teaching and learning, which has vexed educators for nearly a century. The latest versions of this struggle focuses on competing approaches to reading and mathematics. In the case of reading, the conflict hinges on the relative virtues of "whole language" and "phonics" as strategies for ensuring early literacy; in the case of mathematics, disagreements arise over the merits of "traditional" methods emphasizing computation as against "reform" methods that seek to foster a deeper understanding of mathematical concepts.

The controversy over different approaches to instruction in reading and mathematics is cloaked in competing claims about the relative effectiveness of traditional and innovative curricula, but the energy behind the debate derives in large part from deeper disagreements about the nature of childhood and the purposes of education. Defenders of new strategies deride traditional curricula as "jugs and mugs" or "drill and kill," while opponents complain about political correctness and the abandonment of intellectual rigor in favor of "pizza math" and "invented spelling." Advocates of a balanced approach find little common ground in a polarized policy environment (Pearson & Schoenfeld, 2009). Behind these disagreements lie fundamentally different views of the respective rights and responsibilities of parents and the State in the preparation of young people for adulthood. Educators' well-intentioned aspirations to teach the whole child and overcome the disadvantages of birth or station run headlong into some parents' anxieties about the indoctrination or alienation of their children.

The progressive view that schools should cultivate children's unique talents and interests and foster their love of learning by introducing them to new possibilities thus confronts the belief that schools should limit their engagement with students to ensuring that all children master basic skills, and leave matters of feeling and belief to other institutions including the family and the church. Which of these approaches better prepares youngsters for adult success remains more a matter of conviction than of evidence, but the latter is currently ascendant, as schools and education systems move toward ever-greater standardization of curricula and assessments.

Canonical Knowledge

A second front in the curriculum wars has opened over the question whether children should receive an education that features the canonical knowledge required for "cultural literacy" and occupational success under the prevailing social order (Bloom, 1988; Hirsch, 1987), or rather one that reflects and affirms the diverse identities and traditions of specific groups (Banks, 2007). At one level, the debate focuses on the question whether a curriculum emphasizing mastery of familiar and socially legitimated facts and narratives is more likely to produce educational success for otherwise disadvantaged students than one that features facts and narratives more closely aligned with their own prior knowledge and experience. This runs parallel to a similar debate over language of instruction, and the question whether it is more important for children to master English or to master curriculum content in their own languages (Smitherman, Villanueva, & Caragarajah, 2003; Gándara, 2010).

At a deeper level, however, the conflict revolves around the question whether canonical knowledge and the status hierarchy that it reflects should be open to challenge at all (D'Souza, 1998; Gitlin, 1996). The explicit defense of "the canon" as a bastion against multicultural incursions appeared most visibly in resistance to campaigns by students and others on university campuses to broaden the literature curriculum to include more female and minority authors, and fewer "dead White males," but similar disagreements have emerged in school districts as well (Graff, 1993; Berubé, 2007). Analogous conflicts have erupted with regard to the social studies curriculum, as opponents square off over the appropriate approach to issues ranging from slavery and the treatment of Native Americans to the internment of Japanese Americans and the relative standing of variously flawed historical figures in history textbooks (Nash, Crabtree, & Dunn, 2000).

Science and Religion

Another flash point for the curriculum wars is the dispute between science and religion, which erupted into open and occasionally violent conflict at several points in the 20th century. The *Scopes* trial in 1926 brought this dispute into sharp focus, as the state of Tennessee sought to defend a law forbidding the teaching of evolution in the public schools, but the underlying conflict has flared up regularly in the years since. In the 1970s, for example, protests by fundamentalist Christians against the innovative social studies curriculum "Man: A Course of Study" were organized across the country, and violent protests against the adoption of textbooks perceived to undermine "traditional" values closed the schools in Kanawha County, West Virginia. With reference to the protesters in Kanawha County, Marty and Appleby (1993, p. 467) observe:

> Among the principles they wanted to preserve were the following: the "traditional" patriarchal family; belief in God, the American political system, the free enterprise economic system, and the history of America as "the record of one of the noblest civilizations that has existed"; and the need for study of the traditional rules of grammar.

Disputes over the teaching of evolution persist, currently focused on ensuring a place in the curriculum for competing "theories" of human origins including Intelligent Design. Controversy over evolution has lately been joined by controversy over global warming, with demands for the inclusion of competing "theories" of climate change in the curriculum. These disputes make the headlines regularly, as states across the country wrestle with the articulation of curriculum standards and the adoption of textbooks.

Sex, Gender, and Sexuality

A final front in the curriculum wars pits contrasting views on how public schools should address questions of sex, gender, and sexuality in a rapidly changing cultural environment. As noted above, the protesters in Kanawha County included defense of the "patriarchal family" among their guiding principles, and the treatment of girls and women in schools and in curriculum materials continued to stir conflict in subsequent decades as obstacles to girls' educational and occupational success were successively dismantled.[3] As the struggle to preserve traditional gender roles has wound down in a nearly complete defeat for the supporters of patriarchy, its place in the curriculum wars has been taken by an equally impassioned defense of the "traditional" family against the usurpations of same-sex parenting and the notional "homosexual agenda" in public schools.

Parallel conflicts over "sex education" continue as well, as efforts to include materials that address questions ranging from human physiology to contraception to the prevention of AIDS in public school curricula almost invariably produce local controversy. Efforts to bar teaching about sex that acknowledges that young people are or might become sexually active have been matched by efforts to develop "abstinence-only" curricula, which continue to receive generous federal funding even in the presence of strong evidence that such curricula are ineffective in changing sexual behavior (Doan & Williams, 2008).

Summary

At the end of the day, the curriculum wars reflect deep and, ultimately, irreconcilable disagreements about the purpose of schooling and the respective rights of parents and the state. On the one hand, schooling is profoundly conservative, providing young people with the skills and knowledge they will need to take their places in the prevailing social and economic structure. On the other hand, though, schooling is at least potentially subversive, offering young people the opportunity to look beyond their present circumstances and aspire to change prevailing social arrangements.

As the State has become more inclusive and intrusive in the wake of the *Brown* decision, many parents have become increasingly assertive in defending their right to guide their children's moral and intellectual development against the perceived encroachments of the secular State. Despite their ubiquity, these generally reflect value conflicts that can be adjudicated through the regular political system. At the limit, though, they represent potentially significant challenges to State legitimacy and the prevailing regime (Plank, 2006).

Those who perceive themselves to be losing in the curriculum wars have resorted to both "voice" and "exit" in their efforts to turn the tide (Hirschman, 1970). On the one hand, they continue to mobilize in protest, seeking to ban books that challenge "traditional" values, to protect the patriotic account of American civilization against critique and dissent, and to incorporate alternative "theories" of human origin and climate change into scientific curricula. On the other hand, growing numbers of parents have withdrawn their children from the institution of public education into educational institutions more sympathetic to "traditional" values, including home schooling (Lugg & Rorrer, 2009) and "traditional virtues" charter schools. Meanwhile, the larger trend toward a standardized curriculum for all students has continued unimpeded.

Conclusion

Periodic skirmishes in the curriculum wars invariably attract public notoriety, in large part because they reflect very different and ultimately irreconcilable beliefs about the nature of childhood and the appropriate role of schooling in preparing young people for adulthood. Recent efforts to revise the social studies curriculum in Texas to minimize the importance of some historical figures (e.g., Thomas Jefferson) and magnify the importance of others (e.g., Ronald Reagan) are of a piece with the ongoing struggle over the teaching of evolution in Kansas, and also with campaigns across the country to ensure that young children receive instruction in phonics. These and other flare-ups in the curriculum wars divert the media and draw outraged partisans to the ramparts, but in fact they are little more than a colorful sideshow, of almost no lasting consequence for the dramatic changes that have occurred in the curriculum over the past half-century.

In spite of the intractable ideological tensions that characterize the U.S. education system, and the virtual impossibility of decisive victories or defeats in the curriculum wars, the curriculum has undergone momentous changes since 1954. In this chapter we have argued that these changes have come about in response to the large social and economic trends unleashed by the Supreme Court's *Brown* decision and the launch of *Sputnik*. Over the course of the intervening half-century, these trends have steadily and perhaps inexorably pushed toward the adoption of national standards and the development of a national curriculum, intensely focused on the mastery of basic skills in English and mathematics and largely drained of local character or controversy. The curriculum wars continue to get the headlines, but the underlying trends toward standardization and homogenization proceed without serious impediment. Whether this will benefit American children or American competitiveness remains to be proven.

Notes

1 Japan, humiliated by the forcible "opening" of its society and economy to western commerce and influence in 1868, created a national education system that imitated the best features of the systems developed by its principal western competitors, including Germany and the United States (Passin, 1965).
2 Ben Jonson and John Milton both depreciated William Shakespeare for his limited proficiency in Latin.
3 The campaign to ensure equitable treatment for girls has advanced to the point where some now question whether boys might need affirmative assistance in the education system (Whitmire, 2010).

References

Banks, J. A. (2007). *Educating citizens in a multicultural society* (2nd ed.). New York: Teachers College Press.

Berubé, M. (2007). *What's liberal about the liberal arts? Classroom politics and "bias" in higher education*. New York: W.W. Norton.

Bloom, A. (1988). *The closing of the American mind*. New York: Simon & Schuster.

Bowles, S., & Gintis, H. (1977). *Schooling in capitalist America*. New York: Basic Books.

Brown v. Board of Education of Topeka. 47 U.S. 483 (1954).

Bruns, B., Mingat, A., & Rakomotalala, R. (2005). *Achieving universal primary education by 2015: A chance for every child*. Washington DC: The World Bank.

Burch, P. (2009). *Hidden markets: The new education privatization*. New York: Routledge.

Callahan, R. E. (1962). *Education and the cult of efficiency*. Chicago: University of Chicago Press.

Darling-Hammond, L., & Baratz-Snowden, J. (2005). *A good teacher in every classroom: Preparing the highly qualified teachers our children deserve*. San Francisco: Jossey Bass.

Doan, A. E., & Williams, J. C., (2008). *The politics of virginity: Abstinence in sex education*. Westport, CT: Praeger.

D'Souza, D. (1998). *Illiberal education: The politics of race and sex on campus*. New York: Free Press.

Elementary and Secondary Education Act, P.L. 89-10. 89th Congress.

Featherman, D. L., & Vinovskis, M. A. (2001). *Social science and policy-making: A search for relevance in the twentieth century.* Ann Arbor: University of Michigan Press.

Frankenberg, E., Siegel-Hawley, G., &Wang, J. (2010). *Choice without equity: Charter school segregation and the need for civil rights standards.* Los Angeles: Civil Rights Project/Proyecto Derechos Civiles at UCLA.

Gándara, P., & Hopkins, M. (2010). *Forbidden language: English learners and restrictive language policies.* New York: Teachers College Press.

Geiger, R. L. (1993). Research, graduate education, and the ecology of American universities: An interpretive history. In S. Rothblatt & B. Wittrock (Eds.), *The European and American university since 1800: Historical and sociological essays* (pp. 234–259). New York: Cambridge University Press.

Ginsberg, R., & Plank, D. N. (1995). *Commissions, reports, reforms, and educational policy.* Westport, CT: Praeger.

Gitlin, T. (1996). *The twilight of common dreams: Why America is wracked by culture wars.* New York: Holt.

Goldin, C., & Katz, L. F. (2008). *The race between education and technology.* Cambridge MA: Belknap Press of Harvard University Press.

Graff, G. (1993). *Beyond the culture wars: How teaching the conflicts can revitalize American education.* New York: W.W. Norton.

Hirsch, E. D. (1987). *Cultural literacy: What every American needs to know.* New York: Houghton Mifflin.

Hirschman, A. O. (1970). *Exit, voice, and loyalty: Responses to decline in firms, organizations, and states.* Cambridge MA: Harvard University Press.

Johnson, B. J., Jr. (2003). Those nagging headaches: Perennial issues and tensions in the politics of education field. *Educational Administration Quarterly, 39,* 41–67.

Katz, M. B. (1975). *Class, bureaucracy, and schools.* Westport CT: Praeger.

Katznelson, I., & Weir, M. (1988). *Schooling for all: Class, race, and the decline of the democratic ideal.* Berkeley: University of California Press.

Kline, M. (1973). *Why Johnny can't add: The failure of the new math.* New York: St. Martin's Press.

Loveless, T. (2009). *Tracking and detracking: High achievers in Massachusetts middle schools.* Washington DC: The Thomas B. Fordham Institute.

Lugg, C. A., & Rorrer, A. K. (2009). The politics of (im)prudent state-level homeschooling policies. In W. G. Sykes, B. Schneider, & D. N. Plank (Eds.), *Handbook of education policy research* (pp. 805–818). New York: Routledge.

McNeil, L. (2000). *Contradictions of school reform: Educational costs of standardized testing.* New York: Routledge.

Marty, M. E., & Appleby, R. S. (1993). *Fundamentalisms and society: Reclaiming the sciences, the family, and education.* Chicago: University of Chicago Press.

Meyer, J. W., & Hannan, M. T. (1979). *National development and the world system: Educational, economic, and political change, 1950–1970.* Chicago: University of Chicago Press.

Nash, G. B., Crabtree, C., & Dunn, R. (2000). *History on trial: Culture wars and the teaching of the past.* New York: Vintage.

National Center on Education and the Economy (NCEE). (1990). *America's choice: High skills or low wages!* Rochester NY: Author.

National Center on Education and the Economy (NCEE). (2007). *Tough choices or tough times.* San Francisco: Jossey Bass.

National Commission on Educational Excellence (NCEE). (1983). *A nation at risk: The imperative for educational reform.* Washington DC: US Department of Education.

No Child Left Behind Act, Pub.L. 107-110, 115 Stat. 1425, enacted January 8, 2002.

Nye, J. S., Jr. (2004). *Soft power: The means to success in world politics.* Cambridge MA: Perseus Books.

Oakes, J. (2005). *Keeping track: How schools structure inequality* (2nd ed.). New Haven, CT: Yale University Press.

Oakes, J., Muir, K., & Joseph, R. (2000). *Coursetaking & achievement in mathematics and science: Inequalities that endure and change*. Madison, WI: National Institute of Science Education (NISE).

Oakes, J., & Saunders, M. (2008). *Beyond tracking: Multiple pathways to college, career, and civic participation*. Cambridge, MA: Harvard Education Press.

Passin, H. (1965). *Society and education in Japan*. New York: Columbia University Press.

Pearson, P. D., & Schoenfeld, A. H. (2009). The reading and math wars. In W. G. Sykes, B. Schneider, & D. N. Plank (Eds.), *Handbook of education policy research* (pp. 560–580). New York: Routledge.

Peterson, P. E. (1981). *City limits*. Chicago: University of Chicago Press.

Plank, D. N. (1986). The ayes of Texas: Rhetoric, reality and school reform. *Politics of Education Bulletin, 13,* 3–6.

Plank, D. N. (2006). Unsettling the state: How 'demand' challenges the U.S. education system. *European Journal of Education, 41,* 13–27.

Plank, D. N., & Boyd, W. L. (1994). Anti-politics, education, and institutional choice: The flight from democracy. *American Educational Research Journal, 31,* 263–281.

Plank, D. N., & Davis, T. E. (2009). Economics and the state's role in education. In D. Brewer & P. McEwan (Eds.), *International encyclopedia of education* (economics section) (pp. 347–353). New York: Elsevier.

Ravitch, D. (1995). *National standards in American education: A citizen's guide*. Washington DC: The Brookings Institution.

Ravitch, D. (2001). *Left back: A century of battles over school reform*. New York: Simon & Schuster.

Ravitch, D. (2010). *The death and life of the great American school system: How testing and choice are undermining education*. New York: Basic Books.

Reich, R. B. (1992). *The work of nations: Preparing ourselves for 21st century capitalism*. New York: Vintage.

Rowan, B. (2006). The school improvement industry in the United States: Why educational change is both pervasive and ineffectual. In H-D. Meyer & B. Rowan (Eds.), *The new institutionalism in education* (pp. 67–86). Albany: State University of New York Press.

Schlesinger, A. (1992). *The disuniting of America: Reflections on a multicultural society*. New York: W.W. Norton.

Schultz, T. W. (1975). The value of the ability to deal with disequilibria. *Journal of Economic Literature, 13,* 827–846.

Smith, M. S., & O'Day, J. (1991). Systemic school reform. In S. H. Fuhrman & B. Malen (Eds.), *The politics of curriculum and testing: The 1990 Yearbook of the Politics of Education Association* (pp. 233–267). London: Falmer Press.

Smitherman, G., Villanueva, V., & Caragarajah, S. (2003). *Language diversity in the classroom: From intention to practice*. Carbondale: Southern Illinois University Press.

Tyack, D. (1974). *The one best system: A history of American urban education*. Cambridge, MA: Harvard University Press.

Weber, E. (1976). *Peasants into Frenchmen: The modernization of rural France, 1870–1914*. Stanford, CA: Stanford University Press.

Whitmire, R. (2010). *Why boys fail: Saving our sons from an educational system that is leaving them behind*. New York: AMACOM.

Wirt, F. M., & Kirst, M. W. (1972). *The political web of American schools*. Boston: Little, Brown.

9

PATH DEPENDENCE IN GERMAN AND AMERICAN PUBLIC EDUCATION

The Persistence of Institutional Difference in a Globalizing World

Heinz-Dieter Meyer

The American public school system was designed to provide a "common school" shared educational experience to all school-aged children. This is not the basis for public schooling in other countries. For example, the German tri-partite system is meant to provide distinctly different educational tracks for working-class, technical-class, and ruling-class aspirants. Important distinctions also include different governance structures and differences in the articulation of the linkages between lower and higher education. In both nations these institutional underpinnings were formed in the early 19th century. They have persisted largely unchanged for more than a century.

The difficulties of changing such basic founding assumptions are exemplified by the German experience of American Occupation following World War II. Beginning in the 1960s, German economic expansion prompted calls for softening the demarcation lines between the three educational tracks by making technical and higher education more accessible to children of working-class parents, and calls to open Germany's class-structured system for greater mobility and inclusion garnered support. This move towards a democratic opening of German public education centered on the introduction of a new institutional model, the comprehensive school (*Gesamtschule*), borrowed partly from American experience. The latter was to integrate the three tiers of secondary schools—the Hauptschule (the new name for the Volksschule), the Realschule, and the Gymnasium—to diminish the elitist bias of the traditional secondary education system. Yet, proponents of the Gesamtschule confronted the same resistance to inclusion that the American occupiers had experienced 25 years earlier, as the German "dual" system of tracked schooling was promoted by business leaders as one means for the young nation to secure its international competitiveness. The analysis here offers clues to recurrent frustrations of education policy making by surfacing some often-ignored obstacles of institutional change. Deeply institutionalized beliefs (Douglas, 1986)—the national ideologies or "folk psychologies" of education (Bruner, 1996) that define how the members of a national community think about schooling—often put limits on policy change.

Second, it offers a counterpoint to some oversimplified models of globalization. Unlike some globalization theorists who stipulate a gradual convergence of mass education towards a single, globally dominant (American) model, I find that institutional persistence counterbalances and even trumps global convergence. The German school system of the early 21st century remains strongly shaped by its 19th century predecessor with a few signsof converging on an American style common school model.

Path Dependence and Institutional Analysis—Some Essentials

In his poem "The Road Not Taken," Robert Frost describes a traveler who confronts a juncture in the road and, "being one person," must choose. The traveler looks for reasons to prefer one road to the other but must admit that they are hard to distinguish ("both that morning equally lay / in leaves no step had trodden black"). As for the possibility to come back and visit the road not taken, "knowing how way leads on to way," he realizes it is unrealistic. Standing at a critical juncture, we know all too often that we must choose, though we have little grounds on which to base a choice; yet any choice will have lasting consequences.

Frost's poem is a good analogy for the problem of institutional path making. Like travelers, nations confront critical junctures in their development where policy makers must choose one way or another. The choice often has long-term consequences, constraining the range of future options, and distinguishing one nation from more or less distant fellow nations. Lipset (1996), following Weber (1949), suggests the image "of a nation's history starting as a game in which the dice are not loaded at the beginning, but then become biased in the direction of each past outcome ... Each time the dice comes up with a given number, the probability of rolling that number again increases" (p. 24).

This chapter explores the educational path making of nations. An institutional "path" is shorthand for a distinct, stable, interlocking set of institutions with a long life expectancy that exerts great inertial pull on the behavior of social actors and constrains their future options (David, 1985, 1986; Brian, 1989). These constraints are often shaped by arbitrary precedent or historic accident. Education within one path confronts different problems, opportunities, and tradeoffs than education in another, which once may have been equally accessible. How these different opportunities and constraints coalesce into stable institutional arrangements and how they affect and limit our efforts for change is the topic of this chapter

Path dependence promises to explain the kind of educational inertia policy analysts have often lamented: "When the same problems persist despite changes of leadership and many successive reform efforts, the inescapable conclusion is that the problem is built into the basic [institutional] arrangements... Many reform initiatives appear plausible but are quickly marginalized or worn down by the existing system of habits and incentives" (Hill, 1999, p. 422).

To address these problems, we must "bring history back in." The path-dependence literature emphasizes the importance of fine-grained historical analysis to understand lock-in effects, which not only lock in certain practices and behaviors, but also beliefs. Once evoked to legitimize an institution, ideas and beliefs are institutionalized and switching from one set of beliefs to another is very hard.

Because each successive institution is grafted on to the set of existing ones with which it must fit and cohere, a nation's educational path over time takes on a certain distinctive shape and form. This emphasis on local and idiosyncratic factors conflicts with the widely shared view that institutions are somehow evolving towards efficiency. No such assumption is made here. History, as March and Olsen (1984) have put it, is not efficient. Lock-in occurs whenever a particular social practice or technology is sufficiently entrenched so as to hinder or prevent switching to an available alternative practice, even a technically superior one. In the case of technological path dependence, the factors that contribute to entrenchment run the gamut from contractual commitments and the damages resulting from breaking a contract, investment in durable equipment that switching would devalue, training and retraining, to the costs of weighing the costs and benefits of alternative designs (search costs) (Shapiro & Varian, 1999). In case of institutional lock-in, the forces contributing to lock-in are less clearly understood.

Among the likely suspects are the costs of rebuilding trust and loyalty with a new coalition of actors, but also the costs of switching to a new set of ideas and beliefs. In the United States a host of writers has argued that the lower educational branches have been imprisoned by "one best way" thinking (Tyack & Cuban, 1995; Clark 1985a,b; Tyack 1974). This notion that there is an efficient, a one best way to organize and administer public education is so deeply rooted in the system that it has survived even the most promising reform efforts and, as recent studies have shown, continues to influence the mentality and everyday habits of administrators and teachers (Stigler & Hiebert, 1999). Some lock-in aspects of the American public education system are local control and strict, American-style separation of church and state. They are arguably also among factors that prevent sustained reforms of American public schools, sometimes in paradoxical ways. For example, despite its intent to the contrary, local control opens public schooling to unaccountable forces of central intervention (Meyer, 2010). Similarly, the separation of church and state excludes proven reform energies from being applied to the system even where their religious impetus is secondary to the public benefits (Boyd & v. Geel, 2002; Boyd & Lugg 1996).

Paradoxically, at the same time, American higher education continues to be the envy of the world (Heidenheimer, 1997; Geiger, 1986). Most Americans accept as normal that higher education is the financial responsibility of private individuals. They willingly pay large amounts of money for their children's higher education. By contrast, proposals that would require private payments of even minute fractions of the American tuition costs send Germans into the streets in droves. Conversely, most Germans have accepted for almost two centuries that students are selected at age 10 or 12 into irreversibly different career paths, a notion that bewilders Americans, to say the least.

Similarly, Germans hold fast to Froebel's idea that kindergarten is the space for play, unencumbered by pressures to perform, while many Americans believe in "the earlier, the better" when it comes to teaching literacy and numeracy. These beliefs are simply *there*, and the work they do in legitimizing and reproducing certain institutions is done silently and behind the scenes (Westney 1987).

Efforts to understand how these beliefs and ideals influence policy are aided by a rich history of cross-national comparison and borrowing between the United States and Germany. The institutional interaction between Germany and the United States in the field of education exhibits a high degree of frequency, intensity, and historic continuity (Geitz & Heideki, 1999). Many important educational institutions, including the common school, the pre-school, and the high school have been built with an awareness of the practices and institutions in the other nation.

Path Dependence and the Institutionalization of Beliefs

The last decade has witnessed a remarkable revival in institutional studies (North, 1990; Powell & DiMaggio, 1991; Granovetter 1985; Meyer & Rowan, 2006), and not infrequently schools and universities served as paradigm cases for organizational scholars looking for alternatives to the rational-bureaucratic view of organizations (Meyer & Rowan, 1977, 1978; Rowan & Miskel, 1998). A subset of this literature has begun to address the role of ideas and beliefs in the formation and operation of institutions (Goldstein & Keohane, 1993; Ziegler, 1997; Campbell, 1998; Greif, 1998). Some of these studies focus on the hysteretic nature of institutions; their tendency to snap back into their original form after the force of an external intervention (an "education reform," for example) has passed. The view of institutions emerging from this literature is at odds with the prevailing notion of institutions as "structures," i.e., sets of constraints and rule-of-the-game type instructions that shape the behavior of individuals by affecting their cost-benefit calculus. The structural view of institutions suggests that reform and policy change are mainly a matter of replacing a given set of rules and constraints with a new one. As a result, much policy analysis revolves around how to change incentive structures to reward the desired and sanction undesired behaviors. By contrast, the cultural view of institutions suggests that lasting institutional changes are unlikely as long as the *ideas* and *beliefs* that are culturally shared among the individuals operating in the compass of a given institution are left untouched. Because these ideas and beliefs go often unchallenged and are rarely made, they reassert themselves after the force of the external change effort is spent and the institution often emerges unscathed from the effort to reform it. For this reason any thorough institutional reform must include a reflection on the beliefs that underlie a given institution. If a good deal of what ordinarily passes for education reform admittedly only perpetuates the malaise which it is meant to overcome, it is, as Tyack and Cuban (1995) have suggested, because the reform rarely reaches the "deep structures" of those institutions, i.e., their cultural foundations (Crowson, Boyd, & Mawhinney, 1996).

A cultural view of institutions focuses systematically on their moorings in *particular* (locally bounded) ideas and beliefs. A key tenet of this view is that *institutions institutionalize beliefs*. It suggests that we conceive of institutions as cognitive and mental relay stations that simultaneously store and transmit ideas and beliefs. Thus, institutions constrain the behavior of individuals not just through rules and sanctions, but also (and often more powerfully) by shaping the ideas and beliefs that propel them into action. We might say that the effects of institutions reach *deeper* than the standard institutions as rule-of-the-game metaphor suggests, affecting not only the self-interest of social actors, but their beliefs and their cognitive and emotional habits as well. These cognitive and emotional habits propel men and women into action. Unless they are changed, the institution will remain unchanged.

Thus, a path can be said to consist of four elements:

1. A unique point of origin, or idiosyncratic founding conditions. Small differences between the origins of an institutional path in different countries can produce large consequences later.
2. Particular, idiosyncratic ideological foundations and legitimizing discourses.
3. Characteristic socio-economic and institutional arrangements.
4. Unique historic events.

Together, these four elements are likely to produce idiosyncratic institutional arrangements, which shape, influence, and limit the possible range of future behaviors.

Institutional Paths of Education in Germany and the United States

Institutional path-dependency is well illustrated by reviewing a few select milestones and junctures in the American and German public education systems: the founding moments in the early 19th century, the critical juncture when the two systems literally "cross paths" and intersect after World War II, and the more recent period of continuous reform near the close of the 20th century. Despite the two systems' increasing mutual awareness and some surface convergences, the deep structure of the two nation's institutional arrangements remains largely intact and distinct.

Germany

From its founding in 1810 to the late 1960s, Germany had three distinctive educational tracks. The *Gymnasium* provided a classical education for elites and was the prerequisite for university. The *Volksschule*, literally the people's school, was attended by the majority of students and prepared for a life in the trades. An intermediate type of school, the *Realschule,* focused on advanced technical training for the professions.

The basic outlines of the German school system emerged during a brief period of reform led by Wilhelm von Humboldt (1767–1835). He required university-level training for high school teachers and modernized the structure and curriculum of the *Gymnasium*. Humboldt also proposed a qualifying examination, the *Abitur,* for university admission. The system's capstone was the university in Berlin that now bears his name. It was founded on the principles of academic freedom, the unity of teaching and research, and self-government by the professors.

The Founding Conditions

Humboldt reluctantly accepted the call to serve as the head of education reform after Prussia was dealt a devastating defeat by Napoleon on October 4, 1806, at Jena. Prussia's glory seemed to end with Napoleon's victory. In this moment of national defeat, William III took counsel not from the military or clergy, but from reform-minded civil servants and scholars with Freiherr vom Stein and Wilhelm von Humboldt at the center.

If 1806 marked the moral defeat of a budding nation, it also opened a window of opportunity for change. The philosopher Johann Gottlieb Fichte—a follower of Kant who was going to become the first president of the university of Berlin—seized on the moment most forcefully. He understood that the defeat could be turned into a new beginning. While the nation was militarily and politically defeated, its culture and education were a "free space" that was unoccupied. Speaking from the lectern of the University of Jena, Fichte made himself the spokesman of a national, anti-Napoleonic movement. In his "Address to the German Nation," he outlined a program of national rejuvenation through spiritual and cultural means. The key measure to be taken was a total overhaul of Germany's education. Fichte advocated a reorganization of schools along Pestalozzi's lines who, in turn, had been strongly influenced by Rousseau's (1782/1979) revolutionary ideas about education. The German government was, in Fichte's (1808/1878) forceful argument, defeated by the French occupants, but Germany's language and culture remained free. Thus the task of defending and resurrecting the broken German nation turned on education.

To this task administrators and scholars around Wilhelm von Humboldt turned with gusto. With able associates like Schleiermacher and von Süvern, Humboldt became the chief engineer of turning the new humanism into viable institutional reform. Beginning in 1808 they streamlined and systematized Prussian educational institutions—from the first grade of the *Volksschule* to the university state examination. A decade later the system had acquired the reputation as the most efficient system of schooling in Europe. By 1840 it was the most widely visited by foreign experts. By 1871 the widely admired system was credited with being the main cause for Prussia's victory over France. According to a widespread sentiment in France, the French were "defeated by the German schoolmaster."

Education as Lever for National Rebuilding

The key of Fichte's proposals was to use a revamped, streamlined education system to address two urgent needs: (a) to promote German national identity vis-à-vis its Western neighbors; and (b) to advance the recovery from the destruction and trauma of the French occupation in areas where no occupying power can effectively control another nation: its language, culture, and education. The main contribution of the *Reden* is to connect the diverse themes of *Bildung*, national identity, and national resistance and renewal against the occupation and suggest a feasible line of action pivoting on building a centralized, state-controlled education system. "Let freedom vanish for some time from the visible world; let's give it refuge in our innermost thoughts... Let us not with our body also have our mind be subjugated and suppressed and thrown into prison" (Fichte 1878, p. 193) Or: "Defeated we are... The fight with weapons is concluded; there emerges, if we want, the new fight of principles, of morals, and of character" (Fichte, 1878, p. 217).

Rousseau's moral and emotional education, Kantian ethics, Herder's culture, the nascent anti-Napoleonic nationalism, and Pestalozzi's experiments all fused into an activist agenda of educational rebuilding—this heady mix of revolutionary philosophical ideas and large-scale institutional reform was to establish and defend German nationhood against foreign military occupation and ideological dependence.

Finally, Humboldt and his peers were committed to a philosophy of knowledge and education that differed significantly from the Anglo-American concept of gentlemanly breeding and professional preparation. The term *Bildung* connoted a concept of cultural self-perfection through the life-long engagement with culture, knowledge, and the arts.

One of its underlying assumptions was that throughout his life the individual is engaged in a struggle between higher and lower selves, higher and lower inclinations. For the higher inclinations to win out required a continuous struggle for self-perfection, which was, by definition, open-ended. The model of high culture was Greek antiquity (as opposed to Roman antiquity, which was already a corruption of the Greek model; and as opposed to French civilization which falsely placed appearance over essence, as Rousseau had so clearly demonstrated).

United States

Partly inspired by the Prussian education system, Horace Mann began a campaign to replace the loose, unregulated, fragmented, and decentralized New England school system by a uniform, centralized, coherent and common one. The "common school" became shorthand for this uniquely American view of schooling to uplift and assimilate a culturally heterogeneous population, with a denominational version of Protestantism as the shared ideological platform. The first purpose of the common school promoters was more equality and social justice. As Horace Mann put it:

> According to the European theory, men are divided into classes—some to toil and earn, others to seize and enjoy. According to the Massachusetts theory, all are to have an equal chance for earning, and equal security in the enjoyment of what they earn.... The operative or laborer of the present day has no employment, and therefore no bread, unless the capitalist will accept his services. The vassal had no shelter but such as his master provided for him. Not one in five thousand of English operatives, or farm laborers, is able to build or own even a hovel; and therefore they must accept such shelter as Capital offers them. (cited in Cremin, 1957, p. 85)

This change meant centralization, secularization, and taxation—three big departures from a tradition of decentralized, locally controlled schooling. Inevitably, such a project would run into strong resistance by anyone who opposed centralization, secularization of the school's religious mission, and higher taxes.

To appreciate the significance of the common school idea, it is important to recall what problem it was designed to solve. For decades schooling in New England was more like a quilt than an evenly woven cloth. Yet, the results were quite impressive. Many Americans had no reason to be particularly unhappy with their messy and disorganized system of schooling, which satisfied the needs of a largely rural society. The call to centralize and systematize this loose arrangement of educational venues did not come from the agrarian middle classes of New England. It was made by the emerging class of urban intellectuals and reformers who believed that the uneven and disjointed nature of the system conflicted with the imperatives of equality and democracy. Some reformers pointed to the fact that the United States had a system of higher education that served the upper classes well, while general education was relegated to second-class status. As Noah Webster put it in 1790: "The constitutions are republican and the laws of education are monarchical" (cited in Kaestle 1983, p. 6).

Resistance Against School Centralization

To many Americans of the early 19th century, the common school idea was an open invitation to secularize education and place it under the control of big government. Since its implementation implied higher taxes, expanded government, and weaker religious impact, the number of groups who resisted the common school was impressively large. Poor rural towns had no money to support a more comprehensive, and more expensive system of schools; for many the idea to raise taxes to educate "other people's children" was akin to "reaching into neighbor's pockets to finance one's own children's education." Many defenders of local autonomy saw a centralized school system, governed from Boston rather than their local town, as a threat to their local self-government. The members of the various Protestant groups and sects saw a religiously uniform school system as a vehicle of secularization. Unlike local schools that could follow the beliefs of the preponderance of the local community, common schools would have to teach a watered-down version of Protestantism, something that would satisfy no one. Whereas Protestants were concerned that the common school would no longer teach the specific sectarian version of their beliefs, non-Protestant groups, especially Catholics, saw Horace Mann's project as a way to establish Protestant dominance over all other religions. Non-Anglo-Saxon ethnic minorities who used schooling as a means to pass their cultural and language heritage to their children likewise were suspicious of the idea to centralize and standardize the system. Last, but not least, upper-class families were not keen to have their children mix with, as John Locke and Thomas Jefferson had called it, "the rabble." One upper-class student quoted his father as saying that he would "rather send me to jail than to public school in Boston" (Kaestle, p. 59). The children of the well-to-do did not need improved schools for their upbringing. The private education they enjoyed was far superior to anything the public system could provide.

Thus, in the early 19th century few social groups saw the need for a reform of the magnitude Horace Mann envisioned, and the resistance against a system of public schools was formidable. To forge a strong coalition in favor of public schools a compelling rationale was needed.

Mass Immigration: A Window of Opportunity for Change

A key event in the acceptance of a centralized and secularized, tax-supported public school was the mid 19th century mass immigration, which rendered impossible the continuation of gradual assimilation of the newcomers through the established institutions of church and township. Not only were the immigrants too numerous to be readily absorbed into American culture. Their cultural and ethnic origin also put them directly at odds with the dominant Anglo-Saxon Protestants, who saw the mass immigration as a threat that would cause civic disorder, urban riots, and religious segregation. Coincidentally, the new factories in the nascent New England textile industry needed laborers that could not readily be found among the ranks of rural Americans. To be useful for factory work, owners sought workers with English language skills socialized to American standards of discipline and authority. Seen against that background, some of the upper-class resisters saw the common school in a new light. Perhaps such an institution could provide the necessary assimilation and socialization that would turn these newcomers into more reliable members of American society—both civically and economically (Bowles & Gintis, 1986; Katznelson & Weir, 1985). The coincidence of institutional change and mass immigration was not limited to Massachusetts. As Ravitch (2000) pointed out, "… each major reorganization of the school system was the result of intense political struggle, and that each of these battles coincided with a huge wave of new immigration" (p. xxix).

With mass immigration, the rhetoric of social reformers like Horace Mann, who described the common school as "protection of society against the giant vices which now invade and torment it"; as well as a "great equalizer of the condition of men; source of civilization, of economic prosperity" (1891, p. 233) fell on more fertile ground. Protestant hegemony, combined with social egalitarianism, defines school as engine of social progress, the instrument to transform nominal democracy into real democracy. The only way this works, however, is by stretching the compass of moral consensus, by building an ever-wider roof under which a growing disparity of beliefs would fit. Inevitably, the larger the roof, the shallower the convictions that united all Americans. Yet, this increasingly thin blanket of shared convictions would inevitably invite the resurgence of religious sectarianism.

Summing Up: Different Origins and Purposes of Public Schooling in the Two Countries

The public school is a contested project in the United States, uncontested in Germany. It is organized in a decentralized manner in the United States, and centralized in Germany. It is common here, and elitist there, espousing a philosophy of equality in the former and of class distinctions in the latter. Whereas Americans founded an institution that was to be a common school based on principles of common values, even if weakly held, schooling in Germany was institutionalized in the name of *Bildung*. While the common school strives to make better citizens for a better republic, *Bildung* is focused on the self-perfecting individual—conceived as a philosopher or artist, not the bourgeois.

Reaffirmation Trumps Reeducation (1945–1950)

For many decades, both systems developed in their respective tracks, which had been carved out during their 19th century founding moments. The case we will consider now is the American attempt to install an American-style high school in Germany. This historically unique episode provides a one-of-a kind natural experiment and test of the idea of path dependence. It was a time, after all, when the two systems engaged each other, each trying to get the other to see the virtues of its ways. In theory, conditions were ideal for institutional export. If ever a nation was in a position to implant its educational model on foreign soil, the post-war period during which Germany was under military and political control of the United States should have guaranteed success (Tent, 1982; Bungenstab, 1970; Heinemann, 1981).

A foreign occupying army in a devastated, defeated, and demoralized nation holding, for the time period in question, almost unlimited power in its zone of operation was attempting to abolish the *Gymnasium* and to replace it by an American-style comprehensive high school. Globalization theory would predict some significant success in that venture.

Potsdam and Reeducation

Under the Potsdam agreement, the American occupying forces and the American military government were committed to a policy of "reeducation" to ensure that "German education shall be so controlled as completely to eliminate Nazi and militarist doctrines and to make possible the successful development of democratic ideas" (Tent, 1982, p. 37). The prevailing opinion among Americans was that the German school system was an elite system that made "the submission and lack of self-determination [possible] upon which authoritarian leadership has thrived" (*Report of the United States Education Mission to Germany*, 1946, p. 19). Accordingly, American intervention in German education began (in June of 1946) with an order to purge the universities of all former supporters of National Socialism. On the school-level, the problem went far beyond filtering out compromised teachers and administrators. In the American view, it was not only a group of particular individuals who were tainted by the German past, but an entire institution. To assess the problem and to recommend guidelines for change, the U.S. government turned to an expert-commission under the direction of George F. Zook, a professor of European history and former U.S. Commissioner of Education. The 10 members of the commission were mainly selected for representing American educational organizations; familiarity with Germany ranked second. The group toured Germany in August and September of 1946. On October 12, 1946, the commission submitted its 50-page report to General Clay and the American public. In it the commission judged the *Gymnasium* to be an "anachronistic survival of an aristocratic-military tradition," which inoculates "habits of uncritical obedience" (*Report of the United States Education Mission to Germany*, 1946, p. 1). It recommended replacing the German school system by a comprehensive school for which the American high school served as model.

On January 10, 1947, Lucius Clay ordered the submission of school reform plans by April 1 of that year. Finding that their requests were met with months of foot-dragging by the German authorities, the Allied Control Authority issued its directive #54 on June 25, 1947, which essentially turned the recommendations of the Zook report into military law. At the height of the ensuing conflict, the American military government repeatedly threatened to dismiss responsible German officials who, in the American view, stalled and disobeyed those laws, threatening to take the reform of schools into its own hands. Yet, after two years of intense dispute and controversy, the American side, in effect, conceded defeat. One of their spokesmen noted that "[t]he true reform of the German people comes from within. It will be spiritual and moral. The organization or the structure of schools, for example, is less important for the future of the Germans and the world, than what is being taught, how, and by whom" (Schmidt & Fichter, 1971, p. 167). The military government dropped its attempt to impose a high school-type model and Germans rebuilt their traditional class-based school system with the humanistic Gymnasium as its centerpiece, thus affirming the "peculiar nature and value of our education system," as Alois Hundhammer, a key figure in the anti-reeducation movement, put it (in Tent, 1982, p.. 145).

The Zook Report: The Common School Meets the Gymnasium

How did Americans decide that the German school system needed to be changed and how did they settle on their own school as the proper model? The American policy of reeducation was not only a response to the almost impossible task of returning a defeated and demoralized nation to civil life. It was also the result of one nation looking at a foreign institution through the eyes of its homegrown institution and asking for a make-over in the image of itself. What the Americans saw was an institution shot through with the spirit of class inequality and the anachronistic ideals of a pre-democratic age. What they wanted was an institution that would prepare students for democracy, as opposed to a "school system, where class distinctions are emphasized in the very organization of the school and the authoritarian inculcation of subject matter is still widely prevalent in teaching methods" (*Report*, 1946, p. 1).

A number of things disturbed and irritated the American observers. First, was the fact that "80% [of students] dropped out somewhere during the eight-year course" (Report, 1946, p. 18). Since they were selected into a vocational and an academic educational track at age 10—a choice that determined their future working-class or upper-class careers—Americans counted every student who was not channeled into the academic track as "drop-out." The small group of students who made it to the terminal degree, the *Abitur*, were seen as a select group socialized to rule over the 80% they left behind. The segregation by social class, which the school reflected, also was visible in a two-class teacher education system, with lower school (*Volksschul*) teachers trained at the teacher training institutions (*Pädagogische Hochschule*), and the others at the university.

Last but not least, the Americans believed that the German school system did not and could not prepare students for democracy. Because it fostered segregation by social class and by religion, the German school system offered "no possibility of a common school life" (Report, 1946, p. 19). The curriculum at the elite *Gymnasium* was long on history and classical languages and short on subject matter the American observers deemed important to prepare students for participation in democratic society. Tuition payments (*Schulgeld*), though modest, appeared to further stack the odds against the non-propertied classes.

Based on this assessment, the Commission recommended that "elementary, secondary and vocational schools should be united to form a comprehensive school system" (Report, 1946, p. 20). Higher and lower schools should be integrated to offer "an elastic organization of the curriculum in core subjects and elective courses" (p. 22). "The present curriculum of the secondary school seems crowded with subjects, heavy with academic tradition, and in most respects remote from life and ill-adapted to the future needs of the pupils" (p. 23). This was to be remedied by greater attention to the social sciences, vocational and commercial studies, and home economics. In addition, vocational education should take place within the high school (as opposed to the dual system); vocational schools ought to be upgraded so that graduates had access to the university; and "teacher dominated classes" ought to give way to an atmosphere of "democratic living." Classes should cease to be "heavy with academic tradition" and no longer be taught by "academicians withdrawn from community concern."

Yet, while the common school ideal was dominant among the Americans, it was not unopposed. Criticism came from various quarters, including the U.S. Assistant Secretary of State (Tent, 1982, p. 119). Yet, the most powerful opponents turned out to be a group of Chicago scholars. This group of émigré scholars went on record that the humanistic tradition of education in Germany was empirically, but not intrinsically wedded to a system of social and class segregation, and that Humboldt's ideals of *Bildung* were not only not obsolete, but the proper basis on which to reorganize German education.

In the immediate aftermath of their social and military catastrophe, German school authorities had to reach back far into German history to find precedents on which the new educational policy could be built. In Bavaria—the major front in the struggle over reeducation—some of the early ordinances to re-establish confessional schools referred back to 1926 or even 1883 (Trent, 1982, 174). The desire to take up and continue a tradition from the unblemished part of Germany's history did not stop at party lines. During their brief reign in power, the social-democratic government in Bavaria (until end of 1946) did not want to abolish the traditional three-pillared structure (*Dreigliedrigkeit*) of German schools.

Hundhammer's War

The consensus for educational continuity that prevailed across the political spectrum was a challenge to the American military government. In the emerging conflict between the Bavarian government and the military government, the Bavarian minister of culture, Alois Hundhammer, became the chief spokesman and strategist leading the campaign against reeducation and for the affirmation of Germany's educational tradition. A staunch conservative and adroit politician, Hundhammer met the American occupants flexible in detail, but firm in his principles, which he articulated with power and eloquence. In an interim report (*Zwischenbericht*), about the progress of education reform which he presented to the military government on March 7, 1947, he conceded the need for equal access, but insisted on the special role of the *Gymnasium* to further the needs of "all truly gifted" students. In Hundhammer's view, the implementation of meritocratic principles was possible only within the limits set by the *"natural hierarchy of talent."* The truly gifted make up only a small group of students and those do not emerge from the different classes in equal proportions. No civilizational measure can erase this biological inequality, not even the alteration of our so-called two-track system in favor of a comprehensive school (*Einheitsschule*).

In defending his interpretation of the German educational tradition, Hundhammer could also draw on the Bavarian Constitution, whose article 132 established that the "diversity of vocations is decisive for the structure of the education system" ("daß für den Aufbau des Schulwesens die Mannigfaltigkeit der Lebensberufe maßgebend ist"), meaning that the school system had to mirror and reproduce the socio-economic differentiation in lower and upper classes. And: "The start of the higher school [Gymnasium] must not be delayed beyond the developmentally justified age (about ten years of age)" (in Klafki, 1984, p. 178).

Three weeks later Hundhammer presented the Bavarian ministry's Education Reform Plan, which amounted to an unambiguous rejection of American reeducation. The latter implied a "total turn-over and radical break with a century-old culture from which our education system emerged" (Hundhammer in Klafki, 1984, p. 179).

Despite its diplomatic wording, this was a defiant rejection of everything the American military government OMGUS (Office of Military Government, United States) intended to accomplish in education. It was also a refutation of existing military law. As a response, OMGUS increased its pressure. A senior OMGUS officer Van Wagoner (a former governor of Michigan) explained to the Bavarian authorities that the military government considered its reeducation declarations "an order." At the height of the conflict, OMGUS issued military orders to bring the German authorities into compliance with its reeducation policy. The key points on which it insisted were that there be a six-year elementary school for all (Tent, 1982, p. 191) and that there be no instruction in Latin. Unless these orders were carried out, OMGUS would impose its own educational system (p. 195). General Clay repeated that "equality of opportunity in education is essential to a sound democracy" (pp. 135–136).

Summary

In no other field of reconstruction did the Americans encounter a mass movement rallying to the defense of the tradition whose watchwords proved to be so deeply rooted in the shared beliefs and affections of the Germans. The result was that very minor issues (whether certain groups of children ought to begin to study Latin in fifth or seventh grade) came to demarcate a line which to cross was equal to national betrayal or suicide.

One hundred and forty years after *Bildung* was institutionalized, the idea was still very much in the hearts and minds of Germans, capable of coordinating and framing their thought, of evaluating alternative educational designs, and of galvanizing them into action. Similarly, 100 years after Horace Mann articulated the vision of the democratic school as a common, inclusive one, which educates students irrespective of wealth and creed, that idea of school as the great lever and promoter of equality and democracy was also still very much alive in the minds of the Americans; so much so that they believed their own ideas about schooling would allow the Germans to overcome a presumably disastrous cultural heritage.

In both cases, the main agents of the conflict are enthusiastic, highly motivated protagonists of contingent, culturally specific ideas. Men and women on each side—reasonable, highly educated persons of good will—who saw their way of doing things as the one best system. Both groups were applying and acting on deeply entrenched cultural blueprints. Instead of cosmopolitanism,

Hundhammer wrapped himself in the mantle of Humboldt, and Zook in the mantle of Horace Mann.

The Gesamtschul-Reform

In the ensuing period, the major challenges to both nations stem from insufficient inclusion of heterogeneous student populations. In the United States, African Americans, special needs students, and Asian and Hispanic ethnic minorities struggle for inclusion with various degrees of success. In Germany, the main efforts for access and inclusion target the segregation of working-class children and, more recently, the segregation of immigrant children (especially of Turkish descent) into the lower educational track. In both countries, these formerly excluded groups make significant strides toward inclusion, while key path-dependent institutional commitments prevent full and complete integration.

In Germany, a key institutional reform effort was the attempted introduction of the integrated comprehensive school (*integrierte Gesamtschule* or *Gesamtschule* for short). The starting point for the *Gesamtschule* was a recommendation issued by the German Education Commission (*Bildungsrat*) in 1969. The objective was to improve "education for democratic citizenship" through integration of the hitherto distinct three branches of the public school. The promoters of the *Gesamtschule* avoided allusions to the *Einheitsschule* (united school) for which there had been agitation on the Left during both the Weimar Republic and in Berlin during the occupation.

The German Education Commission recommended setting up 40 *Gesamtschulversuche* across West Germany. The plan was to create a basis for a "scientific" analysis as to what works and what does not.

The educational reform, detailed in the *Strukturplan* (Structural Plan), was approved in 1970 by the Council of Education and by each education minister of the several states. The main components of the reform program were (a) the reorganization of the upper level of the *Gymnasium*, (b) the recruitment of more students into colleges and universities, and (c) the establishment of the comprehensive school (*Gesamtschule*). The latter was to integrate the three tiers of secondary schools—the *Hauptschule* (the new name for the *Volksschule*), the *Realschule*, and the *Gymnasium*—to diminish the elitist bias of the traditional secondary education system.

However, the *Bildungsrat* had only advisory authority. Thus, implementation of the plan became subject to the cross-fire of political conflict. Left-leaning provinces (Laender), those governed by the Social Democratic Party (SPD), generally supported the plan, while those governed by the more conservative Christian Democratic Union (CDU) did not. Where there was resistance against the plan, this resistance had a popular basis rooted in the attachment to the Gymnasium that had also fueled the resistance against the Allies' reeducation plans.

A report by Brauns and Steinmann (1997, p. 27), members of the prestigious German social research institute ZUMA, confirms the idea of a high degree of inertia in the German system, along with partial reforms in opening access:

> In contrast to many other countries, the basic structural features of the German educational system have remained relatively unchanged by the educational reforms. The attempt of designing a comprehensive system, for example, has only been realised in a few number of Länder, on a limited scale and on trial basis for experimental purposes. Basically, the traditional three-tiered system of secondary education has been kept.

But even though the *Gesamtschulreform* fell short of the original plan, it marked a change in the German education system. The boundaries of a tri-partite system that was rigidly class-based were softened and became more penetrable. Socioeconomic status lost some of its power to predict educational opportunities.

The number of students attending institutions of higher education rose from just over 200,000 in 1960 to about 1.9 million in the 1992–93 academic year. Between 1959 and 1979, 20 new universities were built, and university academic staff increased from 19,000 to 78,000. About 34% of all students graduated with the *Abitur* in 1990, compared with only 11% in 1970. Yet, for many, the new opportunities led to disappointment. The number of dropouts had quadrupled from 14,000 in the mid-1970s to 60,000 two decades later.

This democratic opening was largely endogenously produced (see also Heidenheimer, 1997). Rather than one country imitating another, Germany responded within the constraints of its institutional configurations to its own view of problems. In Germany, an unprecedented economic expansion (*das Wirtschaftswunder*, the economic miracle) followed the devastation of the 1940 and the stagnation of the 1950s. The economic expansion showed up a shortage of qualified personnel, especially in the technical and upper staff levels. The Left-liberal forces used their political capital from having opposed Hitler to press for an opening of the still tightly elite-controlled school system. Aided by the economic need to draw on broader reservoirs of "manpower," they succeeded in softening the rigid class barriers. The hitherto irreversible sorting into one of three tracks was softened. Still, where the Left-liberal coalition intended the *Gesamtschule* to replace the *Gymnasium*, it merely managed to complement it within rather narrow bounds of state and region.

Discussion: Implications for Policy and Theory

The above analysis has shown that the German school system remains wedded to key features of its institutional origin in a class-based tracking and sorting model. Different founding conditions, different dominant beliefs, different

Table 9.1 Comparison of USA and German Schooling Models

	USA	GERMANY
Basic Ideology	Assimilation ("common school"), education for citizenship; economic opportunity;	Cultural induction (Bildung as elite cultural capital); class-based preparation for lower or upper class occupations
Institutional Model	Tayloristic factory	Government bureaucracy
Fault Lines	public education comparatively highly contested; strong legal leadership (supreme court) weak professional leadership;	School as a 'top down' cultural project; upward mobility requires cultural capital; Hauptschule as "Restschule" (residual school) increasingly devoid of legitimacy
Path Dependent Policy Inertia	Cumulative disadvantage of class and race excludes students in urban centers from equal opportunity; Local control	Three-tiered structure ("Dreigliedrigkeit") well and alive; negatively affects especially foreign born immigrant children

class-structures have given rise to distinct path differences which have persisted over a long historical period (see Table 9.1).

Two Paths of Education

The German and the American institutions of education are two of the world's most admired and influential systems of education. And while they have influenced each other over a period of almost two centuries, they have also been shaped by singular cultural forces. By studying the processes by which they have influenced each other, we are able to discern what is unique about them.

The German system was, by common consent, created in a brief period of immensely productive institutional fermentation. When William III took counsel not from the military or clergy, but from the scholars with Wilhelm von Humboldt at the center, the road to an unprecedented story of cultural rejuvenation, centered around the nation's educational institutions, was cleared. Eight weeks after signing the Peace of Tilsit, William III signed an edict stipulating the construction of a university in Berlin.

Wilhelm von Humboldt was at the helm of a newly created Prussian ministry of Kultus, directing, with a handful of associates and friends, a general overhaul of the Prussian education system. Humboldt retired after only 18 months in office, but not without leaving a legacy of educational innovations that—for better or worse—shape the way Germans view education to this day.

The American educational system did not spring full-blown from a single historic act of institution building, but eventually assumed an equally definite and coherent shape. Until about 1880, its various branches of higher and lower schools and colleges developed in relative independence of each other. But when the modern American university assumed definite shape in the two decades following the Civil War, the high school also found its final form. Institution building in the lower schools was prompted by the problems associated with rapid urbanization, industrialization and, most keenly felt: cultural assimilation. The slogan of the movement addressing these needs was common schools.

Germans were quite comfortable with the three-tiered class system prevailing in Germany (separating people into the peasantry and urban laborers, the bourgeois middle classes, and the landed aristocracy) and did not mean to challenge it. Neither was religious inclusiveness of great concern to the mainly protestant German educational institution-builders. Catholicism was deeply entrenched (rather than being a minority religion as it was in the United States) and the vast majority of Protestants were of Lutheran creed. Instead of accommodating sectarian pluralism, the German founders could assume that both Protestant and Catholic religion would be respected in Prussian/German schools. Last not least, where Humboldt affected reforms which reached deep into the curriculum, Horace Mann, the head and spokesman of the common school movement, largely focused on creating a coordinated educational delivery system. In lieu of a ministry of education for which the "limited government" creed of the United States left no place, the schools were to be coordinated by a state-wide "Board of Education."

To be sure, neither Humboldt nor Horace Mann created institutions out of thin air. Humboldt's radius of action was limited by a well-established three-tier system of education bearing the stamp of a rigid system of social classes that had been codified 14 years earlier in the Prussian Landrecht of 1794.[1] Where Humboldt's reforms were constrained by rigid class divisions, Mann had to take established traditions of local and sectarian educational control into account. Especially in Massachusetts, the state which pioneered formal education in the United States, education had from the outset been synonymous with religious and moral formation—a process jealously guarded by the largely puritan clergy.

Thus the Prussian and the American group of educational reformers found themselves confronted by different tasks. Creating a socioeconomically inclusive common school was neither a problem nor an option for the circle of reformers around Humboldt. Their chief task was to forge the existing institutions into an integrated whole to be supervised from the academic top, an institutional system that would answer to the call for national revitalization in an occupied and devastated country in the spirit of *Bildung* and classical humanism.

On the other hand, very few Americans saw reasons to be unhappy with the inchoate network of colleges and academies then in existence. Nor were they likely to think about common schools and colleges in the same context, the former being places for elementary learning, the latter for the preparation of gentlemen to the professions.

Understanding Policy Differences

Path dependence defines the horizons of policy making and helps understanding elements of persistent policy inertia. In Germany a continued commitment to elite-formation through *Bildung* has meant that the acquisition of cultural capital has been a major hurdle to upward mobility, especially from the lower to the higher tracks in the tri-partite school system. Among the inertia-producing, retarding factors in the United States are local control and an ideology of one best system. Arguably, both institutional blocks owe their continued vitality to exclusive class-interests. In the United States, local control survives and thrives because it affords privileges to the wealthy who can bend an otherwise egalitarian public school system in their favor (Meyer, 2009a, 2010). In Germany, the *Gymnasium* is the key lever for the reproduction of the *Bildungsbuerger*, a class whose distinct status is based not on money, but on access to cultural capital.

In both countries, the gravitational pull is toward inertial reproduction of the inner-city and *Hauptschul*-educational ghettos. To break the inertia is certainly not impossible, but it requires insight into the deep roots that both institutional features have in either system.

Implications for Theory

As I have argued elsewhere, educational and organizational policies exhibit strong path dependent inertia not often recognized in studies of globalization (Meyer, 1995, 1997, 1998, 2009). Frequently, globalization research is conducted at a level of generality at which recognizable institutional variations and differences are obscured. This can convey the erroneous impression that the comprehensive American high school and the *Gymnasium*, the German dual system and the American vocational education, the American graduate school and the French *Grandes Ecoles* were all instances of the diffusion of the same essential model of formal education (see also Meyer, 2009 ; Benavot & Resnik 2006). One of the main shortcomings of globalization research is that recognizable actors are absent and the groups and people pushed around by the globalization agenda never fight back. It is clear, however, that, in the cases of reeducation and the attempted introduction of the *Gesamtschule*, people did not passively accept the imposition of new models of education.

Note

1 According to this code, Prussia's population was divided into four socially and politically distinct classes: peasants and laborers, the commercial classes, clergy, professors and civil servants, and the nobility proper (many of whom were active in the military and top level civil service). Only the latter two classes were *satisfaktionsfaehig*, meaning that they had the requisite social standing to be admitted into noble "society," including the right to settle their affairs by duel.

References

Benavot, A., & Resnik, J. (2006). Lessons from the past: A comparative socio-historical analysis of primary and secondary education. In J. E. Cohen, D. E. Bloom, & M. B. Malin (Eds.), *Educating all children: A global agenda* (pp. 123–230). Cambridge, MA: MIT Press.

Bowles, S., & Gintis, H. (1986). *Schooling in capitalist America*. New York: Basic Books.

Boyd, W. L. (2003). Market forces, globalization, and pressures for school choice. *PSBA Bulletin, 67*(3), 14–17.

Boyd, W. L., & Lugg, C. (1996). Reflections on a Pennsylvania Case: Religion and the Politics of Educational Reform. *Politics of Education Bulletin, 23*(3–4), 2–5.

Boyd, W. L., & v. Geel, T. (2002, September 4). Vouchers and the entanglement of church and state: Thoughts on the Zelman decision. *Education Week, 22*(1), 46, 49.

Braudel, F., & Matthews, S. (1982). *On history*. Chicago: The University of Chicago Press.

Brauns, H., & Steinmann, S. (1997). *Educational reform in France, West Germany, the United Kingdom and Hungary*. (Working Paper AB I/21). Mannheim, Germany: Mannheim Centre for European Social Research.

Brian, A. W. (1989). Competing technologies, increasing returns, and lock-in by historical events. *Economic Journal, 99*(397), 116–131.

Bruford, W. H. (1975). *The German tradition of self-cultivation: 'Bildung' from Humboldt to Thomas Mann*. Cambridge, UK: Cambridge University Press.

Bruner, J. (1996). *The culture of education*. Cambridge, MA: Harvard University Press.

Bungenstab, K.-E. (1970). *Umerziehung zur Demokratie*. [Reeducation for democracy] Düsseldorf, Germany: Bertelsmann.

Campbell, J. L. (1998). Institutional analysis and the role of ideas in political economy. *Theory and Society, 27,* 377–409.

Clark, B. R. (1985a). *The high school and the university. What went wrong in America, Part I. Phi Delta Kappan, 66*(6), 391–397.

Clark, B.R. (1985b). *The high school and the university. What went wrong in America, Part II. Phi Delta Kappan, 66*(7), 472–475.

Cremin, L. A. (Ed.). (1957). *The republic and the school. Horace Mann on the education of free men*. New York: Teachers College Press.

Crowson, R. L., Boyd, W. L., & Mawhinney, H. B. (Eds.). (1996). The politics of education and the new institutionalism. London: Falmer.

David, P. A. (1985). Clio and the economics of QWERTY. *American Economic Review, 75*(2), 332–337.

Douglas, M. (1986). *How institutions think*. Syracuse, New York: Syracuse University Press.

Fichte, J. (1808/1878) *Reden an die deutsche Nation*. [Address to the German nation] Leipzig, Germany: Philipp Reclam jun.

Geiger, R. J. (1986). *Private sectors in higher education: Structure, function, and change in eight countries*. Ann Arbor: University of Michigan Press.

Geitz, H., & Heideki, J. (Eds.). (1999). *German influences on education in the United States to 1917*. Cambridge, UK: Cambridge University Press.

Goldstein, J., & Keohane, R. O. (Eds.). (1993). *Ideas and foreign policy. Beliefs, institutions, and political change*. Ithaca, NY: Cornell University Press.

Granovetter, M. (1985). Economic action and social structure: The problem of embeddedness. *American Journal of Sociology, 91,* 481–510.

Greif, A. (1998). Historical and comparative institutional analysis. *American Economic Review, 88*(2) 80–84.

Heidenheimer, A. J. (1997). *Disparate ladders. Why school and university policies differ in Germany, Japan, and Switzerland*. New Brunswick, NJ: Transaction.

Hill, P. T. (1999). Supplying effective public schools in big cities. In D. Ravitch (Ed.), *Brookings papers on education policy* (pp. 419–462).Washington, DC: Brookings Institution Press.

Kaestle, C. F. (1983). *Pillars of the republic*. Boston: Hill and Wang.

Katznelson, I., & Weir, M. (1985). *Schooling for all*. New York: Basic Books.

Klafki, W. (1984) Restaurative Schulpolitik 1945–1950 in Westdeutschland [Restorational education policy 1945–1950 in West Germany]. In H. Kemper (Ed.), *Theorie und Geschichte der Bildungsreform* (pp. 173–186). Hanstein, Germany: Forum Academicum.

Lipset, S. M. (1996) *American exceptionalism. A double-edged sword*. New York: Norton.

Heinemann, M. (Ed.). (1981). *Umerziehung und Wiederaufbau. Die Bildungspolitik der Besatzungsmächte in Deutschland und Österreich* [Reeducation and reconstruction: Education policy of the occupying forces in Germany and Austria]. Stuttgart, Germany: Klett-Cotta.

Mann, H. (1891). *Life and works of Horace Mann*, Vol. IV, Boston: Lee and Shephard.

March, J. G., & Olsen, J. P. (1984). The new institutionalism: Organizational factors in political life. *American Political Science Review, 78*, 734–749.

Meyer, H.-D. (1995). Organizational environments and organizational discourse: Bureaucracy between two worlds. *Organization Science, 6*(1), 32–43.

Meyer, H.-D. (1996). Ideological continuities and discontinuities in American public education. Parameters of a new consensus. In M. Minkenberg, & R. Dittgen (Eds.), *The American impasse: The United States at the end of the cold war* (pp. 215–237). Pittsburgh, PA: Pittsburgh University Press.

Meyer, H.-D. (1997). Local control: American experiences with educational autonomy. *Bildung und Erziehung, 2*, 137–153.

Meyer, H.-D. (1998). Fröbel or 'Head Start'? - Religion and social ccience in the institutionalization of early childhood education in Germany and the United States. In H.-D. Meyer, M. Minkenberg, & I. Ostner (Eds.). *Religion and social policy — comparative perspectives.* Jahrbuch für Europa- und Nordamerikastudien [Yearbook for Europe- and Northamerica studies] (2nd ed., pp. 225–252). Opladen, Germany: Leske und Buderich.

Meyer, H.-D. (2009a). Institutionelle Isomorphie und Vielfalt—Zu einer ueberfaelligen Korrektur in der Bildungsforschung. [Institutional isomorphism and diversity—Regarding an overdue correction in education research]. In S. Koch & Schemman, M. (Eds.), *Neo-Institutionalismus in der Erziehungswissenschaft* (pp. 292–308). Wiesbaden, Germany: Verlag fuer Sozialwissenschaften.

Meyer, H.-D. (2009b, May). Meaning what we say and saying what we mean: Disambiguating decentralization, *American Journal of Education*, 457–474.

Meyer, H.-D. (2010). Local control as a mechanism of colonization of public education in the United States. *Educational Philosophy and Theory, 42*(8), 830–845.

Meyer, J. W., & Rowan, B. (1977). Institutionalized organizations: Formal structure as myth and ceremony. *American Journal of Sociology, 83*, 340–363.

Meyer, H.-D, & Rowan, B. (2006). *The New institutionalism in education.* Albany: State University of New York Press.

Meyer, J. W. (1977). The effects of education as an institution. *American Journal of Sociology, 83*(1), 55–77.

Meyer, J. W., & Rowan, B. (1978). The structure of educational organizations. In M. W. Meyer and Associates (Eds.), *Environments and organizations* (pp. 78–109). San Francisco: Jossey Bass.

North, D. C. (1990). *Institutions, institutional change and economic performance.* New York: Cambridge University Press.

Powell, W. W., & DiMaggio, P. J. (1991). *The new institutionalism in organizational analysis.* Chicago: The University of Chicago Press.

Ramirez, F. (2003).The global model and national legacies. In K. Anderson-Levitt (Ed.), *Local meanings, global schooling* (pp. 239–245). New York: Palgrave Macmillan.

Ravitch, D. (2000). *The great school wars.* Baltimore: The Johns Hopkins University Press.

Report of the United States Education Mission to Germany. (1946). Washington, DC: United States Government Printing Office.

Rousseau, J. J. (1979). *Emile.* New York: Basic Books. (Original work published 1782)

Rowan, B., & Miskel, C. G. (1998). Institutional theory and the study of educational organizations. In K. L. Seashore (Ed.), *Handbook of research on educational administration* (pp. 359–383). San Francisco: Jossey Bass.

Schmidt, U., & Fichter, T. (1971). *Der erzwungene Kapitalismus* [Enforced capitalism]. Berlin, Germany: Wagenbach.

Shapiro, C., & Varian, H. R. (1999). *Information rules. A strategic guide to the network economy.* Boston: Harvard Business School Press.

Somers, M. (1996). Where is sociology after the historic turn? Knowledge, cultures, Narrativity, and historical epistemologies. In T. McDonald (Ed.), *The historic turn in the human sciences.* Ann Arbor: University of Michigan Press.

Stigler, J. W., & Hiebert J. (1999). *The teaching gap: Best ideas from the world's teachers for improving education in the classroom.* New York: Free Press.

Strang, D., & Meyer, J. W. (1993). Institutional conditions for diffusion. *Theory and Society, 22,* 487–911.

Tent, J. F. (1982). *Mission on the Rhine. Reeducation and denazification in American-occupied Germany.* Chicago: The University of Chicago Press.

Tyack, D. (1974). The one best system. Cambridge, MA: Harvard University Press.

Tyack, D., & Cuban, L. (1995). *Tinkering toward utopia. A century of public school reform.* Cambridge, MA: Harvard University Press.

Weber, M. (1949). *The methodology of the social sciences.* Glencoe, IL: The Free Press

Westney, D. E. (1987). Imitation and innovation. The transfer of Western organizational patterns in Meiji Japan. Cambridge, MA: Harvard University Press.

Ziegler, J. N. (1997) Governing ideas. *Strategies for innovation in France and Germany.* Ithaca, NY: Cornell University Press.

PART V

Major Efforts to Improve School Performance

Douglas E. Mitchell

The two chapters of Part V provide contrasting takes on important strategies that are being used in efforts to produce an overall improvement in the performance of the nation's schools. Kenneth Wong and Emily Farris review recent developments in the historical tension between education and civic governance. The Progressive and Urban Reform movements of the early 20th century were largely successful in separating educational governance systems from those responsible for the rest of local civic policies. Local civic governance remained with mayors and city councils, while protectionist educational governance was given over to school boards and school superintendents who were insulated from partisan politics through non-partisan, off-year elections and the development of teacher tenure laws to secure teacher employment rights. Wong and Farris draw our attention to substantial reconsideration of this pre-1950 consensus as, particularly in the nation's largest cities, mayors have become actively engaged in school governance and management. At the same time, interpreters of urban policy and governance have highlighted the importance of political *regimes*—coalitions of ideologically compatible civic elites whose political power and support for specific policy commitments account for the overall direction of policy decision making. This chapter asks the provocative question: Should we bet on the integrated executive governance control exercised by mayors and their appointees, or on the development of a school *performance regime* of community elites devoted to school improvement to bring about the very substantial improvements in public education needed to really leave no child behind in the 21st century?

Robert Crowson, Claire Smrekar, and Jo Bennett tackle the question of substantial school improvement from a very different direction. Whereas Wong and Farris look at the problem primarily in terms of how the power to control is distributed, Crowson and colleagues focus on the kinds of services needed to substantially improve the schools' capacity to support high level learning for all students. Looking back at the relatively brief period when political consensus endorsed the development of integrated children's services within the school setting—joining health, welfare, recreation, community organization, and other important support services into an integrated service delivery model— these authors pose anew the proposition that educational attainment cannot be produced through educational services alone. They anticipate growing support for an integrated services model that makes schools the coordinating agency to provide leadership in a system of holistic child support and development.

As other chapters in this volume make clear, these are not the only systemic approaches to improving educational success, but they do share in common a continued belief in the importance of local integration of services and the expansion of the educational mission to include other community and social services that are an essential part of child nurture and development. Both of the chapters stress the importance of community coherence and integration, implicitly raising a question about whether the relatively invasive policy demands from more centralized policy makers can reach the level of integrated service delivery needed for educational success.

10

GOVERNANCE IN URBAN SCHOOL SYSTEMS

Redrawing Institutional Boundaries

Kenneth K. Wong and Emily Farris

Speaking before a gathering of mayors and superintendents in March 2009, U.S. Secretary of Education Arne Duncan urged the mayors to assume greater responsibility for improving public education (Quaid, 2009). Secretary Duncan took the position that mayors can provide steady and strong leadership to raise school performance in urban schools. At other public events, the secretary made reference to his experience as CEO of Chicago Public Schools in engaging outsider organizations to manage and turn around the district's lowest performing schools. Secretary Duncan's remarks illustrate the growing interest in mayoral accountability in a climate of declining public confidence in urban schools. How schools are governed, in other words, has gained national attention.

Notwithstanding the U.S. Secretary of Education's remarks, school governance has received ongoing attention in both the reform community and the scholarly literature. To be sure, mayoral involvement represents the latest effort to reform urban school governance in the United States. Over the last four decades, school systems have faced various major challenges. In the 1960s, urban schools were under enormous pressure to integrate minority students, equalize resource allocation, and expand minority representation in the school board and the school administration. City schools were found to be heatedly political—with major battles over desegregation, decentralization and community-control, income-class cleavages, within-district allocations of resources, and labor-management relations. Since the early 1990s, the charter school movement has been successful in gaining school autonomy. Charter school legislation has been adopted in over forty states and charter schools currently enroll about 2 million students. With the passage of the No Child Left Behind Act of 2001, schools that fail to meet state standards of proficiency are required to adopt restructuring strategies, including staff replacement and reopening of schools under alternative management.

As urban school systems manage new policy and political challenges, school governance has remained remarkably stable for about a century. Urban districts are generally governed by elected school board members whose non-partisan elections are held separately from the regular municipal or national election. The elected board appoints the superintendent and exercises broad fiscal authority. The superintendent assumes the role of the chief administrative officer and oversees the central office as well as the schools in the district. Principal selection and teacher hiring are handled by the district's central office. In other words, organizational hierarchy with top-down command tends to define school governance in urban districts.

divided

While the hierarchical model continues to dominate, urban school governance has become increasingly diverse in recent years. In this chapter, we first provide the current context that facilitates greater public attention to governance reform at the district level. Our central observation here is that, given growing public concerns for educational accountability, the shift toward stronger district-wide governance is directed to reform objectives for improving school performance and to broadening stakeholder engagement. Second, the chapter examines two analytical perspectives on system-wide governance and politics, namely *regime theory* and *integrated governance* with mayoral accountability. These perspectives provide alternative accounts of how institutional boundaries are shifting to enable mayoral leadership and broader civic engagement. The design, rationale, implementation, and policy consequences following from each of these perspectives are discussed. We conclude with a discussion on the broader implications of governance reform.

Organization Stability in School Districts

Despite expansion of state and federal influence in educational policy and practice, in American public education, local governance prevails (Fusarelli & Cooper, 2009). While the number of school districts has changed significantly over the years, district governance and administration have remained remarkably stable. The dominant mode for the selection of school board members is a nonpartisan election held in an off year from the local general election. Board members can be elected from sub-districts or district-wide (at-large). Term limits are not usually placed on board membership. These elections are frequently uncontested and usually involve very low voter turnout. Even fewer voters are likely to attend board meetings, which are often held on a monthly basis. Given the low political interest in school board politics, many researchers note the dominance of civic elites and interest groups in these elections (Zeigler & Jennings, 1974; Moe, 2005; Hess & Leal, 2005). However, a few exceptions are found in major cities. Although an overwhelming majority

[handwritten margin note: How is this working for these districts?]

of school boards are popularly elected, those in Baltimore, Boston, Chicago, Cleveland, New York, Philadelphia, Providence, Trenton, and several other cities are appointed either by the mayor or jointly by the mayor and the governor (Wong & Shen, 2009).

District-level governance is often defined in terms of a strong professional management model. At the top of the district bureaucracy is the school superintendent, who assumes educational, managerial, and fiscal responsibilities for the entire district. To provide daily services to a large number of students, the school system tends to adopt a bureaucratic structure—centralization of decision making, routinization of task performance, and standardization of resource generation and allocation. The urban district resembles a complex hierarchical structure, with centralized authority and line departments. The organization's insiders enjoy autonomy from outsiders' influence because the former possesses expertise and information on how the system operates. External pressures from state and federal government are largely accommodated through an internal division of labor, which is characterized by specialized bureaus in which program administrators are insulated from one another. When allocating resources, the lay school board largely follows the recommendations made by professional administrators (Danzberger, Kirst, & Usdan, 1992).

The superintendent and his or her central office staff also exercise a great deal of influence on the schools. In most districts, the school board and the superintendent recruit and replace the school principals. Teacher recruitment, with a few exceptions, is generally processed at the central office. Most schools lack discretion over their own budgetary allocations. The centralized bureaucratic model has served several important functions in the public school system: it manages competing political demands, routinizes service delivery, distributes comparable resources to schools across neighborhoods, enforces national and state mandates on academic standards and equity issues, and, above all, provides organizational stability to a complex operation that serves a diverse clientele (Wong, 1992).

An independent local school district that is free from general governmental control is consistent with the American ethos. An autonomous school system reflects strongly held public beliefs in democratic, nonpartisan control over public education. The public has traditionally equated local control with district-wide board authority in the constitutional-legal framework of educational governance. In comparing private and public schools, Chubb and Moe (1990) characterized public school governance as "direct democratic control."

Multiple Challenges on Accountability

The stability of district governance faces growing tension in a context of changing political and policy conditions. First, urban school districts are seen as increasingly cost inefficient. In their study of New York City prior to the reform initiated by Mayor Michael Bloomberg in 2002, Ravitch and Viteritti (1997, p. 22) observed, "Most of the necessary functions are over administered and under supervised." Substantial resources are used to support central services instead of being allotted to the schools themselves. While New York's problems may be unique, virtually all urban districts have to face the question of whether some of the centralized functions can be better performed at the school level or by outside organizations.

Related to the issue of efficiency is the rigidity of a single pay schedule that does not allow for differential compensation for differential teacher performance. Until very recently, the teachers' union has been successful in turning performance-based compensation into a "non issue." In recent years, however, with the public becoming more impatient with school performance, several governors and state legislatures are beginning to experiment with differential compensation. Florida and Texas, for example, provide individual cash bonuses to teachers for standardized test results. Arizona, Minnesota, and North Carolina connect part of the teacher salaries to student achievement. In Minneapolis and Denver, union leadership actively participated in negotiating with the management to redesign the teacher compensation package. Denver's ProComp Agreement did not eliminate collective bargaining. Instead, it gained voters' approval for new taxes to pay for the expanded salary schedule that takes into account four factors: knowledge and skills, professional evaluation, market incentives, and student growth. In other words, performance-based governance has gained public support.

Urban school systems have been slow in responding to the socio-demographic shifts in their communities. Since the 1960s, civic and community-based organizations have directed their efforts to diversify the makeup of the school leadership, which presumably would improve policy responsiveness. Despite these efforts, fewer than 10% of the nation's school superintendents are minorities and fewer than 15% were women. Many districts are looking for ways to expand the pipeline of a more diverse teaching force.

Finally, there is the ongoing challenge of raising student performance. In a global economy, policy makers, business leaders, and parents often see graduates of public schools lacking academic preparation for the labor market or post-secondary education. The public's perception is reinforced by the moderately low ranking of the United States in international assessments. The Third International Mathematics and Science Study, for example, ranked American eighth graders around the middle in comparison with their peers in all industrialized nations (Commission on Mathematics and Science Education 2009). There is also growing public awareness that state-developed proficiency standards are much lower than those established by the National Assessment on Educational Progress (NAEP).

plus, some states' standards are more rigorous than others!

Partly in response to these public concerns, the federal government enacted the No Child Left Behind Act of 2001 to hold students, schools, and districts accountable for student performance. For persistently low performing schools, the district must make arrangements to implement one of the following alternative governance structures:

- Reopen the school as a public charter school;
- Replace all or most of the school staff (including the principal) who are relevant to the failure to meet adequate yearly progress;
- Enter into a contract with a private management company, with a demonstrated record of effectiveness, to operate the public school;
- Turn the operation of the school over to the state; or
- Any other restructuring arrangement that makes fundamental reforms to improve student academic achievement.

These mounting accountability pressures have created new demands for changes in school governance. In several large cities, popularly elected political leaders, such as mayors and governors, have taken formal control over the school system. Parental support for choice-based programs tends to grow in low-income minority neighborhoods where traditional public schools are not meeting the academic standards.

In other words, the educational system has entered a phase of institutional transition, where the politics of the status quo is subject to mounting pressure to face growing public demand for accountability. Consequently, districts and schools are adopting different models of restructuring. For example, according to a study on school restructuring in California (Center for Education Policy 2006a), of the 271 schools reported on their restructuring efforts, 76% chose school governance change, 28% focused on staff replacement (e.g., 120 teachers in 13 schools in Oakland were involuntarily transferred out), and 14% contracted an outside organization to operate their schools. Another study on restructuring in Maryland found that of the 63 schools implementing restructuring plans (Center for Education Policy 2006b), 46 used a "turnaround specialist" (e.g., in Prince George's County, District Regional Directors serve as turnaround specialists, in addition to their responsibility for school improvement within their region), 10 focused on High School Reform, and 5 reconstituted their instructional staff.

New Institutional Boundaries in School Governance: Two Perspectives

As reform advances in system-wide governance, two perspectives emerge to facilitate our understanding of the political conditions that matter: regime theory and integrated governance. Both perspectives aim at strengthening the institutional capacity of the school system. The two perspectives differ, however, in emphases on formal governmental institutions and performance-based accountability. Regime theory pays primary attention to the governing process by specifying the role of nongovernmental institutions in sustaining a governing coalition. According to this perspective, public officials need to develop power arrangements that ensure other key stakeholders are able to contribute to the collective goals of the system. Regime theory, however, recognizes different types of regime politics, including some that resist school reform. In contrast to the regime theory, where multiple centers of power continue to make decisions, integrated governance, led by mayors, focuses on holding a single, elected office accountable to the public for student achievement and management performance. While the mayor is expected to engage other key stakeholders, he or she is seen as uniquely positioned to overcome power fragmentation, to raise system performance and strengthen public confidence. While these perspectives can be complementary in specific settings, we will examine the rationale, implementation, and effects of these two strands separately for analytical purpose.

Governing Regimes

Beginning in the 1950s, political scientists engaged in significant empirical and methodological debates over where power lies in local government. On one side of the debate, sociologist Floyd Hunter (1953), using "reputational" approach, found a group of elites in the private sector dominating the power structure of "Regional City"—Atlanta, Georgia, in the 1940s. On the other side, political scientist Robert Dahl (1961) developed the pluralist model of power in his study, *Who Governs*, of decision-making in New Haven, Connecticut. Dahl argued that no one individual was able to exert influence across all policy decisions in the city, although they might be powerful in one area. Dahl's account of politics as power diffused sparked a number of critical responses throughout the political science discipline, particularly in the subfield of urban politics, with works such as Bachrach and Baratz's analysis in Baltimore (1970) and Diane Pinderhughes' study of Chicago (1987).

In the 1970s and 80s, studies on urban political economy developed as an alternative to the elitist versus pluralist debate (Molotch, 1976; Logan & Molotch, 1987; Peterson 1981). These newer approaches varied significantly in their assumptions but all urged scholars to pay closer attention to the economic forces structuring local decision-making. In *City Limits* (1981), for example, Peterson argued that urban policy decisions are significantly constrained by the propensity for cities to compete for capital and labor and to maintain their land value. While recognizing the necessity for competition, Wong's (1990) comparative analysis of policy making in Baltimore and Milwaukee found that leadership and governing culture affected local policies in housing, community development, and education. These works laid the groundwork for a new urban theory: regime theory.

Building on the work on political economy, regime theory has emerged as a dominant paradigm in the urban politics field (Mossberger &Stoker, 2001, p. 810) and has been increasingly utilized by urban education scholars. Regime analysis touches fundamental questions of politics, such as the nature of power and potential for democratic governance in a growingly complex world (Fainstein & Fainstein, 1983; Jones & Bachelor, 1986; Elkin, 1987; Stone, 1989). Stone's analysis of urban regimes in Atlanta represents the first comprehensive treatment of this perspective (for a collection detailing Stone's numerous contributions to the field, see Orr & Johnson, 2008).

Stone's account of Atlanta describes "the actions of various elements of the Atlanta community in bringing together, challenging, and modifying the informal arrangements through which Atlanta was governed" (1989, p. ix). Regime theory's explanatory power lies in its ability to describe how local governments develop policy capacity within the limited resource constraints they operate. Stone explains that Atlanta was governed by a regime, which he defines as "informal arrangements by which public bodies and private interests function together in order to be able to make and carry out governing decisions" (p. 6). In an urban regime, leaders in the public and private sectors form coalitions of collective resources in order to achieve the policy goals of the city.

Urban regimes are informal but stable partnerships among resource providers (Stone 1989). Urban regimes are understood by their capacity to act, their set of actors and the relationship among the actors (Stone, 1989, p. 179). Two primary needs motivate regimes:

(1) institutional scope (that is, the need to encompass a wide enough scope of institutions to mobilize the resources required to make and implement governing decisions) and (2) cooperation (that is, the need to promote enough cooperation and coordination for the diverse participants to reach decisions and sustain action in support of those decisions). (Stone 1989, p. 6)

The relative influence of the actors in the regime relies on the importance of the resources they add to the governing arrangement for a policy output. Urban regime looks closely at which actors must be involved to carry out policy for the city.

The goal of the policy determines the requisite resources and partners necessary for the governing coalition. In many instances, city government creates partnerships with the private sector in order to execute public policy (Stone, 1989; Elkin, 1987). The business community members are frequently regime partners due to their unequal share of resources in cities (Stone 1989; Imbroscio, 1998). This is also observed frequently in urban education with the corporate business elite (Cuban & Usdan, 2005; Lipman, 2003; Ray &

Mickelson, 1990; Shipps, 1997). However, the power of business is often insufficient for reform in the public schools (Henig et al., 1999; Mickelson, 1999; Shipps 2006).

Urban regime theory understands power as a capacity to accomplish policy goals rather than its ability to control actors. Stone (1989) describes his conception of power as a "social production model" which differs from the traditional "control model" of the previous community power debate of Dahl and Hunter. Stone explains, "[t]he power struggle concerns, not control and resistance, but gaining and fusing the capacity to act—power to, not power over" (1989, p. 229). According to regime theory, public officials must develop the power to govern in conjunction with other resource providers.

Common understandings of urban public schooling are especially open to this definition of power. Numerous studies over the years have established that no office holder, such as the superintendent, mayor, or school board member, has sufficient power over the urban system to bring about reform (Counts, 1928; Cuban, 1976; Danzberger, Kirst, & Usdan 1993; Hess 1999, Pois 1964; Rich 1996). Moreover, reform coalitions have been found to fail when they only briefly invest resources in schools (Cuban & Usdan, 2003; Rich & Chambers, 2004; Tyack & Cuban, 1995).

The appeal of urban regime analysis to scholars has been its ability to explain urban politics and urban education reform by incorporating both political and economic influences, resolving prior debates over elitism, pluralism, and economic structural constraints in urban politics. Regime analysis understands local actors as constrained by their environment but also as capable of reshaping that environment through coalitions in their governing arrangements.

Applying Regime Theory to Urban Education

For regime-oriented researchers examining urban districts, their broad area of concern is the civic capacity needed to create a stable reform-oriented regime. Drawing on an 11-city study, Stone and his colleagues examined urban school reform efforts in terms of the relationship of school systems to both the structure of political authority in the cities and the resources available of local civic groups (Stone, 1998; Stone, Henig, Jones, & Pierannunzi, 2001). In almost all cities they examined, civic mobilization fell far short of full capacity needed for substantial reform. Though there was variation among the eleven cities in the degree of reform, none had a comprehensive program of positive reform in effect. Pittsburgh, Los Angeles, and Boston scored at the upper end for local civic capacity; Baltimore, Houston, Washington, DC, and Detroit scored in the middle; and Denver, Atlanta, St. Louis, and San Francisco at the lower end. Ideally, scholars would have found high levels of civic capacity indicated by a coalition brought together, engaging its members in discourse and activities focused around the issue of educational improvement.

Fourth ranked Baltimore, examined by Marion Orr, shows the difficulty of implementing civic capacity for educational reform (Orr 1998; see also Orr 1999). Baltimore had a profusion of small-scale experiments, several of them considered successful and widely praised. Also, Baltimore's key players—the mayor, governor, state board of education and state superintendent, local community and business organizations like Baltimoreans United in Leadership Development (BUILD) and the Greater Baltimore Committee—all actively pushed for reform. Yet, Baltimore was not able to successfully implement large-scale efforts due to intergroup conflicts centered largely on race. Given the political and administrative control of the city's school system by African Americans, members of that educational community saw restructuring as a threat to their limited power base. Although the idea of educational improvement remained high on the Baltimore agenda, the stakeholders of the regime were only loosely aligned and faced obstacles in holding together civic capacity needed for comprehensive reform.

Several studies find that reformers face the difficult task of forming a coalition capable of organizing fragmented public and private sector resources and altering the relationships needed to pursue reform (Henig et al., 1999; Shipps, 2003, 2006; Stone, 1998; Stone et al., 2001). Based on their review of case studies, Stone and his coauthors (1998) developed a typology of regimes which is associated with education policy and politics: employment and performance regimes. In the previous example, Orr (1998) found an employment regime in Baltimore where African Americans, rather than pushing for education reform, instead joined the regime, as it provided them with jobs and a power base. In an employment regime, regime leaders often try to maintain the status quo of the school governing system. The members of an employment regime are "those groups who materially benefit from the existing governance and teaching arrangements" (Shipps, 2003, p. 857).

Similar to the notion of an employment regime, Rich's study (1996) of Detroit, Gary, and Newark found that the school bureaucracy was highly skilled at resisting efforts of change in order to maintain its power base and the status quo. Rich spent almost five years collecting data through interviews with school personnel, school activists, board members, and the mayors of the respective cities, though these interviews were not as extensive in Newark where the board members refused to participate. Rich examined why school reform failed even after black politicians were elected. Though Black politicians now had political power in these cities, their political capital did not translate into the necessary changes needed to improve urban schools. Rich found that the school bureaucracy was highly skilled at resisting efforts of change in order to maintain its power base and the status quo, like an employment regime.

In contrast, Stone and his coauthor's (1998) alternative regime, the performance regime, consists as an activist agenda, aiming at creating substantial improvement in education universally. Performance regimes bring together the resources of both public and private (including also for-profit and nonprofit) organizations that share a common goal of school improvement. Stone explains that changes alone in the district's internal leadership will not bring about a performance regime; instead, he observes, that more resources and sources of popular support are needed to develop and sustain such a regime. Scholars overall agree that these regimes are typically the most difficult to develop and maintain. Their difficulty lies in the number and type of actors that must engaged for a period long enough to create significant change in a city's educational politics and policies. The coalition and resources needed for a performance regime was outside the civic capacity of any of the cities Stone and his colleagues studied at the time. Stone argues that "[performance] regimes now exist only in embryonic form is a sign that politically they are hard to bring about" (1998, p. 14).

In examining the public-private governing coalitions, other researchers have expanded the typology of education regimes. Drawing on her case-study work on Chicago school politics, Shipps (2003) builds on Stone and his colleagues' understanding of the employment regime and describes two additional types of activist regimes, market regime and empowerment regime. In terms of ranking the difficulty of creating and sustaining regimes, Shipps ranks the regimes from employment, market, empowerment, to performance. Shipps uses the single case study of Chicago, but traces its urban education reform efforts over time to map out the different types of education regime.

In examining the role of business in the education reform efforts in Chicago, Shipps develops the idea of a market regime, which "shifts the incentives and rewards for both adults and children from the professional and bureaucratic expectations that dominate government run schools to the economic and survival consequences of markets" (2003, p. 850). She identifies two subtypes of market regimes: entrepreneurial and corporate. Entrepreneurial market regimes center primarily on school choice reforms, with parents seeking to be decision makers as core members of the regime. Corporate market regimes utilize the business community in employing similar methods of corporate restructuring, with efforts such as downsizing, replacing superintendents with CEOs, and increasing measures of accountability.

Empowerment regimes focus less on the corporate role and instead seek "to alter the power relations among adults working in and concerned with schools. It does so to spur new thinking about, and experimentation with, old problems" (Shipps 2003, p. 850). This regime also has subcategories – regimes that suggest decentralization as a means to empower parents and school-level educators, and regimes that advocate centralization through methods like mayoral control.[1] Its primary participants include parents or teachers, politicians, and bureaucrats.

In her history of school reform, Shipps (2003) found the ideas behind an empowerment regime in the creation of Local School Councils (LSCs) in Chicago. The concept of parent empowerment through these councils was developed in the mid-1970s and enacted in 1988 as a form of site-based management. Even with Chicago's recentralization in 1995, LSCs remained as a local governing body, a testament to the democratic ideas underpinning the empowerment regime. However, their record on student performance is mixed and hard to trace. More empirical research and more cases of this regime type are needed to see if empowerment regimes can reach their goals of greater equity and democratic responsiveness.

Bulkley (2007) adds a fourth regime type to the typology developed by Stone, Shipps, and others with the same method of a case study. Bulkley assesses the political and policy changes in the Philadelphia School District resulting from the 2001 state takeover and the subsequent hiring of a new district Chief Executive Officer, Paul Vallas. Bulkley's analysis identifies a contracting regime, a new type of market-based regime of public-private interaction. The regime consisted of Vallas, as CEO, and his official oversight body, the School Reform Commission (SRC), and a group of state and local appointees including the local teachers' union. Bulkley found limited incorporation of parents and the business community in the regime, however. Vallas and the SRC utilized contracting to create partnerships between private and nonprofit actors and the public officials governing the school system. In the case of Philadelphia, central to the district's strategy for reform was the use of private sector organizations to attempt reform.

Regime theory is not restricted to understanding urban governance at the local level. It has been used by Burns to examine state-district relations. In his first study, Burns examined the governor's role in Hartford, Connecticut, using urban regime analysis. He found the local actors to be limited in their "capacity to address educational problems," whereas the governor "controlled the financial and institutional resources that Hartford's educational system needed" (2002, p. 66). Burns expands the scope of regime theory to actors outside the traditional urban context, increasingly important analysis as more states become involved in local education issues.

In his examination of the state of New Jersey's takeover of Newark's schools, Burns (2003) builds on his previous work, which determined urban regime analysis understates the role state governmental actors play in urban education reform. The Newark case describes how state government became motivated to be involved at the local level, to reform a poorly performing school district. The new regime paired local, White business elites with statewide politicians over a shared concern that the African American school establishment was unwilling and unable to reform its patronage system. Despite the new regime, Burns found that Newark has done little in the way of improved student performance.

The application of urban regime theory to education reform has become increasingly diffused as researchers depicted types of regimes in various cities at different moments in time. Most scholars examined above rely on the case study method to conduct urban regime analysis. While a single case study is limited in its ability to generalize, its strength lies in its ability to thoroughly describe how structural factors and politics jointly shape urban education reform. Clearly, there is a need to expand the empirical base to see if different types of regime are applicable beyond a single case within a specified time frame. Future research should continue adding cases like Stone and his coauthors (1998, 2001), using historical analysis like Shipps (2003), and should consider using mixed methods to examine the various types of regimes.

Integrated Governance: Mayoral Leadership and Educational Accountability

As the former CEO of the Chicago Public Schools, U.S. Secretary of Education Arne Duncan identified mayoral leadership as a supportive condition for improving urban schools. Secretary Duncan's policy position came at a time of growing public interest in mayoral accountability as a viable strategy to improve public school governance. In 2006 and 2007 the Gallup Poll surveyed the public's view on mayoral control in schools. In 2006, only 29% was in favor, but in 2007 that number had jumped to 39%, with 42% of parents in favor (Rose & Gallup, 2007, p. 38). The Obama administration's support for mayoral involvement is likely to broaden local interest in this strand of district governance.

As a governance framework, mayoral accountability *integrates* school district performance and the electoral process at the system-wide level. The education mayor is ultimately held accountable for the system's performance, including academic, fiscal, operational, and management. For too long and in too many large urban districts, governance constitutes a structural barrier for progress. Many urban districts are exceedingly ungovernable, where fragmentary centers of power tend to look after their own particularistic interest (Wong, 1992). Consequently, the independently elected school board has limited leverage to advance collective priorities, and the superintendent lacks the institutional capacity to manage the policy constraints established in state regulations and the union contract. Mayoral accountability aims at addressing the governing challenges in urban districts.

As an institution, mayor-led districts no longer insulate from the city's social, civic, and economic sectors. The education mayor identifies public education as a core component in improving the city's quality of life as well as its long term economic growth. The education mayor also expands both formal and informal learning opportunities for school children through multiple partnerships with cultural and civic organizations. Aside from these functional benefits, mayors, like any elected politicians, are keenly interested in leaving behind an institutional legacy. Fixing dysfunctional schools and building the district capacity enable mayors to advance long term institutional purposes. In other words, the education mayor is not simply a vote maximizer to get re-elected but also an institution builder.

we would only hope!

Currently, several urban districts are under formal mayoral leadership. These include New York, Chicago, Boston, Cleveland, Washington, DC, Providence, New Haven, and Harrisburg. Baltimore and Philadelphia are jointly governed by the mayor and the governor. In recent years, mayors and mayoral candidates in Dallas, Houston, Memphis, Seattle, Syracuse, St. Paul, Rockford (Illinois), and Stafford (Texas), among others, have expressed an interest in more formal involvement in public education. Mayors in Rochester and Milwaukee have stood behind a legislative proposal to formally take charge of the school district. In Los Angeles, after a long legal and legislative battle, Mayor Villaraigosa gained control over three clusters with a total of 40 schools. Since his candidates were elected to the school board, Mayor Villaraigosa establishes de-facto control with a 4–3 majority of his close allies. In Detroit, the newly elected mayor David Bing endorsed the notion of mayoral control during his electoral campaign. In Nashville, mayoral interest in school reform has never been stronger. In his state of the city address in April 2009, Mayor Karl Dean of Nashville highlighted education reform as his top priority. He has supported Teach for America and the New Teacher Project for recruiting teachers to the district. He also wanted to expand alternative schooling options for students who are over aged and under credited. In advocating for a more "aggressive" reform agenda, Mayor Dean told the city that "I think about and work on our schools every single day, and I'm not going stop until I'm convinced that we have a system that gives all of our students, regardless of race and economic status, an opportunity to graduate from our schools ready to succeed in college and careers" (Dean 2009, p. 6). In other words, the number of districts under mayoral governance is likely to grow in the next few years.

Chicago provides a good example of how the mayor-led system operates. The Chicago School Reform Amendatory Act, which took effect in July 1995, reverses the trend toward decentralization of authority over school operations and redesigns the governance arrangement so that power and authority are now integrated. The 1995 law suspended the power of the School Finance Authority, eliminated the School Board Nominating Commission, and diminished the ability of the local school councils to operate independently of board policy. Mayor Richard Daley sought greater control of schools, as he considers education to be one of the essential services that will keep middle-class residents in the city. A strong public school system, in his view, can also attract businesses to Chicago.

Integrated governance in Chicago is characterized by (a) a reduction of competing authorities (such as the School Board Nominating Commission) and a coordination of activities in support of system-wide goals and standards, (b) mayoral appointment of school board members and selection of top administrators, (c) powers granted to the school board to hold local school councils accountable to system-wide standards in professional conduct.

The 1995 legislation left intact some features of the previous decentralized arrangements, but it reduced competing institutional authority and recentralized administrative authority. As a result of the 1995 reform, appointment decisions emanating from the mayor's office closely link the board, top administration, and the mayor's office. The 15-member board was decreased to five, and the mayor was given the authority to appoint the board's president and its members and the chief executive officer in charge of the schools. Daley picked Paul Vallas, his former budget director, to serve as the CEO from 1995 to 2001. The top appointments in the central office made between July 1995 and February 1998 reflect a diversity of expertise, with over 40% of the appointees coming from the private sector, nonprofit organizations, and city agencies. In areas not directly related to educational services, such as finance and purchasing, over 60% of the appointees came from outside of the school system.

A particularly important feature of the 1995 reform law was an eighteen-month moratorium on teachers' strikes. The Chicago Teachers' Union has been an assertive demand maker since the late 1960s, when it obtained the right to collective bargaining. Since 1970, strikes have often resulted in school closings. For example, 11 school days were lost in 1970, 10 days in 1980, 2 days in 1985, and 19 days in 1990. Using both the threat of a strike and the strike itself, the teachers' union has been able to obtain multiyear contracts with terms that favorably preserved their work conditions (Wong, Shen, Anagnostopoulos, & Rutledge 2007). Under the new political conditions following the 1995 reform, Mayor Daley sought and succeeded in getting labor peace.

The Vallas administration seemed to have turned around the school system. The CEO and his team restored public confidence and gained strong support from the media, businesses, and civic groups (Wong, Shen, Anagnostopoulos, and Rutledge 2007.) Since the mayor took over the schools, social promotion was eliminated and standardized test performance has steadily improved every year at both the elementary and the high school level. The mayor's board has signed two four-year teachers' contracts that sustain labor peace, and the Vallas administration has begun to implement a more rigorous academic curriculum in the high schools. Because of Chicago's academic success, President Bill Clinton praised the district two years in a row in his State of the Union messages. Arne Duncan, the current U.S. Secretary of Education, succeeded Vallas to serve as the CEO in the Chicago school district for seven years. His tenure, too, saw steady improvement in student performance.

Promising Evidence on School Improvement

To be sure, Secretary Duncan's comments reflect his extensive first-hand experience as the Chief Executive Officer of one of the first mayoral control districts, Chicago. More importantly, Secretary Duncan's position on mayoral accountability is informed by measurable progress in urban districts that are under mayoral control.

In *The Education Mayor: Improving America's Schools*, Wong, Shen, Anagnostopoulos, and Rutledge (2007) conducted a comprehensive empirical analysis on the effects of mayoral control on student outcomes and management performance. The study examines 104 big-city school systems (including 12 that were under mayoral control) located across 40 states, and we synthesized standardized achievement data from thousands of schools between 1999 and 2003. The study examines multiple years of data by using a mixed methods approach, applying both statistical models and conducting in-depth case studies that connect the macro policy conditions to the micro level practices in a sample of urban classrooms. The following paragraphs highlight and update a few of the study's key findings.

Wong and his associates (2007) have taken an interest in evaluating the effects of mayor-led systems as a distinct type of turnaround strategy, *relative to the independently elected governance structure that would have been in place otherwise.* Can we generalize about the achievement effects of this reform strategy beyond a specific setting? In an analysis of a U.S. Department of Education longitudinal school achievement database of over 100 urban districts, Wong et al. found that mayor-led school systems are positively related to standardized elementary reading and math achievement, even after statistically controlling for previous achievement and a host of demographic background variables. The results of the statistical analysis suggested that if a district moved from an elected board to a board with a majority of its members appointed by the mayor, that district would see, relative to other districts in the state, an increase of approximately 0.15 to 0.19 standard deviations in elementary reading and math. While not likely to move the district above the state mean in the short run, these improvements are nonetheless significant.

A promising effect of mayoral accountability lies in the academic improvement of the district's lowest performing schools, such as the lowest 25th-percentile schools. To be sure, these schools consist of a higher concentration of students eligible for free and reduced-price lunches. In most cases, these schools are also educating greater percentages of African American students than the overall district average. Despite these structural challenges, lowest 25th-percentile schools in mayor-controlled districts show steady progress in the percentage of students who were tested proficient in the state annual benchmarking-grade assessment during 1999 and 2003. For example, the lowest 25th-percentile schools in Baltimore's third-grade reading improved from 5.6% to 32.7%. In math, Chicago's fifth-grade math improved from 10.4% to 27.5% in the lowest performing schools.

Mayoral control, as suggested in the data from 1999 to 2003, seemed to show mixed results in narrowing the achievement gap between schools in the highest 25th percentile and those in the lowest 25th percentile.

Further, an absence of checks and balances (such as the lack of a school board nominating commission) were found to have a negative effect on student performance during 1999 and 2003. These cautionary findings, however, need to be revisited as current data becomes available. Wong and Shen, for example, are in the process of beginning a follow-up study by updating the 100-district data base. At the same time, additional in-depth analysis of a sample of mayoral control districts will provide descriptively rich evidence on what works under what governing circumstances.

An example of a district that shows evidence on mayoral accountability is New York City. As the city completed its seventh year of mayoral control in June 2009, student performance showed progress. While there seems to be general agreement on the city's academic gains in state assessment, there is disagreement on the NAEP assessment. For example, historian Ravitch observed that NYC "made no significant gains in reading or mathematics between 2003 and 2007" on the NAEP (2010, p. 88). Further, Ravtich concluded that "mayoral control is not a guaranteed path to school improvement" in part because "two of the three lowest-performing cities [on the 2007 NAEP] had had mayoral control for more than a decade" (p. 91). In other words, the debate on whether student test scores are appropriately controlled for their prior achievement as well as other socioeconomic characteristics will continue.

At the same time, an analysis of NYC's NAEP assessment suggests this mayoral district has been making measurable progress on narrowing the achievement gap. In fourth-grade mathematics on the NAEP test in 2007, low income students in NYC outperformed their urban peers in all the other 10 urban districts in the NAEP urban assessment, despite the fact that NYC has a much higher concentration of low-income students taking the test. Of all the fourth graders who took the NAEP math assessment, NYC had a much higher percentage of low-income students (87%) when compared with other central cities (71%). In eighth-grade math in 2007, low-income students in NYC outperformed low-income students in 7 of the 10 other urban districts in the NAEP urban assessment. Of all the eighth graders who took the NAEP math assessment, NYC had a much higher percentage of low-income students (86%) when compared with other central cities (65%).

In math, the racial gap in NYC continued to narrow while other central cities experienced a widening racial gap in NAEP score points during between 2003 and 2007. The Black-White gap in eighth grade reduced from 36 to 30 score points, while the Hispanic-White gap dropped from 29 to 26 score points. Likewise, the Black-White gap in fourth grade reduced from 25 to 22 score points, while the Hispanic-White gap dropped from 24 to 18 score points.

In reading, the racial gap in NYC steadily narrowed between 2002 and 2007. In fourth-grade NAEP reading scores, the Black-White gap was reduced from 34 to 26 score points. The Hispanic-White gap was narrowed from 38 to 29 score points. In eighth-grade NAEP reading scores, the racial gap in NYC was comparable with other central cities, even though the district slightly widened the gap between 2003 and 2007. NYC's racial gap in eighth-grade reading was comparable with the racial gap in other central cities during this period. For example, NYC's Black-White gap of 30 score points in 2007 was slightly lower than the gap in other central cities (31 score points). NYC's Hispanic-White gap of 20 score points in 2007 was lower than the gap in other central cities (28 score points).

Turning to management improvement, integrated governance enables strategic resource allocations. Mayor-led districts are not spending more, as found in our analysis of 10 years of district finance and staffing patterns (Wong et al., 2007). These districts are spending differently over time—re-allocating resources to instruction and instructional support (as opposed to spending in the central administration). Further, mayors are able to facilitate strategic partnerships to improve management efficiency. Education mayors seem able to leverage cooperation, or sometimes, even concessions, from the school employees' unions. Regarding management efficiency and fiscal discipline, districts under mayoral control have showed improvement in the system's bond ratings over time, maintained labor peace (there has been an absence of teachers' strikes in mayoral control systems), and a streamlined central bureaucracy by shifting staffing resources to the sub-district or school cluster levels.

Integrated governance also broadens the human capital pipeline at both the system and the school levels. At the central administration, there is a broadening of expertise to fill key positions in budgeting, operations, facilities, and management. For example, 40% of the newly recruited managerial staff in Chicago during the first two years of mayoral control came from state and local governmental agencies and non-profit sectors outside of education. Many were drawn from non-traditional leadership ranks, including Joel Klein (a private sector attorney), Paul Vallas (former city budget director), Michelle Rhee (head of New Teacher Project), and Arne Duncan (a former professional basketball player). At the operational level, mayors are more likely to bring in diverse service providers to address challenging issues, such as contracting out the lowest performing schools to Education Management Organizations (EMOs) or Charter Management Organizations (CMOs). When it comes to improving principal and teacher quality, mayors actively seek alternative sources, including New Leaders for New Schools, Teach for America, New Teacher Project, and other mid-career professional tracks.

Mayoral accountability both broadens public engagement and benefits from additional checks and balances. Mayoral control does not mean an absence of checks and balances, instead, mayoral accountability tends to generate wider public attention to the needs of public schools. When mayor gets involved, education becomes a city-wide priority. While community organizations seek more transparency, local newspapers are more likely to report on the mayoral role. Because of mayoral involvement, other governmental stakeholders, such as city council and state inspectors, are ready to spend more attention to education. In Washington, DC, the City Council Chairman has played a growingly visible role in education issues following mayoral control.

Mayoral accountability is, of course, most prominently visible in the regular municipal electoral cycle. Voters now can assess if the education mayor meets their expectations on school performance. For example, the last school board election prior to mayoral control in New York City had a voter's turnout of merely 4%. As Mayor Bloomberg sought an unprecedented third term, education became a key issue in the 2009 campaign. Polls suggested that a majority of the New York City voters did not want to return to the system prior to mayoral control. Further, as part of the system of checks and balances, the legislature adopted a sunset provision. In New York, the legislature reauthorized mayoral control until 2015.

Despite electoral accountability, integrated governance as a reform strategy is viewed as producing mixed results in public engagement. In New York City, the panel for educational policy that replaced the school board was seen as "a rubber-stamp for the mayor and the chancellor" (Ravitch 2010, p. 78; also see Viteritti, 2009). In Chicago, standardization on principal hiring has reduced the influence of the Local School Councils on selecting site-level leadership. Using an independent nominating commission, a practice that has been institutionalized in Boston and Providence, has not become the rule for selecting members of the school board in districts that are under mayoral control. As these concerns gain political support, integrated governance will evolve to broaden public engagement on governance reform issues. There needs to be greater transparency and more channels of direct communication between the parents and the school administration. These and other efforts to fine-tune the process of public engagement will strengthen the institution of mayoral accountability.

Conclusions

This chapter examines two prominent perspectives on schools governance, namely, the regime theory and integrated governance. While these two perspectives tend to overlap in many substantive aspects, such as the convening role of the mayor, they tend to differ on several analytical dimensions. As suggested in Table 10.1, integrated governance places the mayor at the center of the governing structure, which in turns is held accountable for district performance by municipal elections. Regime theory tends to allow for multiple entities, both formal and informal, in sustaining a governing coalition. While integrated governance seems more ready to intervene in low-performing schools, regime theory is less clear on this issue.

Clearly, in studying urban education governance from a regime perspective, scholars assume multiple sources of power are needed to accomplish urban

Table 10.1 Regime Theory and Integrated Governance as Analytical Perspectives

Analytical Dimensions	Regime Theory	Integrated Governance
Governing Structure	Multiple Entities (Formal/Informal)	Mayor at the Center
Strategic Focus	Sustain a Coalition	Performance Outcomes
Source of Accountability	Negotiated Terms	Citywide Mayoral Elections
Degree of Public Engagement	Varies by Regime	Varies by Cities
Intervention in Low-Performing Schools	Less Direct	More Direct

governance. Regime analysis defines the different types of regimes by the relationships between these sources of power. For many policy arenas like education, regime analysis argues that informal power is as important as formal governmental power in achieving a regime's goals. One of the strengths of the perspective is that it pays special attention to who controls key resources in a community. Regime analysis sees resources as issue-specific, meaning that the resources and groups that come together to try to improve transportation are different from those needed to improve education. Hence, researchers focus as much on informal-formal relations as on inter-governmental relations on an issue-by-issue basis. Built into the theory with its various typologies is an understanding that some regimes will not meet their reform goals, due to a lack of required resources or leadership.

Integrated governance assumes instead that it is possible for the mayor to pull together political will, technical knowledge, and managerial skills to support public schools. By integrating all sources of power into the office of the mayor, this governance arrangement reduces the fragmentary tendency that is often a result of the distribution of political power among competing interests in an urban system. Integrated governance argues that the office of the mayor can leverage informal sources of power that might be needed. This perspective emphasizes the coordinating and the accountability functions of the mayor in aligning city agencies to improve public education. Nonetheless, the integrated governance perspective has yet to fully consider how a mayor might be ineffectual in accomplishing his or her reform priorities.

The education system in the United States is increasingly defined by accountability-based politics. The public, policy makers, and organized interests have increased their demands for improvement in district-level governance as well as student performance. Clearly, district-level governance is in transition in the era of accountability. While many communities maintain their tradition of nonpartisan, popularly elected school boards, urban districts that are perceived as low performing are under multiple pressures to improve the quality of governance. Though political and civic leaders have yet to fully mobilize broad-based support for human development issues, as expected by regime theory, reformers have made many efforts to improve management and accountability, such as distributing report cards on school and district performance. Governance reform, especially under mayoral leadership, is designed to respond to public demands to improve accountability.

From the regime perspective, the stability of the public-private coalition may face growing tension in the current climate of heightened accountability. Further empirical research needs to address several issues. What are the conditions necessary to bring about an institutional transition from an employment to a performance regime? Which institutional actors would lead such a transition? Is it likely for organized interests in both the public and the nonpublic sectors to yield to collective goals? And how do we measure progress made under regime governance? Since many of the regime-oriented studies are based on descriptive rich case studies, it would be important for researchers to expand the work using larger scale data base.

From the integrated governance perspective, a broader public engagement strategy needs to be taken into consideration. While mayors have shown measurable improvement in financial management and academic improvement generally, they face several challenges in sustaining their gains. How do mayors institute formal channels for ongoing citizen participation in schooling decisions? The Local School Councils in Chicago offers a more radical example of parental involvement. But a number of mayoral districts are now moving toward advisory parental councils. Further, incumbent mayors need to consider institutional safeguards beyond their tenure. There have been concerns on whether future mayors may be able to manage the district challenges. With proper institutional safeguards, mayoral accountability can ensure a stable policy system that aims at student performance.

U.S. Secretary of Education Duncan's call for mayoral control in March 2009 may turn out to be an interesting moment in the history of urban school governance. Throughout much of the 19th and 20th centuries, urban districts were dominated by a single governance model—a professional educator as superintendent selected by an elected school board that operates outside of the regular municipal electoral cycle. Only in the last 15 years do we see the emergence of mayoral accountability as a viable alternative governance model at the district level. While all mayors are politicians, the education mayors are keenly focusing on outcome performance and data transparency. As *The Education Mayor* and other recent studies suggest, districts that operate successfully under the integrated governance framework are moving toward site-based teacher hiring, stronger incentives on adult accountability, a diverse pool of professional talents, labor peace, stronger fiscal discipline, more school choice, a greater number of external providers, and higher degree of public confidence. These programmatic initiatives promise to create the necessary conditions for raising student performance in our urban school districts.

Note

1 Chicago was one of the first cities to give its mayor, Richard M. Daley, control over the schools, showing some of the overlap between the two models of reform presented in this chapter, as Shipps builds in mayoral control into her regime typology.

References

Bachrach, P., & Baratz. M. (1970). *Power and poverty: Theory and practice.* Oxford, UK: Oxford University Press.

Berry, J. (1999). *The new liberalism.* Washington, DC: Brookings Institution Press.

Bierlein, L. (1997). The charter school movement. In D. Ravitch & J. Viteritti (Eds.), *New schools for a new century.* New Haven, CT: Yale University Press.

Bulkley, K. (2007). Bringing the private into the public. Changing the rules of the game, and the new regime politics in Philadelphia public education [Special issue]. In K. Bulkley & L. Fusarelli (Eds.), The politics of privatization in education. *Education Policy, 21*(1), 155–184.

Burns, P. (2002). The intergovernmental regime and public policy in Hartford, Connecticut. *Journal of Urban Affairs, 24*(1), 55–73.

Burns, P. (2003). Regime theory, state government, and a takeover of urban education. *Journal of Urban Affairs, 25*(3), 285–303.

Center on Innovation and Improvement. (2006a, September 25–26). *Report on Restructuring.* Presentation at the Institute for School Improvement and Education Options, Des Plaines, IL.

Center on Innovation and Improvement. (2006b, September 25–26). *Report on Restructuring.* Presentation at the Institute for School Improvement and Education Options, Des Plaines, IL.

Chubb, J., & Moe, T. (1990). *Politics, markets and America's schools.* Washington, DC: Brookings Institution Press.

Commission on Mathematics and Science Education (U.S.). (2009). *Opportunity equation: Transforming mathematics and science education for citizenship and the global economy.* New York: Carnegie Corporation of New York.

Counts, G. (1928). *School and society in Chicago.* New York: Harcourt, Brace.

Cuban L. (1976). *Urban school chiefs under fire.* Chicago: University of Chicago Press.

Cuban, L., & M. Usdan. (Eds). (2005). *Powerful reforms with shallow roots: Getting good schools in six cities.* New York: Teachers College Press.

Dahl, R. A. (1961). *Who governs? Democracy and power in an American city.* New Haven, CT: Yale University Press.

Danzberger, J., M. Kirst, & M. Usdan (1992). *Governing public schools: New times, new requirements.* Washington, DC: Institute for Educational Leadership.

Dean, K. (2009, April 23). *State of metro address.* Office of the Mayor, Metropolitan Government of Nashville and Davidson County Tennessess.

Elkin, S. (1987). *City and regime in the American republic.* Chicago: University Of Chicago Press.

Fainstein, N., & S. Fainstein. (1983). Regime strategies, communal resistance, and economic forces. In S. Fainstein (Ed.), *Restructuring the city* (pp. 245–282). White Plains, NY: Longman.

Fusarelli, B., & Cooper, B. (Eds.), (2009). *The rising state: How state power is transforming our nation's schools.* New York: Teachers College Press.

Henig, J., R. Hula, M. Orr, & D. Pedescleaux. (1999). *The color of school reform: Race, politics, and the challenge of urban education.* Princeton, NJ: Princeton University Press.

Hess, F. (1999). *Spinning wheels: The politics of urban school reform.* Washington DC: Brookings Institution Press.

Hess, F., & Leal, D. (2005). School house politics: Expenditures, interests, and competition in school coard elections. In W. Howell (Ed.), *Beseiged: School boards and the future of education politics* (pp. 228–253). Washington DC: Brookings Institution Press.

Hunter, F. (1953). *Community power structure: A study of decision makers.* Chapel Hill: The University of North Carolina Press.

Imbroscio, D. L. (1998). Reformulating urban regime theory: The division of labor between state and market revisited. *Journal of Urban Affairs, 20,* 233–248.

Jones, B., & L. Bachelor. (1986) *The sustaining hand: Community leadership and corporate power.* Lawrence: University Press of Kansas

Lipman, P. (2003). *High stakes education: Inequality, globalization and urban school reform.* New York: Routledge Falmer.

Logan, J., & H. Molotch. (1987). *Urban fortunes: The political economy of place.* Berkeley: University of California Press.

Mickelson, R. (1999). International business machinations: A case study of corporate involvement in local educational reform. *Teachers College Record, 100*(3), 476–512.

Moe, T. (2005). Teacher unions and school board elections. In W. Howell (Ed.), *Beseiged: School boards and the future of education politics* (pp. 254–287). Washington DC: Brookings Institution Press.

Molotch, H. (1976). The city as a growth machine: Toward a political economy of place. *The American Journal of Sociology, 82*(2), 309–332.

Mossberger, K., & G. Stoker. (2001). The evolution of urban regime theory: The challenge of conceptualization. *Urban Affairs Review, 36*(6), 810–835.

No Child Left Behind Act of 2001, Public Law 107-110, 107th Cong., 1st sess. (January 8, 2002).

Orr, M. (1998). The challenge of school reform in Baltimore. In C. N. Stone (Ed.), *Changing urban education* (pp. 93–117). Lawrence: University Press of Kansas.

Orr, M., & V. Johnson (Eds.). (2008). *Power in the city: Clarence Stone and the politics of inequality.* Lawrence: University Press of Kansas.

Peterson, P. (1981). *City limits.* Chicago: University of Chicago Press.

Pinderhughes, D. (1987). *Race and ethnicity in Chicago politics: A reexamination of pluralist theory.* Champaign: University of Illinois Press.

Pois, J. (1964). *The school board crisis: A Chicago case study.* Chicago: Educational Methods.

Quaid, L. (2009, March 31). *School chief: Mayors need control of urban schools.* Associated Press.

Ravitch, D. (2010). *The death and life of the great American school system how testing and choice are undermining education.* New York: Basic Books.

Ravitch, D., & Viteritti, J. (1997). New York: The obsolete factory. In D. Ravitch & J. Viteritti (Eds.). *New schools for a new century* (pp. 17–26). New Haven, CT: Yale University Press.

Ray, C., & Mickelson, R. (1990) Corporate leaders, resistant Yyuth, and school reform in sunbelt city: The political economy of education. *Social Problems 37*(2), 178–190.

Rich, W. (1996). *Black mayors and school politics: The failure of reform in Detroit, Gary and Newark.* New York: Garland.

Rich, W., & Chambers, S. (2004). Cleveland: Takeovers and makeovers are not the same. In J. R. Henig & W. Rich (Eds.), *Mayors in the middle: Politics, race, and mayoral control of urban schools* (pp. 151–172). Princeton, NJ: Princeton University Press.

Rose, L., & Gallup, A. M. (2007). *The 30th Annual Phi Delta Kappa/Gallup Poll of the public's attitudes toward the public schools, 2007.*Bloomington, IN: Phi Delta Kappan.

Shipps, D. (1997). The invisible hand: Big business and Chicago school reform. *Teachers College Record, 99*(1), 73–116.

Shipps, D. (2003). Pulling together: Civic capacity and urban school reform. *American Educational Research Journal, 40*(4), 841–878.

Shipps, D. (2006). *School reform, corporate style: Chicago 1880–2000.* Lawrence: University Press of Kansas.

Stone, C. (1989). *Urban regimes: Governing Atlanta, 1946–1988*. Lawrence: University Press of Kansas.

Stone, C. (Ed.) (1998). *Changing urban education. Lawrence: University Press of Kansas*.

Stone, C., Henig, J. R., Jones, B. D., & Pierannunzi, C. (2001). *Building civic capacity: The politics of reforming urban schools*. Lawrence: University Press of Kansas.

Tyack, D., & L. Cuban. (1995). *Tinkering toward utopia: A century of public school reform*. Cambridge, MA: Harvard University Press.

Viteritti, J. (Ed.). (2009). *When mayors take charge*. Washington, DC: Brookings Institution Press.

Wong, K. (1990). *City choices: Education and housing*. Albany: State University of New York Press.

Wong, K. (1992). The politics of urban education as a field of study: An interpretive analysis. In J. Cibulka, R. Reed, & K. Wong (Eds.), *The politics of urban education in the United States* (pp. 3–26). London: Falmer Press.

Wong, K., & Shen, F. (2009, October 14). Mayors can be 'Prime Movers' of urban school improvement, research perspective. *Education Week,* 29(7), 11–13.

Wong, K., Shen, F., Anagnostopoulos, D., & S. Rutledge, S. (2007). *The education mayor*. Washington, DC: Georgetown University Press.

Zeigler, L. H., & Jennings, M. K. (1974). *Governing American schools*. North Scituat, MA: Duxbury.

11

EDUCATION AS CIVIC GOOD

Children's Services Perspectives

Robert L. Crowson, Claire E. Smrekar, and Jo Bennett

Introduction

Two events from the 1950s continue to shape a debate over improving education through services to children and families. The *Brown v. Board of Education of Topeka* decision regarding school desegregation introduced an array of still-active concerns over student-enrollment composition and the socio-economic circumstances of schools as predictors of equal opportunity. The continuing debate shows that community context matters. A second event, the launching of *Sputnik*, expanded ongoing discussions of a school's instructional quality as a predictor of effectiveness, economic productivity, and leadership. School achievement outcomes matter.

More than a half-century later, efforts are continuing (and indeed increasing) toward a workable match between expectations of both equal opportunity and instructional effectiveness. A short-hand phrase much in vogue today, "the achievement gap," captures the essence of these ongoing efforts quite cleanly—a connection much in keeping with the expectations of No Child Left Behind (NCLB) legislation.

This shared concern over the provision of both opportunity and achievement (equity and excellence) is much enlivened, however, by a rather deep split in perspective—a split between those who believe the schools can, versus those who believe the schools cannot, do-it-alone in reducing the gap. On the can side, there is the belief that the schools can be sufficiently improved to perform well academically whatever their community context. On the can't-do-it-alone side, the claim is that standards-based reforms and in-school improvements in instructional quality aren't enough. The schools require complementary efforts to strengthen capacities and supports for learning within the family and in the surrounding community (see Rothstein, 2004; Rothman, 2007). The position here is that there are many children's learning difficulties stemming from conditions of concentrated poverty, poor health, inadequate nutrition, and other external forces. Reducing the achievement gap, it is claimed, requires help for the school via strengthened school-community relationships, particularly through a vehicle of "wrap around" social and health services for individual students and their families, brought more effectively to bear in improving scholastic performance.

This chapter examines anew the can't-do-it-alone perspective within the current national framework of expectations for both equality of opportunity and instructional effectiveness. Following a brief historical examination of the development of services coordination as a social movement of some consequence, the chapter discusses three contemporary points-of-departure in a decided renewal of interest in the children's services phenomenon, as a route toward both improved learning and improved opportunity. The three contemporary efforts conceptualize services as (a) vital elements of social context and capital development for communities in the interest of instructional improvement; (b) the foundations of viable and varied partnerships for learning between schools and their communities; and (c) sources of very direct and focused supports for improved classroom learning through community linkages.

Background: The Services Coordination Movement Historically

Informative historical summaries of the services coordination idea as a social movement have been prepared by Smrekar and Mawhinney (1999), by Fusarelli (2008), and by Fusarelli and Lindle (in press). The idea is credited with roots in the Progressive Era and the settlement houses of the late 19th and early 20th centuries. A wide variety of family services, many with an emphasis upon literacy education, were provided by the settlement houses to impoverished immigrant families in the most congested of newcomer neighborhoods (see Philpott, 1978). During the Depression years of the 1930s, the services idea gained added attention, as the local school came to be recognized as a convenient place to "house" services (especially health services) that were hard for families to afford in tight economic times. The idea of a "community school" also developed in the 1930s—with the school regarded as a center for community recreation, adult education, holiday celebrations, and sometimes such services as family counseling and/or legal aid.

Federal aid to education and the War on Poverty in the 1960s and '70s had a decided services impact, particularly for groups of people targeted for compensatory aid. Health services (including mental health) continued to be dominant, but food services, counseling, after-school programs, youth centers, and even some "outreach" to families in need also became part of the services menu. The separate idea of *coordinating* services to children and families, however, received impetus from a series of events in the late 1980s and early '90s. These were, particularly: (a) a report on the "Conditions of Children in California" (Kirst. 1989) that identified the fragmentation characterizing children's services in that state; (b) an interest among a number of well-known private foundations in supporting services integration initiatives (e.g., Kellogg, Annie E. Casey, Mott, Danforth); (c) some arguments in favor of services coordination by influential authors (e.g., Schorr, 1988; Levy & Copple, 1989; Melaville & Blank, 1991; Kagan, 1993; Dryfoos, 1994); plus, legislation in New Jersey, Kentucky, and California that pioneered statewide integrated services programs (see Crowson & Boyd, 1993; Smrekar & Mawhinney, 1999; Fusarelli, 2008).

However, as the children's services effort expanded during the 1990s, a number of studies and reports came to light indicating just how very difficult the implementation of services coordination can be (Chaskin & Richman, 1992; Crowson & Boyd, 1993; White & Wehlage, 1995; Cibulka, 1996). Cross-agency tensions were evident between the differing professions, with their separate organizational support structures. Tensions surfaced as well in attempts to redefine the role of the school in some settings toward a more family-supportive "outreach" relationship with the community (Cibulka, 1996). Projects were also hindered by communications and information breakdowns, "turf" issues, funding and space inadequacies, a limited knowledge base, inadequately focused leadership, and a slow development of clientele buy-in (Crowson & Boyd, 1993).

Additionally, a serious blow to the movement came from some evaluative conclusions of non-effectiveness among a few of the projects, with a consequent pull-back of funding from some influential foundations (White & Wehlage, 1995). With a loss of funding from previously supportive foundations, the services coordination effort in the United States lost much of its momentum by the end of the 20th century. Additionally, the initial effect of No Child Left Behind, toward state and national standards plus test-based accountability, was to re-focus school-improvement attention inward to school and classroom rather than outward to the community.

Quite interestingly, the integrated services idea gained increasing attention in the United Kingdom just as it was winding down in the United States. With the resonating themes of inter-agency working and "joined-up government," the notions of full-service schooling and community-focused schooling caught on well in the UK; these constructs continued to have considerable appeal well into the 21st century (see Riddell & Tett, 2001; Dyson, 2009).

A catch-phrase introduced in the early 2000s by then Prime Minister Tony Blair linked the idea of joined-up government into the idea of a "new localism" in educational policymaking. The new localism in the UK has represented a devolution of power to local governmental agencies, but only within a framework of national priorities and goals.

Specific foci of the new localism in the UK include more freedom for community initiatives in improving the overall responsiveness of public services to children and family needs, plus more community governance and direct engagement in implementing national goals. Local authorities are specifically encouraged to wrap multiple services around shared problems such as health, police, housing, employment, and education (Powell, 2004; Storey & Farrar, 2010).

Perhaps in part because of the continued interest in and saliency of joined-up thinking "across-the-pond," but more because of our own deepened concerns in the United States regarding ongoing achievement gaps, the integrated services concept is currently receiving attention anew in American education. And, indeed, the phraseology of a new localism is catching-on as well in the United States, including an emphasis upon local adaptations to national goals. With this renewal of interest in locally-delivered, coordinated services, there is a belief that the achievement gap cannot be reduced by the schools acting alone; there must be a much deepened school-community relationship. However, because the focus in this renewal of interest is more directly upon achievement (and gap-reduction) rather than simply the coordination of services for families and their needs, there is also a decidedly new priority. As Kirst (2008, p. 3) has framed it: "The hope may lie in connecting outside services for children and families to *classroom instruction* [our emphasis here] in a coordinated and interactive manner." This classroom learning approach, he continues, is indeed "the basis for some cautious optimism in closing the achievement gap."

Indeed, any optimism must be cautious to be sure. It may be prudent to contrast the documented, positive benefits of parent involvement activities that focus upon students' skill development and academic growth (Clark, 2002; Henderson, Mapp, Johnson, & Davies, 2007; Reynolds & Clements, 2005; Swap 1993) with what is known—virtually nothing—regarding the effects of coordinated services upon learning outcomes.

To be sure, the new, more direct focus upon improving academic outcomes through a services coordination approach has rejuvenated the movement. It is not yet clear just what sets of services, partnering arrangements, and delivery mechanisms offer the best opportunity for improved academic achievement. Nor is it apparent whether the best approach involves potentially promising partnerships across multiple policy domains—such as housing, health care, and workforce development—all typically arranged in a rather siloed pattern of separate funding and program autonomy. As noted above, solid linkages between coordinated services and improved learning are yet to be agreed upon or understood.

It is imperative, however, to consider what we have learned from other services-based, academically-focused, national initiatives, including after-school programs. A critical lesson may be offered by the national evaluation of the 21st Century Community Learning Centers Program (U.S. Department of Education, 2003). This federal initiative provided funding for after-school programs featuring academic, recreational, and cultural enrichment elements. But the core goal was clearly stated: all 21st Century programs must make academic activities and skill development designed to "advance student achievement" the centerpiece of these after-school initiatives (U.S. Department of Education, 2003). The key findings from the national evaluation, however, noted little influence of 21st Century after-school programs on academic performance. The centers changed where students spent their after-school hours (greater safety), and the peers with whom they interacted (better behavior), and parent involvement increased (U.S. Department of Education, 2003). The report underscored the problems of low attendance among students, inadequate staffing, low academic program content and quality, and limited partnerships with community agencies. It seems safe to assume that the recommendations from this national evaluation of after-school programs offer a framework for examining the challenges of a learning-focused coordinated services initiative.

We proceed now to examine three differing perspectives or points-of-departure that have characterized current directions in services coordination to date, asking what each might promise in helping children learn. The three perspectives discuss the services movement within the emerging frameworks of community development for school improvement, community supports for classroom learning, and school-community partnering for instructional improvement.

Improving the Community Context for Learning

Drawing from earlier emphases upon expanded notions of school community (Bronfenbrenner, Moen, & Garbarino, 1984; Hobbs, 1978), two significant elements in the initial approaches to children's services coordination signaled (a) a renewed appreciation of an ecological relationship among schools, families, and communities; and correspondingly, (b) a strong sense that the ecological connections embedded in services to families in high-poverty circumstances were lacking in adequate child development. A patchwork of delivery systems for poor children plus a fragmentation of professional and organizational supports for families were just not meeting current needs (Kirst & McLaughlin, 1990). Families, schools, and neighborhoods are intertwined, but deliveries of health care, adequate nutrition, good housing, safe streets, clean clothing, and adult caring are not (Crowson & Boyd, 1993).

There was an implicit achievement message in this initial thinking about improved and hopefully coordinated services. The message was that hungry, inadequately clothed and housed, and unhealthy children are academically challenged learners. Additionally, such other services as parks and recreation offerings, safe neighborhoods, and a range of after-school options can be just as educative and important to a child's development as the local school (Littell & Wynn, 1989). Quite often these amenities too, however, are little to be found (e.g., well-kept playgrounds, community policing, adequate street-lighting). If these neighborhood forces and services can somehow be both provided and linked, observed Mario Fantini (1983), the powerful result could be a strong "network of learning environments."

With an implicit notion of improved learning and a more direct message of facilitating child and human-capital development through efforts to "network," the services idea gained measurable momentum and credibility. Contributing factors included an array of projects with sizeable foundation support; an impressive provision for Family Resource Centers in Kentucky's school-reform legislation; state legislation in New York and New Jersey mandating coordinated family and children's services; new "Children's Budgets" in state expenditures; experimentation in a number of urban systems (e.g., Cities in Schools); plus a "bandwagon" effect of plans, guidelines, handbooks, reports, and proposals from professional associations and universities.

As the movement developed, there was no common denominator for experimentation, in either the range of services or the location of facilities. Health-related services were frequently provided—as often were such services as family counseling, daycare, parent education, and some categories of family assistance (e.g., providing food, finding shelter, finding employment). The location of projects was variously on-site or co-located at a local school, school-linked but not actually at the school, or community-based with a broadened focus that often covered more than one school. Each of these models had its pluses and minuses. On-site projects were not infrequently placed in portable facilities on the school grounds, with attendant problems in finding a niche and role-acceptability within the regular routines and workday of schooling. School-linked and community-based projects had the political responsibility of legitimizing themselves as worthy service-available resources for the school—without having much opportunity to interact deeply, often, and directly with school personnel, particularly classroom teachers.

As Smrekar and Mawhinney (1999) have documented, many of the early projects encountered dilemmas in penetrating (that is, bringing new roles to) the institutionalized cultures of schools; learning how to actually collaborate when separately trained professionally; learning how to connect with the community as well as the school; learning the boundaries of service, intervention, instruction, home vs. school, and educator vs. other-professional; plus, simply learning how to survive politically in a turbulent environment filled with other policy initiatives of the time in urban education (e.g., the beginnings of the school choice, standards, test-based accountability, and mayoral-takeover movements).

By the late 1990s, the idea of coordinated children's services began to move away from integrating a provision of varieties of assistance to individual families, toward a more concerted look at community-wide conditions of household need. The ecological frame of reference remained strong, but in the larger sense now that fundamental social circumstances characterizing entire neighborhoods should be the central point of attack (e.g., the quality and condition of the housing stock, residents' sense of safety and security, stability vs. turnover in neighborhood mobility).

Social and cultural capital and processes of community-development, in the course of assisting human capital, began to dominate thinking around children's services late in the 20th century (see Saegert, Thompson & Warren, 2001). A much broadened sense of the problem accompanied this shift. Again, well beyond the needs and characteristics of families, the community's impact upon the educational success of its children was now understood to include such elements as: the quality and availability of housing; the strength of each community's own institutions (e.g., community organizations, faith-based organizations, the business community, public-sector resource availabilities); the poverty and employment circumstances of the community; the criminal-justice characteristics of the community; and the overall depth and stability of the community's culture.

The sense of a target clientele for supportive services and points of intervention was also considerably broadened. Stimulating enterprise and the economic vitality of a community became recognized as an educationally-supportive endeavor (see Kerchner & McMurran, 2001; McGaughy, 2001). Similarly, adult education, employment training, after-school programs for youth, crime-prevention efforts, and the community itself as "place"—all became subjects of much interest in improving children's learning (see Driscoll, 2001; Gonzalez, Moll, & Amanti, 2005; Pena, McGill, & Stout, 2001). Additionally, deepened studies were surfacing around the unique elements of cultural capital that characterize educational success in African American and Latino communities (see Savage, 2002; Tillman, 2005; Valle & Torres, 2000); and, interestingly, foundation support was newly returning to the fray, but now around such topics as *Linking Public Housing to Neighborhood School Improvement,* A Report prepared for the Annie E. Casey Foundation (Abravenel, Smith, & Cove, 2006).

The community development approach was much in keeping with President Bill Clinton's urban policy agenda, in funding the Empowerment Zones (EZ) and Enterprise Communities (EC) Program as early as 1995 (see Crowson, 2001; McGaughy, 2001). In their fascinating study of school district involvement in economic development in Pomona, California, Kerchner and McMurran (2001) found that schools can serve significantly as engines of revitalization in their communities. Pomona represented one of the first efforts to map and track the distribution of capital assets and liabilities area-by-area in a school district—noting, as the authors put it, that: "Counting assets as well as liabilities allows the school district and others in the community to begin to see their surroundings as something to be built around, not only as a set of problems and barriers" (p. 59).

Geographic mapping has now emerged as a major tool in understanding the potential of school districts and communities to leverage improvements in their external environments toward improved instruction. Not only economic development but other "spatial variables" that are important to schooling and instructional improvement are being mapped (e.g., sense of place, market baskets of family incentives around choice, the competitive "market" for individual schools themselves) (see Lubienski & Dougherty, 2009). In a commentary on the rapidly emerging technology of geographic mapping (GIS), Henig (2009) notes the potential for a rich research agenda around not only the delivery of needed services to communities but also much added knowledge about the complex interactions between space, place, choice, community, social capital, and the economy in improved schooling generally.

One key aspect of the community-development approach to improved schooling, an aspect very much in keeping with the Clinton-era's Empowerment Zones initiative, has been a concerted effort to help communities develop the capacities to improve their *own* learning environments (see Brooks-Gunn, Duncan, & Aber, 1997; Smrekar, 2009). One direction in such capacity-building has emphasized the importance of social networks of support, connectedness, commitment among neighbors, and the sense of a community-wide responsibility for outcomes (see Chaskin, Brown, Venkatesh, & Vidal, 2001; Chadwick, 2004). A spin-off has been an effort toward community-organizing in a number of neighborhood settings, adding an empowerment of the community vis-à-vis its schools to capacity-building, and indeed an exercise of capacity as an instrument of learning improvement (see Shirley, 1997; 2001).

Another direction in capacity-building emphasizes the importance of *investments* by community institutions (e.g., churches, the health sector, schools, the parks department), plus investments by families and individuals themselves in their neighborhood's welfare and vitality. From an insight shared many years ago, Janowitz (1967) observed that community institutions, including the schools, can often take a stance of "limited liability" vis-à-vis their neighborhood surroundings. They guard their institutional boundaries, divorce themselves from "outside" responsibility, and act bureaucratically and impersonally (just-doing-their-job) with the community clientele.

Quite at odds with such a posture of limited liability, is the suggestion of a revised "theory of the state" by Offe and Ronge (1997, p. 62). In place of limited liability and traditional governmental activities of transfer payments, services, and subsidies, Offe and Ronge claim that governments should *create the conditions* under which individuals and neighborhoods can achieve independent success. Among the conditions would be a program of "public infrastructure investments" in and by community institutions in poor neighborhoods.

One of the most interesting examples of such an effort has been the HOPE VI initiative for public housing, which began in the mid-1990s as an attempt to substantially alter public housing from its patterns of concentrated poverty, dangerous living environments, high population density, and tightly-clustered residential units. HOPE VI offers attractive dwellings, reduced density, a mixed-income population of residents, and supportive resources (e.g., household budgeting and home-buying courses, GED test preparation, employment assistance, neighborhood watch programs, youth centers and programs) (see Smith, 2002; Turbov & Piper, 2005).

HOPE VI offers a significant opportunity to investigate and reinforce a general (but yet to be firmly established) sense that school achievement can be improved by developing neighborhood capacities and overall family environments, by de-concentrating poverty, by encouraging social interaction and added institutional investments. Thus, unlike the federally funded, public housing resident relocation program known as Moving to Opportunity (MTO) the HOPE VI emphasis rests with razing and then revitalizing the *existing* public housing neighborhood. Interestingly, work has only recently been underway to study comparatively (HOPE VI against traditional public housing) just how neighborhood environments might lead to improved school environments and school outcomes. In undertaking such a comparative study, Smrekar (2010, p. 224) observes: "This research should document the ways in which housing density and dispersion, conditions of crime and perceptions of safety, patterns of social interactions and networking, and residents' education and employment patterns may coalesce to produce distinctive patterns of community capacity— with potentially measurable spillover effects for neighborhood schools." While the evidence from the MTO family relocation initiative suggests little if any change in the school composition or academic outcomes for children (Brooks-Gunn, Duncan, Kling, & Sanbonmatsu, 2006), the impact of HOPE VI on school outcomes remains unknown at this point.

Improving the Community's Support of Classroom Learning

The coordinated services movement has typically viewed the relationship between classrooms and children's services in much the same manner that it has tended to perceive the role of the school nurse (an important available resource but a service not directly integral to learning). Health services, family resource centers, community agencies, local volunteers, and other social services were there to be called upon by teachers and administrators when needed. But, typically, unless there was an acute need or crisis situation, the extra set of services was not likely to be tapped. One of the problems in early attempts to coordinate children's services was the difficulty faced by teachers to find any *additional time* for the effort involved in individual student referrals for services, even when the services (e.g., family resource centers) were co-located at the school-site (Crowson & Boyd, 1993). Evidence produced by case studies in Kentucky suggested that family resource center coordinators often operated in physical and programmatic isolation from the instructional, classroom-based activities of the school, and teachers assumed entirely disconnected roles from these centers and the service providers (Smrekar, 1994).

This peripheral positioning of the services coordination dimension is now changing. Against the backdrop of NCLB's emphases upon school performance and test-based evidence of learning, a decided narrowing of focus on academic outcomes has emerged—defining the priorities of numerous federal and state education plans (Fusarelli, 2008). There has been a significant expansion of preschool programs across the nation, seen in many states and communities as a means to reduce the achievement gap (Schaub, 2009). The NCLB legislation itself has placed a premium upon the provision of extra tutorial services to pupils in schools that fail to meet the so-called "AYP" (or Average Yearly Progress) standards of performance. Accordingly, faith-based organizations, Boys and Girls Clubs, Y's, community centers, and tutorial start-ups have proliferated, providing after-school and summer-long tutoring. Libraries are once again in significant demand in communities across the nation—supplying not only after-school daycare for working parents, but also responding to a renewed emphasis nationally upon reading and information retrieval (particularly via the Internet).

Concurrent with the press for higher academic achievement and school accountability, there has been a resurrection of interest in what families of differing socioeconomic circumstances and ethnicity separately bring to early childhood and to in-home preparation for school (Chin & Phillips, 2004; Lareau, 2003; Rothstein, 2004), including language and questioning patterns, reading and storytelling behaviors, nutrition, physical activity, play, and disciplinary expectations. Much aware of education's performance emphasis, many parents (particularly middle-class parents) have helped recently to fuel an entire industry of early learning (with an explosion of instructional CDs, videos, computer exercises, and children's TV). Competition has sometimes been fierce to have one's child accepted into the "best" pre-school in an area. Indeed, parental attention generally to the intellectual development of children, in many community settings thus far into the 21st century, has been rather remarkable.

There can sometimes be more parental involvement or intrusion into the schools, in middle- and upper-class communities, than classroom teachers would prefer (Lareau, 2000). Securing the active participation of parents in their child's education in low-income neighborhoods, however, can be problematic (Brooks-Gunn, Duncan, & Aber, 1997; Furstenberg, 1993; Horvat, Weininger, & Lareau, 2003; Wilson, 1987). Ethnicity and cultural beliefs can play a role, wherein some groups of parents believe they do not have a right to push themselves into the special professional province of the trained educator (Delgado-Gaitan, 1991; Harry, 1992; Lareau, 2000). Parenting from this perspective should stop at the schoolhouse door, giving the expertise of the teacher full authority from that point on. In other circumstances, issues of time and travel, or discomforting differences in education and social class, can also discourage involvement (Smrekar, 1996).

Nevertheless, the newly invigorated services movement around learning has considerably renewed our attention to parental roles in assisting children's achievement in poor communities as well as the more well-to-do (see Brooks-Gunn et al., 2006). And, in communities where traditional beliefs have tended to constrain parental involvement, there are examples of innovative success in bringing parents "in" to the school productively despite matters of cultural hesitancy (see Shirley, 1997, 2001; Smylie, Crowson, Chou, & Levin 1994).

Despite barriers in securing parental involvement in some community contexts, it would be quite erroneous to assume that low-income communities are without significant capacities to support learning (see Smrekar & Cohen-Vogel, 2001). Indeed, note Smrekar and Cohen-Vogel (2001), neighborhood schools can mistakenly assume that community apathy and insufficient local resources are in play, and can act (or fail to act) accordingly, with little effort on their part to tap the many strengths that are to be found and utilized. Faith-based institutions, community organizers, a community's elderly population, local businesses, neighborhood health clinics, city agencies, local athletes, and military veterans, are all potential sources of service and support instructionally within a web of community-based learning environments. These individuals and organizations represent assets for expanding economic and educational opportunities across and within communities, creating what Putnam (2000) calls "bonding" and "bridging" social capital. The new social networks are both productive and instrumental, and assist in creating new channels of information regarding coordinated services, educational programs, and economic support (Foley, McCarthy, & Chaves, 2001).

With an understanding that each community does supply a network of learning opportunities, more and more attention in the services movement has been directed toward assessing just how the schools can best use their communities as instructional resources. A realization, of course, is that not all of the learning in a community environment is supportive of the school's mission. Thus, an added challenge, in using the community effectively is that of pursuing activities to counter negative interferences with instructional goals while simultaneously reinforcing aspects of the community that support the schools. Rather surprisingly, despite much increased interest and attention to community influences on student learning, there is not an exceptionally strong knowledge-base yet to be drawn upon in using the community as an instructional resource.

School-Community Partnering for Instructional Improvement

A partnership model of the school-community relationship is by no means new. Indeed, the community-relations literature is rather well supplied with quite interesting and generally successful examples of collaborative efforts between schools and other agencies (e.g., adopt-a-school programs, school-business and/or school-university partnerships, work-study partnerships, and, of course, school-linked services) (see particularly, Cibulka & Kritek, 1996; Rigsby, Reynolds, & Wang, 1995).

The literature on cross-agency partnering has ample evidence of just how difficult it is to do (see Gray, 1989; Knapp & Associates, 1998). Agencies representing differing professions (e.g., business and education) can have considerable difficulty finding common ground in the use of time, in patterns of workplace behavior and language usage, in diagnosing and treating client needs, in the use of service-related resources, and in judgments of impact (see Guilbeau, 2002).

Nevertheless, a partnership approach to the school–community relationship and children's services is now very much back in vogue. Partnering has returned in full measure to the lexicon of "best practice." The focus, once again under the influence of NCLB, is heavily upon learning and indeed the learning community surrounding schools. An excellent example of the shift in thinking toward service partnerships for learning emerged in the late 1990s in the UK. The development of some 25 education action zones (EAZs) in a number of cities (in 1998 and again in 1999) emphasized community development partnerships for learning among an array of private, voluntary, and public agencies (e.g., business, health, welfare, recreation, church, police, and education). Close partnering with the schools was emphasized, along with the identification of standards for EAZ success—such as achievement gains, improved school attendance, and reduced school leaving (see Power, 2001; Storey, 2005).

Another notable element in the UK program was labeled a "deinstitutionalization of learning" (Power, 2001, p. 24). This was an effort on the part of each EAZ to extend learning beyond the sole responsibility of schools toward extended (and external) learning opportunities, with partnerships throughout the community. Learning agreements in one EAZ reported upon by Storey (2005), for example, included instructional partnerships with a local airport, local engineering and construction firms, a local trucking company, and a number of local retailers.

The interest in creating extended learning opportunities through an array of school–community partnerships has been catching on early in the 21st century in the United States (see Greifner, 2007). A rationale for, and evidence of the potential importance of learning partnerships, comes from the work of Larry Picus (Picus, McCoskey, Robillard, Yao, & Marsenich, 2002), who found that less than half of the money spent on children's education in Los Angeles' various neighborhoods can be accounted for in the funding allocated to neighborhoods by the public schools. After-school and childcare servers, both profit and nonprofit agencies, youth services, city agencies, and of course family-to-family spending provide large amounts of additionally educative resources in each community. Picus et al. suggested a "children's budget" for education community-by-community, bringing all of a city's educative resources to bear in the allocation of services, not just school-to-school resources.

For the United States, the most thorough development to date of school–community partnerships and an improved-learning model in the children's services domain comes from the continued work of a pioneer in the field, Joy Dryfoos (see Dryfoos & Macguire, 2002; Dryfoos, Quinn, & Barkin, 2006). Full-service community schools, as she and her colleagues describe them, typically extend the curriculum of the school well into the community (e.g., with service learning, partnerships with community institutions, extended hours of schooling, summer enrichment, negotiations of added health and social services for families, and use of the school as a catalyst for community improvement).

In response to the recent emphasis placed on institutional effectiveness in public education, Dryfoos has devoted considerable attention of late to a consideration of "outcomes" in full-service schooling. She notes that there is ample space for much discussion around just what standards and measures are most appropriate in assessing services. One option is to concentrate heavily upon "learning supports"—in the form of improved children's health coverage in a community, the availability of early childhood programs, lowered crime statistics, improved housing, and the like. A more direct assessment would focus upon evidence of improved academic achievement —in the form of test-score gains but also improved school attendance, reductions in disciplinary actions, and a decrease in high-risk behaviors. While recognizing the increasing emphasis nationally upon improved test results, Dryfoos urges broad evaluation strategies which are fully cognizant of the underlying problems children bring with them to school and the need for learning supports to address these (Dryfoos, 2000).

While Dryfoos has focused heavily upon the school as a catalyst for partnering and improved learning, Bennett (2008) has reviewed cases of partnering wherein city government takes the initiative. Coordinating city services in the interest of school improvement is often a key part of the rationale among mayors for their "takeover" of the public schools (Edelstein, 2008). Even short of a full takeover, city governments can take actions (as Bennett found in a Kansas community) to provide such services as city-supported afterschool tutoring, summer camp learning experiences, health and dental clinic availability, adult education opportunities, and other services at one-stop centers and neighborhood city halls at the community level.

Bennett and other scholars have observed that partnering for schools and communities benefits much from the support of an intermediate agent, liaison, or advocate—a person who can devote the time and the personal attention needed to cement relationships (see Goldring & Hausman, 2000; Fusarelli, 2008). This suggestion, along with the observation regarding city or mayoral initiatives in the services movement, draws attention to the importance of "civic capacity" (Stone, 1998) in partnering efforts. Without a decided attempt to energize civic capacity, often through focused advocacy or an intermediate agent, there's often little time available to other school personnel "to nurture and maintain effective relationships with external agencies" (Fusarelli, 2008, p. 367).

Much the same theme is expressed by Strike (2008), in suggesting that a shared sense of community (almost in the style of a congregation or parish) needs to accompany the goal-directedness and accountability-mindedness of educational aspirations and achievement outcomes. Strong advocacy and effective partnering in children's services can help to communicate the notion that education is very much a civic good, not just a product of classroom-focused teaching and within- school curricula.

Conclusion

It would be a major mistake in this time of centralized educational reform, notes Henig (2010), to buy into a myth of local obsolescence in public schooling. Local educational agencies are no longer buffered and privileged from strong accountability pressures, but they continue to be key actors for the nation in setting educational policy and in shaping school improvement. They can act most effectively today, continues Henig, if they tap into the larger governmental capacities of their communities, if they are "locally rooted," and if they build strong cross-sector coalitions of support for the schools.

In his own analysis of trends in local schooling, Cunningham (2003, p. 156) also observed that school districts and their schools are increasingly "expected to interact with their communities and local surroundings." They are additionally expected to place more emphasis on "collaborative relationships and assume a shared accountability for well being in their communities" (p. 156). Moreover, continued Cunningham (p. 158), there has been a decided paradigm shift in American education: Governing schools is no longer at the heart of policy and administration in local education, "governing learning" is now the paramount activity.

Cross-sector coalitions, an awareness that the locality is by no means obsolete despite centralizing reforms, plus a focus upon student achievement and direct evidence of learning in school improvement: These are the major forces represented in a decided renewal of interest in children's services. A debate continues around just how much progress in resolving such issues as the achievement gap can be made by the schools on-their-own, versus how much help the schools require from efforts to strengthen the external context for learning in school neighborhoods. Those who advocate anew an improvement of scholastic performance through strengthened communities and added children's services have offered three contemporary approaches.

A *first* approach looks directly at *improving* the overall community context for learning, finding conceptual roots in the well-established literature on ecological relationships between schools, families, and communities as well as the literatures around the importance of generating social and cultural capital plus community-development in general. Although services-coordination in the interest of community-development is not a new strategy, the rejuvenated interest in this approach has been energized by: (a) the nation's 21st-century focus upon evidence of learning and particularly the family's role in learning; (b) new tools of comparison between communities, as evidenced by an emerging technology to geographically map neighborhood assets against liabilities and to study the impacts of asset differences upon the schools; plus, (c) a substantial shift in public policy toward new directions in publicly-supported housing, in countering poverty through employment, and in a "new urbanism" that strives to create a sense of shared community through the networking of families and community institutions.

A *second* approach to children's services has focused more specifically than previously upon the community's *closely linked connections to classroom learning*. Services are now being emphasized that are believed to most directly influence successful school achievement—including particularly an expansion of preschooling and kindergarten, tutoring services, summer-learning camps, lengthened hours of instruction, and many-sided efforts to encourage parents' involvement in their children's learning. Not lost at all in this focus-upon-instruction domain of services provision has been an awareness that local libraries, community centers, faith-based institutions, youth-activity and recreational outlets, health clinics, and safe streets all play additionally important roles in student achievement.

A *third* approach in a rejuvenated model of services provision has focused upon *school-community and cross-agency partnering*. Partnering has long been advocated in the literature of school-community relations, but only recently has a narrowed focus upon learning been the driving force. An added impetus comes from arguments often used by mayors to explain their reasoning for a "takeover" of the schools. The reasoning typically is that city governments can play a helpful instructional role for the schools in overseeing programs of cross-sector assistance to the schools—from city departments of parks and recreation, library services, public health, housing, welfare, public safety, etc.

Another notable element in the new approach to partnering has been a recognition that partnered learning can use the community as its classroom, not just the school. An array of such activities (sometimes referred to as "expeditionary learning") in any one community might include opportunities for service learning, internships with local public- and private-sector organizations, exercises in urban agriculture, work-study experiences, and scientific or environment projects in the community (see Mawhinney & May, 2010).

Finally, the renewed interest in partnering in education has been very much attentive to today's demands for hard evidence—recognizing that community-wide outcomes of achievement gains, lowered dropout rates, safer streets, improved school attendance, and the like can be vital indicators of progress in these No Child Left Behind times.

A rejuvenated movement to bring children's services coordination back into prominence is finding new strength in the recognition that improved classroom learning is a community-wide responsibility and very much a "civic good." Much effort remains, however, to ascertain just how schools and their communities can in practice implement effectively, and implement together, the paradigm shift that Cunningham (2003) foresaw as a necessary shift in local education from governing schools to governing learning.

References

Abravenel, M. D., Smith, R. E., & Cove, E. C. (2006, June). *Linking public housing revitalization to neighborhood improvement*. Washington, DC: The Urban Institute.

Bennett, J. (2008). *Care Ethic in an Urban School*. Unpublished Doctoral Dissertation. Austin, TX: University of Texas at Austin.

Bronfenbrenner, U., Moen, P., & Garbarino, J. (1984). Child, family, and community. In R. Parke (Ed.). *Review of child development research* (pp. 283–328). Chicago: University of Chicago Press.

Brooks-Gunn, J., Duncan, G. J., & Aber, T. L. (Eds.). (1997). *Neighborhood poverty*: *Context and consequences for children* (Vol. 1). New York: Russell Sage Foundation.

Brooks-Gunn, J., Duncan, G., Kling, J., & Sanbonmatsu, L. (2006). *Neighborhoods and academic achievement: Results from the moving to opportunity experiment*. Cambridge, MA: National Bureau of Economic Research.

Brown v. Board of Education of Topeka. 47 U.S. 483 (1954).

Chadwick, K. G. (2004). *Improving schools through community engagement*. Thousand Oaks, CA: Corwin Press.

Chaskin, R. J., Brown, P., Venkatesh, S., & Vidal, A. (2001). *Building community capacity*. New York: Walter de Gruyter.

Chaskin, R.J., & Richman, H. (1992). Concerns about school-linked services: Institution-based versus community-based models, *The Future of Children, 2*(1), 107–117.

Chin, T., & Phillips, M. (2004). Social reproduction and child-rearing practices: Social class, children's agency, and the summer activity gap. *Sociology of Education*, 77(3), 185–210.

Cibulka, J. (1996). Toward an interpretation of school, family, and community conditions: Policy Challenges. In J. Cibulka & W. Kritek (Eds.), *Coordination among schools, families, and communities: Prospects for educational reform* (pp. 403–435). Albany: State University of New York Press.

Cibulka, J. G., & Kritek, W.J . (Eds.). (1996). *Coordination among schools, families, and communities*. Albany: State University of New York Press.

Clark, R. (2002). Ten hypotheses about what predicts student achievement for African American students and all other students: What the research shows. In W. Allen (Ed.), *African American education: Race, community, inequality and achievement* (pp. 155–177). Oxford, UK: Elsevier Science.

Crowson, R. L. (Ed.). (2001). *Community development and school reform*. London: JAI Press.

Crowson, R. L., & Boyd, W. L. (1993). Coordinated services for children: Designing arks for storms and seas unknown. *American Journal of Education, 101*(2), 140–179.

Cunningham, L. (2003). Rethinking the role of the community. In W. L. Boyd & D. Miretzky (Eds.), *American educational governance on trial: Change and challenge. 102nd yearbook of the National Society for the Study of Education (NSSE), Part I.* (pp. 155–176). Chicago: The University of Chicago Press.

Delgado-Gaitan, C. (1991). Involving parents in the schools: A process of empowerment. *American Journal of Education, 100*, 20–46.

Driscoll, M. E. (2001). The sense of place and the neighborhood school: Implications for building social capital and for community Ddvelopment. In R .L. Crowson (Ed.), *Community development and school reform* (pp. 19–41). London: JAI Press.

Dryfoos, J. (2000). *Evaluation of community schools: An early look*. Washington, DC: Coalition for Community Schools.

Dryfoos, J. (1994). *Full-service schools*. San Francisco: Jossey-Bass.

Dryfoos, J. G., & Macquire, S. (2002). *Inside full-service community schools*. Thousand Oaks, CA: Corwin Press.

Dryfoos, J. G., Quinn, J., & Barkin, C. (Eds.). (2006). *Community schools in action: Lessons from a decade of practice*. Oxford, UK: Oxford University Press.

Dyson, A. (2009, April). *Beyond the school gate: Schools, communities and social justice*. Paper presented at the annual meeting of the American Educational Research Association, San Diego.

Edelstein, F. (2008). The evolving political role of urban mayors in education. In J. G. Cibulka, L. D. Fusarelli, & B. S. Cooper (Eds.), *Handbook of education politics and policy* (pp. 179–191). New York: Routledge.

Fantini, M. D. (1983). From school Ssstem to educational Ssstem: Linking the school with community environment. In R. L. Sinclair (Ed.), *For every school a community: Expanding environments for learning.* Boston: Institute for Responsive Education.

Fantini, M. D., & Sinclair, R. L. (1985). Linking school and nonschool education, public policy considerations. In M. D. Fantini & R. L. Sinclair (Eds.), *Education in school and nonschool settings. Eighty-fourth yearbook of the National Society for the Study of Education, Part I* (pp. 1–38). Chicago: University of Chicago Press.

Foley, M., McCarthy, J., & Chaves, M. (2001). Social capital, religious institutions, and poor communities. In S. Saegert, J. P. Thompson, & M. Warren (Eds.), *Social capital and poor communities* (pp. 215–245). New York: Russell Sage Foundation.

Furstenberg, F. (1993). How families manage risk and opportunity in dangerous neighborhoods. In W. J. Wilson (Ed.), *Sociology and the public agenda.* Newbury Park, CA: Sage.

Fusarelli, B. C. (2008). The politics of coordinated services for children: Institutional relations and social justice. In B. S. Cooper, J. G. Cibulka, & L. D. Fusarelli (Eds.), *Handbook of education politics and policy* (pp. 350–373). New York: Routledge.

Fusarelli, B. C., & Lindle, J. C. (in press). The politics, problems, and potential promise of school-linked social services: Insights and new direction from the work of William Lowe Boyd. *Peabody Journal Of Education.*

Goldring, E. B., & Hausman, C. (2000, April). *Civic capacity and school principals: The missing links for community development.* Paper presented at the Annual Meeting of the American Educational Research Association, Seattle, WA.

Gonzalez, N., Moll, L.C., & Amanti, C. (2005). *Funds of knowledge: Theorizing practices in households, communities and classrooms.* Mahwah, NJ: Erlbaum.

Gray, B. (1989). Collaborating: Finding common ground for multiparty problems. San Francisco: Jossey-Bass.

Greifner, L. (2007, January 24). Panel favors extended view of eearning. *Education Week, 26*(20), 1, 25.

Guilbeau, C. (2002). *A case study of a career focus school's partnership with business for student success.* Unpublished doctoral dissertation, Nashville, TN: Vanderbilt University.

Harry, B. (1992). An ethnographic study of cross-cultural communication with Puerto Rican-American Families in the special education system. *American Educational Research Journal, 29*(3). 471–494

Henderson, A., Mapp, K., Johnson, V., & Davies, D. (2007). *Beyond the bake sale: The essential guide to family-school partnerships.* New York: The New Press.

Henig, J. R. (2009, August). Geo-spatial analyses and school choice research. *American Journal of Education, 115*(4), 649–657.

Henig, J. R. (2010). The politics of localism in an era of centralization, privatization, and choice. In R. L. Crowson & E. B. Goldring (Eds.), *The new localism in American education. 108th yearbook of the National Society for the Society of Education (NSSE)* (pp. 350–373). New York: Teachers College Press.

Hobbs, N. (1978). Families, schools, and communities: An ecosystem for children. *Teachers College Record, 79*(4), 756–766.

Horvat, E., Weininger, E., & Lareau, A. (2003). From social ties to social capital: Class differences in relations between schools and parent networks. *American Education Research Journal, 40,* 319–351.

Janowitz, M. (1967). *The community press in an urban setting* (2nd ed.). Chicago: The University of Chicago Press.

Kagan, S. L. (1993). *Integrating services for children and families: Understanding the past to shape the future.* New Haven, CT: Yale University Press.

Kerchner, C. T., & McMurran, G. (2001). Leadership outside the triangle: The challenges of school administration in highly porous systems. In R. L. Crowson (Ed.), *Community development and school reform* (pp. 43–64). London: JAI Press.

Kirst, M. (Ed.). (1989). *The conditions of children in California.* Berkeley: Policy Analysis for California Education.

Kirst, M. (2008). *A 'Rosetta Stone' for the achievement gap: Integrating outside community services and better teaching could lead to success.* An occasional paper prepared with the support of the School

Finance Redesign Project, Center for Reinventing Public Education, Seattle: University Washington.

Kirst, M. W., & McLaughlin, M. (1990). Rethinking policy for children: Implications for educational administration. In B. Mitchell & L.L. Cunningham (Eds.), *Educational leadership and changing contexts of families, communities and schools. 89th yearbook of the National Society for the Study of Education (NSSE), Part Two* (pp. 69–90). Chicago: University of Chicago Press.

Knapp, M. S., & Associates (1998). *Paths to partnership.* Lanham, MD: Rowman & Littlefield.

Lareau, A. (2000). *Home advantage.* Lanham, MD: Rowman & Littlefield.

Lareau, A. (2003). *Unequal childhoods.* Berkeley: University of California Press.

Levy, J., & Copple, C. (1989*). Joining forces: A report from the first year.* Alexandria, VA: National Association of State Boards of Education.

Littell, J., & Wynn, J. (1989). *The availability and use of community resources for young adolescents in an inner-city and a suburban community.* A report, Chapin Hall Center for Children, Chicago, University of Chicago.

Lubienski, C., & Dougherty, J. (2009, August) (guest editors). Mapping educational opportunity. *American Journal of Education, 115*(4).

Mawhinney, H. B., & May, J. (2010). Localism, learning, and the pressures for accountability in an expeditionary learning focused public charter school. In R. L. Crowson & E. B. Goldring (Eds.), *The new localism in American education, 108th yearbook of The National Society for the Study of Education (NSSE)* (pp. 149–203). New York: Teachers College Press.

McGaughy, C. (2001). The role of education in community development: The Akron enterprise community initiative. In R .L. Crowson (Ed.), *Community development and school reform* (pp. 121–138). London: JAI Press.

Melaville, A., & Blank, M. (1991). *What it takes: Structuring interagency partnerships to connect children and families with comprehensive services.* Washington, DC: Education and Human Resources Consortium.

Offe, C., & Ronge, V. (1997). Thesis on the yheory of the state. In R. E. Goodwin & P. Petitt (Eds.), *Contemporary political philosophy: An anthology* (pp. 60–65). Cambridge, MA: Blackwell.

Pena, R. A., McGill, C., & Stout, R. T. (2001). Community based organizations, Title I schools and youth opportunities: Challenges and contradictions. In R. L. Crowson (Ed.), *Community development and school reform* (pp. 65–99). London: JAI Press.

Philpott, T. L. (1978). *The slum and the ghetto: Neighborhood deterioration and middle class reform, Chicago 1880–1930.* New York: Oxford University Press.

Picus, L. O., McCoskey, J., Robillard, E., Yao, J., & Marsenich, L. (2002). Using student level data to measure school finance adequacy: An exploratory analysis. In C. Roelke & K. Rice (Eds.), *Fiscal policy in urban education* (pp. 181–201). Greenwich, CT: Information Age.

Powell, M. (2004, September). *In search of new and old localism.* A paper prepared for conference presentation, University of Bath, UK.

Power, S. (2001). 'Joined-up thinking': Interagency partnerships in education action zones. In S. Riddell & L. Tett (Eds.), *Education, social justice and inter-agency working: Joined-up or fractured policy?* (pp. 14–28). London: Routledge.

Putnam, R. (2000). *Bowling alone: The collapse and revival of American community.* New York: Simon & Schuster.

Reynolds, A., & Clements, M. (2005). Parental involvement and children's school success. In E. Patrikakou (Ed.), *School-family partnerships: Promoting the social, emotional, and academic growth in children* (pp. 109–127). New York: Teachers College Press.

Riddell, S., & Tett, L. (2001) (Eds.). *Education, social justice and inter-agency working: Joined-up or fractured policy?* London: Routledge.

Rigsby, L. C., Reynolds, M. C., & Wang, M. C. (Eds.). (1995). *School-community connections.* San Francisco: Jossey-Bass.

Rothstein, R. (2004). *Class and schools.* New York: Teachers College Press.

Rothman, R. (Ed.). (2007). *City schools.* Cambridge, MA: Harvard Education Press.

Saegert, S., Thompson, J. P., & Warren, M. R. (Eds.). (2001). *Social capital and poor communities.* New York: Russell Sage Foundation.

Savage, C.J. (2002, Spring). Cultural capital and African American agency: The economic struggle for effective education for African Americans in Franklin, Tennessee, 1896–1967. *The Journal of African American History, 87,* 206–233.

Schaub, M. (2009, February). The expansion of early childhood education. *American Journal of Education, 115*(2), 337–341.

Schorr, L. B. (1988). *Within our reach, breaking the cycle of disadvantage.* New York: Anchor Books.

Shirley, D. (1997). *Community organizing for urban school reform.* Austin, TX: University of Texas Press.

Shirley, D. (2001). Linking community organizing and school reform: A comparative analysis. In R. L. Crowson (Ed.), *Community development and school reform* (pp. 139–169). London JAI Press.

Smith, A. (2002, October). *Mixed-income housing development: Promise and reality.* Cambridge, MA: Joint Center for Housing Studies of Harvard University.

Smrekar, C. E. (1994, Winter). The missing link in school-linked social service programs. *Educational Evaluation and Policy Analysis, 16*(4), 422–433.

Smrekar, C. (1996). *The impact of school choice and community: In the interest of families and schools.* Albany: State University of New York Press.

Smrekar, C. (2009). *Neighborhood revitalization and neighborhood schools: The impact of HOPE VI in public education.* A Research Grant Proposed to the Annie E. Casey Foundation, Peabody College, Vanderbilt University.

Smrekar, C. (2010). Public housing reform and neighborhood schools: How local contexts must matter. In R. Crowson & E. Goldring (Eds.), *The new localism in American education, 108th yearbook of the National Society for the Study of Education (NSSE)* (pp. 204–233). New York: Teachers College Press.

Smrekar, C., & Cohen-Vogel, L. (2001). The voices of parents: Rethinking the intersection of family and school. *Peabody Journal of Education, 76*(2), 75–100.

Smrekar, C., & Mawhinney, H. B. (1999). Integrated services: Challenges in linking schools, families, and communities. In J. Murphy & K. S. Louis (Eds.), *Handbook of research on educational administration* (2nd ed., pp. 443–461). San Francisco: Jossey-Bass.

Smylie, M. A., Crowson, R. L., Chou, V., & Levin, R. A. (1994, August). The principal and community-school connections in Chicago's radical reform. *Educational Administration Quarterly, 30*(3), 342–364.

Stone, C. (1998). Civic capacity and urban school reform. In C. Stone (Ed.), *Changing urban education* (pp. 250–273). Lawrence: University of Kansas Press.

Storey, V. A. (2005, July). *The eye of power: Partnership dynamics and their impact on an area based initiative in England.* Unpublished doctoral dissertation, Vanderbilt University, Nashville, TN.

Storey, V. A., & Farrar, M. (2010). The new localism in the UK: Local governance amid national goals. In R. Crowson & E. Goldring (Eds.), *The new localism in American education, 108th yearbook of the National Society for the Study of Education (NSSE)* (pp. 30–55). New York: Teachers College Press.

Strike, K. A. (2008). Liberty, democracy, and community: Legitimacy in public education. In W. L. Boyd & D. Miretzky (Eds.), *American educational governance on trial: Change and challenges, 102nd yearbook of the National Society for the Study of Education (NSSE), Part I* (pp. 37–56). Chicago: The University of Chicago Press.

Swap, S. (1993). *Developing home-school partnerships.* New York: Teachers College Press.

Tillman, L. C. (Ed.). (2005, October). Pushing back resistance: African-American perspectives on school leadership [Special Issue], *Educational Administration Quarterly, 61*(4).

Turbov, M., & Piper, V. (2005). *HOPE VI as a catalyst for neighborhood change.* Washington, DC: The Brookings Institution.

U.S. Department of Education, Office of the Under Secretary. (2003). *When schools stay open late: The national evaluation of the 21st century learning centers.* Washington, DC: Author.

Valle, V. M.. & Torres, R. D. (2000). *Latino metropolis.* Minneapolis: University of Minnesota Press.

White, J., & Wehlage, G. (1995). Community collaboration: If it is such a good idea, why is Ii so hard to do? *Educational Evaluation and Policy Analysis, 17*(1), 23–38.

Wilson, W. J. (1987). *The truly disadvantaged.* Chicago: University of Chicago Press.

PART VI

Looking to the Future of Public Schooling

Douglas E. Mitchell

The two chapters of Part VI provide an overview summary of how education policy has been shaped in the past and the powers and processes that are likely to be shaping and reshaping public education in the next several decades. Dorothy Shipps offers a sweeping summary of the education policy reform story of the 20th century. She reviews not only the major changes that have accompanied the intense centralization of power and initiative in the hands of the federal government, but also the changing public mood and belief system that supports this remarkable shift in the locus of policy control. Identifying the key policy entrepreneurs who have managed the shift in control and the critical moments of change, Shipps tracks the relentless march from dispersed localism to concentrated centralism. Every major policy change of the last half century has contributed to this shift, she argues: desegregation, collective bargaining for teachers, the Cold War struggle to keep up with the Soviet Union, globalized economic and political competition, quality and accountability movements leading to the federal dominance firmly established in the No Child Left Behind rendition of the Elementary and Secondary Education Act. The apparently decentralizing tendencies of choice, vouchers and charter schools are seen here as in line with the centralizing tendency—this time the centralizing of a market based policy ideology that seeks to impose competitive pursuit of centralized goals. New players in the education policy arena, particularly large foundations and privately supported think tanks, have collaborated in the pursuit of strongly centralized control. Even as they promote the ideology of market competition, they endorse the movement toward a national consensus of standards-based accountability for results.

The final chapter provides a more prospective framework for summing up of the core ideas developed throughout this volume. In this chapter the editors have gathered together the primary themes developed and offer some concluding thoughts on what is likely to unfold in the next several decades. They note, for example, that apart from a broad agreement that the last half century has sharply centralized education policy control at the federal and state levels, education policy change has been far from single minded in content or direction. There is serious concern regarding whether America's schools have the structural strength and integrity needed to respond effectively to centralized policy control. There has also been a sharp retreat in the willingness of the judiciary to protect constitutional rights and equitable access to educational opportunities. Experiments in executive controlled mayoral takeover of big city schools have left it uncertain whether there is either enough executive power or a sufficiently supportive political regime to sustain reform initiatives. Globalization is a source of influential pressure, but apparently not strong enough to redirect historically rooted national cultures. While it is pretty clear that educational success will require coordinating schooling with health, safety, recreation, child welfare and other community services—it is not clear that any agency has the capacity to bring off this coordination. Finally, it does not seem likely that escalating pressure for standards and test-based accountability or raising the level of enthusiasm for using competitive market forces to redirect schools will provide either the ideas or the energy needed to build the better schools we have been promising over the last six decades. Indeed, it just might turn out that David Tyack's *The One Best System* will not see fundamental improvement despite harsh criticism and frantic efforts.

Reference

Tyack, D. (1974). *The one best system: A history of American urban education.* Cambridge, MA: Harvard University Press.

12

THE POLITICS OF EDUCATIONAL REFORM

Idea Champions and Policy Windows

Dorothy Shipps

Waves of reform have altered the politics of education over the past three decades, substituting one stratified governance system for another. New actors now dominate educational policy arenas. Parents, locally elected school boards, and community groups are less vital policy actors than they were in the decades before 1980. They have been replaced by coalitions of policy elites—notably political executives, corporate leaders, think tank advocates, and foundation officials—who are accustomed to wielding influence in state capitals and Washington D.C. Simultaneously, much educational decision making has been relocated from local districts to higher levels of government. Local authority to make policy has been reduced while state and federal government authority is enhanced and the United States now has a national education policy. This chapter explains those momentous changes as reactions to widespread social disruption following reform in mid-20th century and reformers' dissatisfaction with weak implementation and results of court-ordered civil rights gains. I argue that the combination of new actors and new policy arenas has altered how policy is made and, consequently, what is possible. This change in the policy process has political feedback: It reinforces the credibility of unorthodox ideas about school reform that would have been unthinkable only three decades ago, and provides unprecedented opportunities for nationally organized interest groups to influence educational policy.

Evidence that the public is being won over to this new governance structure can be found in public opinion polls. Trust in American governing institutions, Washington D.C. in particular, has been low since the 1970s. Americans nonetheless want more federal and state intervention in public education than ever before. The proportion of Americans who thought the federal or state government ought to have the "greatest influence in what is taught in the public schools" doubled from 1980 to 2008, from 9% to 20%. Those preferring state or federal influence to local control grew from 21% to 50% over the same period. Americans who put their primary faith in local control dropped from a strong majority (68%) to less than half of the public (46%). A combination of federal and state funding was preferred by nearly three quarters of the American public in 2008, up from little over 50% two decades ago. Support for federal financing as the single "best way" to fund public schools also grew from 24% in 1986 to 37% in 2008 (*Phi Delta Kappan*, 2010).[1]

A somewhat lagging indicator of public acceptance is the gradual turn in public perceptions of education's greatest problem. Between 1970 and 1985, when asked to identify the most serious problem facing education, most Americans consistently offered (unprompted) a "lack of discipline," arguably reflecting their concerns about an emboldened youth culture evident in many communities. A close second was some version of desegregation/busing/integration, reflecting local policy struggles in response to civil rights demands and court orders. In the transition years from 1986 to 1991, the central problem had switched to a more extreme variant of indiscipline: drug abuse. An average of nearly 31% of the public believed it to be the paramount educational concern, with lack of discipline still a strong second.

But in the decade of the 1990s, as educational policy making was being institutionalized in state and federal policy arenas, and when Americans met their first "education" presidents, governors and mayors, new problems surfaced. In four of the next nine years "lack of funding" topped public concerns about education.[2] After 2001, the new worry had solidified. Every year since then, in pluralities that grew to 32% by 2009, the public has identified insufficient funding as education's most pressing need (*Phi Delta Kappan*, 2010). More dollars than ever before are spent on education, so why this problem? One could argue that it reflects the shift from local worries over student behavior and grassroots politics to bigger, less tractable concerns about how schools can obtain the resources needed to meet ever-increasing expectations set by distant state and federal policy makers.

We have these new politics of education partly because the composition of educational policy communities has been altered by uncommon alliances among political executives, businessmen, ideologically committed intellectuals, and foundation officers, all of whom developed or rekindled an interest in education during the 1980s.[3] They shaped unorthodox policy instruments while sympathetic state and federal legislators authorized the new directions, bypassing the nation's 15,000 local school districts.

One result has been a turning away from cautious incrementalism in which broadly democratic, if fiercely contentious, processes of policy making once prevailed. Traditional improvement strategies like expanded access or increased resources are maligned as reform charades. Policy making since the 1980s has instead been characterized by abrupt, often misunderstood shifts in the policies being enacted. Policy makers now embrace policy instruments that rely on incentives, competition and bottom-line accountability, while standards, high stakes testing, vouchers, charters, and performance bonuses have become synonymous with reform. Although largely unknown before enactment, they did not remain mysterious for long. Even as these policies are being enacted, advocates vigorously promote their merits in the media. And within a decade or more, the public has typically come to accept the need for the changes already enacted and at least some of the assumptions behind them (*Phi Delta Kappan*, 2010). We may now be watching the institutionalization of a new policy making equilibrium based on federal norms of policy making behavior and stabilized by a new set of highly invested policy actors.

Shifting Policy Processes

In the early 20th century, the ultimate in educational policy making was rationalism, broadly believed to be the antidote to political corruption and graft. This governing approach relied on inductive reasoning that painstakingly detailed ideal processes, measured effort, set improvement goals, and rewarded conforming contributions. It owed much to the view of industrial efficiency practiced and promoted by Frederick Winslow Taylor. The Taylor system had a laudable goal: to "confer prosperity on worker and boss alike, abolishing the ancient class hatreds" (Kanigel, 1997, p. 1). It was to be accomplished by carefully observing and measuring workers on the job so that "scientific" inductive evidence of their contribution to the productive process could be recorded and used to determine their compensation: a system of incentives whereby workers might earn a share of profits according to their productivity. The Taylor system recast class-based animosity as a technical problem amenable to research evidence. Educational policy, it was widely believed, should follow suit (Shipps, 2006).

Notwithstanding its continuing application today, when applied to public schooling, Taylorism performed poorly. Rational, logical processes almost always fell short of implementation expectations. It wasn't that educators or school governors were especially deficient or venal, but rather that all human beings suffered the cognitive limitations of insufficient time and incomplete information. By the mid-1970s few policy makers still believed that the systematic application of rationalism would inevitably produce the best policies, and consequently, educational progress.

A decade or so earlier political scientists had developed these observations into a formal theory that represented the new era's educational policy processes. It was founded on the concept of *bounded rationality*, which asserted that all human beings have cognitive limitations (Cyert & March, 1963; Simon, 1957, p. 1). Unlike the rationalists, these political scientists argued that disbursed knowledge of many types—not merely technical expertise—was required to create satisfactory solutions to policy problems. Technical solutions could not resolve value conflicts; nor could they overcome the objections of those expected to implement changes (Lindblom & Woodhouse, 1993).

School board members, like other policy makers, were faced with insufficient time, incomplete information, and the incessant demands of competing organized interests. Consequently, with this *bounded rationality* they tended to *satisfice*: to aim toward policy outcomes that were publicly acceptable and attainable, but unless the community was small and homogeneous, not optimal from any single perspective (Simon, 1957). Incrementalism, or *muddling through,* as this new view of policy making became known, was a process marked by gradualism and marginal adjustments, avoiding big policy changes that could result in costly, perhaps irretrievable, errors. Incrementalism was also contextualized and path-dependent in the sense that it focused policy makers on ameliorating current ills rather than establishing future goals. This too, encouraged small gradual improvements, which could over time lead to big change (Lindblom, 1959, 1965).

The new perspective accompanied and explicated a series of systemic shocks in the 1960s. Locally organized groups of parents and their neighbors, youth and teachers, religious leaders and their followers supported or opposed policy initiatives aimed at expanding the opportunities and influence of previously disadvantaged groups. These were grassroots movements organized by civil rights, anti-war, counter-culture and union activists, among others (Gittell & Hevesi, 1969; Peterson, 1981). Although local school politics were often fiercely fought, the policy reactions were typically moderate. School board members, like other local policy makers, tended to value consensus and coalition building over abstract issue justification, the organization of political forces, key personnel changes, or shifts in the public mood (Liu, Lindquist, Vedlitz, & Vincent, 2010).

The solutions proposed by district superintendents and school boards during the 1950s, 1960s, and 1970s were small improvements over existing practice. It took intervention from the federal courts to spur more than ritual or procedural reaction. Thus, change played out in small steps. Its slow pace frustrated activists who reacted with louder demands and more radical threats, and counter-coalitions defending the status quo cast every minor deviation as a slippery slope to diminished school quality. Meanwhile, the public grew anxious about the fierce arguments, concerned that the political process was itself destabilizing. Although incrementalism explained school boards tendency to moderation, there were a few truly unprecedented policies set in this era, and political scientists found it harder to explain the exceptions.

One way to explain the difference between incremental and radical reform policies is to distinguish between local policy making on the one hand, and state or federal policy making on the other. These differences were captured as part of study based on the U.S. Congress in the late 1970s (Kingdon, 1995). Also accepting bounded rationality as a limiting constraint on human decision making, this perspective proposed that the norms of Congressional policy making—ambiguity run rampant, with problems and solutions only loosely tethered and policy actors drifting unpredictably through decision venues— are more likely to produce radical change than incremental improvements. That is, in Congress, problems become important to address irrespective of any consensus about how to resolve them and solutions depended on who is present in the agenda-setting process. In the words of one political scientist, federal policy making was *organized anarchy* (Kingdon, 1995, 1999).[4]

This new model of agenda setting envisioned three streams of policy influence. Analysis was redirected away from the decisions themselves and onto the processes by which decisions secured the attention of policy makers. A problem stream includes all the possible problems that might concern legislators, and offers opportunities for public participation in the policy process. A policy stream produced politically palatable and technically feasible solutions, and is dominated by policy elites (Robinson & Eller, 2010). A politics stream consisted of the national mood, regular cycles of elections and budgeting, and the alignment and realignment of pressure groups. "These streams of problems, policies, and politics flow independent of one another. The proposals are generated whether or not they are solving a given problem, the problems are recognized whether or not there is a solution, and political events have a dynamics of their own" (Kingdon, 2001, p. 2).

Policy making involves combining a particular issue, like education, with a policy instrument, a generic means to meet goals. Incentive payments, taxes, deregulation, privatization and exhortation are all examples of policy instruments (Howlett & Ramlesh, 1995). At the federal level, issues and policy instruments float around Congress and the courts combining, recombining and mutating. Some solutions in this *policy primeval soup* drown; "others survive and prosper" (Kingdon, 2001, p. 3), depending on the effectiveness of *policy entrepreneurs*—politicians, bureaucrats, expert advisers, or advocacy group leaders—who reframe problems to fit their favored solutions, adapt them to the authority limits of different governmental bodies, and above all, are persistent promoters (Kingdon, 1995).

Politics provides most of the policy-making opportunities. Some can be anticipated, but there are also unpredictable events in the politics stream that offer opportunities for big policy changes if exploited quickly. Their emergence creates brief windows of opportunity that can be exploited or squandered by activist policy entrepreneurs, who have both the will—their advocacy for particular solutions—and the energy to exploit a window of opportunity before it closes.

When policy making relocates from local school districts to the federal government, the policy processes change largely because the actors are different. Elites considered unaccountable interlopers in local policy making are drawn to the more distant policy venues where they have greater influence, and where legislators rely on them to provide solutions to unfamiliar problems. Especially during long periods of exceptionally high political instability, the same bounded rationality that encourages incrementalism in school districts gives these more distant policy makers reason to take risks. Thus, a shift in policy-making venue from a local school board to Congress permits serious consideration of policy solutions that board members think beyond the pale.

In the 1970s, political analysts were witnessing just such a shift in educational policy-making venues. Instability created by years of civil disruption combined with activists' disillusion and their opponents' outrage. A national mood of uncertainty emerged and sympathy for local activism waned. By the 1980s, this had emboldened educational policy entrepreneurs, including governors and business executives, who had abstained from policy debates during the previous two decades, or as was the case for soon-to-be important foundations and think-tanks, simply did not exist before the 1980s.[5] Many promoted repurposed educational solutions that had been floating around for years, and did so first in state houses and then the Congress.

These new policy actors eventually divided into two loose factions: One promoting incentives and systemic accountability (Smith & O'Day, 1991), the other advocating market competition and discipline (Chubb & Moe, 1990). Psychometricians, curriculum specialists, and survey researchers reduced the technical constraints accountability and market models so that policy makers could consider them both feasible and politically palatable.

The new policies were justified in ways that elevated the credentials of the new policy actors.

Stories of systemic decline in the quality of public education (Stone, 1998) and inadequate global competitiveness (National Commission on Excellence in Education, 1983) argued that serious reform required passing power to national elites whose global perspective would make education a national priority. These elites have shifted public opinion over the last two decades, and educational policies were reoriented. Once demanding local acceptance by the parents and educators who would carry them out, educational policy now only requires nominal acceptance by a growing plurality of the nation's citizens, whether parents or not.

The remainder of this chapter describes some of the key events that led to this shift in policy making processes, from local incrementalism to the norms of federal policy. After describing how these changes occurred, I suggest we are on the verge of a new equilibrium based on the norms of national policy making behavior in which elite insiders dominate policy-making processes, shifts in policy occur abruptly, and policies are sold to the public.

Educational Policy Making in Mid-20th Century

Mid-century public schools were deeply affected by public perceptions. In many tens of thousands of small, middle-class, and homogeneous suburban school districts this meant quiet politics, predictable school board elections, and few controversies. But in as many others, the school board's policy preoccupations came from socio-economically and racially diverse factions of parents, neighbors, teachers, and youngsters, some of whom formed movements that realigned interest group politics. Civil rights activists and educators willing to risk censure to obtain collective bargaining rights were chief among them.

Civil Right Struggles in the Schools

The best-documented and most important mid-century education movement sought Black access to "White" public schools, not only those legally segregated in the 17 Southern and Border states, but also the de-facto segregated districts of the North and Midwest (Orfield & Lee, 2006).[6] In many communities, high school and college students, local religious and community groups in organized coalitions challenged school boards to provide equal access. Their demands were at first brushed aside by school boards unwilling to make any dramatic changes. Soon enough civil rights activists were battling counter-veiling coalitions organized to limit race-based access, sometimes in the name of economy, most often to safeguard urban or suburban real estate values and parents' social investments (Hochschild, 1984; Hochschild & Scovronick, 2004; Orfield & Eaton, 1996). Such conflicts paralyzed many school boards and the deadlock further frustrated activists.

Appeals to higher levels of governing authority soon followed, and seemed at first to portend radical change. Overturning six decades of legal precedent by ruling that segregated schooling could never be equal, the Supreme Court ruling in *Brown v. Board of Education* (1954) nevertheless had a different policy effect: It reinforced rather than challenged local authority. Dozens of subsequent court decisions questioned the wisdom of local districts' policy choices even as they reinforced their authority to make them. In so doing, the courts enabled the substantial desegregation of Southern and Border states that had racially segregated schools as a matter of policy, and simultaneously absolved the rest of the nation's de facto segregated school boards from any specific obligation. Although routinely called upon by activists, it is especially telling that state legislatures took almost no policy initiative in local desegregation arguments (Hochschild & Scovronick, 2004).

Notwithstanding the nightly news, local school boards consistently responded with caution. Torn between constituencies and more subject to contentious electioneering than ever before, school boards adopted incremental improvements over existing practice by carving out small areas of agreement between the warring sides to the extent that they could legally do so. In the states where Black and White children had been required to attend separate schools, school board members were ordered to reverse those policies or risk federal sanctions, including federal troops. The result was desegregation by the same policy means—within-district busing—that had been previously used to segregate students. For students in four Southern states this actually meant *less* busing or a shorter commute, since the nearest school had often been set aside for students of the other race (Hochschild & Scovronick, 2004, pp. 36–37). Then, the proportion of Southern Black students in majority White schools was 2%; it burgeoned to 33% in 1970. By 1991, almost 40% of Southern Black students attended schools where at least half of the students were White. After reaching that apex, however, re-segregation ensued when the threat of federal sanction disappeared. In 2003–04 the proportion had fallen back to 29%, while 44% of Southern Black students attended schools with 90%–100% minority enrollments (Orfield & Lee, 2006, pp. 9–14).

The same reinforcement of district authority in the Midwest and Northeast reified, rather than altered, de facto segregation. These regions had created relatively small homogeneous school districts aligned to segregated neighborhood borders, each governed independently. Consequently, these states never experienced the desegregation levels of the South, but saw an intensification of segregation. An average of nearly 4% more Black students attended majority minority schools in 2003 than was the case in 1991 when about 70% did so. Nationwide, in 2003, the typical Black student (as well as the typical Latino student) attended a school where more than half of the students were of their own race (Orfield & Lee, 2006, pp. 9–14). The most likely hope for widespread integration in these regions was mandatory busing across district lines, a policy that lay outside the interests of all but the most homogeneously liberal school boards and was largely prohibited by the Supreme Court in 1974 (*Milliken v. Bradley*, 1974). Court decisions that were shortly reversed complicated the policy landscape, creating uncertainty among local (and state) education actors and diminishing the likelihood that districts would feel the need to comply (McDermott & Jensen, 2005, p. 52).

If desegregation was not to involve wholesale change, a process of gradual implementation was begun. Just after the 1964 Civil Rights Act was enacted, its implementing successor the 1965 Elementary and Secondary Education Act (ESEA) was passed in Congress.[7] ESEA provided states with incentive funding if they would target disadvantaged children. For the most part, the money was used for pull-out programs and not viewed as a lever for radical policy change, even as it officially recognized the disproportionate needs of disadvantaged children, a large plurality of whom where Black and Hispanic (McDonnell, 2005, p. 24).

In districts where busing was fiercely resisted, other incremental policies were adopted to placate activist's demands. Identifying a few schools as *magnets*, a status that permitted some curricular freedom and extra resources, allowed cautious, slow moving districts to begin desegregation by attracting White student volunteers to a handful of minority-neighborhood schools (Fraga, Rodriguez, & Erlichson, 2005; Goldring & Smrekar, 2000). Unlike busing, magnet schools received federal funding for many decades, although they enrolled less than 1% of students nationally by 2005. In its support of magnets, the federal government also concurred that "support of the same traditional decision makers is most critical to the achievement of the court's goals" (Fraga et al., 2005, p. 124). Over the long run, magnets proved no more successful than busing: Their level of integration declined between 1983 when 60% were integrated, to 2003 when 43% were experiencing increasing segregation (Frankenberg & Siegel-Hawley, 2008, pp. 12, 15). This strategy had largely dropped its desegregation goals by the 1990s.

The Struggle for Collective Bargaining

During the same era, another momentous movement for teachers' rights was reaching its apex. Northern urban teachers had been organized into unions— some even affiliated with the AFL—since the early 20th century, but none had achieved stable salaries and benefits through those collaborations (Murphy, 1990). Just as the civil rights movement was at its most active, several big city union leaders, frustrated by salaries and benefits that were handed out and rescinded at will by board members, determined the time was ripe to seek collective bargaining rights. Although it was not inevitable, this choice put teachers at odds with civil rights activists. Feeling in the crosshairs of another value conflict, board members often played one set of demands against the other; either resisting teachers' demands for unionization and collective bargaining while reluctantly changing bus routes to desegregate schools as happened in the South, or giving teachers collective bargaining rights to serve as a bulwark against challenges from Black activists.

Collective bargaining took its first small step in New York City under the activist leadership of Albert Shanker, the labor organizer who became the United Federation of Teachers (UFT) president in 1964 and simultaneously the American Federation of Teachers (AFT) president by 1974. Shanker's success paved the way for a rapid spread of political action by teachers seeking bargaining rights elsewhere. By 1967 there were 105 teachers' strikes in districts across the nation. One year later, the National Education Association (NEA) dropped their opposition to collective bargaining, and the battleground became conflict between union organizations over the right to represent teachers in district negotiations. The NEA won more contests than did the AFT, which was more attractive to big city teachers including those in Detroit, Philadelphia, Chicago, Boston, Kansas City, Cleveland, Washington D.C., Newark, and Toledo, among others (Kahlenberg, 2007; Murphy, 1990).

New York City's example demonstrates that collective bargaining was won and expanded incrementally despite often-rancorous clashes. During the mid-20th century, about one third of all workers were union members and their right to organize was broadly supported by the Democratic Party. By 1962, President John F. Kennedy had even signed an Executive Order allowing federal employees to join unions and bargain collectively. The topic had been hotly debated within dozens of teacher associations in New York City, but after Shanker's small UFT held a one-day strike in 1961 that would involve no more than 10% of the city's teachers, Democratic Mayor Robert F. Wagner appointed a committee of labor leaders to advise him (and the appointed board) on a response. Predictably, they recommended collective bargaining.

The decision to embrace collective bargaining was, if anything, over-determined. Teachers throughout the city had voted four-to-one to adopt bargaining in December 1961, and subsequently voted the UFT their sole agent.[8] Although strikes were technically illegal, striking teachers received no sanctions. Moreover, one third of workers, and likely parents, were themselves union members. In June 1962, after a second one-day strike, the school board signed a collective bargaining agreement. While collective bargaining constrained the board's managerial prerogatives, it also turned the majority of the district's employees into negotiating partners as invested in local school board governance as were board members themselves.

New York City also set the pattern for securing teachers' influence at the expense of Black civil rights demands. Notwithstanding UFT support for the 1963 march on Washington D.C., Shanker's personal commitment to voting rights in the South, and his claim that "teachers, like blacks had been treated in a second class way," UFT proposals for desegregating New York City schools were cautious, little different from the school board's (Kahlenberg, 2007, p. 43). They relied on "the first magnet schools," and opportunistic distinctions like declining to endorse a massive 1964 student-led integration boycott while simultaneously agreeing to support individual teachers who refused to cross the civil rights picket line (Kahlenberg, p. 57). When Black parents protested the appointment of a White principal to Harlem's Intermediate School 201 that White students refused to attend, Shanker backed the central school board, even though he recognized that the conflict between the two powerful movements could "destroy the civil rights movement" (p. 71).

No longer willing to seek integration with reluctant Whites, many of New York City's Black activists demanded direct control of their neighborhood schools. Political decentralization was a more direct threat to school board governance than collective bargaining. Even so, White corporate supporters and the liberal Republican Mayor John Lindsey, both induced by the Ford Foundation, and all fearful of a violent Black reaction, concurred with activist's demands (Levin, 1970). Under great pressure, the school board agreed to take the small step of establishing three demonstration community control districts. But Brooklyn's Ocean Hill-Brownsville district declined to establish UFT's magnet schools, and within one year, teachers were again on strike over the school board's failure to support them over the activists in the magnet controversy, and a separate UFT demand that teachers be permitted to expel disruptive students from their classes.

Black activists saw both policies as an attack on community control. The school board cautiously balanced the two interests: negotiating a teacher's settlement for higher salaries and benefits while retaining the Ocean Hill-Brownsville community district's discretion. Still dissatisfied, the UFT organized its longest and most polarizing strike: 36 days at the beginning of the school year in 1968. Shanker's insistence that social class, not race, was at the heart of educational inequity fractured liberals, conservatives, the civil rights movement and the city's media. UFT teachers and Black activists hurled racial epithets (the large majority of NYC teachers were Jewish) and fists at one another. Yet the school board remained calm, if ineffectual, consistently seeking a cautious middle ground in the face of the fierce public debate.

In a harbinger of an era yet to come, New York City's race and class conflicts were adjudicated in the state capital, where the UFT aligned with conservative legislators and Republican Governor Nelson Rockefeller to defeat a bill that would have created community control districts across the city's five boroughs. Busloads of minority parents proved no match for hundreds of teachers who had proven their willingness to shut down the schools. The legislative resolution was a modification of the existing school board system, in which a central board kept most power, notably the authority to hire teachers, while 30 elected sub-district community boards were created to oversee about 20,000 students each. One hope was that the community boards would tamp down local conflicts before they threatened social peace. But the same boards were granted the authority to hire patronage employees (e.g., custodians), leading to their inevitable denunciation for corruption. Ten years later, the schools were declared "no better and no worse" under this form of decentralization (Kenneth Clark quoted in Kahlenberg, 2007, p. 121). Both the lack of improvement and corruption were used in 1996 to curtail community board powers, and again in 2001 to eliminate them altogether.

Unionists opposed civil rights activists for both strategic and partisan reasons. Shanker allied with anti-unionist Republicans because making deals with powerful executives was the easiest way to acquire basic, bread-and-butter gains for teachers. It also positioned teachers unions a counterweight to the civil rights movement, suggesting that teachers, unlike Black activists, sought a seat at the table but would not challenge the legitimacy of local district governance.

Even so, like the gains of the civil rights, union organizing had limits. Unions made most headway in the Northeast and Midwest where de facto segregation endured, but were less successful in the South (and parts of the West), where segregation had been de jure, and integration had seen initial gains under federal mandates and school board governance.

Small changes that could be incrementally expanded year-after-year, or abandoned just as easily, were precisely the solutions school boards adopted in these tumultuous times. Boards were, after all, deliberative bodies mandated to hold open meetings and expected to reflect the values, and the value conflicts, of the local community. School board members were themselves diverse: One might represent a city's unionized workers, another a particularly impoverished Black ghetto, while still others represented business or religious organizations or ethnic neighborhoods. Their very diversity combined with the competing pressures of civil rights and teachers' rights activists (among others) to narrow the space of consensual agreement. No one could say with majoritarian certainty what the most important problem was, or how it should be addressed. Little wonder then that board members stuck to small deviations from existing practice: new bus routes, a few magnet schools, more formalized means of setting salaries. As each of these small policy changes became routine services its inspirational motivation was lost. At the same time, it was just such incremental policy choices in districts large and small throughout the nation that helped spur a new politics of education.

For a new brand of reformers who came of age since 1980, the continuing influence of these 'traditional' interests is a central part of their public education critique. Many believe the continuing influence of unions and civil rights groups amounts to a form of policy capture. Even before the various local New York State unions united in 1972—an accomplishment Shanker saw only as a prelude to national unity and even greater power for teachers—one conservative commentator described the UFT as "the most powerful lobbying group ... able to essentially write entire sections of the state's education law" (Sol Stern quoted in Kahlenberg, 2007, p. 122). Civil rights organizations have been similarly identified with the status quo in school district policy making (Rich, 1996). Today, civil rights organizations and teachers unions, no less than school boards, superintendents, and bureaucrats are central to what contemporary reformers have named the *education blob*: "the more than 200 groups, associations, federations, alliances, departments, offices, administrations, councils, boards, commissions, panels, organizations, herds, flocks and coveys, that make up the education industrial complex" (Allen, 2009).

The Sputnik Challenge

To be sure, these years witnessed a few policy shifts led by elites without ties to local school boards. The most famous was enabled by a swing in the national mood from post-war satisfaction to anti-communist paranoia, when the Soviet Union launched the first *Sputnik* satellite in 1957. The policy response—the declaration of a technology gap that required more rigorous scientific and mathematics curricula—was more characteristic of later policy initiatives than typical of its own era. Policy entrepreneurs leading scientific organizations and in higher education took advantage of the mood shift to declare the U.S. way of life "doomed" (Schmeck, 1957). Some even argued for a special set of schools for the top 5% of students capable of benefiting from high quality technological education, ironically echoing the Soviet model (Ryan, 1958).

Soon thereafter, Congress passed the National Defense Education Act. It reimbursed districts for purchasing science and foreign language lab equipment, teacher training in math, science, and foreign languages, career counseling, and adoption of new science and math curriculum mostly developed through the National Science Foundation.[9] Scientists responded to the incentive program by creating technically sophisticated, inquiry-based and inductive curricula. The physics curriculum proved a poor fit for the schools of the day and by 1980 was judged to be present in no more than 4% of the nation's high schools (Hechinger, 1980). Similarly, the "new math" in several incarnations was also judged highly controversial among parents—as well as some mathematicians—and a pedagogical failure, while the "new biology" ran into objections by parents who thought it contradicted their religious views, and the whole "alphabet soup" of new curricula faded away (Kline, 1973; Lazerson, McLaughlin, & McPherson, 1984).

Unlike other movements of the era, these curricular changes had no public advocates, nor did the public understand these curricular changes. The higher education faculty and scientists who participated were not closely aligned with K–12 educators, nor did they have a public to whom they felt themselves accountable. There was no concerted effort made to convince parents of their value. In these ways the *Sputnik*-inspired curricular reforms were different from other attempts at educational policy change in the era. Their impact would become apparent only a decade or two later (Apple, 1983; Lazerson et al., 1984).

By the 1980s, when the political conditions of educational policy making were being refashioned, policy entrepreneurs could point to the *Sputnik* experiments as a valuable precedent, lacking only more attention to salesmanship. This is a process that policy entrepreneurs know as *softening up the public*. Contemporary entrepreneurs also learned that Congress was more amenable to their wholesale changes than were the more conservative and politically accountable local school boards. Independence from local politics and less accountability to parents and local communities made state legislatures and the Congress better venue choices for legislation that sought fundamental change. In hindsight, it would prove possible to say that once the federal Rubicon was crossed in the early 1980s, incremental policy making based on a narrowly defined consensus among widely competing interests in 16,000 local districts proved no match for the insider politics of Washington DC and the 50 state capitals.

Entrepreneurial Policy Making Since the 1980s.

The current era of educational policy making began with a political re-orientation. Small groups of entrepreneurial leaders took advantage of the political uncertainty created by contradictory court rulings on civil rights, incentive legislation like ESEA, and the new power of teachers unions. Recognizing that civil rights activists and union leaders had achieved more success by circumventing the highly contentious politics of local school boards, new policy entrepreneurs sought their influence almost exclusively in state and federal venues.[10]

This meant operating in political arenas characterized by opaque, often ambiguous, negotiations between elected officials and lobbyists, during a time when state departments of education lacked the capacity to define and implement reforms and the new federal Department of Education was politically weak and vulnerable. Entrepreneurial presidents and governors, corporate executives, foundation executives and think-tank colleagues proposed that federal standards and market-oriented policy instruments be adapted to educational settings. Longstanding race and class disparities would be reframed to fit their proposed solutions. But the public was "so reluctant to embrace the economic and educational reforms recommended by leadership" that the entrepreneurs simultaneously embarked upon a campaign to shift public opinion (Immerwahr, Johnson, & Kernan-Schoss, 1991, p. 5). Their policies manifest today as federal and state laws providing incentives for meeting various forms of standards and accountability one the one hand, privatization and choice on the other.

State and Federal Standard Setting

The re-orientation began during the Republican landslide election of 1980. Presidential candidate Ronald Reagan had vigorously campaigned to shrink government in favor of market-based policy approaches. In office he deregulated industry, devolved federal responsibilities to state governments, broke unions, and introduced private sector competition. In addition, he argued that the recession then gripping the nation could only be overcome if the wealthy kept their money for investments expected to eventually "trickle down" the socio-economic ladder. This meant across-the-board regressive tax cuts, which reduced the federal share of education spending by 30% over his two terms (Kahlenberg, 2007, p. 238; McDonnell, 2005). Reagan repackaged the remaining funds in the form of "block grants," which let states decide how to spend federal dollars and removed much of ESEA's equity incentive. Deferring to states obviated the need for a strong federal Department of Education, which Republicans proposed to abolish. When pressured to encourage reformers, Reagan advocated market-based ideas like merit pay, parental choice, tuition-tax credits, and vouchers, a set of non-incremental policy solutions that did not rely on federal resources. The ideologically committed president surprised many when, in 1983, he nonetheless lent his support to a manifesto commissioned by his Education Department Secretary, Terrell Bell (Boyd, 1988; Manna, 2006).

The *A Nation at Risk* report (National Commission on Excellence in Education, 1983) cast education as a federal responsibility. It was written by, according to one participant, a politically "problematic" collection of individuals who represented virtually no membership groups and lacked any federal representative (Holton, 1984, p. 3). Their unusualness proved an asset for activist governors; the report reflected reform trends already begun in several Southern states when the commission began meeting in 1981. Governors, long accustomed to bargaining with corporate leaders for jobs by providing tax and infrastructure incentives, had listened to business leaders' arguments about education being another keystone in economic development and inter-state competition. Among them the Southern Regional Education Board governors sponsored legislation to make the changes business executives had sought, including mandatory minimum high school competency tests and improving the capacity of state departments of education to intervene in struggling school districts.[11]

For example, Florida Governor Bob Graham had appointed a commission to assess the quality of secondary education in 1980. It was chaired by the "maverick" head of the Kettering Foundation, Frank Brown, who believed, along with the state's corporate leaders, that Florida's public schools slowed economic development. He blamed local school boards, "which have responsibility for setting graduation requirements, [but] have not kept the school system abreast of the needs of the State, the nation or the students," and under-qualified teachers (Gould, Scott, Starobin, & Verdier, 1984, p. 4). The Brown Commission report called for state legislation to abrogate local school board authority to set graduation standards and negotiate teacher wages. The recommended legislation mandated statewide high school course requirements—three to four years of classes in each of four basic subjects—more time in school, merit pay for teachers, and an end to school-based decisions on student promotion, dubbed "social promotion" (Gould et al., 1984, pp. 3–5). The heads of Florida's 100 largest corporations, The Council of 100, promoted the new standards plan, which passed in 1983 with unprecedented support from the Associated Industries of Florida, the state's most powerful business lobby. Two months after the first Florida bill was introduced, *A Nation* echoed virtually all the Brown Commission's recommendations.

A Nation at Risk (National Commission on Excellence in Education,1983) adopted the Southern states' economic arguments as a national concern: The country's public schools must have higher standards before the nation can compete for jobs in the global economy. The manifesto forcefully reframed the problems of public education to fit this solution, offering a compelling crisis-oriented counter-narrative to the existing race and class-conflict stories that had underpinned education policy making for two decades.

The core problem became a loss of will: "Shoddiness ... is to often reflected in our schools and colleges ... A trend that stems more from weakness of purpose, confusion of vision, underuse of talent, and lack of leadership," than a lack of knowledge or institutional capacity. Its solution harkened back to the Sputnik focus on "excellence" or "high expectations and goals for all learners." It sought no less than "the goal of creating a Learning Society," in which individual students and educators are responsible for striving beyond current performance and every school has the obligation to hold them accountable for the results. Among the means mentioned to recover education's moral purpose, the report pointed to a "tradition ... that the Federal Government should supplement State, local, and other resources to foster key national educational goals," and "the federal government has *the primary responsibility* to identify the nation interest in education" (National Commission on Excellence in Education, 1983, italics in original).

Rapid shifts in state education policy followed. Requirements for high school graduation tests, increased numbers of required courses, certification exams for teachers, and/or longer school days were adopted in all but a handful of states within two years (McDonnell, 2005). The policy action was in state capitals, but the federal government kept track of the changes by rating the states one against another in a wall chart, to "validate state-by-state comparisons as means of holding state and local school systems accountable for education" (Ginsberg, Jay, & White Plisko, 1988, p. 1). Heretofore used for sorting students, achievement tests would soon replace the wall chart for the purpose of rating and ranking states. Within a dozen years, these tests became the new indicator of educational performance, a common ruler against which districts, schools and students were judged.

A Nation (1983) had not only validated the ideas state governors and powerful state business lobbies, but also lifted the profile of national education policy (McDonnell, 2005). Most educators, still wedded to local policy making, dismissed it as uninformed.[12] But Shanker correctly foresaw that education's key policy actors had changed, the arenas of action had shifted, and the rationale for reform would abandon the race and class equity concerns of the past. More than anything, he wanted a seat at the new policy table (Kahlenberg, 2007, pp. 276–280).

Since then the table has been set by U.S. presidents, with governors and business executives as regular guests. George H. W. Bush, styled himself the "education president" to enhance his domestic policy credentials. His Education Secretary, the former Tennessee Governor Lamar Alexander, convened a governor's education summit that developed a list of national education goals, and subsequently a National Education Goals Panel to "oversee the development and implementation of a national education progress reporting system" (Manna, 2006, p. 81). The federal Department of Education also funded the first development of voluntary national content standards by professional associations, and proposed America 2000, in which progress towards standards would be voluntarily measured in three grades (4th, 8th, 12th). The unprecedented federalization sparked a "firestorm" of public controversy. National standards would then be marketed to a skeptical public and educational establishment for nearly two decades because "the politicians whose leadership and endorsement were needed ... senators, Congressmen and governors ... determined that it was [still] political suicide" (Ravitch, 2010, p. 18).

When William J. Clinton, former governor of Arkansas, became president in 1992, he leaned so heavily on his National Governor's Association advisors that it angered Congressmen and their staff on both sides of the isle (DeBray, 2004, p. 69). Although he extended America 2000 to Goals 2000, adding incentive grants to states, he also convinced Congress to omit its "opportunity to learn" standards, which governors feared might embolden constituents to hold state governments responsible for poor school performance and perhaps demand more state resources (Manna, 2006, p. 110).

ESEA was subsequently reshaped in the image of Goals 2000. For the first time, federal incentive funding was made conditional upon states developing complex sets of curriculum and student performance standards. A federal timetable routinized and tracked the states' detailed plans for standard development and test alignment, but few met the deadlines, only 17 had done so by 2001, and another four were judged "out of compliance" (McDonnell, 2005, p. 31).

In theory, disadvantaged students were held to the same standards as all others, in hopes that common standards would close achievement gaps since civil rights strategies like busing were no longer thought publicly palatable or technically feasible (O'Day & Smith, 1993; Smith & O'Day, 1991). "Raising and enforcing academic standards in failing schools" was by then cited by both Blacks (77%) and Whites (82%) as a preferred approach to improving education (Farkas & Johnson, 1998, pp. 26–27, 34).[13] Just three days after his inauguration, Republican President George W. Bush confirmed this new federal education agenda. Adopting standards and tough-love accountability would be sufficient, the new president argued, to overcome "the soft bigotry of low expectations" (McDermott & Jensen, 2005). Equity, it was by now comprehensible to say, could only be fostered by accountability.

Notwithstanding party differences, G. H. W. Bush, Alexander, Clinton, and G. W. Bush agreed on education policy more than they disagreed. Like the others, G. W. Bush had been the governor of a Southern state active in education reform and had called upon business leaders and fellow governors for advice, to the near exclusion of the educational establishment (DeBray, 2004). Governors may have been active, but nearly two decades of entrepreneurialism in which dozens of business-led task forces initiated rewrites of state and federal education laws had not satisfied corporate leaders (Allan, 1989; Berman & Clugston, 1988; Borman, Costnell, & Gallagher, 1993; Business Roundtable Public Policy Committee, 1990; Fosler, 1990; Fowler, 1990). By the close of the 20th century, 80% of business executives told pollsters the nation's schools remained "seriously" off track, and 95% said more funding would be wasted without further reorganization (Farkas, 1992, pp. 1, 6, 10, 14). Having been subjected to an informational campaign, the public was also by then softened up to the need for test-based accountability, national standards, and the importance of education to the economy, as well as to the benefits of market-based alternatives.[14]

The No Child Left Behind Act of 2002 distilled these ideas into several basic tenets, the first three being logical extensions of *A Nation at Risk*, and adapted as federal law in America 2000 and Goals 2000. They were standards-based mandated annual testing of all students in grades three-to-eight and high school (reflecting Texas law), teacher competency standards, and greater flexibility for innovation and assistance for low-performing schools (reflecting Reagan's block grants and Clinton's small "Ed-flex" waiver policy passed in 1999). Now in near-unanimous agreement that performance gaps could be narrowed by consequential accountability, but nevertheless mistrusting of state-by-state implementation, Congress required that distinct subgroups of students—disadvantaged, minorities, Limited English Speaking—make Annual Yearly Progress (AYP) or the school was to face sanctions. Hoping to check states inclined to set low AYP goals, all were required to participate in the National Assessment of Educational Progress (NAEP), a heretofore voluntary national sample of student performance tests instituted decades earlier. Business executives were delighted, publishing another of a series of "tool kits" for corporate leaders that purported to help them take advantage of NCLB opportunities (The National Business Roundtable, 2002).

Although the two-decades long unfolding of national educational policy making and entrepreneurial advocacy by political executives and business leaders has been institutionalized, that does not mean the problems of public education are closer to resolution that when policy making was local and incremental. By the standards used today to evaluate hundreds of well-funded reform ideas, nothing has the consistent success of desegregation and the first wave of Great Society legislation, weakly implemented though they were. The only sustained period of narrowing the White-Black performance gap was between 1971 and 1980 (Barton & Coley, 2010). One reason is likely that the standards based system envisioned in the early 1980s and fully adopted by Congress under NCLB left out crucial "opportunity to learn" standards, the law's moral imperative. In theory, these standards would have ensured that the schools, teachers and the system as a whole had the capacity to deliver high-quality instruction to all children (National Council on Educational Standards and Testing, 1992). In no small part, this resulted from state governors' outsized influence.

Market-Making in Education

Governors and corporate executives were not the only actors whose voices roared after the shift from local to federal policy arenas. Foundations and think tanks, many quite new, became vociferous advocates for market-based initiatives in the entrepreneurial era. They too, used political uncertainty to press for new policy instruments. Like Reagan, their policy ideas relied on deregulation, market competition and consumer choice. For some, this was an attempt to harness entrepreneurial creativity for social improvements. For a better-resourced, more tenacious group, it was an opportunity to prove that markets were better at delivering social services than government bureaucracies.

President Reagan was one of the earliest ideologically committed advocates of parental choice, a stance his second Secretary of Education, William Bennett, embraced wholeheartedly. In addition to advocating the still-unpopular and poorly understood vouchers and merit-pay ideas, he revived the policy of tuition tax credits to parents who send their children to private schools, an idea unsuccessfully championed in Congress by Senator Daniel Patrick Moynihan a few years earlier. Like tax cuts, tax credits favored those whose income was high enough to pay taxes, as opposed to the working poor whose incomes fell below any potential benefit. Consequently they did little for the nation's worst schools.

Reagan's opinion of vouchers was "directly influenced by Milton Friedman's ideas," which were premised on the assumption that private competition could improve the quality of public schools (Kahlenberg, 2007; Ravitch, 2010, p. 117). The libertarian economist had written a famous essay in 1955, arguing that government should provide compensation to parents for the expense of enrolling their children in any school they chose, predicting that this would create a vibrant and diverse market of schooling options. Nearly three decades later, he became one of Reagan's White House advisors, but the action since then has again been in the states. Free-market policy entrepreneurs promoted vouchers where binding ballot initiatives were permitted and sympathetic foundations were active. In the view of critics, they took advantage of "golden opportunities" to replace destroyed or failed public schools with the "radical social engineering" of private corporate schooling (Kenneth Saltman quoted in Gabbard & Macrine, 2008). Voucher experiments targeted to disadvantaged have been tried in several cities and one state since: Milwaukee (1990), Washington D.C. (1993–2003, 2003-2010), Cleveland (1995), New York City (1997), Florida (1999), and New Orleans (2008).[15] The experiments have produced wildly disparate claims of increased student performance and no benefit (see Harris and Witte, this volume). For the most part, neither the contentious evidence nor the ongoing entrepreneurialism has convinced the public, although time and advocacy may soften the remaining opposition (Farkas, Johnson, & Foleno, 1999).[16]

Instead, for Reagan and most advocates since, educational choice and privatization has come to mean charter schools. In theory, a charter school's contract permits the regulatory freedom of a contractual relationship in exchange for attaining lofty student performance goals by using innovative means. Charter schools may be new creations or, in some states, public schools may secede from the school district to operate under a charter contract. Charters may be self-managed or managed by for-profit or nonprofit organizations, linked in a network or through a company and can be formed by anyone able to persuade the authorizing government agency. In practice, relatively few charter schools have been closed for failing to meet performance standards (Bulkley,

2001). Their appeal is not based on their ability to improve student performance, which remains in doubt. Nor on their value as an "interesting but incremental and uncontroversial reform in service delivery" as some had hoped, but rather because charter schools "occupy a pivotal position in an ideologically polarized strategic debate," about whether markets or governments are best suited to delivering socially desirable public services (Henig, 2008, p. 34; Zhang & Yang, 2008). Or as one market-oriented advocate put it "Should government buy or make education?" (Lieberman, 1989). This polarized debate is especially ripe for policy entrepreneurship, which uses evidence as ammunition, seeks small opportunities to instantiate change, and relentlessly pursues a long-term policy goal.

In 1988 a teacher named Ray Budde came up with the charter idea. It was initially promoted by Al Shanker to encourage teachers' development of "innovative" schools, akin to magnet schools. Five years later, Shanker watched Education Alternatives Inc. (later reorganized as TesseracT Group Inc.) exploit the idea to form an "education industry" of privately run contract schools in Baltimore. He correctly foresaw business-run charters would render unionization more difficult to achieve (Bracey, 2002; Kahlenberg, 2007; Ravitch, 2010, p. 123).[17] Meanwhile, partly because of Shanker's early endorsement, the Democratic Party's centrist faction, the Democratic Leadership Council (DLC), embraced charter schools in 1993. The DLC's most famous member, President Clinton, immediately initiated a federal charter intended to demonstrate re-invented, customer-friendly government, and championed an increase in funding to $137 million in 2000, when there were 1,700 such schools nationwide (Bracey, 2002, p. 65).

Both presidents G. W. Bush and Barack Obama have since promoted charter schools. Bush wanted NCLB to close persistently low- performing schools and give their students vouchers; he got "reconstituted" schools as charters. Charter legislation now exists in 40 states and their number rapidly expanded to 5000 by 2009 (Center for Education Reform, 2009). Obama too seeks more charters. His DOE is requiring that states applying for federal grants commit to radical increases both to "encourage educational entrepreneurship" and "increase the supply of high-quality educational options" (U.S. Department of Education, 2010, p. 37).

Like the expansion of standards and accountability, charter growth has relied on a loose alliance among a small group of national interests, in this case free-market oriented think tanks and foundations. The Heritage Foundation, The Cato Institute, The Manhattan Institute, The Hoover Institution, and The American Enterprise Institute all support and publicize advocacy research on charter schools and other market-based education policies. In 1993, the Heritage Foundation spun off the Center for Education Reform, an advocacy organization devoted entirely to promoting charter schools, when only 17% of all the newspaper articles on educational choice in the *New York Times, Wall*

Street Journal, Washington Post, Boston Globe, and the *Los Angeles Times* mentioned charter schools. By 1994, the proportion had shot up to nearly 65%. Between 1994 and 2004, 70% of school choice articles have discussed charter schools. Much of this publicity was funded by foundations, which also supported almost half of all the research studies of the best-known researchers of charter schools (Henig, 2008, pp. 147, 184–185).

For example, one journalist concluded that the Bill and Melinda Gates Foundation (assets $60 billion) spent $100 million on charter management organizations between 2000 and 2005 even as it funded nearly every organization in the educational establishment plus the National Governor's Association to "broaden and deepen its reach" (Robelen, 2009, quoted in Ravitch, 2010, p. 210). Similarly, the Walton Family Found*ation* spent $108 million on charter schools and other school choice programs in 2007 (45% of all its giving), including $32.9 million on three charter school operators, many tens of millions on individual charter schools, and $7,150,000 on charter advocacy organizations (p. 202).

The growth of charter schools should not be confused with demonstrated evidence of their efficacy or efficiency. Data on their performance is kept less systematically than on public schools, but when analyzed as a contrast between two sectors, charter schools come out no better or worse than traditional public schools (see Harris and Witte, this volume). The most optimistic interpretation of charter school performance reflects the advocates' belief that they demonstrate the efficacy of markets and competition in providing public services. Detractors point out that the enrollment in charter schools has far fewer special education, non-English speaking, and unmotivated students than do the regular schools, so at par results mask worse-than-typical performance (Henig, 2008).

The Eli and Eydth Broad Foundation and the Gates Foundation have also focused also on another form of privatization: a set of "diverse providers" of educational services. These mostly non-profit organizations offer one or two educational services, like alternative teacher and leadership training, curriculum, school turnaround services or the management of charter schools, charging districts or the state a fee. The market for external support services was $1.4 billion in 2004. Nearly all this philanthropic funding is focused on a handful of urban districts under state and/or mayoral control to shield the outside service providers (and the foundations) from school board politics and local interest groups. This market-creation strategy, dubbed "venture philanthropy," requires foundations to actively collaborate in grant making. They provide progressively larger amounts of funds to a shrinking number of provider organizations. Foundation executives believe they have more influence over outside groups this way (Reckhow, 2010). Even so, huge obstacles remain for the development of a truly alternative set of educational service delivery mechanisms. The strategy of concentrating resources to increase influence may render the diverse provider network homogeneous, and the evidence of performance improvements still remains limited to a few highly touted and unusual schools and organizations, which have not yet changed educational practice (Ravitch, 2010; Reckhow, 2010).

Conclusion

The standards-testing-accountability regime is now established national education policy: supported by the current presidential administration, large Congressional majorities, and a plurality of citizens. Like his predecessors, President Obama has deferred to the governors, specifically the NGA's Common Core State Standards Initiative, launched in summer 2010 with 48 pre-committed states. He encouraged the adoption of national standards by providing a huge increase in federal grant dollars, dubbed Race to the Top, to motivate states to compete with one another by demonstrating their implementation commitments (Klein, 2010; U.S. Department of Education, 2010). Foundation and think tank influence also remains strong. Obama has encouraged greater privatization by adopting the foundations' current criteria of success—career and college readiness—as his contribution to national standards. For advice, he routinely turns to foundation executives and entrepreneurs from the diverse provider network. And many high level DOE employees come from the diverse provider community, including Education Secretary Arnie Duncan, himself a bootstrapped education leader with no formal education training (U.S. Department of Education, 2010). In these ways and others, the current federal administration promises to institutionalize the shift from local to federal policy making, and to public schooling that is increasingly reliant on private, contracted services and resources.

To be sure, NCLB, charters, and diverse providers are only the latest in a series of incremental policy solutions that began with a paradigm shift in 1983. But the apparent continuity should not blind us to the fact that these policies were only enacted because there had been a radical redistribution of authority between local and federal governments, and a reconsideration of whose ideas are considered credible reform, and whose measure of success is adopted (Baumgartner & Jones, 1993). As of this writing, the United States is in the midst of the worst recession in three decades and is suffering a politically unacceptable level of national debt. A policy process that severely limits the access and influence of all but a handful of elite policy actors combined with these signals of decreasing fiscal flexibility to portend a new educational policy equilibrium. This means a new stability in how policy is made, where, and by whom. It will not be the incrementalism of the past—local, public, democratic, contentious, and slow to change. The new policy stability will be based on the norms of federal policy making—agenda setting by entrepreneurs, behind-the-scenes negotiations, policy solutions that must be sold to the public, and a stable collection of policy insiders who forge legislative compromises and allocate resources.

This new equilibrium will raise political questions heretofore not confronted in U.S. education: How will parents and other citizens voice their opinions when the rules and resources are determined through the complex, uncertain, and often opaque norms of policy making in Washington DC? If school boards continue to make policy incrementally in spite of national changes, will poorly performing districts decline even further while districts that win grants and meet standards gain disproportionately? How will privately supported markets and service providers be incentivized to focus on students, instead of their district customers or foundation sponsors? If external educational vendors become as powerful as the educational establishment once was, will policy makers have the will to regulate them, either to rein in overall costs or to ensure quality control? Analogs to such questions have long troubled American health care policy analysts and befuddled even the most ambitious politicians. The political difficulties of solving these problems in health care do not foreshadow easy answers in education.

Notes

1 The Phi Delta Kappa/Gallup Polls conducted yearly since 1969, less frequently before, are good sources of historical polling trends because the same questions are asked over time. The wording of the PDK/Gallup Poll questions summarized here are respectively: "Should the federal government in Washington have more influence or less influence in determining educational programs in local public schools?" "Who should have the greatest influence in deciding what is taught in public schools here—the federal government, the state government, or the local school board?," and "There is always a lot of discussion about the best way to finance the public schools. What do you think is the best way to finance schools? By means of local property taxes, by state taxes, or by taxes from the federal government in Washington?"

2 The new concern vied with lack of discipline, or more occasionally drug abuse or violence/ gangs.

3 These same groups were also crucial actors in the years when our local systems of schools were being developed, roughly 1880–1930.

4 John Kingdon (1999) argues that this need not be the case in other nations because they do not have our distinctive limited-government orientation, and are more comfortable allowing bureaucrats to regulate public services.

5 The largest foundation in the world, the Bill and Melinda Gates Foundation, was founded in 1994 by Gate's father, taken over by Bill and Melinda Gates in 2000. Libertarian and free-market foundations include the John M. Olin Foundation founded in 1953 but became active in 1969, the Lynde and Harry Bradley Foundation, which became active in 1985, the Walton Family Foundation founded in 1987, the Annenberg Foundation established in 1989, and the Eli and Eydth Broad Foundation begun in 1999. Older, more established and less engaged education funders include the W.K. Kellogg Foundation in 1930, the Lilly Endowment in 1937, The David and Lucile Packard Foundation in 1964, and the PEW Charitable Trusts formed between 1948 and 1979. Think tanks engaged in education policy instrument development and entrepreneurship include recent entrants: the conservative Heritage Foundation, which was established in 1973, the Cato Institute in 1977, the Manhattan Institute begun in 1978 and reorganized in 1981, and the Center for Education Reform in 1993. More established conservative foundations active in education include the Hoover Institution founded in 1919, and the American Enterprise Institute, whose business leaders settled in Washington, DC as a lobby in 1943.

6 Southern states are defined as the 11 in the Confederacy, and the border states in the Union during the civil war but that were slave states, including Delaware, Kentucky, Maryland, Missouri, Oklahoma, and West Virginia, plus Washington, DC.

7 Title IV of the Civil Rights Act gave the Justice Department authority to outlaw admission discrimination and authorized it to reimburse states, school boards, and institutions of higher education for training of educators on issues of discrimination. ESEA was a part of President Lyndon Johnson's War on Poverty, and funded "educationally disadvantaged" children under its "Title 1" (renamed "Chapter 1" under the Reagan administration).

8 The Teachers Guild, which hired Shanker as an organizer, had about 2,000 teachers of the city's roughly 50,000. On March 16, 1960, the United Federation of Teachers was formed when the Guild merged with a high school teachers union, bringing their numbers to about 4,500.

9 There was also a less well-funded effort to improve social studies education along the same inquiry-based lines, but it garnered almost no public funds and barely got off the ground.

10 The one exception was in a few big cities where businesses, foundations and think tanks held an access advantage and where these groups were permitted to test out their policy ideas. This was often accompanied by a governance shift to mayoral control in order to avoid the contentious legislative politics of school boards (see Wong and Ferris, this volume.)

11 Colorado and Washington state also had activist governors.

12 Among the education groups dismissing the report were the NEA, the National Association of Secondary School Principals, the National Association of State Boards of Education, the American Association of School Administrators, the Council of Chief State School Officers, and the National School Boards Association, among others.

13 By 1998, 55% of Black parents still approved of busing for integration, which 41% said would make schools better; but 78% of White parents opposed to busing, with 72% having concluded that racial integration "makes little difference" in the quality of education.

14 In 1990, the survey research firm Public Agenda was commissioned by The Business-Higher Education Forum to track public opinion about the connection between the economy and education. Throughout the decade, Public Agenda conducted local public information campaigns preceded and followed by focus groups and surveys in various U. S. cities (see Farkas, 1992; Farkas, Johnson, & Foleno, 1999; Immerwahr, Johnson, & Kernan-Schoss, 1991; Johnson, 1995; Johnson & Immerwahr, 1994).

15 There was a small privately funded voucher experiment in Washington, DC prior to 2003, which was supplanted by the first federally funded one under President H. W. Bush. President Barach Obama slates it to sunset in 2011.

16 Even the court cases that adjudicated whether state funding might go to religious schools in voucher programs have been at odds. The Florida experiment permitted funding to religious schools, but the state's Supreme Court ruled that unconstitutional in 2006.

17 TesseracT Group Inc. filed for bankruptcy in 2000.

References

Allan, J. (Ed.). (1989). *Can business save education? Strategies for the 1990s.* Washington, DC: Heritage Foundation.

Allen, J. (2009). Why we call it the BLOB. *Blob Watch* Retrieved March 1, 2010, from http://www.edreform.com/About_CER/BLOB_Watch/index.cfm

Apple, M. W. (1983). Work, gender, and teaching. *Teachers College Press, 84*(5), 611–628.

Barton, P. E., & Coley, R. J. (2010). *The black-white achievement gap: When progress stopped* (Policy Information Report). Princeton, NJ: Policy Evaluation and Research Center, Educational Testing Service.

Baumgartner, F. R., & Jones, B. D. (1993). *Agendas and instability in American politics.* Chicago: University of Chicago Press.

Berman, P., & Clugston, R. (1988). A tale of two cities: The business community and educational reform in California and Minnesota. In M. Levine & T. Roberta (Eds.), *American business and the public school: Case studies of corporate involvement in public education* (pp. 121–149). New York: Committee For Economic Development, Teachers College Press.

Borman, K., Costnell, L., & Gallagher, K. (1993). Business involvement in school reform: The rise of the Business Roundtable. In C. Marshall (Ed.), *The new politics of race and gender: The politics of Education Association Yearbook* (pp. 69–83). Washington, DC: Falmer Press.

Boyd, W. L. (1988). How to reform schools without half trying: Secrets of the Reagan administration. *Educational Administration Quarterly, 24*(3), 299–309.

Bracey, G. W. (2002). *The war against America's public schools: Privatizing schools, commercializing education.* Boston, MA: Allyn and Bacon.

Brown v. Board of Education of Topeka, Kansas. 347 U.S. 483 (1954).

Bulkley, K. (2001). Educational performance and charter school authorizers: The accountability bind [Electronic Verstion]. *Educational Policy Analysis Archives, 9.* Retrieved October 1, 2010, from http://epaa.asu.edu/epaa/v9n27/html

Business Roundtable Public Policy Committee. (1990, September 11). *Essential components of a successful education system:* The Business Roundtable

Center for Education Reform. (2009, November). *National charter school and enrollment statistics.* Retrieved March 29, 2010, from http://www.edreform.com

Chubb, J. E., & Moe, T. M. (1990). *Politics, markets and America's schools.* Washington, DC: The Brookings Institute.

Cyert, R. M., & March, J. G. (1963). *A behavioral theory of the firm.* Englewood Cliffs, NJ: Prentice Hall.

DeBray, W. H. (2004). *Politics, ideology and education: Federal policy during the Clinton and Bush administrations.* New York: Teachers College Press.

Farkas, S. (1992). *Educational reform: The players and the politics.* New York: Public Agenda.

Farkas, S., & Johnson, J. (1998). *Time to move on: African-American and white parents set and agenda for public schools.* New York: Public Agenda.

Farkas, S., Johnson, J., & Foleno, A. (1999). *On thin ice: How advocates and opponents could misread the public's views on vouchers and charter schools.* New York City: Public Agenda.

Fosler, S. R. (1990). *The business role in state education reform.* New York: The Business Roundtable.

Fowler, S. R. (1990). *The business role in state education reform: Report prepared of the Business Roundtable.* Washington,DC: Committee on Economic Development

Fraga, L. R., Rodriguez, N., & Erlichson, B. A. (2005). Desegregation and school board politics: The limits of court-imposed policy change. In W. G. Howell (Ed.), *Besieged: School boards and the future of education politics* (pp. 102–128). Washington, DC: The Brookings Institution.

Frankenberg, E., & Siegel-Hawley, G. (2008). *The forgotten choice? Rethinking magnet schools in a changing landscape.* Los Angeles: UCLA.

Gabbard, D., & Macrine, S. (2008). Review of Kenneth J. Saltman, 2007, capitalizing on disaster: Taking and breaking public schools. *Education Review: A Journal of Book Reviews* Retrieved March 29, 2010, from http://edrev.asu.edu/reviews/rev727.htm

Ginsberg, A. L., Jay, N., & White Plisko, B. (1988). Lessons from the wall chart. *Educational Evaluation and Policy Analysis, 10*(1), 1–12.

Gittell, M., & Hevesi, A. (1969). *The politics of urban education.* New York: Praeger.

Goldring, E., & Smrekar, C. (2000). Magnet schools and the pursuit of racial balance. *Education and Urban Society, 33*(17), 17–35.

Gould, S., Scott, E., Starobin, P., & Verdier, J. (1984). *Governor Bob Graham and the improvement of Florida's education system* (Instructional Case No. C16-83-574). Cambridge, MA: John F. Kennedy School of Government.

Hechinger, F. M. (1980, January 29). About education: Solving the case of the missing scientists [Electronic Version]. *New York Times.* Retrieved February 10, 2010, from http://select.nytimes.com

Henig, J. R. (2008). *Spin cycle: How research is used in policy debates, The case of charter schools.* New York: The Russell Sage Foundation.

Hochschild, J. (1984). *The new American dilemma: Liberal democracy and school desegregation.* New Haven, CT: Yale University Press.

Hochschild, J., & Scovronick, N. (2004). *The American dream and the public schools.* New York: Oxford University Press.

Holton, G. (1984). A nation at risk revisited. *Daedalus, 113*(4), 1–27.

Howlett, M., & Ramlesh, M. (1995). *Studying public policy: Policy cycles and policy subsystems.* Toronto: Oxford University Press.

Immerwahr, J., Johnson, J., & Kernan-Schoss, A. (1991). *Cross-talk: The public, the experts and competitiveness.* New York: Public Agenda.

Johnson, J. (1995). *Assignment incomplete.* New York: Public Agenda.

Johnson, J., & Immerwahr, J. (1994). *First things first: What Americans expect from the public schools.* New York: Public Agenda.

Kahlenberg, R. D. (2007). *Tough Liberal: Albert Shanker and the battles over schools, unions and democracy.* New York: Columbia University Press.

Kanigel, R. (1997). *The one best way: Frederick Winslow Taylor and the enigma of efficiency.* New York: Viking.

Kingdon, J. W. (1995). *Agendas, alternatives and public policies* (2nd ed.). New York: Harper Collins College.

Kingdon, J. W. (1999). *America the unusual.* New York: Worth Publishers.

Kingdon, J. W. (2001). *A model of agenda setting with applications.* Paper presented at the Second ANnual Quello Telecommunications Policy and Law Symposium, Washington, DC.

Klein, A. (2010, August 23). State policymakers talk standards, Race to the Top, ESEA. *Education Week* Retrieved from http://blogs.edweek.org/edweek/campaign-k-12/2010/08/school_chiefs_and_govs_talk_es.html

Kline, M. (1973). *Why Johnny can't add: The failure of the new mathematics.* New York: St. Martin's Press.

Lazerson, M., McLaughlin, J. B., & McPherson, B. (1984). New curriculum, old issues. *Teachers College Record, 86*(2), 299–319.

Levin, H. M. (Ed.). (1970). *Community control of schools.* Washington, DC: The Brookings Institution.

Lieberman, M. (1989). *Privatization and educational choice.* New York: St. Martin's Press.

Lindblom, C. E. (1959). The science of "muddling through" *Public Administrative Review, 19*(2), 79–88.

Lindblom, C. E. (1965). *The intelligence of democracy: Decision-making by mutual adjustment.* New York: Free Press.

Lindblom, C. E., & Woodhouse, E. J. (1993). *The policy making process* (3rd ed.). Englewood Cliffs, NJ: Prentice Hall.

Liu, X., Lindquist, E., Vedlitz, A., & Vincent, K. (2010). Understanding local policymaking: Policy elites' perceptions of local agenda setting and alternative policy selection. *The Policy Studies Journal, 38*(1), 69–91.

Manna, P. (2006). *School's in: Federalism and the national education agenda.* Washington, DC: Georgetown University Press.

McDermott, K. A., & Jensen, L. S. (2005). Dubious sovereignty: Federal conditions of aid and the No Child Left Behind Act. *Peabody Journal of Education, 80*(2), 39–56.

McDonnell, L. (2005). No Child Left Behind and the federal role in education: Evolution or revolution? *Peabody Journal of Education, 80*(2), 19–38.

Milliken v. Bradley, 418 U.S. 717. (1974).

Murphy, M. (1990). *Blackboard unions: The AFT and the NEA, 1900–1980.* Ithaca, NY: Cornell University Press.

The National Business Roundtable. (2002). *Using the No Child Left Behind act to improve schools in your state.* Washington, DC: The National Business Roundtable.

National Commission on Excellence in Education. (1983, April). *A nation at risk: The imperative for educational reform.* Retrieved August 22, 2010, from http://www2.ed.gov/upubs/NatAtRisk/index.html

National Council on Educational Standards Testing. (1992). *Raising standards for American education* (No. ISBN-0-16-036097-8). Washington, DC: U.S. Department of Education, OERI.

O'Day, J. A., & Smith, M. S. (1993). Systemic Reform and Educational Opportunity. In S. H. Furhman (Ed.), *Designing coherent educational policy: Improving the system* (pp. 250–312). San Francisco: Jossey-Bass.

Orfield, G., & Eaton, S. (1996). *Dismantling desegregation*. New York: New Press.

Orfield, G., & Lee, C. (2006). *Racial transformation and the changing nature of segregation*. Cambridge, MA: The Civil Rights Project, Harvard University.

Peterson, P. E. (1981). *City limits*. Chicago: University of Chicago Press.

Phi Delta Kappan. (2009, 2010). PDK/Gallup Poll of the Public's Attitudes Towards the Public School Retrieved February 15, 2010, from http://www.pdkintl.org/kappan/poll.htm

Ravitch, D. (2010). *The death and life of the great American school system: How testing and choice are undermining education*. New York: Basic Books.

Reckhow, S. (2010). Disseminating and legitimating a new approach: The role of foundations. In K. E. Bulkley, J. R. Henig, & H. M. Levin (Eds.), *Between public and private: Politics, governance, and the new portfolio models for urban school reform* (pp. 277–304). Cambridge, MA: Harvard Education Press.

Rich, W. (1996). *Black mayors and school politics: The failure of reform in Detroit, Gary and Newark*. New York: Garland.

Robelen, E. W. (2009, December 23). 'Race to the Top' driving policy action across states. *Education Week* Retrieved August 23, 2010, from http://www.edweek.org/ew/articles/2009/12/23/16states.h29.html?qs=Race+to+the+Top

Robinson, S. E., & Eller, W. S. (2010). Participation in policy streams: Testing the separation of problems and solutions in subnational policy systems. *Policy Studies Journal, 38*(2), 199–215.

Ryan, J. R. (February 18, 1958). Prefer quality over quantity in engineers, scientist urges [Electronic Version]. *New York Times*. Retrieved February 10, 2010, from http://query.nytimes.com/

Schmeck, H. (1957, October 8). Nation is warned to stress science: Faces doom unless your learns its importance, Chief Physicist says [Electronic Version]. *New York Times*. Retrieved February 10, 2010, from http://query.nytimes.com/

Shipps, D. (2006). The science and politics of urban education leadership: Toward a reorienting narrative. In D. E. Mitchell (Ed.), *New foundations for knowledge for education policy, politics and administration: Science and sensationalism* (pp. 181–210). Mahwah, NJ : Erlbaum.

Simon, H. A. (1957). *Models of man: Social and rational; mathematical essays on rational human behavior in a social setting*. New York: Wiley.

Smith, M. S., & O'Day, J. (1991). Systemic school reform. In S. Fuhrman & B. Malen (Eds.), *Politics of curriculum and testing* (pp. 233–267). Bristol PA: Falmer.

Stone, D. (1998). *Policy paradox: The art of political decision making* (2nd ed.). New York: Norton.

U.S. Department of Education. (2010). *A blueprint for reform: The reauthorization of the Elementary and Secondary Education Act*. Washington, DC: Office of Planning, Evaluation and Policy Development, U.S. Department of Education.

Zhang, Y., & Yang, K. (2008). What drives charter school diffusion at the local level: Educational needs or political and institutional forces? *Policy Studies Journal 36*(4), 571–591.

13

WHAT HAVE WE LEARNED ABOUT SHAPING EDUCATION POLICY?

Douglas E. Mitchell, Dorothy Shipps, and Robert L. Crowson

Federalization of educational governance over the last 60 years is the most prominent common theme explored by the authors contributing to this volume. There are distinct dimensions to this shift in policy-making power: (a) centralization and concentration of power at higher levels of governance, (b) shifting from specialized educational governance to what Wong and Farris identify as "integrated civic governance" mechanisms, and (c) efforts to disperse power by introducing market mechanisms into local education delivery.

Centralization. All the authors in this volume offer some evidence that policy-making power has shifted sharply toward state and, especially, federal policy makers. All see that responsibility for setting standards and enforcing consequences has moved from more than 18,000 districts in mid-century to the 50 states in the 1980s. And, by 2002, the federal Department of Education (DOE), an agency that did not even enjoy cabinet status until the late 1970s, had taken over responsibility for providing core direction to the nation's 90,000 schools. Mid-twentieth century state governments had delegated virtually all of their constitutional responsibility for education policy to local school districts. By the first decade of the 21st century, however, states find themselves pressured by federal mandates, competing with one another for federal incentive grants, and looking to Washington for fiscal bailouts. As Betty Malen has noted, policy-making power is not necessarily a zero-sum game in which increased federal authority means equally reduced state or local authority. By aligning themselves with the federal agenda, state agencies have become better resourced and more powerful in their efforts to influence local educators. The framework offered by Wong and Farris offers a similar take on the growing power of big city governments. A convergence of policy priorities aligning city government and federal interests has strengthened the role of general civic governments at both levels.

The authors of this volume offer several different perspectives on why educational policy has moved so thoroughly into the mainstream of Washington, DC, politics. Whether they judge the trends reported here to be the logical extension of an inexorable process begun long ago or see them as a more recent manifestation of local government failure and shifts in the public mood, they all acknowledge the new political reality. For those who take an institutional view (e.g., Malen, Cohen and Moffitt, Hannaway and Mittleman, and Shipps) centralization is explained by a combination of persistent weaknesses in local school structural capacity and the emergence of strong new state and national institutions: teacher unions, entrepreneurial think tanks, well-endowed foundations, education oriented governors, etc.

Those taking this longer view tend to believe that the 19th-century exhortatory urging and land grant provisions for schooling started a process of federal intervention that gave way to broad and sustained regulatory activity beginning in the 1960s. Early federal policy initiatives—the vocational education act of 1917, the National Defense Education Act of 1958, the Elementary and Secondary Education Act of 1964—were relatively isolated categorical programs; generally lacking in significant consequences for regular educators. They did, however, whet the appetites of federal policy makers for expanded influence and conditioned local educators to expect support to flow from the nation's capitol. These early federal education policies were gradually seen as relatively weak levers, unable to substantially raise school performance or create educational equity. Thus began a search for ever more potent policies, and stronger language with which to describe what was needed and why.

One important enabling condition for this long-term shift in the locus of authority is the vast expansion of our capacity to collect and interpret detailed information about school operations and performance. Careful tracking of school segregation and integration data in the early 1960s laid the foundations for judicial intervention in racial and other forms of school segregation and neglect. Following James Coleman's landmark study of the equality of educational opportunity, state and federal judges and politicians came to value and use massive and reasonably well-analyzed data on school finance, school staffing, student graduation rates. Most recently, as Hannaway and Mittleman point out, detailed monitoring of student achievement data has made it possible, if still controversial, to trace achievement outcomes to social and demographic factors affecting learning and link outcomes to the ability of teachers to provide "value added" achievement gains for their students. Only in the last two decades has it been possible to track hundreds of variables for millions of students and disaggregate the data by classroom, school, student demography and other variables important to understanding how and where learning is taking place.

A national dialog about how to use this data to improve schooling emboldened a range of national interests and institutions, most of which felt more comfortable lobbying general purpose governments in the states and Washington, DC than debating local school policy in contentious school board meetings. Beginning in the 1980s, federal policy began to coalesce on common standards and accountability tools like common tests, and "whole-school" reform requirements for federal funding eligibility so that educators would feel responsible for ensuring that low-performing students succeed (Kaestle & Smith, 1982; Smith & O'Day, 1991). Most recently, the Obama administration, in Race to the Top, has move teacher quality and supervision to the center of the federal agenda.

For those whose analyses are more issue focused (e.g., Mitchell and Mitchell, Brown and Cooper, Plank and Johnson, Crowson, et al.), the centralization of policy power is seen as a national response to issues that are increasingly serious and quite intractable at the local level. For example, school desegregation was, and still is, both a local problem and a national issue, but only the federal courts and other national actors were able to mobilize the political will and enforcement resources needed to address this issue, if only for a few decades. Similarly, when Cold War national security anxieties and international economic competition became focal issues, it seemed only obvious to content area experts that standardized national policies would be needed to responsibly address the these emergent realities. When it became evident that the War on Poverty was being lost for lack of sufficiently robust child development strategies to lift the next generation out of poverty, it once again, became evident that only a national policy strategy could hope to address the issue adequately.

For authors who look at centralization from the perspective of global social and political developments (e.g., Plank and Johnson, Meyer) the growth of federal power is seen as the natural consequence of geo-politics. The world has become intensely competitive in both political and economic terms, and nation states are the competing units. Access to energy, wealth, jobs, influence over social values, the protection of human rights, and the preservation of national cultures all dictate that nation states take increasingly direct control over all of the elements of economic and political development. From this perspective, education is an essential element in global competition and development. In short, education is too important to be left to educators, even if the nationally centralized policies are not very successful in solving productivity problems or closing the gaps between students at the bottom and top of any nation's performance distribution.

Integrated civic governance. The second broad governance change identified throughout this volume is a sweeping reversal of the Progressive era and Urban Reform movements' commitments to put educational governance under the control of specialized educational governance agencies (non-partisan local school boards) and apolitical executive administrators (school superintendents) who were expected to act in the best interests of children and families. During the first half of 20th century, these reformers largely succeeded in separating school governance from partisan politics by convincing the nation that educational policy should be the province of civic-minded "trustees" and politically insulated executive managers. Their reforms were particularly successful in school systems, though many cities also underwent "good government" reforms that weakened mayors and created strong city managers who were to professionally manage a workforce protected by civil service laws aimed at preventing political abuse.

Close reading of the chapters in this volume suggests that integrated governance goes far beyond a few big cities. Whereas it was once taken for granted that education should be divorced from party politics to shield school employees from partisan pressures, stave off patronage employment and insider contracts, and professionalize decision making, politicians and political parties are now expected to have educational platforms. As Shipps notes, this agenda-setting activity, once the purview of district and state school superintendents, is now associated with political executives: mayors, governors, and at the federal level, the president of the United States.

There are several reasons for this shift in governance authority. One is the growing belief that quality education is now essential for maintaining national security, economic productivity, cultural integrity, and international status. These concerns have trumped historically powerful commitments to providing children with *in loco parentis* school environments that sheltered them from the harsh realities of the adult world and provided support for largely private nurture and child development. This willingness to let national and international anxieties overrun sheltered school nurturing has been mightily strengthened by public recognition of the frequency of child abuse and neglect and the racial and class biases found in far too many schools.

Another reason why policy making has been moving into the hands of general purpose government agencies is the substantial research that documents the vulnerability of state and local education agencies to special interests—religious parochialism, union capture, business influence, and racial and social class biases are too well documented to ignore. These biases are particularly troublesome because Progressives sought specialized education governance precisely because it was expected to transcend bias and would represent disinterested civic values. Perhaps even more important than school boards' tendency to reinforce local social biases is the point made so clearly by Cohen and Moffitt that educational governance agencies at all levels of government have been unable to build an instructional and curricular infrastructure strong enough to support implementation of robust standards, whether or not they are aligned with local biases.

At the same time, researchers have embraced institutional and political regime theories that recognize that schools are embedded community agencies, not just enclaves of professional service delivery. Where bureaucratic and scientific management theories attribute organizational effectiveness to rational processes that address the logic of task performance, institutional and regime theories see productivity as powerfully influenced by inter-organizational and environmental relationships—especially clients' confidence and support from political coalitions of interested community members. From this analytical perspective, specialized education governance appears to be too isolating, too insensitive to community and client interests, and unable to draw upon the intelligence and support that are the stock in trade of politicians and interest groups.

The most basic contributor to shifting power toward general purpose governing agencies is the same one that encourages federalization. In response to general disappointment with the track record of educational change and improvement efforts over the last six decades, political policy makers are looking for change. As Betty Malen notes, they are convinced that one important mechanism for encouraging change is to alter who is in charge. After more than half a century of tediously slow progress in the nation's "crash program" to fix the public schools, empowering new governors, including taping their different knowledge and skills, is both symbolically and substantively important.

As we appraise the likelihood that placing governance in the hands of general purpose government agencies will increase school performance, we also need to recognize the risks. These changes aim to reverse the century old and hard won successes of the Progressive and Urban Reform movements. Too often teachers were patronage workers, budgets were deflected from educational purposes, anti-intellectual curricula were used, and constitutional rights of students and employees trampled. Whether a return to integrated civic governance will signal a return to neglect and abuse is unknown. Perhaps access to high-quality and well-managed information systems will enable citizens to hold public officials accountable in ways that were not possible a century ago. But the recent jailing of a few governors and congressmen for corruption suggests that this might not be easy.

It is also important to remember integrated governance structures facilitate negotiation for policy agreements and support among the interested parties seeking to influence electoral and governance successes. These negotiations involve idea champions and policy entrepreneurs who constantly seek to capitalize on opportunities to tie their preferred policy solutions to the currently recognized policy problems, even if those solutions do not really address the problems. The negotiation process means, as Cohen and Moffitt argue, that policy adoptions are the cause of political actions as well as the result of them. The policy winners want a robust politics of implementation; the losers pursue a politics of resistance, evasion or reconsideration. It is too early to tell whether the move from specialized education governance to general purpose governance of education will mean a more coherent, high performance and stable school system. Wong and Farris display some confidence that it will, other authors voice more caution. Without a deep understanding of learning processes, child development dynamics, student behavioral management, curriculum content and sequencing, and other core issues in educational program design and management, general purpose agencies may be inclined to demand results that no one knows how to produce; or even whether they can be produced.

Another important aspect of reliance on general purpose governance agencies for education policy making is the potential for abrupt and surprising changes in direction that arise as education policy problems compete with policy problems in other important sectors of society. Beginning with the early observations by Downs (1972), analysts of governmental policy making have recognized that attention to specific policy problems tends to be intermittent, characterized by what Downs called "issue attention cycles." This tendency to shift attention from one issue to another occurs even when the problems that need to be addressed are persistent and unresolved. It is true, that overall interest in education as a policy domain has remained high over more than half a century. Some might take to mean that issue-attention cycles of policy making in education are not following this pattern. A closer look, however, makes it quite clear that policy-making has shifted back and forth between education and other policy sectors such as health, foreign relations, economic recovery, crime, etc. Moreover, the continuing high interest in education has not meant that the whole range of education policy problems is constantly receiving attention. Rather, education policy attention has, as Downs predicted, shifted rapidly from topic to topic: from incentives to mandates, from testing to credentialing, from equality as access to equality through outcome accountability, from reading to STEM subjects, from higher performance to greater efficiency, from the needs of gifted students to those of the educationally handicapped, from discipline to academic learning, from school program content to teacher quality, from integrated children's services to algebra for all, from vocational preparation to college for everyone. As policy makers become more general, the tendency for short attention spans is compounded by the need to address a broader array of issue areas.

Market mechanisms. Education policy-making power has also been restructured by dispersing decision-making authority from governments to markets. The theory behind this dispersal is that market forces will stimulate innovation and improve efficiency. Harris and Witte provide us with an "Economics 101" description of the underlying assumptions and the expected consequences of exposing public schools to various forms of market competition and risk. Elementary economic theory predicts that, if given a choice, consumers of various services will opt for the highest quality obtainable at the lowest cost available. Market providers of desired goods and services will be motivated to improve quality and increase efficiency in production so as to gain a larger market share and thus maximize income and profits. As Harris and Witte note, the seminal work of Chubb and Moe (1990) seems to have provided the decisive argument for why market based policy making is superior. They see political decisions by democratically constrained government bodies like school boards as inherently risk averse, and compromised by self-serving bureaucrats who attend too much to the internal distribution of benefits, not enough to the quality of services provided. The evidence is quite mixed, but enthusiasm for the potential of markets to deliver higher quality services at the same price (or similar quality more cheaply) remains strong.

Drawing on these assumptions, a wide variety of educational markets have developed over the last half century. Traditionally, real estate prices have played a powerful role in allocating different levels of educational service based on the prices families are willing and able to pay for housing. This is partly the result of local property tax funding of schools, a pattern of finance that is slowly eroding. Private schools, both religious and secular, along with home schooling have also provided options for families, and have developed their own niche markets. The marginal cost increase in terms of tuition and increased parental effort are seen by a modest, but growing, number of families to be rewarded with greater student learning (or at least preferred learning content) and/or greater access to prestigious post-secondary education and employment opportunities.

Over the last few decades, open enrollment systems, vouchers, magnet schools, and charter schools have been added to the mix of options available to some, but certainly not all families. Indeed, as Shipps and Malen note, elaboration market-based educational service delivery has been a major theme in both rhetoric and action among the strengthened and centralized federal and state policy makers. Theoretically, the market mechanisms being used to restructure school operations appear to clash directly with the centralization of policy making and the resurgence of direct political control of the schools as described above. State and national standards and their more or less well-aligned tests of student achievement are pressuring all service providers to produce the same levels of educational attainment, in the same curricular areas (except, perhaps for those students with the talent and family support needed to substantially exceed baseline learning goals). But the fact that few charters, for example, have been closed for poor performance, as both Malen and Shipps relate, beggars this theoretical argument, especially since the extant research suggests that charters, on average, produce no better performance than do traditional schools. Some market advocates see the potential for a clash over standards and performance as a relatively minor problem because market contributions to improved efficiency and effectiveness in service delivery are of substantial value even if they do not include changing the content of the school curriculum or the nature of its learning goals. In due time, more detailed and complete information about the achievement effects of market competition for students will, no doubt, be forthcoming.

The dispersal of policy making into market arenas suggests we also need to look at the mix of market and government services that will be provided in some ideal future, and the source of funding in these markets. No one seems to be seriously proposing that the system of compulsory, government funded, education be abandoned in favor of a market place that would only create schools where families are ready and willing to come up with the actual costs of schooling. The depth of continued support for compulsory education is easily recognized in the way policy makers and the general public view early school leaving (i.e., dropping out). Both the public at large and the policy-making community remain firmly convinced that students need more education than many voluntarily seek. The desire for educational attainment (10th grade, high school diploma, college graduate, post-graduate) varies, but so does the desire for educational rigor. Significant groups of secondary school students are regularly engaged in negotiating with teachers for a reduction in educational demands; giving more cooperative classroom behavior in exchange. If a significant group of students, for whatever reasons, desires fewer years or lower standards rather than more and higher quality education, it is not unreasonable to expect that market vendors will lower standards to meet the demand. Consequently, most arguments that take seriously market in schooling, anticipate a need to regulate those markets. But we know very little about what needs regulating and what does not. Moreover, some proportion of market advocates, and many vendors in established markets, as Shipps suggests in her discussion of diverse educational providers, can be expected to resist all regulation beyond an initial contract as a fundamental perversion of market benefits.

As policy-making authority has become more centralized, and shifted more towards general purpose government officials it has become evident that the real client for marketed educational services are the taxing authorities paying for them and regulating them. The federal government, for example, is currently putting up a tiny fraction of the total cost of public education, but federal policy makers are not at all bashful about making demands regarding what that small fraction should buy. The George W. Bush administration's No Child Left Behind law imposes content standards and record keeping. The Obama administration's Race to the Top is requiring changes in teacher evaluation and is pushing for national standards and testing programs. State governments too have requirements in the form of curriculum standards for textbook and professional service delivery providers and charter authorization laws, among dozens of other requirements. As Shipps asks, what will it take to ensure that providers of educational services attend to the diverse needs of students over the requirements of the contracting agencies? Compounding this, many of the voucher programs are preventing families from augmenting the value of the voucher because that would mean using government funds to augment private advantages.

Three other topics deserve specific attention in this summing up chapter: (a) the role of globalization in setting the education policy agenda; (b) the near universal overlay of standards and test-based accountability policies on top of regulation and resource controls; and (c) a final reflection on the ways in which education policy is characterized by both abrupt abandonment of previously high profile policies and rapid imposition of new initiatives.

Globalization and the policy agenda. We have already remarked on some aspects of the ways in which economic and political globalization have led to an anxious concern that national security and prosperity demand radical improvement in educational productivity —especially improvement in basic skill test scores and more advanced training in science, technology, engineering and mathematics, the so-called STEM subjects. The 1983 publication of *A Nation at Risk* by the Commission on Excellence convened by the Reagan administration is widely seen as the break through moment when the civil rights focus on equity and the Progressive emphasis on child nurture and development came to an end, replaced by sharply escalating anxiety about the nation's future economic and political security. Intriguingly, policy debates have needed a comparison country on which to focus when responding to globalized pressures. At first it was Germany and their engineering prowess, then variously on Japan and its rapid economic growth, Finland and its high tech industrial successes, then Singapore and other Asian nations with their high mathematics test scores. India had its turn as the place to which we are outsourcing many high technology jobs. Today, it is the power of the Chinese economy (and their ownership of a huge chunk of America's federal debt) that stirs global competition anxieties. What is important about these global anxieties is that they have come perilously close to turning the American Dream into an American Nightmare—a preoccupation with our vulnerability and a replacement of the rugged individualist American adventurer with a harried and troubled American consumer.

The two chapters in this volume that give explicit attention to the effects of globalization have very different takes on what it means for education policy and practice. Plank and Johnson see the driving power of globalization as defining a new American education curriculum so starkly that algebra has become the "new Latin" and replaces child development with achievement production as the central criterion of educational success. Heinz Dieter Meyer doesn't argue this point directly, but he makes it clear that long-term embedded cultural structures make it impossible to simply graft on to a national education system new educational programs and priorities, no matter how much circumstances might demand them. He suggests that educational programs have to evolve starting from these deeply embedded structures and following the logic of national cultures, norms and aspirations. Anxious imposition of new policy directions that are at odds with these underlying cultural elements are likely to breed confusion and resistance rather than compliance and implementation.

Standards and test-based accountability. There is little more thoroughly recognized by the authors represented in this volume than the fact that education policy today is intensely committed to the use of curriculum standards and high-stakes test-base accountability policies to control schools. The most recent upsurge in this as a set of policy instruments is the development of the econometric principle of "value-added" evaluation of individual teacher's work performance. As Hannaway and Mittleman report, even the hide-bound resistance of the powerful teacher unions appears to be melting away before the pressure. Earlier efforts to hold teachers directly accountable for student success were generally abandoned when confronted with evidence of evaluator bias, unreliable test score data, and an inability to tell what kinds of handicapping conditions limited the amount of academic achievement that could be expected in any given classroom. Powered by a new confidence in the adequacy of testing instruments and an enormous growth in the ability to record, store, analyze, and report on vast quantities of academic and demographic data has rekindled policy commitment to direct and precise evaluation of just what each individual teacher has been contributing to each and every child in their charge.

Policy churn and program abandonment. We end by remembering where we started in the development of this reprise of education policy formation over the last six decades. We began with William Lowe Boyd's remarkable list of surprising shifts in education policy. His list (see chapter 1) notes not only what is new in education policy, but also what has been abandoned, by neglect, replacement or contrary policies. He observed that belief in policy control over the productive processes of education has been abandoned, along with specialized governing arrangements. General purpose policy makers focus on goals; they expect professionals to attend to specific practices. Thus, process-based policies are replaced by outcome specifications and accountability mechanisms. Boyd also observed the abandonment of attention to resource inputs in favor of measureable outcomes; the end of teachers as professional civil servants and their reinvention of themselves as unionized workers; an end to the doctrine of *in loco parentis* responsibility for students to debates over their constitutional rights. He remarked on the end of education as expression of local cultural beliefs, replaced by the notion of evidence-based and odds-calculating educational treatments. He noted the abandonment of the idea of student tracking or channeling toward differentiated educational goals (though the practice is far from gone). And he detected that Americans' confidence in professional governance, and in schooling as secular gospel extolling the vitality of the American Dream, has withered away in favor of politically dominated policy systems seeking national political and economic security.

Most of the attention given to his observations in this volume has focused on where the new policy initiatives and governance structures come from and what we might expect of their implementation. As we look back over the insights to be garnered from these chapters, however, we are struck by how little attention scholars and policy makers give to post mortems on the policies that are being abandoned. What has been lost, we wonder, by abandoning the governance and policy-making system, which David Tyack (1974) so insightfully characterized as *The One Best System*? The problems and concerns voiced to justify the new policy system needed serious attention, and the old system seemed to many to be incapable of producing needed changes. Yet in 1950, American schooling was the envy of the world, and few then would have thought it so quickly discredited. Even as we aggressively pursue the policy changes reviewed in this volume, it might be helpful to ask about what has been lost, as well as what has been gained, by the dramatic changes in power allocation and policy-making processes now governing the American school system.

References

Chubb, J. E., & Moe, T. M. (1990). *Politics, markets, and schools.* Washington, DC: Brookings Institution.

Downs, A. (1972, Summer). Up and down with ecology: The 'issue attention cycle.' *The Public Interest, 28,* 38–50.

Kaestle, C. F., & Smith, M. S. (1982). The federal role in elementary and secondary education, 1940–1980. *Harvard Educational Review, 52*(4), 384–408.

Smith, M. S., & O'Day, J. (1991). Systemic school reform. In S. Fuhrman & B. Malen (Eds.), *Politics of curriculum and testing* (pp. 233–267). Bristol, PA: Falmer.

Tyack, D. (1974). *The one best system: A history of American urban education.* Cambridge, MA: Harvard University Press.

CONTRIBUTOR BIOGRAPHIES

Jo Bennett is an assistant professor at Wichita State University in the Educational Leadership Doctoral Program. Her area of interest is community and parental relations, creating a sense of community in schools, and exploring the intersection of policy implementation and the experience of schooling. She has worked especially with issues concerning second language learners.

Carolyn A. Brown, PhD, is an Associate Professor of Educational Leadership, Administration, and Policy in the Graduate School of Education at Fordham University. She has been a teacher, a school administrator, and an educational consultant. Her research focuses on the influences of education policy on teachers and administrators.

David K. Cohen is the John Dewey Professor of Education at the School of Education and Professor of Public Policy at the Ford School of Public Policy, at the University of Michigan. He recently co-directed the Study of Instructional Improvement, a large longitudinal study of efforts to improve teaching and learning in reading/language arts and mathematics in high-poverty elementary schools. He taught at Harvard and Michigan State before coming to the University of Michigan. His most recent book, with Susan L. Moffitt, *The Ordeal of Equality: Did Federal Regulation Fix the Schools?* (Harvard University Press, 2009), is an analysis of federal efforts to use Title I of the 1965 ESEA to improve K–12 education.

Bruce S. Cooper, PhD, is professor of education leadership at the Fordham University Graduate School of Education, New York City, and editor of *Private School MONITOR.* He is co-author of a forthcoming book, *Blurring the Lines:*

The Case of Religious Charter Schools with Janet Mulvey and Arthur Maloney. Other books of include *Home Schooling in Full View*, and recently, *Handbook of Education Politics and Policy*, co-edited with Lance Fusarelli and James Cibulka. He was president of the Politics of Education Association from 2004–2008.

Robert L. Crowson is a Professor of Education and Policy with the Department of Leadership, Policy, and Organizations, Peabody College, Vanderbilt University. Before joining the Vanderbilt faculty in 1994, he served as a member of the faculty of the University of Illinois at Chicago, with a joint appointment in Urban Planning and Education. His PhD was earned from the University of Chicago. Professor Crowson's research interests include the study of large-city schools and their politics/ organization, particularly relationships between schools and their surrounding neighborhoods or communities. His recent books include *Successful Schools and the Community Relationship* (with Ellen Goldring and Katherine Taylor Haynes), 2010; and *The New Localism in American Education* (co-edited with Ellen Goldring), 2010.

Emily Farris is a fourth year PhD candidate at Brown University. From Birmingham, Alabama, she received her BA in Political Science and Urban Studies from Furman University and MA from Brown University. After completing her masters, Emily taught third grade in Baton Rouge, Louisiana, through Teach for America. Her current research interests address issues related to American urban and racial politics. Her dissertation work focuses on questions of ethnic representation among Latino locally elected officials.

Jane Hannaway is Senior Fellow and founding Director of the Education Policy Center at the Urban Institute, where she oversees the work of the Center and is a member of the Institute's senior management team. She is also Director of CALDER (National Center for the Analysis of Longitudinal Data in Education Research), a federally funded national research and development center. Hannaway is an organizational sociologist whose work focuses on educational organizations, in particular the effects of education reforms on school policies and practices and ultimately on student outcomes. She previously served on the faculty of Columbia, Princeton, and Stanford Universities and was a senior researcher with the Consortium for Policy Research in Education (CPRE). Dr. Hannaway has authored or co-authored/edited seven books and numerous papers in education and management journals.

Douglas N. Harris is Associate Professor of Educational Policy and Public Affairs at the University of Wisconsin at Madison. His research considers the efficiency and equity of K–12 and higher education programs, ranging from market and test-based accountability to issues of school segregation. His work on segregation and peer effects has been cited in the national media and court cases; and he served on the National School Board Association's task force on desegregation. He is also the author of the forthcoming book on educator performance measures and "value-added" (Harvard Education Press, 2011) and is known for his research on the nature of the relationship between teacher credentials and teacher performance. In higher education, he is co-directing (with Sara Goldrick-Rab) two large-scale randomized trials of college financial aid programs. His more than 30 studies have been published in academic publications such as *Brookings Papers on Education Policy, Journal of Policy Analysis and Management, Educational Evaluation and Policy Analysis, Economics of Education Review, Education Economics,* and *Teachers College Record.*

Bob L. Johnson, Jr. After serving at the University of Utah for 20 years, Bob is now professor in the Department of Educational Leadership and Policy at the University of Alabama. His research interests focus on understanding the defining and distinguishing features of schools as organizations and how these inform leadership, policy, change and reform. He has published in several leading journals in the field of educational leadership and policy. His latest work is a book entitled *Decision Making For Educational Leaders: Under-examined Dimensions and Issues,* recently released by SUNY press. He is also the immediate past editor *Educational Administration Quarterly.*

Betty Malen is a Professor in the Department of Education Policy Studies at the University of Maryland, College Park. Her research brings the discipline of political science to the examination of education problems and relies heavily on the effective application of case study designs and qualitative research methods. Her work addresses the political determinants and the substantive effects of prominent education reforms (e.g., choice, decentralization, professionalization of teaching, high-stakes accountability policies, pay for performance initiatives) and the impact of various policy shifts on distribution of power within and across federal, state and local units of the education system.

Heinz-Dieter Meyer is Associate Professor of Education Policy at the State University of New York (SUNY) Albany. His research focuses on the impact of culture and institutions on education. Among his recent publications are "Unpacking the Contingencies of Decentralization" (*American Journal of Education*), "The New Institutionalism in Education" (with Brian Rowan), and "Education between State, Markets, and Civil Society" (with Bill Boyd). Meyer grew up and went to school in a still largely class-segregated Germany. On a recent study tour of German schools he was surprised to see how much of that class segregation still remains intact.

Douglas E. Mitchell is Professor of Education at the University of California, Riverside. He is past-president of both the Politics of Education Association and the Sociology of Education Association and recipient of the Stephen K. Bailey Award for research contributions to the politics of education. Education politics and policy have been the focus of his research and scholarly writing. Published writings include more than 100 books, journal articles, and monographs covering topics in social science theory and utilization, school program and policy analysis, state legislative decision-making, labor relations, teacher incentive systems, public support for public schools, school desegregation, and school board elections.

Tedi K. Mitchell holds a PhD from the University of California, Riverside. She is a lecturer in school law and has written on student due process and freedom of expression rights. She has also studied and written on teacher training and induction programs.

Joel Mittleman is a Research Assistant in the Urban Institute's Education Policy Center. A graduate of Swarthmore College, he majored in Economics with minors in Education and Public Policy. At the Urban Institute Joel has worked on several projects, including the federal evaluation of the Teacher Incentive Fund and a National Science Foundation funded project evaluating high school reform in North Carolina.

Susan L. Moffitt is the Mary Tefft and John Hazen White Sr. Assistant Professor of Political Science and Public Policy. Before joining the faculty at Brown, she was a Fellow at the Center for American Political Studies and a Robert Wood Johnson Scholar of Health Policy Research, both at Harvard University. Her research examines the politics of information gathering, distribution and use in government agencies, with particular emphasis on K–12 education policy and pharmaceutical regulation. Her first book, *The Ordeal of Equality*, coauthored with David K. Cohen, was published by Harvard University Press in 2009. Some of her other scholarship has appeared in the *Journal of Politics*, the *Journal of Law, Economics and Organization*, the *American Journal of Education*, and numerous edited volumes

David N. Plank is Executive Director of Policy Analysis for California Education (PACE) and Professor (Research) in the Stanford University School of Education. Before joining PACE in 2007, he was a Professor at Michigan State University, where he founded and directed the Education Policy Center. His current research interests focus on the role of research in the education policy process, and on the shrinking role of the State in national education systems. He has worked as a consultant in education policy development for the World Bank, USAID, the United Nations Development Program, the Organization for Economic Cooperation and Development, and the Ford Foundation, and for ministries of education in countries in Africa and Latin

America. He has published six books and numerous articles and chapters in a variety of fields, including history of education and economics of education. His most recent book is the AERA *Handbook of Education Policy Research* (2009), which he co-edited with Gary Sykes and Barbara Schneider.

Dorothy Shipps has taught education policy analysis at Baruch College, City University of New York and Teachers College, Columbia University. She is the author of *School Reform, Corporate Style: Chicago 1880–2000* (2006), and co-editor with Larry Cuban of *Reconstructing the Common Good in Education* (2000). In addition, she has published on school reform, mayoral control, and the civic capacity needed to institutionalize reform. In 2000, she was honored as a Carnegie Scholar, and in 1994 as a Warren Weaver Fellow at the Rockefeller Foundation. Her PhD is from Stanford University and her MA in Asian Studies is from the University of California at Berkeley. Her current research examines the political implications of mayoral control and high-stakes accountability on New York City principals and explores how urban neighborhood capacity differs conceptually from school level SES.

Claire E. Smrekar is an Associate Professor of Public Policy and Education at Vanderbilt University and an Investigator with the National Center on School Choice. She received her doctorate in Educational Administration and Policy Analysis from Stanford University. Dr. Smrekar conducts qualitative research studies related to the social context of education and public policy, with specific reference to the impact of social class structures on family-school community interactions, social capital development, and social networks in traditional public, private, and choice schools. Her work has been funded by the Danforth Foundation, the Spencer Foundation, the W.T. Grant Foundation, and the U.S. Department of Education. Professor Smrekar is the author of numerous journal articles, book chapters, and reports, and has authored three books, most recently: *From the Courtroom to the Classroom: the Shifting Landscape of School Desegregation*, published by Harvard Education Press in 2009.

John F. Witte received his BA degree from the University of Wisconsin-Madison in 1968. Following three years as a naval intelligence officer ,he attended graduate school at Yale University, where he received a Masters of Philosophy (1974) and a PhD (1978) in political science. Since 1977 he has been a Professor in the Department of Political Science and the Robert M. La Follette School of Public Affairs at the University of Wisconsin - Madison. He was Director of the Follette School from 1998 to 2001. He has been a fellow at the Russell Sage Foundation in New York and at the Center for Advanced Study in the Behavioral Sciences at Stanford. He has been a visiting professor in Hungary, Poland, England, Australia, and New Zealand. His research interests include policy analysis, democratic theory, with specialties in education and tax policy and politics. He has authored or co-authored eight books and over 75 articles, book chapters, and reports. His current research is on charter schools, open enrollment, and a new longitudinal study (through 2011) of the Milwaukee voucher program.

Kenneth K. Wong chairs the Education Department and holds the Walter and Leonore Annenberg Chair at Brown University. Wong is a national figure in shaping the research and policy agenda on urban educational reform, equity issues, and governance. He is the recipient of the 2007 Deil Wright Best Paper Award given by the American Political Science Association. Author of about 100 articles and several books, he serves on the editorial board of leading education policy journals. His recent books include *The Education Mayor: Improving America's Schools,* published Georgetown University Press, and *Successful School and Educational Accountability,* published by Pearson.

INDEX

Page numbers in italics refer to figures or tables.